᯽ ᯽ ᯽ ᯽ ᯽ ᯽ ᯽ ᯽ ᯽ ᯽ ᯽ ᯽ ᯽ ᯽ ᯽ ᯽ ᯽ ᯽ ᯽

Women and Men

in Renaissance Venice

WOMEN AND MEN

IN RENAISSANCE VENICE

Twelve Essays on Patrician Society

STANLEY CHOJNACKI

The Johns Hopkins University Press ✣ Baltimore and London

This book has been brought to publication with the generous assistance
of the Gladys Krieble Delmas Foundation.

The Johns Hopkins University Press
2715 North Charles Street
Baltimore, Maryland 21218-4363
www.press.jhu.edu

Library of Congress Cataloging-in-Publication Data will be found
at the end of this book.
A catalog record for this book is available from the British Library.

ISBN 0-8018-6269-8

Contents

Acknowledgments

To publish essays written over the course of one's adult life produces an autobiographical, faintly valedictory sensation. Revisiting the essays gathered here in order to bring them into a consistent format (and to remove some of the more glaring solecisms) gives them a kind of finality that invites reflection on the three-decade-long experience of writing them. The deepest impression the editing has left me with is of the places and people associated with them. All scholarship has intellectual, local, and social dimensions, and I surely am no different from other scholars in seeing all three as consisting of some elements that have changed and others that have endured throughout the years of my involvement with the documents and ideas on display here. The intellectual consistencies and changes over the years are evident in the essays themselves, with an itinerary of my route through them provided in the introduction. Here, I want to acknowledge the places and people who have made the collection of material and the puzzling through to interpretations an enriching experience, and more of a collaborative enterprise than appears in the essays themselves.

Thanks first of all to the generosity of the many institutions that supported the research that went into the essays. Fellowships from the National Endowment for the Humanities, the American Council of Learned Societies, and the John Simon Guggenheim Memorial Foundation allowed me sustained periods of research; and a generous grant from the Gladys Krieble Delmas Foundation made possible a pivotal research trip to Venice in 1978. Over the years I have also benefited from grants from the American Philosophical Society, Michigan State University, and, as I write this, now from the University of North Carolina at Chapel Hill. A

vii

Herodotus Fellowship in 1971–72 at the Institute for Advanced Study, Princeton, gave me the chance to realize what my research notes told me about Venetian women. Nearly two decades later, in 1989–90, the National Humanities Center awarded me a Mellon Fellowship and the friendship of its incomparably helpful and welcoming staff. It was during that year at the NHC that I began to understand the connection between the political history of Venice's regime and the relationships of the men and women of its ruling class. I got a lot of help from the other fellows, above all from my friends in the Solitude and Creativity Group: Brenda Meehan, Gloria Pinney, Melvin Richter, and Bertram Wyatt-Brown. All these people made my year at the NHC the inauguration of the most satisfying and productive period of my career.

During my graduate student years at Berkeley I began accumulating an enduring debt to Gene Brucker, my friend and mentor since those days. He once advised me that it can be repaid only by helping students and younger scholars when I get the chance. Nobody has given me as many chances to be helpful as I have given Gene Brucker over the years, and he has never failed me, whether as advisor, colleague, patron, or friend. Only his other students and the other scholars who have come under his generous wing can grasp how much I have received from him over the decades. At Berkeley I was lucky enough also to work with William Bouwsma, from whom I learned that thoughtful reflection can lead to better history writing. I wish I could apply the lesson better than I do, but its value has been with me since I learned to cherish it in his work and in, on my part, halting and uncertain conversations that Bill Bouwsma generously endured with me during those years in Berkeley.

From my first arrival in Venice in 1964 friends and colleagues have made the experience of living and working there fulfilling both personally and professionally. The staffs of the Marciana Library and the Archivio di Stato helped a bewildered graduate student explore the riches of those places and have continued to solve mysteries and give guidance. Luigi Lanfranchi and Maria Francesca Tiepolo were welcoming and generous directors of the Archivio, and over the years archivists and the staff of the photography section there have gone out of their way to give me indispensable assistance. I want to single out Bianca Lanfranchi Strina, Giustiniana Migliardi O'Riordan, Claudia Salmini, Sandra Sambo, Michela dal Borgo, Giovanni Caniato, Alessandra Schiavon, Bruno d'Alberton, Michele d'Adderio, Gervolino Petenà, and the late Sergio Barbieri and Lino Boschetto. Among fellow researchers who have become colleagues and comrades, sharers of ideas and paleographical skills, and sometimes stimulating controversialists, I want to mention Federica Ambrosini, Benjamin Arbel, Anna Bellavitis, Adolfo Bernardello, Philippe Braunstein, Patricia Fortini Brown, Linda Carroll, Matteo Casini, Monica Chojnacka, Salvatore Ciriacono, Gigi Corazzol, Gaetano and the late Luisa Cozzi, Giorgio Cracco, Élisabeth Crouzet-Pavan, Nicholas Davidson, Robert Davis, Rebecca Edwards, Joanne Ferraro, Dieter Girgensohn, Beth and Jon Glixon, Rona Goffen, Paul Grendler, James Grubb, Jean-Claude Hocquet, David Jacoby, Margaret King, Michael Knapton, Marion Kuntz, Patricia and George Labalme, Ralph Lieberman, Kate Lowe, Martin Lowry, Ivo Mattozzi, Sarah Blake McHam, Reinhold Mueller, Edward Muir, Brian Pullan, the late Donald Queller, Dennis Romano, Guido Ruggiero, Juergen and Anne Markham Schulz, Anne Jacobson Schutte, Sally Scully, Jutta Sperling, Alan Stahl, and Maria-Teresa Todesco.

Working and living in Venice for long and short periods has always been a happy experience thanks to the enduring friendship and hospitality of Ivo and Rossella Mattozzi. My *compare* Luciano Mozzato first invited me into his house in 1965, and ever since, he, Anna, and their sons, Roberto and Andrea, have been my Venetian family, sharing their home, their vacations, and their experiences as a family over more than three decades. Their friendship has made Venice for me more than a site of scholarship and a monument of beauty and civilization; it is an *ormeggio* of affection and belonging.

These essays also bear the marks of the friendship and generous collegiality of many other scholars. I am especially grateful for favors, collaboration, and ideas to Susannah Foster Baxendale, Judith Bennett, Daniel Bornstein, Judith C. Brown, Natalie Zemon Davis, Robert Finlay, Margery Ganz, Elisabeth Gleason, Sarah Hanley, John Headley, Patricia and the late David Herlihy, Julius Kirshner, Christiane Klapisch-Zuber, Thomas Kuehn, John Martin, Jo Ann McNamara, Carol Bresnahan Menning, Anthony Molho, Mary Pardo, Debra Pincus, Michael Rocke, Domenico Sella, Alison Smith, Webster Smith, Gordon S. Stewart, Sharon Strocchia, Susan Stuard, Emily Z. Tabuteau, Richard Trexler, Ronald Weissman, Merry Wiesner-Hanks, and Ronald Witt.

I am also grateful to scholars who gave me the opportunity to publish several of the essays in their original form: Susan Stuard, Mary Erler and Maryanne Kowaleski, Marilyn Migiel and Juliana Schiesari, Barbara Hanawalt, Claire Lees, Ellen Kittell and Thomas Madden, Trevor Dean and Kate Lowe, and Judith Brown and Robert Davis. At various stages in their gestation, many of the essays were tried out as invited papers, and I wish to express my gratitude to all the sponsors and to the audiences whose suggestions made them better.

The late Felix Gilbert and Frederic C. Lane gave me needed correction and encouragement during my early years as a historian. Their greatness as historians was equaled only by their kindness as senior friends and advisors. I was lucky to know them and the humane, high-principled way in which they lived and worked.

I owe a special debt to Benjamin G. Kohl. A Fulbright colleague during my first trip to Venice and a steady friend and wise colleague ever since, Ben Kohl has given me encouragement that has been more important to my scholarship than he can ever know. I want to thank him for that and for his critical role in the publication of these essays, pushing me to explore the possibility of publishing them with Henry Y. K. Tom, whose deft competence and urbane patience as my editor at the Johns Hopkins University Press have now brought the project to fruition. In preparing the book I have also been lucky to have the graceful editorial guidance of Grace Buonocore. My thanks also to Melissa Franklin-Harkrider for her ingenuity in helping me prepare the essays for publication.

My daughters, Laura Noren and Monica Chojnacka, have been my delights from the time I first began to study Venice. They have been my dear companions and sometime research helpers ever since. Their affection and loyalty and now their adult friendship have enriched my life on two continents.

For the last ten years Barbara J. Harris has been a discerning critic, a bracing example of scholarly dedication, and a loving and sensitive source of encouragement. It is thanks to her that the work from the 1990s included in this volume represents a victory of persistence over hesitancy and uncertainty. It is her doing, too, that during this decade I have learned how scholarship and personal fulfillment can merge into the deepest happiness. I dedicate this book to her.

Women and Men

in Renaissance Venice

Introduction:

Family and State,

Women and Men

THE ESSAYS GATHERED in this book were written over a quarter of a century, from the early 1970s to the late 1990s, a time in which the way historians study the society of late medieval and Renaissance Italy was transformed by attention to gender and the experience of women. For that reason it seems to me a good time to take stock of the themes and findings that I put into the essays, setting them out in a brief overview that prepares the reader for the more detailed treatments in the essays themselves. Along the way I take note of the way my approach to the place of women in society has evolved between the earliest and the more recent ones. There are changes of interpretation, too, which owe a great deal to the large literature on gender, the family, and the state produced by other scholars during that quarter century. Sticking to a line of re-search for more than two decades inevitably means learning from col-leagues, being corrected by them, sharpening one's thinking in the light of their work. That has certainly happened in my case. So reviewing my own work from three decades also gives me the opportunity to comment on some ways in which the essays collected here converge with and di-verge from other writing in the field.[1]

In a nutshell, the book examines the relationships that gave coherence to the ruling class of Venice from the mid-fourteenth to the early six-teenth century, the early Renaissance. Each of the essays has its own emphasis, but in one way or another all deal with two dynamics that I think shaped the political and social evolution of the Venetian regime during that century and a half: the shifting boundaries between the pri-vate realm of the family and the state's expanding efforts to set down rules for social relations; and the interactions of individual women and

1

men, as these were influenced not just by the imperatives of family and government but also by the varied and unpredictable circumstances of individual experience, especially in marriage. Hovering over the entire book is the premise that in an exclusive governing class like Venice's patriciate, the concerns of private life influenced the course of political development while government action stimulated adaptation, sometimes conformist, sometimes dissenting, by families and individuals living their relationships. The focal point of these reciprocal influences was the women of the patriciate. Venice's government moved with growing aggressiveness during those 150 years to shape social activity, in the interest of civic order and the deeper entrenchment of the patrician regime. At the same time, nobles sought to promote their families' position by pursuing desirable marriage alliances with other nobles. Marriage was the most deeply involving of a family's undertakings, and although it was a demarcator among men, at its essence marriage was the movement of women. So the central thread in the evolving social culture of Venice's patrician regime from the 1300s to the early 1500s, as traced in these essays, runs through the circumstances, activities, and relationships of married women.

My understanding of the subject has evolved since the 1970s, as historians' interest in women and gender in Italy has grown. The two earliest of the essays collected here, Chapters 5 and 6, were written in a scholarly near vacuum, as is clear from the sparseness of the bibliographical references in the notes. I have chosen not to bring the bibliography up to date, despite the vast increase in writing on the subject, because the approach and the ideas in those essays reflected the scholarly environment of the early 1970s.[2] To be truthful, I wrote those articles in order to dispose of material that, at the time, I considered tangential to my main interest but which kept seizing my attention in the archives. My original aim in studying late medieval Venice was to search for a social explanation for the republic's exceptional political stability and what at the time was considered the cohesion and discipline of its ruling class.[3] The subject still claims my interest, now with a perspective that puts women very much at the center of it. But in the late 1960s and early 1970s, as I was attempting to understand the patriciate by reconstructing the pattern of relations of one of its largest clans, the Morosini, the crowded and influential presence of women in the sources seemed a side issue, even a distraction from the matter at hand. However, as evidence of their involvement in the ordering of relationships and family life kept piling up, it soon became clear that the wives and daughters of the Morosini were impossible to ignore. More than that, the documentation of their wealth and their preferences in using it offered unexpected purchase on relations within and between lineages, which, after all, was the intended object of my research. Accordingly, in "Patrician Women" and "Dowries and Kinsmen" I represented the women of the Morosini as being so important to their families, and having such substantial legal and economic resources, that they could influence the behavior of their male kin, natal and marital, and on that basis contribute to the cohesion of the patriciate.

Except for one short interpretative piece that built on those two essays, I wrote nothing more on patrician women for a decade.[4] When I came back to the subject, it was in a transformed environment. The second half of the 1970s had seen an outpouring of writing on women in early modern Europe, and now there was a conceptual charge to it, a master issue, which gave the subject a crackling intensity. Lauro Martines's pioneering 1974 article on Florentine women, like my "Patrician Women" and "Dowries and Kinsmen," had offered a positive picture of women's status and influence. So had Richard Goldthwaite's 1972 delineation of changes in Florentine family life as a result of the trend toward more inward-looking palace architecture.[5] But already a less optimistic verdict on women's position in early modern Europe was making a formidable impact. Lawrence Stone's monumental *The Family, Sex, and Marriage in England, 1500–1800* (1977) advanced a characterization of the early modern period as the "reinforcement of patriarchy." Several of the essays gathered in Natalie Zemon Davis's influential 1975 collection gave a nuanced assessment of the situation of women in early modern France, which was marked by an unresolved tension between oppressive gender structures and female agency.[6] In Italian historiography a particularly pessimistic interpretation emerged. In one three-year period Diane Owen Hughes interpreted the reinstitution of the Roman dowry in the high Middle Ages as effectively disinheriting women, Margaret King recounted examples of suppression of women's intellectual ambitions, and Joan Kelly issued her negative evaluation of the overall effect of the Renaissance on women.[7] In the same year (1978) as Hughes's essay, Julius Kirshner and Anthony Molho's accounts of the Florentine dowry fund, the Monte delle Doti, posited a matrimonial culture in which family considerations of social advantage and honor left little room for the interest, let alone the assertion, of women.[8]

From these beginnings, scholarship on women in Italy boomed in the 1980s. A series of studies early in that decade vastly expanded the range of the subject. Samuel Cohn published the first of his studies of working-class women in Florence in 1981; in the same year Bianca Betto examined the place of women in a long study of the marriage strategies of one Venetian noble clan; Thomas Kuehn began elucidating the legal restraints surrounding Florentine women; Diane Hughes examined the gender implications of sumptuary legislation in an essay of 1983; and, most significantly, in those same years Christiane Klapisch-Zuber inaugurated her powerful series of writings on the exploitation of Florentine women.[9] So, when I returned to the subject in the mid-1980s, it was in a vastly different historiographical environment. Scholars had found new approaches to the study of women's experience, but more important than that, they had assembled a bulging record of female subordination to male authority, in the household and in governmental and legal institutions.

The record those studies traced was largely one of men acting upon women. Much of the writing was based on prescriptive sources reflecting the intellectual, legal, and governmental ideology of patriarchy.[10] Other work recounted the aims of men planning family strategy.[11] Still other studies found evidence of the disadvantages faced by women in civil and criminal courts.[12] From the perspective afforded by these records, women appeared not only subordinated but silenced by male intentions in private and public arenas. There was less emphasis, however, on reconstructing the activities of women in this environment, on accounting for female practice and listening to women's voices amid the patriarchal discourse. That left hanging the question of whether the quotidian activities of women, especially their dealings with men and family, corresponded in actual practice to the purposes and principles voluminously displayed in the documentation of male intentions. It was a crucial question, for two reasons. Not only are women's activities critical to a rounded assessment of gender in the Italian cities, but they also go to the heart of the family and kinship arrangements that for two decades have been central to scholarship on the urban elites.[13]

According to the main interpretive line, male dominance among the urban elites was keyed to men's placement in a patrilineal structure that provided them with social and economic support, political alliances, and a sociocultural identity. In return for these advantages men were expected to contribute responsibly to the prosperity of their lineage, and to the extent that their womenfolk figured in their activities it was as an instrument to be deployed for the purpose of enhancing the social placement of the lineage or its contributory individual component, the family. If it were to be discovered, on the other hand, that women played more than a passive part in relations within and between families and between themselves and their menfolk, then the vertically unilineal configuration of kinship would be challenged along with the view of women as helpless instruments of men's strategies. Just such discoveries began to appear in the mid- and late 1980s. My 1985 article "Kinship Ties and Young Patricians" (Chapter 10) found Venetian patrician mothers taking an active role in enlarging their sons' kinship affiliation into a bilateral orientation that associated them with both their father's and mother's families. Then, in an essay of 1988 (Chapter 7), I offered evidence that women's capacity to employ their growing dowry wealth according to their own preferences led their natal families and their husbands to regard them with growing respect, solicitude, and affection, thereby increasing the women's social and cultural influence. At about the same time three new essays gave nuance to the Florentine case. In 1987, Heather Gregory presented documentation showing that parents' keenness to enhance the family's interest by means of their daughters' marriages was perfectly compatible with concerned provision for the girls' well-being. The following year, Elaine Rosenthal portrayed Florentine women as certainly subject to legal restrictions but at the same time capable of acting independently, influentially, and with the collaborative encouragement of their husbands. And in 1989 Sharon Strocchia showed that women's use of their dowry wealth to fund commemorative masses displayed a distinctive female family orientation less lineage-centered than that of men, to which they had the economic means of giving tangible expression.[14]

The effect of these writings was twofold. They complicated the picture of patriarchy in the Renaissance cities by showing that, although institutionally subordinate to men, women of the propertied classes nevertheless possessed the resources and determination to act on their own, often with the support of men. They also enlarged our understanding of the organization and functioning of kinship in the urban elites by documenting a distinctive female social orientation, personally fashioned and responsive to claims of affection and loyalty, which cut across the patrilineal structure promoted by the institutional framework and the strategies of heads of families.

Writing on gender in the Italian cities continues to follow the two main tracks beaten in the 1980s. Despite the appearance of a sharp contrast, however, in reality they are complementary elements of a full understanding of gender among the urban elites. One track gives greatest prominence to the forces oppressing women, amassing documentation of their economic disadvantages, legal inferiority, subordination to family interest, and exclusion from public life.[15] This scholarship emphasizes the structures of patriarchy, the organized and enduring campaign of men and institutions to restrict women's experience by implementing the ideology of male dominance. Although the experience of women is its object, it is really about the intentions of men. The other track devotes itself to women's life in practice, observing how they actually lived in their subordinate position. The practitioners of this approach are interested in exploring the ways in which women managed to exercise agency under the patriarchal umbrella.[16] They bring forth evidence of women making choices, employing wealth, influencing men and other women, carving out individual spheres of autonomous action.

At first glance these two tendencies seem to be polar opposites, in both interpretation and method. Yet they really are complementary; indeed, each is necessary for the other to be meaningful for our understanding of gender in operation. The discovery that women could exercise choice and have an impact on the men, women, and children in their social worlds becomes significant only against the background of the vast array of constraints on their activity. The ceaseless efforts of men and institutions to tighten the patriarchal screws, to reinforce the restrictions on women with new policies and practices, become understandable in light of the evidence of women's influential agency in practice. The dialogue among historians today reflects the dialogue between structure and practice that engaged the men, women, and institutions of the time. It is the nourishing, creative, uncertain discourse of gender.

The seven essays from the 1990s reflect my own growing awareness of that productive dynamic. Chapters 5, 6, and 7, written in the 1970s and 1980s, reported my findings about women's activities in practice, emphasizing their ability to make a tangible impact on their social worlds. Chapters 8, 9, and 12, written in the early nineties, continued that approach, describing ways in which women and men carved out their individual lives amid the imperatives and opportunities presented by the sociopolitical situations in which they found themselves, and in the circumstances of their engagement with other women and with men, especially in the uncertain intimacies of family and marriage. They show women and men making effective choices in conscious contact with their worlds and with each other. The most recent of the essays, Chapters 1–4, reverse that perspective. They focus on how the institutional settings of people's lives changed, in response to political circumstances but also to the pressures from individuals and families promoting their private interests. The meaning of gender seems to me to be found in the patterns of change produced in that interaction between persons, families, and larger institutions. Certain elements are constant: biological maleness and femaleness, the family, the state, patriarchy itself. But as the essays in Part 1 illustrate, they are in ceaseless movement. Masculinity and femininity take on different meanings in the face of altered economic and cultural dynamics and when individual women and men confront the varied and ceaselessly changing circumstances of their lives. The family by its nature undergoes its cycle of development, marked by constantly evolving relations among its members. And the state itself was not a fixed entity but in the period from the later fourteenth through the early sixteenth century went through a great expansion of its reach into society and its capacity to take hold. In these circumstances patriarchy itself was protean and adaptive, a contingent product of changing structures and the varied and unpredictable responses to them by women and men constructing their identities in changing contexts.

IN THIS BOOK, the context is the distinctive environment of Venice and the vicissitudes of its evolving patrician regime. So before launching into a discussion of the main themes of the essays, I want to say a few words about the particulars—some would say peculiarities—of Venice's political and social order, in order to help fill in the background of gender structures and relations there. In several of the essays I identify the turn of the fourteenth century as the pivotal moment in the social and political maturation of the patrician regime. The events of the period from the 1380s to the 1430s brought about the definitive establishment of a closed hereditary ruling class. It was accomplished by a powerful surge of governmental assertiveness in regulating private life, especially the ways in which patricians (or nobles) and their families organized their social relations and domestic concerns. The main purpose of this expansion of state power was to ensure the exclusiveness of the patriciate. The government's means of achieving it was to install solemn procedures formalizing men's assumption of their private and public roles as nobles and to impose status requirements for their wives and mothers and regulations for their families' marriages.[17] Thus, from around 1400 the political and social structure of the regime was fashioned and, over time, elaborated in terms of the vital passages and personal experiences of women and men. Gender identity—what it meant to be a male or a female noble—became the basic material in the fabric of the patrician regime and patrician society. Then, in the first decades of the sixteenth century, gender gave practical focus to the ideological statements then emerging as part of the regime's self-consciousness in the midst of crisis.[18]

For that reason, an understanding of gender relations and individuals' experience of them in Venice begins with the laws and customs set down from 1400 onward. But equally and reciprocally, it entails studying how women and men responded to them. While all Venetians felt the government's efforts to shape individual behavior and social interaction, it was the nobles whose activities were the chief target of the new policies. The impulse behind state direction of gender relations arose from a concern to toughen the impermeability of the ruling class from without and promote orderly relations among the families within it, especially between its richer and poorer elements.[19] In addition to instituting official requirements and procedures for demonstrating patrician status, the legislation of the fifteenth and early sixteenth centuries created guidelines for nobles to follow in their social interactions. The most critical of these were the marriage arrangements that nobles zealously pursued in their quest for status and advantageous social connections. The principal bait in the pursuit was dowries, which from the late fourteenth century rose relentlessly. It is not surprising, therefore, that the most sensitive flashpoint in the whole range of encounters between noble families and a government increasingly assertive in social matters was the contracting of marriage.

The political context was critical to gender relations in Venice; so was the distinctive position of the patriciate. In his recent overview of scholarship on women in Renaissance Italy, Samuel Cohn emphasizes the riskiness of generalizing about society on the basis of any one social group, especially the urban elites, which have attracted most scholarly attention.[20] His admonition is equally valid in reverse: the elites demand particularly sensitive attention because of their intimate relationship with the state, whose efforts to regulate their social behavior were one of the hallmarks of government growth in the Renaissance.[21] This is compellingly true of Venice's nobles, with their special stake in their government's gender policies and vice versa. A dowry-limiting law of 1420 was addressed exclusively to nobles and *cittadini,* the stratum of merchant-bureaucrat citizens immediately below the patriciate.[22] The only members of the *popolo* mentioned in the act were wealthy men whose daughters could furnish large dowries to noble husbands. In reality, though, non-nobles could rarely afford large dowries, and the difference in scale between patrician and popular dowries created a vast gulf between the classes regarding their marriage practices. A comparison of mid-fifteenth-century dowry recoveries by noble and non-noble widows quickly shows the difference.[23] The median amount among 253 popular dowries was 208–10 ducats, and only 18 (7.1%) of them were as high as 1,000. Contrast that with 122 patrician dowries recovered during the same period: the median was 1,066⅔ ducats, five times larger than the *popolano* median, and the smallest noble dowry of all, 400 ducats, was nearly twice the median non-noble dowry.[24] In fact, only 28 of the 122 noble dowries (22.9%) were smaller than 1,000 ducats. Where marriage was concerned, not only were patriciate and popolo different sociopolitical categories in the eyes of the state, but they dwelt in different economic universes. The stakes of dowry regulation were higher for noble families, and the potential social tensions posed by noble marriage practices featuring dowry competition were more worrisome for the government. The import of relations between the patriciate as a group of interacting families and the patriciate as the agent and object of government makes it essential to examine the relationship between these two dimensions of the ruling class as a distinctive dynamic, apart from the rest of the population.[25]

The interplay of structure and practice is the field on which families dealt with the state, and women and men dealt with each other and with the urgings of state and family regarding gendered behavior.[26] That four-sided dynamic became clear to me only during the writing of the essays that appeared in the mid-1990s, and the particular role of the state in the dialogue over gender is featured only in the four most recently written ones, those in Part I. I placed them first to emphasize the importance of the family-state-individual gender dynamic and also to acknowledge the importance that historians, especially in Italy, have in recent years attached to the role of government in Renaissance Italy. Politics, especially the emergence of the "Renaissance state," was for decades a staple of scholarly interest, but from the 1960s it gave way to social questions, stimulated by impulses from sociology and anthropology.[27] It was that shift that led to the study, first, of the family and kinship ties in the Italian cities, then, fueled by second-wave feminism in the 1970s, of women and of gender issues discussed above. The essays in Part I thus represent an effort to connect the vibrant study of gender with the recently renewed interest in the development of the state. Viewing the growth of government as influenced by its concern with male and female identity is still unusual in scholarship on the state, although a large body of theoretical and empirical writing, chiefly on non-Italian subjects, has explored the reverse influence, that of the state on gender.[28] For the most part, scholarship on government in Italy has concentrated on the establishment of regional states dominated by large metropolitan centers such as Milan, Florence, and Venice and on official measures to reinforce or restrain, or both, the power of *ceti dominanti,* the ruling groups.[29] Yet, as I argue in Chapter 1, much of the state's energy in dealing with the paradoxical oligarchical elites—who governed the state but were also objects of the state's ordering tendencies—was channeled into policies on the most gender-sensitive issue of all, marriage.

Marriage was the hinge that connected governments and elite families, and the arena in which gender roles took practical shape in the twisting pathways connecting state, family, and individual women and men. Chapter 2 tracks the progression of laws aimed at shaping the marital practices of Venetian nobles, starting with the early-fifteenth-century legislation mentioned above and following the story to the early 1500s. The expanding body of regulations displays the state's developing principles regarding male responsibilities and female property. It underscores the importance that Venice's government assigned to mothers as determinants of patrician status and notes the problems that family marriage strategies created for masculine identity, a subject explored further in Chapters 9 and 12. At the core of the government's initiatives on marriage was its determination to deal with the insistent, intractable issue of dowries. It was the array of problems opened up by dowries which drove governments into making marriage policy in the first place, leading to the often tense dialogue between official authority and the private interests of families. The dowry is the thread that connects all the essays, to each other and to the main preoccupations of the scholarship on gender in Italy.

Dowries were a crucial indicator of a family's position in the political and social environment. That led to edgy relations with public authority over the right of families to pour into daughters' dowries as much of their wealth as they chose; from 1420 a sharp cleavage divided Venetian noble families that favored government restraints on dowries from others that opposed them.[30] Dowries were the marker that differentiated between noble levels of wealth, between families, and between children, both male and female. Like other Italians, Venetians faced the problem of rising dowry levels by restricting the number of daughters who married. Those whose marriages would have eroded their sisters' dowries were forced to take the veil, a practice that sometimes led to moral disorders in convents.[31] Because nobles put a high premium on marrying within the patriciate, even for men, brothers were subjected to the same restrictions on marriage as their sisters. As the stock of potential noble brides was narrowed by the rising dowry standards, men also were forced into permanent bachelorhood, although, unlike women, they had plenty of alternative sexual outlets, producing illegitimate sons whose efforts to join the ruling class were a perpetual problem for government officials.[32] Of course, some women willingly embraced the religious life, and some men avoided marriage as a matter of choice, but the principal reason for restricting marriage to only some sons and some daughters was the limits that dowry inflation put on the capacity of families to satisfy all their children who wanted to marry, at least within the patriciate. In this very direct way, the rise in dowries broadened the range of gender roles and identities for men as well as women.

Whether that variety enabled men and women to choose the vocation that suited them is one of the most controversial issues in the scholarship on women. Paralleling the much discussed spectacle of girls being forced into convents, many historians have dwelt on the coercive aspects of arranged marriages. There has been little research on family pressure forcing men to marry, but the view that young women were thrust into arranged marriages with little regard to their needs or preferences is a canon of the field.[33] Underlying it is a vast body of evidence demonstrating that alongside the economic and political prospects of their sons, the marriages of their daughters were the primary concern of families. Historians differ on the motives that led them to strive for the best possible matches, and the main division among them concerns the interests of the daughters. The most widespread view is that the stakes of good marriages were so high that fathers and brothers had no choice but to conscript their nubile women into strengthening their family's position, with little regard for the women's preferences. For some historians the main objective was an advantageous alliance with a desirable son- or brother-in-law and his family; for others it was to promote family honor by arranging suitable marriages for daughters.[34] In either case, the needs of the family were the dominant consideration, and compared with it the inclinations of a teenage potential bride were of little account.

Few historians would discount the powerful impact of social and cultural imperatives on families' plans for their children, but some, including myself, maintain that the well-being of daughters also had its place in marriage strategies.[35] In this view, not only mothers and other female relatives but fathers and brothers also took their womenfolk's preferences and their prospects of a secure wifehood into consideration alongside the material benefits or enhanced status that a prospective marriage might bring. Those mothers, fathers, and brothers acted out of both affection and practical interest. The question of affection as a motivating element in families' provision for their daughters (and for that matter their sons) has received little attention. Several of the essays below address it, but it remains a largely unexplored aspect of family relations, whether between parents and children or between siblings or spouses. A more pragmatic consideration operating on families has received attention, however—the fate of the dowry after the wedding. In this line of interpretation, rich dowries not only attracted desirable sons-in-law but also benefited the marrying daughters. A good marriage from the standpoint of the influence or prestige gained by the families of brides also served the interests of the daughters themselves by placing them in honorable and wealthy surroundings.[36] More to the point, a large dowry, presumably draining a large part of a family's estate, could give a daughter substantial wealth. Scholarship on Florence and elsewhere is ambivalent on the question. Diane Hughes and Isabelle Chabot in particular argue that the dowry regime, by making a woman's marriage portion her only claim on her father's estate, effectively disinherited women, while others discern more favorable effects on women's economic position.[37] But in Venice, as I document in Chapter 7, the escalating keenness of families to provide their daughters with respectable dowries sometimes effectively disinherited sons. And, crucially, the dowries ended up in the possession of the daughters when they were widowed or of the designated heirs of women who predeceased their husbands; this last point is the subject of Chapter 4.

Parents' generosity with dowries and women's rights to their restitution put the entire question of dowry inflation, marriage strategy, and attitudes toward daughters in a different light. They focus attention on the total span of a marriage rather than the circumstances of its beginning, taking into account the different stages of the marital experience and giving special regard to what I call the "uxorial cycle," the long evolution of a married woman from young bride to mature widow, with all the stages in between. Widowhood has come under increasing scrutiny, and historians' varied approaches to it have produced contrasting assessments of its effects on the women who experienced it in the Italian cities.[38] But there is consensus on the sharply different characters of widowhood and bridehood and, though to a lesser degree, on the importance of considering the whole span of a woman's wifehood when assessing its effects on her. One aspect of that long-term experience emphasized in this book is the continuing relationship between a married woman and the family that assembled a dowry and found a husband for her—however much or little it consulted her feelings on the matter. Whatever their personal sentiments toward her, which were at least as likely to be affectionate as callous, they had a keen interest in her dowry, which could come back to them in the form of business investments or outright bequests from their daughters. For their part, married and widowed women kept up a lasting connection with their families of birth, to whom they often turned for practical help, for example, in the execution of their wills, the administration of their estates, and, as described in Chapter 4, the recovery of their dowries. Yet, once again, generalization across city-state boundaries is risky. A case in point: in Florence, unlike Venice, wives were not free to bequeath their dowries to beneficiaries of their own choosing but were required to leave the entire dowry to their children or husband.[39] Such variations in the institutions of gender meant that women's lived experience of gender was different from place to place. Women's proprietorship of their dowries appears in the essays as the key to their economic standing and thus to their relationship with their families, with society, and with the state. Whether enjoying possession of them as widows or anticipating it as wives, married women were the principal beneficiaries—and, ultimately, benefactresses—of rising dowry levels. Chapter 7 explores the psychological effects of this economic weight on the men in a married woman's life, giving special emphasis to the wisdom that married women's families of both birth and marriage saw in staying in their good graces. But it and other essays also treat its practical consequences, in giving tangible form to women's distinctive social orientation and in the influence it gave them in the raising of their children, particularly in the matter of the children's vocational choice.

In a famous image, Christiane Klapisch-Zuber depicts upper-class Florentine wives as belonging to neither their family of birth nor that of marriage but as being merely "passing guests" in each. The only ways in which wives were connected to the two families were, at the beginning, as the currency of marriage alliances and, at the end, as the object of a tug-of-war over their dowry wealth—with opprobrium from the losing side in either case.[40] The picture of their Venetian counterparts which emerges in this book is very different. In Venice, not only did married women keep up relationships with both their natal and their marital families, but they also mediated between them, drawing them together in collaborative activities: for example, by naming members of the two families as executors of their wills and by enlisting both in the launching of their sons into adult life.[41] Even in the delicate matter of the way they disposed of their dowry wealth, they tended not to opt for one side or the other but benefited both sides. Where there were children to be provided for, mothers destined the bulk of their estates to them, but even caring mothers bestowed largesse upon their blood relatives as well. This was the practice that induced fathers and brothers to cultivate their relationships with their married womenfolk.

Sisters did the same. The means and motives that led married women to nurture bilateral ties with their male kin also enabled them to maintain female networks of mutual loyalty and generosity. Although they provided for their sons, the biggest impact of their dowry wealth was on the marriage prospects of their daughters. The contributions of mothers to their daughters' dowries is discussed at length in Chapter 2 and elsewhere in this book, as well as in other scholarship.[42] Women also added to the dowries of their nieces, daughters of both brothers and sisters. The enduring ties between married sisters warrant more study, but evidence, some presented here, shows that even the separation into two marriages did not put an end to their relationship.[43] Those spreading female networks are shadowy in the sources and further obscured by the emphasis in Italian society on the vertical connections down the male line, which were reinforced by public and private institutions and are therefore most visible in the documents. However, the combination of women's economic substance and the bonds they forged with other women makes female relationships a formidable counter to the formally agnatic organization of society.

It would be difficult, however, to construct a typology of women's networks because of the differences among the experiences of individual women. Those differences are a primary reason why the study of women—and for that matter the gender experiences of men, too—cannot be confined to the search for general tendencies but must take into account the varied ways in which women and men acted within, and against, rules and customs and norms in constructing their individual lives.[44] In matters of gender identity women and men both dwelt in a world of contingencies. This was especially true of women who married. In addition to the basic fact that marriage put a wife in a familially ambiguous position, her social world was constantly reconfigured during the decades of her marriage, especially by deaths in her natal family and births into the marital one, and then deaths again at the end of her marriage and afterward during widowhood. Even more variable were her relationships with the people in her life. Many a young wife regarded her parents with abiding affection and loyalty, but others showed resentment over their placement in marriage with a stranger, or indifference to them as they bonded with their husbands. A woman's brothers might harbor bitterness toward her because of the dowry she had extracted from the patrimony they regarded as their birthright, but they also might benignly enjoy the advantages of their connection to her husband. Her children might be forsaken as she abandoned them for a second marriage, or be guided by her into a prosperous adulthood.[45]

Out of these wide-ranging responses to family circumstances emerge the open-endedness of individuals' experience of wifehood and husbandhood and the elusive role of the emotions in social relationships. The mystery of sentiment sits uneasily alongside the efforts of historians to find uniformities, trends, the patterns that give coherence to reconstructed social experience. Yet the history of marriage is immeasurably enriched by taking account of the vast range of psychological possibilities in a long-term relationship with high economic stakes, a shared interest in children, joint management of a household and other property, and sexual intimacy over years or decades. Difficult though it is, looking into the personal relations of spouses is worth the effort because in addition to opening a window on the internal history of marriage, it can disclose the implications of the rapport between spouses for their broader social worlds.

Historians have pointed out many aspects of marriage among the urban elites which stood in the way of emotional bonding between spouses. One was the age gap, best documented for Florence but true of Venice, as well. While brides were teenage girls, grooms were fledgling or full-fledged adults, often ten or more years older.[46] Moreover, a young husband's commitment to his family of birth was often reinforced by his legal status as a *filius indivisus,* unemancipated from the economic authority of his father, who even controlled his daughter-in-law's dowry.[47] Hovering over these barriers to intimacy were the deep differences between men and women in law and culture. Everywhere, legal codes gave men privileges, for example, precedence to male heirs in inheritance of real estate. This was consistent with the identification of residences with the patri-

lineage, an overlap even expressed linguistically, since the words for lineage or clan and for place of habitation were the same in both Italian
(*casa*) and Latin (*domus*).

Also distancing the women of the patriciate from the men was the
latter's monopoly of politics. Men alone took part in the patriciate's governmental franchise, so that the ruling class was gendered in the activity
that set it apart from other Venetians. This was hardly unique to Venice
or to the Renaissance period. But the fifteenth-century expansion of state
regulation of social behavior added new formal dimensions to male noble
identity. Laws enacted in 1414 and 1430, for example, set up administrative procedures requiring nobles to prove their hereditary claim to patrician status and the political franchise it entailed. By so doing they gave
male nobles an additional official distinction marking them off not only
from popolani but from the women and youths of their own class.[48] Even
the unofficial settings of public life were men's exclusive space. Dennis
Romano was the first to observe how law and custom in Venice reserved
most public areas to men, confining women to certain designated zones,
mainly domestic ones. Foreign visitors in the sixteenth and seventeenth
centuries remarked upon the rarity of the sight of a noblewoman in
public, and women of the patriciate probably spent most of their time
within palace walls in the fourteenth and fifteenth, as well, although
Linda Guzzetti has recently argued that in the Trecento women were
more active in public than the later sources allow.[49] But male dominance
was not confined to public life. Underlying it all was the structure of
domestic patriarchy, the husband's headship of the household. Even unemancipated young husbands could look forward to taking on the position of household head, responsible for its prosperity, its prestige, its
projection into the social world of the patriciate. The economic authority
of husbands even extended to their wives' dowry property; although a
wife's dowry was secured on her husband's estate (see Chapter 4), he
retained administrative control over it as long as the marriage lasted.

In the face of husbandly hegemony, it is not surprising that young
wives often held fast to their natal families. Differences in age, experience,
legal and political standing, and family orientation constituted formidable obstacles to collaborative intimacy between husband and wife, and a
woman in the house and under the dominance of an authoritative husband or husband's father would do well to turn to her parents and siblings
for emotional and legal support. Yet, as the essays below show, married
couples did succeed in establishing relationships of trust and affection.

Nor did close ties between spouses arise only when relations with natal families turned hostile or indifferent. Certainly, they did serve that purpose, but often they blended with continuing loyalties by both husband and wife toward parents and siblings and, often, in-laws, as well.[50] In Chapter 7 in particular I explore the reasons why such wife-husband bonding occurred, pointing to the effects of shared long-term concern for children and the material interests of the family and to the economic and psychological resources that a married woman could count on even in a society so decidedly patriarchal. Both the resources of women and affectionate relations between spouses are controversial subjects. To emphasize them runs against the grain of documented disregard of prospective brides, especially in the marriage market and even, evidently, by women arranging their daughters' matches, as the well-known case of Alessandra Strozzi demonstrates.[51] Although some Venetian women offered their daughters a choice of vocation, others wanted the girls disposed of as quickly as possible, in marriage or a convent, depending on finances and without much apparent regard for their thoughts on the matter. Even when a daughter was allowed to express her preference for marriage, there is little evidence that she participated in the selection of her husband, which was the hardheaded business of fathers and brothers, and of mothers, as well.[52] In these cases the auspices for what we think of as a happy marriage today were anything but favorable.

Time, however, especially the effects of changing family circumstances and the maturing of a teenage bride (as well as, often, her still-young husband) in the years after the wedding, gave husbands and wives ample opportunity to mold collaborative and loving relationships, or to sink into a marriage marked by alienation and hostility.[53] The documents offer examples of both kinds of marriages and of all the gradations in between. That diversity counsels restraint in casting a general verdict on the practical effects on couples of the patriarchal substructure that underlay all relations between individuals and between each person and the pervasive institutional framework. At gender's ground zero, the association between one woman and one man, the effects of male privilege were uncertain, susceptible to the vagaries of material and emotional circumstance and, in marriage, the unchartable mystery of sexual and parental intimacy. Gender relations in practice made uncertain the force of the structures of gender.

Moreover, the structures themselves present a blurry picture, because of the polymorphousness of patriarchy. The very pervasiveness of male privilege and authority gave rise to uncertainty and conflict. The state was a male domain, its laws and policies enforcing the dominance of men. So was the church, building on centuries of misogyny in theory and practice.[54] At the domestic level the mastery of the father and husband was unchallengeable. In the face of this broad patriarchal front, women might seem inevitably fated to inferior status, material disadvantage, and moral dismissal. Yet from the vantage point of an individual woman, patriarchy was less a juggernaut of coalescing male objectives than a cockpit of contending interests, with wives the stake. The state's efforts to shore up the ruling class's dominion and preserve social order, especially within the class, invaded the private realm of marriage and property arrangements. That impinged directly on men's social strategies and economic interests and the ways women fit into them. The principal tactic employed by governments, in Venice and elsewhere, attempting to direct social relations was to direct the traffic in women.[55] Not surprisingly, fathers and husbands resisted governmental usurpation of their prerogatives as heads of families. Or, rather, some did. Others welcomed state policies that supported their family objectives, especially ones that enabled them to compete in the marriage market, such as the Dowry Fund in Florence and laws limiting dowries in Venice, which are examined in Chapters 1 and 2.

The conflicting interests of the men who benefited from state intervention and those who chafed under it were played out in government assemblies, in struggles over the direction of marriage policy. Official regulation of marriage and its property dimensions complicated not only the state's relations with male heads of households but relations between men of different economic and social standing.[56] It also exacerbated an even deeper structural division within patriarchy, that between husbands and fathers. Although they were both parties to the contract that made the marriage, as Klapisch-Zuber and Chabot demonstrate, they cherished rival hopes of the woman whose passage from one to the other was the heart of the matter.[57] It is true that husbands and the fathers and brothers of their wives collaborated after the nuptial ceremonies ended, sometimes giving the impression that the women who linked them together were an afterthought, only marginally related to the real in-law business. In the end, though, the material expression of a woman's loyalty and beneficence was finite, could go in different directions and did so, with the choice up to her, fomenting competition for her favor between the two families and the two domestic patriarchs in her life.

Contending interests thus diffused male authority among rival claimants, giving women space to act on their own, assured of one set of allies in the private sphere as well as in councils of government, for in both Florence and Venice the self-interest of fathers and brothers in the council chambers protected women's dowry rights from abusive grasping by husbands. Yet, although evidence shows individual women appealing to fathers against husbands, or casting their lot entirely with their husbands, most women avoided taking one side against the other. Their orientation was bilateral. They looked in both directions for affection, material support, and their sense of identity, and they inculcated this nourishing bilaterality in their children.[58] Their dowry wealth gave them a powerful instrument—in the case of their daughters often the crucial one—not only for enlarging their children's social orientation but for shaping their adult lives.[59] It enabled them to contribute importantly to their daughters' dowries and induced their husbands to involve them in arranging the girls' marriages, which many did by assigning to their widows complete authority in matrimonial matters.[60] The participation of mothers in the material and moral dimensions of their daughters' marriages created an emotional bond that reinforced the loyalty of married women to their families of origin. Female networks were stretched further still by maternal grandmothers adding their contributions, sometimes quite substantial, to women's dowries, thereby extending the psychological community of young brides to the women of yet another family.

THE BILATERAL INFLUENCE of mothers was felt by their sons, as well. It is one of the chief sources of the distinctive social individuality to be found in the experience of many men, complicating the lineage membership that was their formal anchor in society. Chapter 10 analyzes the collaboration between mothers and their brothers in the Barbarella ritual, which introduced young patrician men into political adulthood. The relationships thus established lasted well beyond the youths' apprenticeship. Evidence here and there in the essays documents the presence of maternal uncles and grandparents in men's activities, and such extralineage collaboration is examined in greater detail in studies not included in this book.[61] Those relationships, complementing the ones men clung to with their paternal uncles and cousins, undermine the view that men's social orientation was resolutely patrilineal. Their cultivation of and resort to their maternal kin and the weight of those connections in the social, economic, and political networks that men designed for themselves deserve more attention than historians, including myself, have given them. In writing many of the earlier essays, I took the position that since men's stake in the lineage was so great—especially so in a status group that based membership on hereditary right through the male line—that was the whole story of their functional and psychological placement in society. But it now seems clear to me that a sharp division that presses men into a model of strict agnation, in contrast with the more fluid orientation of women, underestimates the persistent collaboration between cognates and the influence of wives on their husbands. No doubt, the solid practical benefits that brothers-in-law derived from their relationship were passed on to their sons. But a powerful promoter of male bilaterality was the durable ties between mothers and their natal families, nourished by personal attachments as well as the economic weight that women could put on the scale.

The bilateral orientation of men, together with the rivalries within patriarchy, makes men appear, like women, as complex social figures, moving in a variety of directions according to the peculiar circumstances of individual lives. But that flexibility was always conditioned by the enduring influence of men's lineage orientation. The baseline of social reality for male nobles was their defined place in the patrilineal-patrimonial-patriarchal structure that guided gender and indeed all social and political arrangements in Venice. At the heart of those arrangements was the patriciate's governmental monopoly, which in the Quattrocento provided men with economic benefits from office holding as well as the prestige and power associated with membership in the ruling class. As a result, the meaning of prevailing ideas of masculinity and the relation of individual men to them are bound up with the class's mission of ruling Venice. A man born into a noble family was channeled into a lifetime of passages to progressive stages of privilege associated with his share in that mission. As noted earlier, the fifteenth and sixteenth centuries saw a steady expansion of the government's array of checkpoints to confirm noble male identity. By the early 1500s a man's standing in the patriciate was evaluated, registered, and documented at regular stages from birth to old age.[62] These validations opened the way to successive levels of authority and dignity and by their very nature induced men to conform to standards of behavior, even to certain life courses, that served the collective interest. On the face of it, patrician manhood came down to advantage within limits, a gilded cage accommodating all the men in the ruling class.

The reality was a much less tidy state of affairs. Gaetano Cozzi, Robert Finlay, Donald Queller, and Guido Ruggiero especially have documented political dissension, finagling and corruption in government elections, and sexual nonconformity among nobles so convincingly that the myth of placid noble unanimity has been shattered once and for all.[63] At bottom, the image of collective adherence to a model of selfless discipline was always too glowing to be credible. It also was unnecessary as an explanation for Venice's governmental stability and the patrician regime's endurance. Less romantic interpretations that give due credit to differences and conflicts in the class serve as well—in fact, better. The one most favored by recent historians, for example, emphasizes economic and political domination by an inner elite, able to prevail over the rank and file by cajolery, patronage, and economic allurements, even outright bribes.[64] That dynamic equilibrium is far more congenial to a modern political sensibility, and there is plenty of evidence for it. Equally plausible is the complementary one emphasized in the essays collected here, the thick reticulation of relationships throughout the class, suggested already in the earliest of these essays, Chapter 5. The men of the patriciate saw their well-being as individuals and as heads of families as inescapably bound up with the resources available to them in their family, lineage, and marriage connections. In economic dealings and especially in the quest for government office and the endless business of proving the patrician credentials of family members, the support and testimony of lineal and affinal kin were indispensable; even the laws instituting the tests of noble status explicitly required the testimony of kinsmen.[65]

Yet, although lineage connections were inherited and marriage ties the product of careful calculation and negotiation, the payoff from neither was automatic. Relations had to be nurtured to be useful, and that put a premium on personal rapport, for men as for women. Brothers were doubtless the first line of collaboration for most men, but they could also be rivals or burdens, as illustrated in Chapters 4 and 12. It was therefore important to establish other alliances of cooperation or patronage to ensure a structure of support, especially in the council chamber when the votes were counted. One of the sources of such associations was the bonding with age-mates which men experienced during their young adulthood. As analyzed in Chapter 11, the period from the late teens through the early twenties was a time when young men buttressed their kinship ties with friendships, shared experiences, and group loyalty forged during the liminal period on the brink of manhood.[66] Such bonds gave men, like women, networks of trust and collaboration in which to cultivate individual relationships, choosing them wisely, tending them assiduously, and performing favors in exchange for favors received.

Men were thus not sealed within the lineage but had a hand in fashioning their social worlds, inside and outside the webs of consanguinity and affinity. This produced varied identities within the general category of male patricians. However, differentiation among men was not only the result of personal choice. In a parallel to their sisters' experience, some men had imposed on them forms of masculinity outside the mainstream patriarchal typology. These alternative courses were often dictated by adverse economic circumstances or the calculus of family strategy. The examination of noble bachelorhood in Chapter 12 emphasizes the economic obstacles that closed off to many men the possibility of marriage within the patriciate. The consequences of forced bachelorhood are amply documented by Guido Ruggiero's findings of nobles forming liaisons with women of the popolo and Victor Crescenzi's account of the government's extended campaign against the machinations of nobles to maneuver their illegitimate sons into the patriciate despite the prohibitions excluding bastards.[67] The fathers of many of these interlopers had been denied the chance to head patrician families. They enjoyed the other prerogatives of nobles, and they obviously succeeded in satisfying their sexual desires. But their sexuality was illicit, if not predatory, and bears at least a superficial resemblance to the sexual misbehavior that some noble daughters engaged in behind the convent walls within which they had been enclosed because of the lack of a dowry. However, bachelorhood was not always imposed. Some men embraced a life free of the responsibilities of husband—and fatherhood; others may have declined to marry because of a preference for homosexual relationships.[68]

Men filled all the spaces on a spectrum of male patrician types: young and old, rich and poor, politically active or resolutely private, single or married. Some of these distinctions were smoothed out by time; age certainly was, political activity often was, possibly also sexual interests, as well; and bachelors sometimes eventually married.[69] As with women, changing circumstances changed the direction of men's lives. Also as with women, the compulsions of the structures intended to guide the behavior of the ruling class had a directive influence on men's lives, though they fell far short of pulling all men into step with the regime's purposes. But in another respect as well, the experience of men resembled that of women. The substance of their position in their private and social worlds was shaped by the accidents of personal relationships. Nowhere did this have greater impact than in their relations with their wives. It is paradoxical that the men who formally conformed most fully to the model of the noble patriarch, ostensibly coordinating headship of the household with the regime's rule over patriciate and popolo, in reality had to negotiate the functioning and the economics of the household with their wives. A husband's position in the family was always premised on the domestic perquisites of patriarchy as well as the vast body of legal, political, and cultural biases in men's favor. But how he asserted it in practice, in shaping the family's fortunes in present and future, depended in large measure on the strength or weakness of the marital bond forged by mutual effort or lacking because of incompatibility or outright hostility. The outcome, effectively the concrete reality of husbandhood, was determined by a man's conduct of his relationship with his wife as much as by how a woman lived her wifehood.

The chief message of this book, to sum up, is that men and women in Venice were not merely types to fit into categories like wife, husband, parent, bachelor, and so on. The ways in which individual patricians, female and male, responded to the structural conditions of their ascribed identities and participated in the relationships associated with them were as important to the forging of personhood as the rules and expectations that cultural norms and authoritative institutions laid down for those roles. In the early Renaissance period the state tightened its tentacles around families and individual Venetians, challenging both to devise ways of dealing with greater regulation and stronger mechanisms of enforcement. It was their response to these pressures and to the family strategies devised in response to them which made men and women individual persons. Identity, especially gender identity, was fashioned by individuals dealing with the requirements and allurements associated with the roles assigned to them, and with other persons taking the measure of their own roles. The deck was reshuffled in each case by the variables of wealth, family size, intraclass status, and, finally, psychological disposition and emotional connection.

In a thoughtful essay on this subject, Thomas Kuehn argues that in Renaissance Florence, also, identity was molded in practice by relationships, especially those involving property; and it is in the conduct of those relationships that personhood emerged.[70] That insight coincides with my understanding of gender identity in Venice as it evolved over the quarter century during which the essays in this book were written. But where

Kuehn observes women and men negotiating the substance of their relations with kin and affines via the possible personhoods available in the law, the essays here emphasize the interplay between relationships and the increasingly directive state, making policies and implementing its expanding jurisdictions, sometimes supporting, sometimes restricting the aims of families as they strove to protect their interests in the social world. This book gives special emphasis to the reciprocity of influences between the government's initiatives on marriage and the matrimonial objectives of families. It was in this welter of state and family interests sometimes clashing and sometimes coinciding that individual women and men constructed their place in the world.

A FEW TECHNICAL NOTES: For purposes of uniformity I have cut the original citations in notes to short-title references, easily followed up in the comprehensive bibliography. The same is true of references to primary sources, which are indicated by abbreviations explained in the list of primary sources.

Regarding dates, the calendar year in Venice began on 1 March, so that for Venetians, documents bearing January and February dates belonged to the previous year. I have indicated that by including both years in date references to those months, for example, 1 February 1415/16, in which 1415 is the Venetians' way, 1416 is our way of numbering the year.

Regarding money, Venetians used different moneys for different transactions: gold and silver, ducats and the three lira-soldo-denaro (pound-shilling-pence) systems, currencies and moneys of account. With a few exceptions, which are explained in the notes, I have converted all other moneys to ducats, using the conversion tables in Lane and Mueller, *Money and Banking,* pages 290–91.

PART ONE

The State,

Its Institutions,

and Gender

Gender and the Early Renaissance State

WAS THE ITALIAN RENAISSANCE STATE concerned with gender? Are gender and politics related parts of a historical process? This chapter argues that the answer to both questions is yes and that government and gender converged in Renaissance Italy because of tensions between the public and private interests of the ruling classes. From "the state as a work of art" depicted by Jacob Burckhardt in the mid-nineteenth century to the enduring image of Machiavelli's cunning, amoral prince, innovations in government and subtle statecraft have traditionally ranked among the most prominent features of the Italian Renaissance.[1] Historians' fascination with the state persists in scholarly writing; a recent supplementary issue of the *Journal of Modern History* was dedicated to *The Origins of the State in Italy, 1300–1600*. Since the 1970s, however, a newer wave of research has added the experience of women and the structures that influenced their lives to the inventory of concerns stimulating historians. Although it was not the first entry in the field, the 1977 essay in which Joan Kelly asked, "Did Women Have a Renaissance?" has had the most powerful influence on the direction of research. In the two decades since its publication, scholars have discovered much to substantiate the negative answer that Kelly gave to her question, documenting women's subordinate status in the patriarchal societies of the Italian cities.[2] The landmark event in the maturing of Renaissance gender studies was the publication, first in 1985, of the collected essays of Christiane Klapisch-Zuber.[3] With poignant eloquence they described manifold ways in which women were exploited for male purposes, especially among the ruling class of Florence. Klapisch-Zuber's chief emphasis, like that of most other scholars working in the field, is on the implications for women of the politics of the family and the male lineage.[4] That focus has brought into high relief the instrumentalization of women which was central to the marriage strategies followed by families, usually headed by men, in the pursuit of their social, economic, and political objectives.[5]

Those family objectives are the link between the new scholarship on gender and the perennial interest in the state. The interaction of family, gender, and state emerges in recent writing as critical to Italy's social and political development. Its workings are identified in the very title of Giorgio Chittolini's contribution to *The Origins of the State in Italy:* "The 'Private,' the 'Public,' the State." Chittolini deftly outlines the complex relationship of state and family. From one perspective, the state can be understood "as a system of institutions that operates like an underlying web in which diverse forces [such as "families, kin groups, and factions"] and purposes are interwoven in mutual interdependence": that is, government institutions shaping interaction among private interests. From another angle, though, the state can be imagined as "a political structure formulated in terms of lineages, factions, and groups, organized on the basis of systems of relations and mechanisms of power that are private in nature": private interests shaping government.[6] For Chittolini these are alternative perspectives, although they can also be complementary sides of a single phenomenon. In either case, "it is essential to keep constantly in mind the structures of association, the intentions, and the formal and informal uses of power generated by society in that interplay between 'public' and 'private.'"[7]

The families best positioned to impose their private interests on the functioning of government or, alternatively, to adapt their private aims to the state's policies and procedures were the members of the oligarchical elites. In the activity of the urban patriciates and feudal/courtly aristocracies government and private life overlapped in a public sphere of uncertain dimensions, where families, lineages, and factions colluded and collided.[8] The policies of regimes show the effects of the elites' control of government or princely favor; the sociocultural complexions of the individual states reflect the distinctions fashioned by oligarchies to mark themselves off from the rest of society. Political and social hegemony was not, however, a permanent achievement but the object, continually redefined, of unceasing effort by families to gain or keep it amid the turbulence of the fourteenth to sixteenth centuries.[9] To do so required demonstrating it on two fronts: the political, by participating in government; and the social, by meeting the standards and cultivating the associations befitting members of a ruling class. These two requirements often blended, but they could also be at odds, as individual men and families balanced the demands of political ascendancy against the imperatives and prerogatives of social distinction. The tension between public discipline and private privilege set the state on a new course, that of regulating relationships within and between families, as governing elites sought to secure their status by enacting rules for male behavior, female behavior, and relations between men and women. The state was both the instrument and the regulator of oligarchy, and gender was the terrain on which it confronted the private interests of families. In the following pages, we explore this confrontation, chiefly in the well-studied cases of Quattrocento Florence and Venice but with occasional reference to other states, examining government initiatives with regard to orderly sexuality, women in religion, and marriage.

SUSTAINED INTERACTION between public authority and private life dates from the first great turning point in Renaissance Italy's political history, the last decades of the fourteenth and the first of the fifteenth century. This was the formative period of the territorial states, the most dramatic structural development in early Renaissance politics.[10] It was also the occasion of a burst of new magistracies and regulations within states, aimed at entrenching regimes by assigning identities and roles to social classes, age groups, and genders. The first step was to define the elites themselves. Starting in the late Trecento, humanist writers added to the two traditional criteria of nobility, heredity and virtue, a third: government attribution of nobility based on service to the state.[11] This theoretical innovation coincided with new initiatives by regimes, shaken by the crises of the late Trecento. The policies were designed to consolidate the governmental position of the political elite and to provide mercantile ruling classes, notably those of Venice and Florence, with an ideology of oligarchy that would counter the enduring claims of the older nobility.[12] Elsewhere, an updated feudalism complemented that republican elite ideology. In Ferrara, for example, the Este marquesses used the venerable practice of conferring fiefs to neutralize resistance from the old Ferrarese nobility and rivalry within their own family, by fashioning a new feudal/courtly nobility out of nobles attracted from elsewhere and Ferraresi of obscure origins rewarded for loyal service to the Este.[13] The Ferrarese example, like those of Milan, Venice, Florence, and other states, underscores the interdependence between the new territorial regimes and the elites that increased their wealth and status by participating in the governing of them.[14]

That mutual dependence also influenced the articulation of a new so-ciopolitical order within cities, as nascent and established elites alike found new ways to entrench themselves. As the supporters of the Este were gaining the distinction of Ferrarese nobility along with the material bene-fits of fief holding, the Milanese nobility was being inscribed, in 1377, in an official register, a step in the princely-feudal collaboration then being developed by the Visconti *signori* and later followed by the Sforza when they succeeded to the duchy of Milan in the mid-Quattrocento.[15] Flor-ence's oligarchy strengthened its political dominance after the Ciompi revolt in 1378 by altering electoral procedures to ensure that the most powerful offices would be controlled by the *reggimento* of traditionally dominant families and their clients, while a broad population of lesser guildsmen had the illusion of political franchise. The result was "a separa-tion between participation and power," between "ruling group and ruling class."[16] In Venice, too, in the years around 1400, the ruling patriciate widened the gap between itself and the populace, culminating a century-long sociopolitical evolution, in Dennis Romano's phrase, "from commu-nity to hierarchy."[17] This has been associated with the entrenchment, as in Florence, of a small ruling group within the patriciate, yet there is ample evidence that the patrician rank and file enthusiastically supported new measures that reinforced their class's exclusiveness and replaced ancient prominence with official procedures as the determinant of patrician sta-tus.[18] As in Florence, these developments were a reaction to crisis, though in Venice it was socioeconomic upheaval rather than class conflict. Mas-sive levies of forced loans during the war of Chioggia (1378–81) had devastated the fortunes of many "noble" families (as patricians called themselves) and simultaneously enriched *popolani*, some of whom were subsequently ennobled. The response was a combination of new programs to provide public employment for needy nobles, and tough new require-ments for proving patrician credentials, in order to prevent diffusion of the new prerogatives and a cheapening of noble status by more additions to the patriciate.[19]

In both Venice and Florence, the bolstering of ruling-class exclusive-ness and hegemony was accomplished by legislation authorizing the state to regulate social identity by age and gender. Venetian laws of 1414 and 1430 designed to keep usurpers out of the patriciate focused on the transi-tion from youth to adulthood, setting up official procedures in which young claimants to noble status documented their fathers' patrician cre-dentials, the marital and social condition of their mothers, and their own attainment of the requisite age. This information was entered into ledgers that thenceforth served as the official registry, continually updated, of the patriciate, just as since 1389 awards of citizen status, the rank below nobility, were to be recorded "in a parchment register maintained specifically for this purpose."[20] In Florence, too, the government's "tenacious reorganizing penchant" during the period 1382–1433 "insinuated itself into. . . the most private realms of citizens' and subjects' social lives," and, as in Venice, new record-keeping practices were set up to create an "institutionalized and government-controlled memory of families' wealth [which] enhanced the government's ability to intervene in the private affairs of its citizens."[21] The Florentine initiatives resembled the Venetian in making checks of men's ages the occasion of state acknowledgment of their families' status, further bringing private relationships under the government's documentary purview. In 1429, in an effort to counteract widespread lying about their ages by men eager for the offices on which Florentine patricians, like their Venetian counterparts, increasingly depended for their livelihoods, a law was enacted requiring all candidates for government office to prove their ages by presenting the family *ricordi*. As in Venice, the age proofs were entered into official registers, creating a constantly updated official census of the political class.[22]

Government innovations in both republics thus imposed new requirements for membership in the ruling class and new rigor in evaluating and recording the entitlement of individual families to belong to it, all pivoting on male identity: that of sons laying claim to the oligarchy's governmental franchise at a particular moment, and that of fathers transmitting it over time. Venetian legislation in 1430 required documentation of the identity of the mothers of would-be nobles as well as their fathers, but the emphasis in all these measures was on the patrilineal basis of roles reserved to men. Patriarchy was the principle that linked governmental and private spheres in securing elite hegemony. The ideology of Florence's increasingly aristocratic government after 1382 was modeled on the patriarchal family; in Venice the authority of fathers was enhanced by their inscription as channels of government authority to the family.[23] Moreover, the new documentary initiatives reinforced patriarchy not just for the ruling class but for all fathers, whose status as family heads was enhanced by the official recognition it received from registration in fiscal censuses.[24]

Male identity was also the pivot of state action to promote social order among the populace. The chief mechanism was the criminal justice system, which was overhauled in both cities in the years around 1400. In Florence the turning point was the immediate aftermath of the Ciompi revolt, with the commissioning in 1378 of the Otto di Guardia, which became the symbol and instrument of the centralized oligarchical control then being consolidated by the electoral reforms mentioned above. The essential strategy of the new system was to break down traditional neighborhood-centered mechanisms of dealing with criminality and replace them with an elaborate network of centralized institutions.[25] In subsequent decades magistracies proliferated as the state asserted its control—not least over the conduct of its own officials, whose eagerness for public office often led to private peculation at the expense of the public interest. To impose governmental discipline on them the Conservatori delle Leggi were instituted in 1429.[26]

At the heart of the drive for "organization, centralization, rationalization," in Maria Serena Mazzi's phrase, was control over the volatile potential of sex. In 1403 the state created a special office, the Ufficio dell'Onestà, to regulate prostitution by building and supervising public brothels. The charter of the Onestà reflected a change in Florence's governmental culture which complemented the burgeoning of new magistracies: discarding the old moralizing approach to social behavior, which treated activities such as prostitution as sinful evils to be extirpated, in favor of a secular pragmatism that accepted them as inevitable features of the urban landscape, to be regulated to serve the regime's purposes—"pragmatic flexibility, not repressive terror," as Andrea Zorzi phrases it.[27] The Onestà was explicitly designed to serve the complementary purposes of discouraging sodomy and repopulating the plague-decimated city by encouraging male heterosexuality.[28] But it was also a way of managing the heavy foreign presence among both prostitutes and clients, an unstable element with disorderly potential to be monitored and controlled. To the foreign residents was added another destabilizing force, which Florence shared with other cities: large numbers of young men who, forced to delay or forgo marriage for economic reasons, constituted a sexual threat to respectable women and, it was assumed, became candidates for sodomy.[29] The Ufficiali dell'Onestà dealt with these worrisome presences in the city by giving new institutional force to traditional notions of male and female sexuality, directing male heterosexuality into approved outlets by turning to the government's advantage the multiform circumstances—economic deprivation, wartime upheaval, sexual dishonor—which drove women into prostitution.[30]

Concerns about male sexuality also brought into being another Florentine magistracy, the Ufficiali di Notte, created in 1432 to combat the "abominable vice of sodomy." According to Michael Rocke, stepping up prosecution of sodomy was one aspect of the Florentine oligarchy's "broad effort to manage sexuality and public morality, all part of a more concentrated and efficient program of social control."[31] Although officially sponsored prostitution was premised on a linkage between civic well-being and orderly male heterosexuality, Rocke's researches reveal that Florence's rulers saw benefits in an orderly homosexual activity, as well. Despite rhetorical fulminations against sodomy, in practice the government followed a policy similar to the one on prostitution, of regulation rather than extirpation. Under the new dispensation of " 'benevolent' but more effective control," penalties for sodomy retreated from the ferocious sanctions of the Trecento, castration or death, to steadily decreasing fines: the 1,000 florins decreed in 1408 for first offenders as an alternative to mutilation, death, or exile were reduced to 50 florins in the legislation creating the Ufficiali sixteen years later.[32] Not only were penalties eased, but prosecutions were temperate; only 16 percent of the accused sodomites brought before the Ufficiali were found guilty.[33] As Rocke notes, milder penalties encouraged more prosecutions, bringing sodomy out into the light of day and making it easier to regulate—as well as increasing the likelihood that fines would be paid into the city's depleted treasury. The sodomy investigations of the Ufficiali di Notte, like the state's prostitution policy, put an official label on a sexually identified segment of the population.

Also like the government's prostitution policy, its regulation of sodomy hardened class, age, and gender distinctions. Although patricians came before the Ufficiali, the great majority of the accused sodomites, and, not surprisingly, an even greater proportion of those actually convicted, belonged to lower socioeconomic levels; the government reduced fines in order to ensure that the poor would be drawn within the Ufficiali di Notte's net, giving the state additional purchase on the *popolo minuto*. Those policies are further evidence that the state's purpose was not to deter aberrant male sexual activity any more than it wanted to eradicate prostitution. Recognizing that homosexual urges, like heterosexual ones, were facts of life, Florence's rulers aimed to control sodomy practice by means of sanctions and documentation. The Ufficiali's trial records constitute a continuing census of men actually or allegedly engaged in same-sex erotic activity, just as the registers of age proofs were a roster of the men of the political class and the catasto registers identified all Florentines in their family relationships.

The prosecutions of the Ufficiali di Notte refined the Florentine sociology of gender by adding sexual significance to the age categories outlined in the registration requirements for aspiring officeholders enacted in 1429. Their records reveal that sodomy was an activity of youth: 82.9 percent of the men implicated between 1478 and 1502 were thirty or younger, 93.9 percent forty or younger.[34] The Ufficiali took age into account when imposing sentences, reflecting their culture's conflation of gender and age by letting off lightly or absolving outright all notionally innocent and irresponsible boys under eighteen, even when they performed the active role.[35] The anonymous accusations on which they acted referred to the passive partners, more than 90 percent of whom were younger than twenty, in female terms, sometimes abusively misogynous ones such as "bitch" (*cagna*), "whore" (*puttana*), or *bardassa*, the feminized term for a youthful male prostitute, but often simply as "women." As Rocke notes, such characterizations of youthful partners as "symbolic females" were absent from accusers' references to the older active partners.[36] By recording this vocabulary in their registers, the Ufficiali gave official voice to a discourse in which maleness was identified with maturity, initiative, and mastery; femaleness and youth with passivity, even inculpability. Their prosecutions also reinforced male authority in the private realm: married sodomites haled before the Ufficiali were less than one-third as likely to be found guilty as unmarried men.[37]

In Venice, also, the reinforcement of the patriciate's exclusiveness was accompanied by elaboration and rationalization of the criminal justice system, with special attention to sexual activity. For Guido Ruggiero, the entire period from the mid-fourteenth to the late-fifteenth century was a watershed during which the Venetian government responded to socioeconomic turmoil by formulating an official sexual morality centered on stable family discipline under paternal authority. The unintended result was a reactive "culture of illicit sexuality" which, given shape by the official orthodoxy it was seen as violating, clarifies the configuration of the state's structure of licit sexuality.[38] With greater chronological specificity, Elisabeth Crouzet-Pavan sees the early 1400s as the "turning point in the history of the regulation of behavior," when the state undertook to control the physical space of the city.[39] Critical to that control was the regulation of sexual activity, and Crouzet-Pavan's (formerly Pavan's) account parallels those of Trexler, Zorzi, Mazzi, and Rocke for Florence in locating in the early Quattrocento an expansion of the criminal justice apparatus and "new definitions of order and of crime, or at least by a revised understanding of those two realities." Alluding to the new prosecutorial rigor brought to Florence by the Otto di Guardia and Ufficiali di Notte, she finds that in Venice, too, "a new public morality" fostered increased government intervention in the private sphere.[40]

The policy is most clearly evident in the Venetian prosecution of sodomy, which in the years after 1400 underwent a jurisdictional overhaul and a surge of prosecutorial fervor. Starting in 1406 the powerful Council of Ten withdrew jurisdiction from the hitherto responsible Signori di Notte, whose antisodomy activity in the fourteenth century had been fitful and unproductive, and in 1418 (fourteen years before the creation of the Ufficiali di Notte in Florence) established a Collegio Sodomitarum, or Sodomy Tribunal. Under its authority sodomy prosecutions soared. More cases (twenty) were tried in the first year of the Sodomy Tribunal's operations than had been prosecuted by the Signori di Notte in any *decade* during the fourteenth century, and prosecutions continued to rise, from only 3 in the years 1376–1400 to 31 in 1401–25, 54 in 1426–50, 71 in 1451–75, and 110 in 1476–1500. The state's mobilization against sodomy culminated in 1448 with the creation by the Ten of a special police force under its authority, whose job it was to patrol the city in search of sodomite activity and take suspects into custody for prosecution by the Sodomy Tribunal.[41]

Unlike their Florentine counterparts, sodomites in Venice were dealt with fiercely; active partners were still burned in the Quattrocento (though from 1446 they were decapitated first, to ensure that their souls would rejoin their bodies at the Last Judgment).[42] But the Venetian policy paralleled the Florentine in promoting reproductive male heterosexuality. The preamble to a law of 1496 declared that sodomy worked "against the propagation of the human race." Worries over the city's demographic health blended with anxiety that divine castigation would strike Venice as it had Sodom, since sodomy was "most detestable and most displeasing to the exalted Creator," indeed, that in it the "order of creation is overthrown."[43] The state must therefore do its utmost to allay God's wrath and promote population growth by encouraging the reproductive male sexuality that was the keystone of that proper order, and by pitilessly repressing its opposite, sodomy in both its homosexual and heterosexual forms.[44]

As in Florence, patterns of punishment reflected and reinforced deeply embedded ideas about masculinity and age. While the active partners in sodomite acts suffered the full weight of penalties, their passive partners, usually much younger, were let off lightly or not prosecuted at all.[45] The homosexual experiences of boys could be treated leniently; although destined to become men, they were still outside the authoritative precincts of male adulthood. Ruggiero puts this differentiation into a broader structure of sexual age grading, for males and females, which influenced the imposition of penalties by Venice's criminal justice officials.[46] In that structure full-grown men who diverted their sexual energies from reproductive heterosexuality were regarded as undermining the biological basis of the masculine order that ruled over private and public life. The force of that principle led the Ten to prosecute patrician as well as popolano sodomites. Although scholars differ on the extent to which nobles, especially the well connected among them, suffered the harshest penalties, from the beginning the Council of Ten prosecuted the elite as well as the poor, in the interests of the well-being of the regime, which required "the fidelity and devotion of our people, who are murmuring because they see *populares* punished [for sodomy] while the nobles go free" under the lax rule of the Signori di Notte.[47]

For Crouzet-Pavan the antisodomy policy represents the "new definition of power, of the formation of the Venetian state" in the Quattrocento, the main element of which was an "extension of the public realm."[48] Her emphasis is on the progressive spread of governmental surveillance and regulation of the large and small physical spaces of Venice—all the places, for example, where men might arrange or be drawn into homoerotic acts. The spatial dimension of the state's regulation of sexual behavior was more concretely present to Venetians in the case of prostitution.[49] From 1360 the government had tried to control prostitution by restricting it to a designated area near the Rialto market called the Castelletto. As with sodomy, regulation intensified in the early fifteenth century, especially the 1420s, with laws requiring prostitutes to wear yellow scarves at their necks, to return to the Castelletto at a specific hour, even to avoid drinking wine in taverns not sold by the tavernkeepers themselves.[50] However, by the 1420s the demand for prostitutes' services as well as the legions of women engaged in the trade had forced the government to accommodate other centers besides the Castelletto, which it did without, however, abandoning its determination, in Crouzet-Pavan's phrase, "to make prostitution coincide with control of prostitution."[51]

In a subtle analysis, Dennis Romano also observes that in the late fourteenth century Venice's patricians "were consolidating their control over all aspects of Venetian life, including the cityscape," but he enriches Crouzet-Pavan's perspective by tracing the way the patrician regime "defin[ed] space in gender terms," restricting women to certain locations much as, in Samuel Cohn's reconstruction, in the wake of the Ciompi revolt the Florentine oligarchy broke down the citywide solidarity that had united workers by isolating them in urban pockets of their own, imposing a double reclusion on working-class women.[52] Locating in supervised physical space both open female sexuality and the extramarital sexual activity of male clients of prostitutes, who were mostly foreigners and popolani, Venice's regime attempted to sanitize sexually and socially the married reproduction on which society, especially patrician society, depended.[53]

Like its efforts to repress sodomy, noble and popolano, homosexual and heterosexual, the Venetian prostitution policy was part of the campaign by oligarchies in the late Trecento and early Quattrocento to entrench themselves more firmly in power by clarifying and controlling class, age, and gender identities at their sexual core, wherein lay the key to the orderly continuity of society and regime. As Romano shows, keeping patrician women in their palaces, women of the populace in their neighborhoods, and prostitutes in their designated zones was a fundamental part of this strategy in Venice. Another was controlling the activities of nuns and their sacred spaces. But that objective, in Venice and elsewhere, was complicated by a deep-seated tension between the imperatives of oligarchical regimes and those of oligarchical families, involving the social identities and the vocations, religious and lay, of the women of the elite.

RELIGIOUS WOMEN were objects of state concern in two main ways, behavioral and ideological, and the most anxious issue was the moral tone of convents. Already in 1349, in the climate of devout fear after the Black Death, Venice's government, alarmed by the "abominable frequency with which the crime of fornication is committed in convents," took upon itself responsibility for regulating religious communities.[54] Sexual activities in convents persisted, however, and the government responded by steadily increasing penalties. A measure of 1382 prescribed three years in prison for raping a nun, two years for intercourse with a willing nun, and one year for merely entering a monastery. In 1486 a fine of 1,000 lire was added to the prison term for consensual intercourse, one of 600 lire for unauthorized entry into a convent, six months in prison and 100 lire for disorderly conduct in the vicinity of a monastery, and a draconian three years in prison and 1,500 lire for persuading a nun to leave her convent.[55] The escalating sanctions were unavailing: in 1497 a Franciscan preacher blamed a current outbreak of plague on a catalogue of Venetians' sins, of which "worst of all, whenever a foreign dignitary comes to Venice, they give him a tour of the city's convents, which in reality are not convents but public bordellos."[56]

The progressive harshening of the penalties for sex in convents documents a perennial problem rooted in the social practices of ruling-class families. Many nuns had no motivation to observe the vow of chastity; they dwelt in convents not in response to spiritual callings but because physical or economic obstacles prevented them from marrying.[57] The most important was the relentless rise in dowries during the fifteenth and sixteenth centuries. A growing percentage of girls were taken off the marriage market by a widespread family strategy of marrying off one or two daughters with large marriage portions rather than a larger number with mediocre ones.[58] Because a sexually mature unmarried daughter was considered a peril to family honor, it was better to consign her to a convent, where at least the fiction of chastity would shield her family from the risk of sexual disgrace.[59] The result was forced monacation (the anglicization of an Italian word for entry into a convent). A Venetian law of 1420 noted the "tears and wailing" of girls "imprisoned" within convent walls, and an anonymous Bolognese writer of the mid-sixteenth century described women "forced by their fathers and brothers into convents with meager allowances, not to pray and bestow blessings, but to blaspheme and curse the bodies and souls of their parents and relatives, and to indict God for letting them be born." In the early 1600s the Venetian feminist writer Arcangela Tarabotti, herself a nun, condemned with fierce eloquence the matrimonial system in which fathers, "motivated purely by worldly pride and the desire to pile up riches," forced daughters into convents in order to funnel family wealth into dowries for one or two of their sisters. By Tarabotti's time the practice had grown so outrageous that the patriarch (archbishop) of Venice himself, claiming that 2,000 noblewomen were stored in convents "as though in a public warehouse," proposed relaxing the rules governing convent discipline.[60] But his voice was lost in the noise of state efforts, however unavailing, to enforce strict moral behavior in convents.

The practice of forcing unmarriageable girls into convents highlights the tension between the private interests and the governmental role of elites in matters concerning women. In 1421, to put an end to what

Archbishop Antoninus called a "scandalum populorum," the oligarchs of Florence created yet another magistracy, this one with responsibility to "conserve the morality" of the city's convents. In 1433 its jurisdiction was taken over by the sodomy-regulating Ufficiali di Notte, but all these efforts were in vain because the Florentine elite continued to fill convents to bursting with vocationless daughters.[61] The percentage of Florence's female population living in convents, a mere 1.2 percent in 1336, had risen by 1427 to 6.7 percent overall, 20 percent for daughters of the elite; in sheer numbers, the total convent population in and around the city rose from 906 in 1427 to 2,000 in 1500 and to 2,500 in 1515.[62] The number of convents in the city also climbed steadily, from 16 in 1368 to 26 in 1415, to 30 in 1470, as did the average number of nuns in each convent, from 14.5 in 1377 to 20 in 1428, to 32.8 in 1478.[63] In Venice, there were 31 convents in the 1490s, and just as in Florence, the patricians who in the council hall legislated stern penalties for seducers of nuns nonetheless forced ever larger numbers of their daughters into the unhappy claustra-tion that fostered seduction. It is estimated that by 1581 no fewer than three-fifths of all patrician women were nuns.[64]

However, the sexual fallout of families' marriage strategies was not the only stimulus to state interest in religious women. The special cha-risma associated with female religiosity made them focal points of gov-ernmental ideology.[65] A fifteenth-century Florentine declared that the nuns of his city "spend day and night praying for the most worthy Si-gnoria of Florence," and an abbess in the same city based her appeal for her convent's continued tax exemption on the claim that those prayers, "com-ing as they do from persons of such great religion, are more useful than two thousand cavalry." The government showed its appreciation of the importance of convents by subsidizing their construction costs.[66] In 1398 the doge of Venice rewarded the nuns of the convent of Corpus Christi for their prayers for Venice's civic well-being by interceding personally on their behalf in a property dispute with the marquess of Ferrara. The civic importance of nuns in Venice was most spectacularly displayed at the con-vent of the Vergini, where the doge, the convent's official patron, accom-panied by the entire executive council (Signoria) as well as other patri-cians, symbolically married each newly consecrated abbess in an elaborate ceremony, complete with rings, presided over by the patriarch of Venice. The diarist Marino Sanudo's account of the ceremony in 1506 notes its special significance for patrician women; afterward, he reported, there was a banquet in the convent's refectory for 500 women, "and few men."[67]

For republican and princely states alike, the charisma of holy women was a talisman providing protection and moral validation for the regimes that harbored them. Gabriella Zarri has documented the diffusion throughout northern and central Italy of the phenomenon of "living saints" whose presence at the courts of princes was regarded as beneficial, if not downright crucial, to civic well-being, especially in the atmosphere of crisis in the years around 1500. Duke Ercole I of Ferrara wrote in 1500 that in those tormented times God had provided "many spiritual, pious, and religious persons, especially of the female sex, in order that [Italians] might rise from ruin to sublimity."[68] The sublimity was made concrete by saintly women like Caterina of Bologna, whose prayers were credited with "the deliverance of the city of Bologna from a siege by a Milanese army," and like Osanna of Mantua, who declared herself ready "to be chopped into morsels and roasted in order to save the city of Mantua."[69] Princes exerted strenuous efforts to bring such *sante vive* to their courts and to promote due piety in convents, as a way of gaining moral legitimation and popular support for their regimes. In 1497, for example, Duke Ercole resolved to attract to Ferrara the saintly Lucia Brocadelli. When the Ferrarese ambassador arrived in Viterbo, where Lucia was then residing, to convey his duke's offer, more than 1,000 women crowded the city square to protest, and the leading citizens sent their overlord, the pope, a letter arguing that if Lucia's protective sanctity left Viterbo the city "would be destroyed to its very foundations." But Duke Ercole would not be denied; he offered to found a new monastery for Lucia with accommodations for 100 other holy women, who would join with her in praying for the Ferrarese state. In the end his recruitment efforts were successful, but it took two years of negotiations to get Lucia to Ferrara.[70]

The veneration of religious women as essential to civic well-being inspired governmental initiatives for convent reform in places as varied as Mantua, Milan, Brescia, Mirandola, Perugia, Venice, Carpi, Modena, Ravenna, Bologna, and Piacenza.[71] Yet again and again that principle of state clashed with the social reality of the convent option's importance for elite families with too many daughters. To complicate matters further, even pragmatic parents were emotionally bound to the daughters they put into convents. Roberto Bizzocchi notes that although the oligarchs who governed Florence were indeed concerned about the morality of their city's convents, they stopped short of monastic reforms so strict as to cut their enclosed daughters off completely from affectionate family ties—which raises the tantalizing possibility of families turning a blind eye to sexual activity by daughters forced into convents because of family imperatives.[72]

Doubtless, some nuns were left forgotten and embittered, as the Bolognese commentator quoted earlier claimed, but others kept close ties to their families. Sharon Strocchia has shown how professed women were given tutelage over their marriageable kinswomen, including supervision of their education in reading and writing.[73] Few fathers were as effusively affectionate as the Venetian noble Francesco Morosini, who in 1497 bequeathed an annuity of 25 ducats to his daughter Fiusina, a nun at the observant convent of Santissima Annunziata, "whom I love as my very soul" and whom "I have allowed no harm to befall from the time she entered that convent, in order to be a good father to her, who is my most sweet daughter and my very heart."[74] But his example was common among Venetians: Ermolao Pisani bequeathed 100 ducats to the convent of Santa Giustina to fund an annuity of 10 ducats to "my daughter, *Soror Gabriela*"; Zanetta, widow of Giovanni Contarini, left 400 ducats to her three professed sisters; in wills of 1448 and 1449 Vito da Canal left bequests to three daughters, nuns in three different convents.[75]

Parental attachment to daughters in religious life spilled over into the political arenas dominated by those same families. In 1399 the Dominican reformer Giovanni Dominici, already resented for alienating the patrician nuns of the Venetian convent of Corpus Christi from their families, was accused of challenging the government's control of religious life. The Council of Ten, normally fearsomely firm, was deeply divided whether to proceed against him, reflecting a split in the patriciate between supporters and opponents of his ministry to their daughters, and more generally displaying the complexities and contradictions involved in the interweaving of family ties, political issues, and female religiosity.[76] Another example involved the Roman women who in the early 1400s gathered around the charismatic Santa Francesca Romana. The majority of them were members of formerly politically prominent families that had fallen from power following an abortive coup against Pope Boniface IX in 1398, and their association with Santa Francesca's charitable work provided an alternative prominence to their politically disgraced families.[77] During political struggles between citizens and nobles in mid-sixteenth-century Parma, the Benedictine convent of San Paolo denied entry to the daughters of feudal families: "no matter what means the leading feudatories might try, [the nuns] will never be willing to accept them." In 1533 Corpus Christi in Venice was once again embroiled with the government, this time over the election of a new prioress. According to the papal nuncio, the nuns on the two sides in the dispute between them rallied the support of eighty patrician houses, and it took the Council of Ten to resolve the controversy, by ordering the relatives of the dissident nuns to persuade them to submit to the new prioress "and to indicate in writing their obedience to the most excellent Council of Ten." The princely and noble families of the northern Italian courts also put their stamp on female religiosity, notably in founding and sustaining houses of Franciscan Clarisse (Clares) as convent communities for their own womenfolk. Their power is displayed in the "capture" of the community of Corpus Domini in Ferrara. Founded in the early 1400s by pious middle-class women, in the early 1430s it was taken over by a wealthy noble widow who used her connections with the pope and the Este rulers to reorganize it into a community of Clarisse under the rule of her sister, a nun in the Clarisse motherhouse in Mantua, which had itself been founded in 1420 by the marchioness of that city.[78]

These examples display the contradictory role of convents and holy women in the intertwining of oligarchy, state, and gender. The religious charisma they radiated encouraged regimes to subsidize them as legitimating symbols and prominent families to cultivate them as havens for devout daughters. But the moral disorders that resulted from the use of convents as repositories for unmarriageable upper-class women led governments to assert regulatory authority over them. Women in religion imparted moral stature to the state and evoked moral supervision by the state, contributing doubly to its institutional and ideological development. The key was the crucial importance of convents to the elites: as ostensibly secure "prisons" for excess women, as generously patronized centers of genuine female piety, and as secure homes where families could bestow material and emotional benefactions, and the education of their daughters, on professed kinswomen. Despite the deeply embedded convention that nuns "died" to the secular world, women in religion exerted a multiform influence on the interconnected evolutions of government and oligarchy.[79] But not the greatest influence. The marriages of their sisters were the occasion of even more complicated interweavings of public and private interests in the activities of the state in the late fourteenth and early fifteenth centuries.

IN THEIR DEALINGS with religious women and their efforts to set parameters for orderly sexuality, governments complicated their relationship with domestic patriarchy. The authority of husbands and fathers was the mortar holding together the social order that secured regimes and elites, the main conduit between state and family. But it was also the most formidable antagonist of government regulation of private life and riven by contradictions itself. The state's reliance on fathers reinforced their domestic authority, but it also laid down the rules for their exercise of it. That giving-and-taking fomented tension between public and private interests, between governmental and domestic patriarchy. The greatest source of tension lay in programs launched by regimes in the early Quattrocento both to support and to regulate fathers' arrangements of their daughters' marriages. These programs made fathers grateful beneficiaries of governmental initiatives but also impatient evaders of their terms. Those terms also exacerbated divisions within the elite and added complicating new dimensions to relations between fathers, husbands, and the women who moved between them.

The most creative marriage initiative was the establishment of the Florentine Dowry Fund, the Monte delle Doti, in 1424/25. Designed to alleviate the government's fiscal problems, it was also conceived, like the prostitution and sodomy policies adopted in those years, as a solution to persistent demographic worries.[80] Of all the marriage measures then being enacted in Florence and elsewhere, it was the most practical, providing families with a government-secured investment vehicle for accumulating the dowries that were indispensable for their daughters' marriages. With the Dowry Fund the state inserted itself deeply into the family's basic business, blending governmental and domestic patriarchy in joint management of the destinies of women. However, the government's role involved more than just the financing of marriages; the Monte delle Doti also made the government the guarantor of the family honor that hinged on the transferral of the bodies, and the dangerous sexuality, of women from the authority of fathers to that of husbands. The language of the enabling legislation made female sexuality its basic premise. "Determined to shore up the frailty of the female sex," it stated, the government undertook to ensure that, "provided with dowries, however small, women will be certain to lead virtuous and praiseworthy lives."[81]

Only a few years earlier Venice's government also had inserted itself into dowry transactions, but in the opposite way. Where the Monte delle Doti helped Florentines keep up with dowry inflation, a law of the Venetian Senate in 1420 sought to arrest it, by setting an official maximum of 1,600 ducats for marriage settlements. The rationale was the same: to protect families' property and honor by facilitating the marriages of young women, thereby lessening the forced monacation of tearful daughters and relieving families of the "shame and danger" of having unmarried adult daughters at home.[82] The preamble made clear the Senate's assertion of patriarchal eminent domain over fathers' strategies: since there was "no hope" that fathers would stop competing with each other in dowry size, "it is necessary that such corruption be corrected by our regime." Alongside their new prescriptions for male and female sexuality, the governments of Venice and Florence were claiming the paternal role of guardian of female virtue, family honor, and the orderly movement of women between families.

But measures to facilitate and regulate dowries put regimes at crosspurposes with their own membership and different oligarchical interests with each other, because of the conflicting claims at stake in marriage. For all families, dowries were the best protection against the threat of sexual disgrace that hovered over unmarried daughters, a principle that the Florentine Dowry Fund implemented and which the Venetian criminal courts also applied, ordering rapists and seducers of unmarried girls, deemed guilty of inflicting "the greatest shame and perpetual dishonor" on their victims' fathers, to provide dowries so that the girls might recover their honor. For the bishop of Pistoia, dowries were the means by which girls were "led to honor," a linkage recognized in practice by the Florentine Marco Parenti, who described one woman's dowry as "wealth and honor, which amount to 1,400 [florins]."[83] Private and public observers thus agreed that the surest way for fathers to safeguard their families' sexual honor was by dowering their daughters. The problem was that even with government programs, securing honorable marriages became increasingly difficult for Quattrocento fathers owing to a relentless rise in dowry levels. Upper-class Florentine dowries, which in 1400 ranged from 600 to 900 florins, increased to 1,200–1,600 in the 1460s, and around 2,000 in 1500; overall, between 1425 and 1524 the average dowry soared 83 percent. In Venice the average net patrician dowry (exclusive of *corredo*, or trousseau) rose from 873 ducats in the last third of the Trecento, to 1,230 ducats in the mid-Quattrocento, to 1,732 in 1505–7.[84]

In these circumstances, fathers seized on governmental initiatives that might help increase the dowry possibilities of their marriageable daughters. Thanks to the Monte delle Doti, for example, the investments of 90 and 60 florins that Francesco Tommaso made for his daughters in 1433 turned into dowries of, respectively, 548 florins in 1445 and 500 florins in 1448. Wealthier Florentines also took advantage of the fund; 80 percent of the 1,200 florins that Lucrezia Tornabuoni brought to no less than Piero de' Medici in 1444 came from the account her father had opened for her. The Tornabuoni had lots of company among their fellow patricians: the Adimari made investments for 51 of their daughters, the Rucellai for 94, the Medici for 104, the Strozzi for 113.[85] Even the records of the fund served crafty Florentines seeking to enhance marriage prospects and buttress family honor; many falsely lowered their daughters' ages when opening accounts for them, inventing official documentation of their youthful chastity, the sine qua non for honorable brides. Venice's patricians also turned their government's marriage policy to private purposes. Many post-1420 marriage contracts explicitly proclaimed adherence to the 1,600-ducat ceiling, as the law required, and included marriage portions of exactly that amount. For families whose membership in the patriciate was comparatively recent, or whose economic situation was shaky, meeting an officially set standard for respectable noble dowries was a ready way of demonstrating their intraclass reputability.[86]

Government measures doubtless helped families, but dowry standards were a moving target, because of powerful forces that kept pushing them upward. Among them was the affectionate concern of parents for their daughters' well-being. This meant striving to *alogare* them in the houses of husbands who would give them, in Alessandra Strozzi's phrase, as much "status and nobility" as possible but also to provide for their material well-being over and above their dowries.[87] In 1397 the Venetian noble Giovanni Morosini, who seven years earlier had given his daughter a dowry of 1,000 ducats (which in Venetian law and practice was her personal property), bequeathed her in addition the life income from 10,000 ducats in the state's funded debt (*prestiti*), as well as 2,000 ducats for the dowry of each of her two daughters, who of course were members of a different lineage.[88] Fourteen years later another patrician, Nicolò Mudazzo, left his widowed daughter 3,200 ducats in the state funds, probably in compensation for his use of her dowry when she returned home as a dependent widow (though he declared that the living expenses he had borne for her were a free gift from him). Thanks to his beneficence she ended up with substantial property of her own, bequeathing in her will, drawn up two days after her father's, the dowry-like total of 1,450 ducats to various female relatives, including six married or monacated sisters, but chiefly for her own daughter's dowry.[89] Paternal generosity, complementing that of mothers, gave such Venetian women the means of benefiting not only their fathers' but other lineages, and most especially of enriching their own daughters' dowries, further fueling their increase. Evidence for Florence presented by Isabelle Chabot, Julius Kirshner, and Christiane Klapisch-Zuber conveys a picture of wives and widows whose propertyless dependence contrasts starkly with the social and economic resources of their counterparts in Venice. However, there were in Venice many patrician wives in grim circumstances just as the Florentine picture is blurred by the confident initiatives of the widow Alessandra Macinghi Strozzi, who contributed her own dowry wealth to the dowry of her daughter, and the other widows whose wide-ranging and substantial beneficence is documented by Elaine Rosenthal.[90]

The most insistent pressure pushing dowries upward came not from parental generosity but the imperatives of social honor that pressed on both sides of a marriage alliance.[91] Defending his son in a breach-of-promise suit in 1457, the Venetian noble Jacopo Gabriel declared that "it is unthinkable that the dowry of 350 ducats which donna Orsa [Dolfin, herself a noble] promised my son Giovanni is suitable for a noble of respectable status such as my son; indeed, it would hardly be appropriate for an artisan." He and his brother, he pointedly noted, had received dowries of 2,500 ducats from their wives; by that standard, Orsa Dolfin's 350 ducats were indeed more artisanal than patrician.[92] Alessandra Strozzi, who had made a similarly scornful artisan reference ten years earlier, summed it up: "Whoever takes a wife demands money."[93] And the more prominent the wife taker, the larger his demands and the greater the eagerness of his future wife's family to meet them, regardless of legislated limits.

Not only did the dowry of Jacopo Gabriel's wife set her family and his apart from poorer nobles like Orsa Dolfin, but it also set them above the law. Jacopo and his brother got their 2,500-ducat dowries in the 1430s, which made them gross violators of the 1,600-ducat limit legislated in 1420.[94] Obviously, they found the prestige and profit of getting large dowries, and their fathers-in-law the advantages of a Gabriel marriage connection, more compelling than laws aimed at leveling the matrimonial playing field. They were scarcely alone in spurning government dowry policies. In Venice, as many as one-half of Quattrocento patrician dowries exceeded the legal limit; in Florence, the fathers of more than half of the richest girls of marriageable age declined to open Dowry Fund accounts for their daughters.[95] Their disregard for official norms and programs suggests that government efforts to help hard-pressed families meet dowry standards ironically ended up encouraging dowry inflation: directly, as Antonio Strozzi noted in Florence in 1450, "because of the convenience of the Monte [delle Doti]" for well-placed families seeking to augment other dowry resources; indirectly, because they spurred wealthy families like the Gabriel and their in-laws to distance themselves from their needier fellow patricians by disdaining government restrictions and flaunting lavish settlements given and received.[96]

More than articulating social differences, the marriage initiatives of the early Quattrocento complicated gender relations by imposing a public dimension upon relations between fathers, husbands, and the women who moved between them. The crux of the issue involved what Isabelle Chabot characterizes as the "paradox that struck at agnatic ideology," namely, that although supposedly excluded from an inheritance system whose "material and symbolic identity was exclusively masculine, patrilinear," married women had in their dowries a share of their family's patrimony which inflation was making larger and larger.[97] This vastly complicated property relations between men and women and between families. Chabot and Klapisch-Zuber have described how Florentines responded by devising exchange practices that kept a woman's dowry and trousseau in the hands of either her husband or her father, but the example of Lena Davizzi suggests that not all women were denied possession of their dowries.[98] Recently widowed in 1422, she infuriated her helpless brothers by betaking herself and her dowry to a convent. They were doubly angry because the dowry had been more than her rightful share of the family patrimony in the first place; indeed, amassing it in order to give her "as much ease and honor" as possible had imposed heavy hardship and obligations on them. Unremitting dowry inflation eventually increased women's property to such an alarming extent that Francesco Acciaiuoli would warn the grand duke of Tuscany in 1619 that lavish dowries would end up "shifting all private wealth to women."[99] Doubtless an exaggeration, but anchored in the reality of the conflict inherent in men's need to preserve property in the male line and their desire for honor and connections from marriage. Venetian men also sacrificed to give their women large dowries. One wife acknowledged in 1391 that "my father took so little account of his need to provide for his many children that he gave me a marriage portion worth more than half his worldly goods," and a man noted in 1459 that his married daughter had "received much more than all her brothers will get." Such cases were not rare.[100]

It was the worrisome impact of women's dowries on the wealth of men which underlay government efforts to restrain them, but the state's attention only added to women's economic and social stature. One of the motives impelling the Venetian senators to limit dowries in 1420 was alarm that the fathers who gave their daughters large dowries "gravely damaged and prejudiced their male heirs," and a 1505 law, which yielded to dowry reality by raising the maximum from 1,600 to 3,000 ducats, invited sons to sue their fathers' estates for the equivalent of any excess over the new limit which had gone to their sisters' dowries.[101] The rulers of Pistoia echoed those of Venice and Florence in worrying that "the price of dowries exceeds the substance and patrimony of husbands, and the fathers or brothers of the brides become poor and are stripped bare by them."[102] Such sentiments posed dowry-rich women against their menfolk, but the reality was more complex, because husbands and fathers had competing rather than common interests, and government intervention intensified their rivalry by giving it official expression. The Florentine government seems to have been chiefly supportive of husbands. The revised statutes of 1415 reaffirmed a husband's right to the entire dowry of his predeceased wife in the absence of children; strengthened his control over her nondotal property during the marriage and his right to one-third of it at her death; and bluntly denied wives the right to bequeath their dowries to anyone but husband and children.[103] They also protected the integrity of the patrilineage by forbidding a widow returning to her father's or brother's house to bring her children with her. This last measure betrays the statute writers' sense of the opposing interests of a woman's paternal and marital relations, the conflict between her status as daughter and as wife, which Klapisch-Zuber and Chabot have emphasized.[104] Venice's rulers were instead solicitous of wives' natal families; the penalties for violations of the 1420 law fell on the husbands who received illegal dowries rather than the fathers who gave them, though both sides were liable in the 1505 measure.[105] They had a different worry about richly pursued bridegrooms. When the Senate tried once again in 1535 to stop the relentless inflation, it lamented that young patricians were abandoning the time-honored commercial and maritime traditions of their forefathers, being content instead to live off "these excessive dowries" that their wives brought them.[106]

In the end, the state's efforts to protect the male stake in dowries foundered on the irreconcilability of fathers' and husbands' interests, and the tension between its own efforts to restrain and to support dowries added a third chord to the dissonance. The overlaps and conflicts among the varied interests, public and private, rich and poor, paternal and marital, which were gathered under the umbrella of patriarchy afforded women of the elites the space and resources to pursue their own objectives, and the state's tortuous attempts to sort matters out only underscored women's capacities.

The clearest evidence comes from sumptuary legislation. A Florentine law of 1511 declared that women were spending so much on "disorderly and sumptuous" clothing and jewels that their husbands got "poco frutto" from their dowries; and a follow-up measure of 1516 lamented that the 1511 law was being intentionally misinterpreted "by both men and women." Those complaints echoed Venetian ones that women's extravagant expenditures "on wicked and impractical" adornments "consumed their husbands and sons" or "ruined their husbands and fathers."[107] The government's solution, to require husbands or fathers "or whoever has authority over these women" to restrain them or pay a fine, reveals its own helplessness in the face of the contradictory impulses within patriarchy. Forcing men to stop practices that "ruined" them was unpromising in itself, but its fatuousness was accentuated by men's connivance in the magnificence of their womenfolk, "the status-bearers," in Diane Hughes's apt phrase, "of their fathers' lineage and their husbands."[108]

Generous dowries and trousseaux forced sisters into convents, impoverished brothers, and sparked in-law competition for the property and loyalty of married women, but they also advertised the wealth, status, and honor of the families that gave and received them.[109] Governments may indeed have been determined to rein in expenditures on women, as Catherine Kovesi Killerby has recently insisted, but their initiatives were whipsawed in the cross-purposes of the very men who voted in the council chambers: not only between fathers and husbands but within individual men, themselves likely to be at one time or another—and often simultaneously—husbands, fathers of daughters, and fathers of sons.[110] In the end, the principal effect of the state's efforts to sort out this welter of interests was to bear witness in its own decrees that the inherent rivalry of fathers and husbands made women formidable agents in the marriage practices where public and private life merged.

Moreover, as Giulia Calvi has argued, "hundreds of women were given voice in public institutions, because the state, in its phase of centralization and expansion . . . legitimated these women as its interlocutors." Calvi's own research provides an excellent example. In 1393, as part of its new social interventionism, the Florentine government created the Magistrato dei Pupilli to look after the interests of fatherless children. Among

other procedures, the new magistracy validated widows' assumption of
the family headship vested in them in their husbands' wills. The effect
was to give an official stamp of approval to widows' taking on the patriarchal responsibilities of administering their husbands' property and
raising their children, and thus to make widows participants in the enlarged public sphere. These effects reverberated in the family and the
lineage. According to Calvi, the interaction of widows and the Magistrato
dei Pupilli contributed to a "softening of the formal structure of the patrilineal system," sanctioning "a bilineal orientation that was not only affective and informal, but, indeed, was given shape on the basis of [women's]
prerogatives and roles, the social and juridical importance of which it
explicitly and officially recognized."[111]

The Florentine government's sensitivity to the worrisome potential of
the social ambiguity of well-dowered widows had other effects, as well. At
the same time that the revised statutes of 1415 reaffirmed women's lack of
freedom to dispose of their dowries, they also gave them the right to
reclaim the dowries when widowed, in order to facilitate their remarriage.[112] Nor were the Florentine rulers alone in their attentiveness to
widows. Revised statutes in Milan in 1396 also guaranteed widows' dowries for remarriage, and the wealth going into dowries prompted Venice's
rulers as well to protect the interest of widows and their natal families.[113]
In 1449, noting the "labore magno" that some widows had to go through
to recover their dowries from their husbands' estates, the members of the
Great Council—in their capacity as fathers of daughters rather than as
husbands of future widows—passed a law requiring notaries to deposit in
the government chancery copies of all dowry receipts and wills in which
husbands acknowledged their wives' dowries; recorded in an official register, these would constitute an official record that widows could cite in the
dowry-restitution procedure.[114] Widows were a special category, but in
Venice the government was framing more precise functional identities for
other women, as well. The dowry limitation law of 1420 explicitly exempted widows and unmarried women aged twenty-four or over, both of
whom "should retain the liberty they now possess": evidence of official
awareness of the difficulties such women had in marrying. It likewise
exempted the daughters of wealthy popolani who married nobles, thereby
infusing new wealth into the patriciate; they could bring dowries of 2,000
ducats rather than 1,600. This nuanced attention to distinctions among
women even took in physical characteristics. In 1425 the Senate waived
the dowry ceiling for blind women and in 1444 extended the waiver to

lame or misshapen women, in order that those "whom nature had injured but fortune had adorned could marry."[115]

THE EXPANSION of the state's policies and apparatus of social intervention around 1400 produced official definitions of the roles of men and women in society, fashioning a prescriptive gender structure that hardened the differences between husbands and fathers (and by silent exclusion highlighted the otherness of unmarried male adults) and gave official standing to the variations and nuances of female experience by vocation, age, marital status, and social class.[116] Sumptuary legislation acknowledged the economic leverage of wives; dowry policies showed governmental concern with the disruptive potential of female sexuality; regulating behavior in convents merged civic morality with the consequences of private marriage strategies; the campaigns to regulate prostitution applied official labels and rules to the women in the business; and anti-sodomy policies equated proper masculinity with sexual dominion over women. All these initiatives attest to the state's recognition that the social order necessary to the security of regimes rested in large measure on addressing the troubling uncertainties of the ambiguous and flexible social position of women and of the manifold circumstances of men's relations with them.

The governments of Florence and Venice, and of other states, embarked in the years around 1400 on a wide-ranging effort to regulate politics and society in a way that would secure regimes shaken by recent upheavals. Central to this effort was directive intervention in social transactions with potential for disturbing the orderly stability that ensured the hegemony of elites. The consequence was to move the boundaries between the public and the private, with the state now absorbing within its domain fundamental concerns of the domestic realm. Tracing the long-term trajectory of this process (though with a French-centered chronology different from that offered here), Roger Chartier argues that the "construction of the modern state . . . is a necessary condition for defining a private sphere as distinct from a clearly identifiable public one." His suggestion that the state did not so much take over the private sphere as stimulate the clearer definition of its dimensions and activities is endorsed by Crouzet-Pavan, who sees the effect already accomplished in Venice by the late fifteenth century.[117] Yet persistent resistance to governmental direction argues in favor of the applicability to the Renaissance state of Philippe Ariès's suggestion that the ambitious reach of the early modern state exceeded its capacity to impose its will.[118] In Florence, for example, triumphant Medici partisans in 1512 revoked a dowry limit imposed the previous year, on the principle that "marriages must be free, and that everyone should be free to endow his daughters, sisters and other female relatives as he sees fit and as he likes, because one must be able to arrange his affairs in his way"; in Venice, the Senate's third attempt at dowry limitation, in 1535, was necessitated by the "immoderate dowries" provided by fathers who, in spite of the previous attempt in 1505, "had no respect" for the state's authority.[119]

Aggressive, institutionalized state intervention in the affairs of society in the late fourteenth and early fifteenth centuries and the conflicting private responses to it made the dimensions of the domestic realm an open, contested question, with fatherly and husbandly authority both supported by governments taking over patriarchal prerogatives and resistant to them when government initiatives clashed with the private interests of husbands or fathers, themselves now more clearly differentiated by state action. The divisions and conflicts between patriarchal structures in both their governmental and private dimensions marked out a space where women with economic resources, social support, and personal ability could maneuver their way through, between, against, or with those interests. How they did so and with what success are questions that need much research. But scholarship has already laid the groundwork for a fuller discussion of the relationship between gender and the Renaissance state, that is, for a richer, more integrative political history. Such a discussion, it is to be hoped, would explore not only how expanding government modified gender roles and relations but also the reverse: how new complications and ambiguities in the relationships between men and women, provoked by the momentous political and social developments of the fourteenth and fifteenth—and sixteenth—centuries, influenced the direction of governmental growth in the Renaissance.

Marriage Regulation

in Venice,

1420–1535

IN JULY 1457 two Venetian nobles, Jacopo Gabriel and Pasquale Malipiero, appeared in the court of the patriarch of Venice to defend Gabriel's son, Giovanni, against a breach-of-promise suit brought by the noblewoman Orsa Dolfin.[1] She claimed that in March 1455 Giovanni had married her by touching her hand in the presence of witnesses but had failed to follow through by taking her (*transducere*) to live with him; now she petitioned Venice's highest ecclesiastical tribunal to compel him to complete the marriage.[2] Gabriel and Malipiero's defense strategy was to impeach Orsa's suitability as a wife. "No one of sound mind," they declared, would credit such a marriage, since the two parties were "unequal in every respect."[3] They claimed that at the time of the purported touching of hands she was thirty years old *et ultra*, while Giovanni was only eighteen. Worse, she was "not of good or chaste life and reputation." If Giovanni frequented her, it was not "to contract marriage but to have sexual relations with her, as young men do," and "if he made the marriage— and we have no knowledge of it, indeed we find it impossible to believe that he did so—it was because he was seduced and tricked."[4]

Above all, they stressed Orsa's and Giovanni's social and economic inequality. Giovanni's paternal great-grandfather had left his two sons, Zaccaria, Giovanni's grandfather, and Zaccaria's brother, also named Giovanni, an estate worth 50,000 ducats, which would have put them jointly among the richest 1.5 percent of Venetians.[5] Moreover, the elder Giovanni had married the daughter of none other than Doge Antonio Venier (1382–1400). Though less illustriously married, Zaccaria had left his three sons an estate worth probably more than 80,000 ducats.[6] Equally important, he had negotiated prestigious marriages for them: Marco marrying Doge Antonio Venier's granddaughter; Girolamo, a woman from the Mocenigo lineage, with three Quattrocento doges; and "ego Jacobus," the daughter of his partner on the defense team, young Giovanni's maternal grandfather, Pasquale Malipiero, who would himself be elected doge the following year. These marriages were lustrous because of the paternity and the marriage portions of the brides: Marco received 3,000 ducats, Girolamo and Jacopo 2,500 ducats each. These were exceptionally—and, as we shall see below, illegally—large dowries.

In stark contrast with those glittering credentials, Gabriel and Malipiero dismissed Orsa's paternal grandfather, Luca Dolfin, as a pauper and pointed out that her father, Antonio Dolfin, and his brother, Nicolò, had married commoners ("non nobilem sed plebeiam"). The Dolfin brothers had "always lived in poverty," been elected to few offices in the government, and lacked the means to pay government imposts. Consistent with this sorry profile was Orsa's alleged dowry. "It is unthinkable," Jacopo Gabriel declared, "that the dowry donna Orsa promised my son Giovanni, 350 ducats, is suitable for a noble of respectable status such as my son; indeed, it would hardly be appropriate for an artisan." Indeed, such a meager dowry was itself evidence that Orsa and her allies "thought to gull him owing to the youth's childish innocence." Altogether, "this alleged marriage is anything but equal with regard to the age, status, nobility, wealth, influence, experience [annorum], and other such characteristics of Giovanni and Orsa; on the contrary, it is of great disparity and inequality, as anyone aware of their respective circumstances would conclude."[7]

How the patriarch's court decided Orsa's suit is not known, but the interest of the case lies less in its disposition than in the contrast between Orsa and Giovanni painted by the young man's father and grandfather. They depicted a patrician marriage model based on worldly maturity in grooms, chaste youth in brides—values shared by the Gabriels' counterparts in Florence—and, most emphatically, the wealth and prominence of both contracting families, qualities conspicuously lacking in the Dolfins.[8] The critical indicator of socioeconomic status was thus a record of marriages with distinguished noble (and preferably ducal) families and generous marriage portions. For Jacopo Gabriel and Pasquale Malipiero, to be noble was to marry nobly, that is, richly and prestigiously.

Yet their patrician ideal was not the only one current in Quattrocento Venice. Despite their strenuous arguments to the contrary, Orsa Dolfin also was a patrician.[9] Indeed, for all that Jacopo Gabriel sought to portray his family as more noble than hers, another gauge reversed that ranking.

A roster of Venice's ruling class compiled a century earlier—during the dogeship of Giovanni Dolfin (1356–61), coincidentally—had included the Dolfin among the twelve "noblest" houses, Venice's founders in the distant past and its rulers during the intervening centuries.[10] By contrast, the Gabriel were merely listed among the noble rank and file, with no mention of great deeds or even origins.[11] These differences reveal very different conceptions of nobility: one based on distinction over many centuries, the other on wealth, connections, and political prominence in the present. In the fifteenth century they collided. The supremacy of the Dolfin and twenty-three other ancient houses, called the *case vecchie* or *longhi,* was challenged by a new noble elite, less ancient and historically lustrous but more aggressive and wealthy. The symbol of the change was the newer houses' capture of the ducal throne.[12] Whereas all but one of the doges elected in the two centuries before 1382 belonged to the case vecchie, after that year they would not see one of their number on the ducal throne until 1612. Thus, when Jacopo Gabriel and the doge-to-be Pasquale Malipiero documented the inferiority of Orsa Dolfin's family, they were asserting criteria of nobility which represented a change in the sociopolitical culture of the patriciate, proudly proclaimed in Jacopo's recitation of the doges in his family's recent marriages.

But ducal politics, criteria of nobility, and the culture of matrimony in fifteenth-century Venice are not reducible to contention between a wealthy, new power elite and the older status elite. Surrounding both those groups was a more miscellaneous element, the 150 houses that constituted the noble majority. Including some families of venerable lineage as well as relative newcomers, its members were united by dependence on the economic benefits of noble status and a determination to tighten their monopoly of them.[13] For the men and women of this group, the ancient prominence of the Dolfin and the wealth and connections of the Gabriel were irrelevant or unattainable or both. What they possessed, beyond material need, was the capacity to press their interests in government councils. Their deployment of it between 1420 and 1535 turned the attention of the state to dowries and the women they accompanied, as the chief determinants of nobility.

The complex interactions between the case vecchie, the new "ducal" houses, and the patrician rank and file shaped the structure of patrician society and regime from the later Trecento into the Cinquecento. They were played out at the boundaries between government authority, social interaction, and family interest, blending into one encompassing dynamic the meanings of nobility, government, and the role of women. These were matters of contention in their own right; the persistent refashioning of each with reference to the others gives Venetian society and regime from the fourteenth to the sixteenth century wide-ranging dynamism behind its familiar façade of stasis. The principal thoroughfare through this shifting landscape is legislation on marriage. In increasingly precise enactments, the government refined its definition of nobility and extended the purview of its authority by prescribing the ways in which families were to reproduce themselves and the ruling class. Because of the pivotal role of women, the legislation focused on them. Examining it reveals conflicting interests, public and private, among nobles, within families, and between men and women. The stakes and the discourse framing them changed over the decades, and the government's evolving responses reveal that the most consistent characteristic of "the state" in Venice was its mutability, reflecting unsettled ideas in noble society about daughters, wives, and mothers. To follow the regulation of marriage during those years is thus to follow change and contestation in the relationships between regime and ruling class, government and family, and men and women.

THE TAKEOFF POINT was the first third of the Quattrocento, when a cluster of laws defined noble marriage. In 1422, the Great Council acted to deny noble status to the sons, even legitimate, of noble fathers and mothers of servile or otherwise "vile" status.[14] The stated purpose of the legislation, to prevent "denigration" of the council by unworthy members, was overwhelmingly endorsed, gaining the votes of 422 of the 473 council members present.[15] That near unanimity is in striking contrast with the vote on a forerunner measure of 1376, prohibiting nobles' bastards from inheriting their fathers' status. Though also premised on the need to avoid "denigration of the honor and reputation of our regime [dominii]," it prevailed only on the third reading, and then with a majority of only 51 percent.[16] Unlike 1422, in 1376 there had been no consensus on marriage as the medium of the class's reproduction, or on the mothers of the next generation of nobles. It was expressly to repair this deficiency that the new legislation was proposed. By instituting a requirement that all claimants to noble status document their mothers' identities along with their fathers', it made maternity a determinant of nobility.

Two years earlier, in August 1420, the more restricted and powerful Senate had also moved on marriage, enacting the first limit on dowries.[17] Alarmed by the "wicked practice that has arisen" of ambitious matchmaking fathers pushing dowry levels so high "that many of our nobles cannot get their daughters married" while others compromised the inheritance prospects of their sons, the act's proponents urged imposing a ceiling of 1,600 ducats, two-thirds to count as dowry, the other one-third as *corredo.* The distinction is important. The dowry strictly so called was a daughter's share of the patrimony, to be returned to her or to heirs designated by her at the end of the marriage.[18] But the corredo, originally the trousseau brought by the bride, had evolved by the early Quattrocento into a gift to the husband, retained by him or his estate when the dowry was returned to the wife.[19] Underscoring the distinction, the preamble noted that fathers were earmarking more of the marriage settlement for the corredo at the expense of the dowry, with the result that daughters were losing the inheritances they would otherwise have enjoyed. Limiting marriage settlements thus had two purposes: to prevent fathers from squandering family wealth on their daughters' marriages, and to restrain the tendency toward deemphasizing dowries in order to inflate the corredo premiums with which fathers attracted desirable sons-in-law.

Like the Gabriel-Dolfin litigation, the 1420 dowry law revealed divisions among nobles on marriage and the role of government. Proponents urged state intervention to save, and deter, fathers from the ruinous pressures of the marriage market, because "otherwise these corruptions cannot be extirpated."[20] But others saw government standards as an unwarranted intrusion into private matters. In contrast to the Great Council's overwhelming endorsement two years later of the law excluding low-status women from patrician motherhood, the dowry limitation measure passed the Senate with a majority of only four: 51 votes in favor, 27 against, and 20 abstentions. Four months later the opponents acted to repeal the law, claiming that its unprecedented usurpation of the rights of fathers had thrown the entire marriage market into "such confusion that no marriages are being contracted."[21] Worse, it had caused a "significant loss of honor and freedom [*libertas*] for our state and citizens." The word *libertas* appears four times in the repeal bill, whose proponents declared that only one thing could right the wrong: to nullify the August law, thus "restoring to all our citizens and subjects [*fideles*] their customary liberty in matters of marriage and dowry." Despite the support of 45 of the 126 senators present, the repeal measure failed, but its premises presented a powerful challenge to government regulation of marriage. Against state action to aid embattled fathers, unmarriageable daughters, and sons with bleak inheritance prospects, it claimed the high ground of honor, freedom, and Venetian tradition—as well as orderly matrimonial practice now thrown into disarray by government meddling.[22]

Two contending patrician ideologies were mobilized over government regulation of marriage. On one side were libertarians, invoking Venice's most sacred traditions in their opposition to restrictions on their use of their matrimonial capital. Among them were wealthy and well-connected families for whom large dowries were a means of gaining or consolidating social prominence. Indeed, if Jacopo Gabriel's boasting about the dowries his kinsmen commanded is accurate, such families had a compelling motive for opposing dowry limits: Jacopo and his brother Girolamo were in violation of the law of 1420, both having received 2,500-ducat dowries in the 1430s.[23] Joining them on the libertarian side were case vecchie men loath to lose the dowry-corredo payoff from their marketability as prestigious sons-in-law (although poorer case vecchie men with daughters, such as Antonio Dolfin, welcomed restraints on dowry standards). Finally, wealthy and socially ambitious newcomers also had good reason to resist restrictions on the free marriage market. The father of the bride who brought 3,000 ducats in 1419 to Jacopo Gabriel's eldest brother, Marco, would have chafed under the limit of 1,600 passed the following year.[24] Whether as purveyors or as recipients of large marriage settlements, whether members of distinguished ancient houses or of newly wealthy families striving for status and connections, men with the means and will to advance their family's interest by advantageous marriages had no sympathy with the leveling aims of dowry limitation. For them, the salient mark of nobility was wealth, antiquity, or preferably both, displayed in the marriage market by dowries and corredi conveyed and commanded. Their spokesmen in the Senate, urging repeal, could clothe their interests in the sacredness of the traditional freedom of Venetians to conduct private affairs without governmental interference.

Yet they were greatly outnumbered by noble families hard pressed to keep up with steadily rising dowry standards, who advanced a statist ideology premised on governmental responsibility for the well-being of private citizens. For them, "customary freedom" counted for less than protection from economic distress, and the only agency capable of warding it off was the government. In the language of the August law, the inflation in dowries and corredi "had to be corrected by *regimen nostrum*, since otherwise it cannot be stopped." The appeal to government intervention built on recent precedent. Starting in the 1380s the statist ideology had produced new programs of economic relief for hard-pressed nobles and new procedures for proving patrician status, in order to prevent men of dubious credentials from competing for those programs.[25] The convergence of state and nobility tightened as needy patricians assigned to the government the authority to define and attribute noble status and the responsibility of assuring them of the tangible benefits of possessing it.

Those earlier initiatives targeted men, defining noble credentials in the male line, the masculine role in government, and men's responsibility for providing for their families.[26] In contrast, the marriage laws of the 1420s emphasized the importance of women, in the determination of noble status and in the ominous consequences of dowry competition. In this they gave legislative voice to ideas that the young patrician humanist Francesco Barbaro had expressed only a few years earlier in his treatise *De re uxoria* (1415–16). Barbaro's emphasis on maternal lineage in breeding worthy patricians and his disapproval of large dowries in favor of wifely virtue prefigured the legislation of the 1420s.[27] The law of 1422 dictating status requirements for the mothers of nobles was premised on a class-based notion of female honor. By accrediting only women of a certain economic and social substance as mothers of nobles, it explicitly fortified the bastard-exclusion law of 1376, since respectable women could be relied on not to conceive bastards who, subsequently legitimized, might "denigrate" the Great Council.[28] Other legislation of the time intensified scrutiny of the paternal credentials of claimants to patrician status.[29] Now in 1422 it was deemed just as necessary for officials to ascertain "who is or was the mother" of every would-be noble. Government supervision of marriage was the means of safeguarding the exclusiveness of the patriciate, with the status and virtue of mothers now joining paternal descent as an essential gauge of nobility.

Women also preoccupied the framers of the dowry-restraining law of 1420. Curtailing matrimonial laissez-faire was a way of saving fathers from themselves: not only from the peril into which their alliance seeking threw family finances but also from the morally dangerous effects on their daughters. Large dowries for some girls entailed imprisoning their sisters in convents or, worse, keeping them unmarried at home, an expedient so "dangerous and shameful [that it] was practiced nowhere else in the world."[30] Even women who did marry suffered from their fathers' avidity for desirable sons-in-law, owing to the inflation of the corredo portion of marriage settlements at the expense of the dowry portion, which constituted wives' inheritance. These were the *corruptiones* into which the pressures of the marriage market were leading fathers desperate to meet the ruinous standards set by wealthy families. The measure of the corruption was its effect on the women of the class, whose need was offered as justification for government regulation. This was the first but would not be the last time the state, asserting its concern for patrician daughters and legislating measures designed to protect their interests, overrode the domestic authority of fathers.

On the same day the Senate passed the dowry-limitation law, it adopted three companion measures. One waived the 1,600-ducat limit for *popolane* girls "who contract marriage ties with nobles"; they could bring portions of 2,000 ducats.[31] This was a concession to needy nobles such as Orsa Dolfin's father, Antonio, who had gladly negotiated his casa vecchia credentials for the 2,000-ducat dowry his "plebeian" wife brought him.[32] For all the scorn of men like Jacopo Gabriel and Pasquale Malipiero, the prospect of large dowries from hypergamous brides had wide appeal among nobles: although the 2,000-ducat limit prevailed, one-third of the senators actually favored setting no limit at all.[33] The rival proposals for the dowries of popolane express different patrician conceptions of wifely desirability, one emphasizing birth, the other dowry wealth. They parallel the contrast between the ancient but impoverished Dolfin and the rich and well-connected but until recently undistinguished Gabriel—with an interesting twist. For it was the Dolfin whose status outweighed their current straits and who could thus marry women of the populace without fear of losing it.[34] For newly prominent families such as the Gabriel, however, prestigious alliances, preferably with families with ducal luster and forged by means of large dowries, were necessary advertisements of recently attained status.

The Senate's debate on marriage displayed a range of patrician interests. Setting a limit on settlements protected rank-and-file noble families from the derogatory effects of unrestrained dowry inflation.[35] The higher ceilings extended to popolane brides legitimated fortune hunting outside the patriciate by families down on their luck. And the effort to repeal the newly legislated dowry limit reveals the keenness of the wealthy to benefit from their advantage on the marriage market. But on one thing all interests converged: whether libertarian or statist, they pressed their objectives in the legislative councils of the government, now the arena of debate on noble marriage, on the mothers of nobles, on nobility.

But the Quattrocento state's concern with women was not confined to their parentage and marriage portions. Another law enacted at the session of 22 August 1420 took up inheritances by married women which exceeded the 1,600-ducat dowry limit. In such cases, the excess, if liquid, was to be invested in the woman's name in the state funds (Camera degli Imprestiti), there to remain until her marriage ended; if immovable property, it was not to be sold until the end of the marriage.[36] The stated purpose of the law was to prevent women's nondowry wealth from serving as disguised dowry supplements or otherwise falling under their husbands' control. Although her capital had to remain unredeemed for the duration of the marriage, "a married woman in this situation is at all times free to make whatever use she chooses of the interest income from her *prestiti* or the rental income from her real estate holdings."[37] Confirming women's economic rights—and protecting nondowry female inheritance, often overlooked in scholarship—was the means by which the government sought to set the terms of the economic relationship between families that came together in marriage. That aim surfaced again in 1449 in an act of the Great Council requiring notaries to submit a copy of every dowry receipt they notarized to the government chancery, there to be recorded, with the date of the receipt, in a "large parchment book."[38] The stated reason for the measure was that too often widows lost track of receipts notarized decades earlier, with the result that property rightfully theirs remained in their husbands' estates. The new registration requirement would provide widows with documentation in government records, thus enabling them to recover their dowries without "great effort" (*labore magno*).

The government's sensitivity to the varied circumstances of womanhood is evident in other marriage legislation of the 1420s. A third supplemental measure passed on 22 August exempted widows and unmarried women aged twenty-four and over from the dowry ceilings just enacted.[39] Fathers and brothers themselves, the senators knew that women past adolescence had more difficulty attracting husbands and thus required larger dowries.[40] The same was true of widows. Whether in the famous typology of the "cruel mother" framed by Christiane Klapisch-Zuber,[41] the young widow quickly forced to abandon her children and remarry for the benefit of her brothers, or in the equally likely case of a widow voluntarily seeking security and companionship for herself and her fatherless children,[42] women entering second marriages had to add a premium to their dowries in order to compete for husbands with girls unencumbered by ties to earlier marriages. By tailoring marriage regulation to the phases of the female life cycle, the senators displayed awareness of the nuances of women's roles in relations between and within families. As if to help families avoid the stain of overage female wantonness with which Jacopo

Gabriel and Pasquale Malipiero would seek to taint Orsa Dolfin in the 1450s, the Senate amended its dowry regulations to enable families to avoid the perils to male interest and honor associated with mature, unmarried female relatives living outside convent walls.[43]

With another law five years later, the government further tailored its marriage rules to distinctions among women. On 22 March 1425 the Senate directed the state attorneys, the Avogadori di Comun, to prosecute evasions of the new limits, ordering any husband who received a dowry larger than 1,600 ducats to return the excess to his wife's family and also pay a fine in the same amount.[44] There was one exception: men who married blind women were not held to the legal limit. Eighteen years later, that exemption was extended to husbands of physically misshapen women.[45] These two laws balanced the need to restrain dowries against the importance of marriage for all women, among whom, the Senate recognized, there were distinctions that impinged on their marriageability. The preamble to the latter measure declared its concern for the "subvention" of women with physical disabilities, in order that "those women may also marry who are physically insulted by nature but economically embellished by fortune."[46]

The legislation of the early Quattrocento reveals the centrality of marriage in maneuvers over the meaning of nobility, the issue on which the status, prominence, and material well-being of all patricians hinged. For all segments of the ruling class, the political and social importance of marriage was immense, fueling private and public tensions over the assembling of dowries, to which government councils responded with aggressive new initiatives to regulate patrician marriage. The stakes were vital: to prevent the most vulnerable nobles from being priced out of the noble marriage market, with all the dangers to social and political order which might follow from their loss of status and connections, a concern expressed in other legislation in the same years which underscored the importance of conducting government business "in the most equitable way possible, in order to prevent divisiveness among the nobles of Venice."[47] The means of defusing such problems was to deepen the state's involvement in the business of marriage, which entailed bringing into focus the distinctive characteristics of women, who emerge in this legislation as the articulating medium of governmental direction of social relations, both within the patriciate and between patriciate and *popolo*. The early years of the following century saw a further escalation of marriage legislation, bringing a new ideological significance to the mediating role of women in the state's evolving definition of nobility.

THE FIRST DECADES of the Cinquecento witnessed the blossoming of the "myth of Venice," the body of celebratory writing which attributed Venice's exceptional political stability to a combination of divine favor, constitutional perfection, and the patriciate's wise government.[48] The promulgation of the myth was a response to economic and political blows suffered in the decades around 1500: losses of Eastern possessions to the Ottoman Turks; news of the navigation of non-Mediterranean routes to the East; and, most devastating of all, the shattering defeats of the war of Cambrai.[49] In the face of these reverses, adulatory treatises by learned nobles fashioned an ideology that celebrated Venice's long history of prosperity and stability as evidence of the divinely inspired justice that uniquely marked the government and its custodians.[50] The myth's ideological application was also displayed in legislative language that to the early Quattrocento linkage between the honor of the regime and the genealogical purity of the patriciate added a new element: the divinely mandated and historically proven governing mission of the ruling class. The language appears in a 1497 law of the powerful Council of Ten, which claimed as its mandate "to ensure justice and uniformity [*equabilitate*] among all those who participate in providing peaceful and secure government for our republic, which thanks to God's grace and mercy is prospering."[51]

The chief means of carrying out the mandate was once again regulation of marriage. The best-known measure of the period is the law passed by the Council of Ten in 1506 instituting the famous Libri d'Oro, registers of male noble births.[52] Its main provision was to require nobles to notify the Avogadori di Comun of the birth of sons, whose names were then officially recorded. The rationale resembled that of the law of 1422 disqualifying sons of low-status women: to protect the Great Council from "contamination, blemishing, or any other denigration." But there was something new, as well. Keeping out interlopers was now declared to be critical to the "preservation of the peaceful union" as well as of the "glorious reputation" of the state—a goal that "our most wise forefathers" had "zealously" pursued in their diligent concern for the "common good."[53] The common good was thus construed as resting on concord among the nobles entrusted with the government of Venice, a principle now dignified by the invocation of the past. Crucial to realizing it were the identities of the mothers who bore the sons. Henceforth, an official noble birth certificate would include not only the patrilineal qualification but also "the birthplace and surname of the mother," in order to ensure that she met the criteria established in the law of 1422.[54] Those requirements put the highest value on mothers born of noble families, whose pedigree and virtue were recognizable by all and whose inscription in an official register would be a permanent document of the bilateral patrician bloodlines of their sons, whether born in Venice or abroad.[55]

Uniformity within the ruling class was thus tied more tightly than ever to respectable parentage on both sides. That principle, already institutionalized in 1422, required reaffirmation in the early Cinquecento because of the large number of male nobles prevented from marrying respectably in the competitive matrimonial climate. Despite the official ceiling set in 1420, dowries had continued to grow, sparking new efforts at restraint in the early Cinquecento, as will be noted shortly. Dowry inflation limited the number of patrician girls who could marry, inevitably excluding men from the patrician marriage market in the same proportion, which may have exceeded 40 percent.[56] However, whereas unmarriageable girls most often ended up in convents, permanent bachelorhood left men at large, to enter informal liaisons outside their own class or to satisfy their sexual urges in more disorderly ways.[57] Marino Sanudo reported in his famous *Diarii* the "shame to the Venetian nobility" brought by the marriage in 1526 between the noble Andrea Michiel and the "sumptuous and beautiful prostitute" Cornelia Grifo.[58] It was to counter the insistent efforts of fathers to insinuate the offspring of such *mésalliances*, legitimate or not, into the patriciate that newborn sons and their mothers were now required to be registered in the Libri d'Oro.

The effect was further to refine the definition of nobility. The Libro d'Oro law sharpened the distinction between men who reproduced the ruling class in the officially prescribed way, newly reaffirmed by the Council of Ten, and others who were denied, or who rejected, the generative patriarchy that constituted the fullness of male noble status. The measure of difference was in the origins and surnames of the women with whom nobles fathered offspring, to be made public not, as in 1422, when a noble's son sought to take his place among the male adults in the Great Council but at birth. Approved marriage, producing bilaterally qualified sons, was now proclaimed the medium not only of noble heredity and the patriciate's reputation but of the peace and unity of the regime; and the enforcement of proper marriage was now assigned to the oversight and record keeping of a government magistracy. The act also declared that henceforth entries in the birth registers of the Avogadori di Comun would be the only valid documentation of the credentials of candidates for membership in the Great Council or for government office.[59] The identities of wives and mothers, officially noted at every stage of a noble's political career, were more than ever the measure of a family's conformity to the standards of patrician culture.

Their importance was affirmed even more strongly two decades later. In April 1526 the Council of Ten moved the locus of enforcement from the birth of sons to marriage itself, enacting a requirement that all noble marriages must henceforth be registered with the Avogadori di Comun within one month of the nuptials.[60] As in 1506, at stake was nothing less than "the honor, peace, and preservation of our state," which rested on the "immaculacy and purity" of the "status and order of nobility."[61] Reporting the Ten's deliberations, Marino Sanudo explained that "many bastards have been accorded noble status" and "the doge and the Ducal Council are incensed."[62] Although it was aimed at bastard interlopers, the law's broader effect was to institute a civil marriage procedure for the ruling class. It was an elaborate procedure, requiring the presence of two of the groom's near kin and two of the bride's, all of whom were to swear to the legitimate marriage of the spouses and to "declare the quality of the bride's father and her status"[63]—requirements that were almost certainly a response to the marriage, ten days earlier, between Andrea Michiel and the prostitute Cornelia Grifo. The information thus provided was then to be entered into yet another specially designated register and signed by all three Avogadori di Comun. Henceforth, any young man seeking to establish his noble credentials had to be born of a marriage recorded in that register; lacking that documentation, he would not be recognized as noble.[64]

The Ten represented these measures as appropriate to a well-instituted republic, which, thanks to God's grace, Venice was ("questa per la divina gratia ben instituta Republica"), a phrase canonized in Domenico Morosini's "De bene instituta re publica."[65] In this treatise, written between 1497 and 1509, the politically influential Morosini proposed to reform the government by strengthening the hegemony of an oligarchical elite, who would thus be able to deal with the worrisome problems of too many poor nobles dependent on government jobs and too many young nobles disrupting Great Council sessions.[66] Morosini's emphasis on institutions was echoed, though more optimistically, in the most widely read treatise on

Venice's government, the *De magistratibus et republica Venetorum* of Gasparo Contarini.[67] The vein of political reflection represented by these works, urging institutional adjustments to enhance the governing mission of the patriciate, provided the context of the Council of Ten's efforts to safeguard the integrity of the ruling class by documenting the identities of the mothers of newborn nobles.

In contrast with the legislation of the 1420s, the Cinquecento laws were framed within Venice's most hallowed traditions. The marriage registration requirement of 1526, like the Libro d'Oro law, was associated with precedents set by "our wise and benign ancestors" in their efforts to safeguard the purity of the patriciate.[68] This clothing of governmental innovation in the garb of tradition, a trait described by Angelo Ventura as the "paradox of the Venetian cultural experience," captures the ideological evolution that the patrician regime had undergone since the 1420s.[69] Then, the state's intrusion into marriage making had been opposed by libertarians who based their opposition to dowry limits on what they declared to be the venerable tradition of fatherly autonomy in family matters. In the anxious years after 1500, however, it was the proponents of state regulation anchoring their proposals in the heritage of "sapientissimi progenitores nostri" who, like their descendants in the Council of Ten, were depicted as having always promoted the common good, the stability of the ruling class, and the Almighty's favor by means of resolute government action, now aimed at equalizing the reproductive possibilities of all patrician houses, rich and poor, ancient and recent.

However, the very laws that would subordinate differences of wealth and antiquity to the government's leveling procedures had the effect of sharpening another distinction, that between nobles who married and those who did not. Though designed chiefly to scrutinize the wives and sons of nobles, the registration requirements decreed for marriages and births also certified the passages of noble men into marriage and fatherhood. It was their marriages to respectable women and the births of their sons, both now ratified by official documentation, which secured the purity of the ruling class and its unbroken continuity from revered ancestors to unblemished successors. By thus reinforcing the generative exclusiveness that distinguished nobles from other Venetians, the new requirements enhanced the dignity of domestic patriarchy at the same time as they laid down rules for its exercise. In the process they consigned the growing percentage of permanent bachelors to a second-class patrician status, forever excluded from the ritual experience of registering their marriage and fatherhood, the means by which the sacred mission of the ruling class was to be perpetuated. Further stigmatizing such men, the extramarital heterosexual options available to them, the women with whom they consorted, and the illegitimate offspring of their unions were officially represented as polluting threats to the nobility's most sacred traditions.[70]

Proclaiming an ideology in which successful government was premised on ancient tradition and divine prescription, the laws of 1506 and 1526 converted the hitherto private events of birth and marriage into civil acts, involving official certification of the men and women who were the agents of the transgenerational continuity of their own lineages and of the patriciate itself. As in the early Quattrocento, those initiatives were coupled with new efforts to restrain dowries. In the aftermath of the dowry law of 1420, the official ceiling of 1,600 ducats became the standard patrician dowry, as many fathers saw conformity with an official norm of noble behavior as a way of affirming their families' status; but it failed utterly to keep men of ambition and means from providing much larger portions. Nearly one-half of a group of 122 midcentury dowries recovered by widows or their heirs were larger than the official maximum of 1,066⅔ ducats (that is, the two-thirds portion of the 1,600-ducat limit designated for dowry as distinct from corredo), and many doubled or even tripled it.[71] By the late 1490s, Sanudo reported, "conspicuous private wealth produced many marriages with sizable dowries, because it is now the prevailing practice to give large dowries, almost all greater than 3,000 ducats and some reaching 10,000 and more."[72] In the face of this relentless surge the Senate in 1505 passed a second dowry-limitation measure, raising the maximum to 3,000 ducats, "including all furnishings, personal effects, gifts, corredo, and all other items."[73] The near doubling of the limit, during a period when the salaries of domestic servants and galley oarsmen remained stable, indicates how powerful the upward pressures on settlements had been since 1420.[74] But the differences between the two laws involved more than concession to irresistible family urges. In 1505, the Senate's determination to restrain dowries began the process that would make marriage a civil act in 1526, and led it to revise women's traditional inheritance rights.

The new law gave the state preemptive control of marriage. Whereas in 1420 penalties had been aimed at contracting families discovered after the fact to have violated the dowry limits, the parties were now required to register their contract with the government before the nuptials. A written copy of every marriage contract, containing the exact language used (*la forma de le parolle usate*), had henceforth to be registered before the Avogadori di Comun within eight days of its signing. Once the Avogadori verified its conformity with the new limit, they were to have it recorded verbatim in a parchment register designated for that purpose and "kept under lock and key in the Avogadori's possession."[75] The state thus introduced a documented civil procedure as a required part of the nuptial process, which until 1505 had been conducted away from government oversight: contracts were normally not drawn up by notaries; and even the dowry receipts that husbands gave their wives, though usually notarized, had not come under official scrutiny until passage of the 1449 law, noted above, requiring notaries to file copies of all dowry receipts they drew up.[76] Now, however, betrothals not only were to be public events but would require official approval to proceed beyond the signing of the contract.

The requirement was given teeth. Failure to comply would result in a 100-ducat fine for the broker of the marriage and a 500-ducat fine for the fathers of the two spouses, all of whom must appear in person before the Avogadori to swear to the accuracy of the copy registered.[77] But a far tougher sanction targeted the marrying women. Henceforth, no widow would be allowed to reclaim her dowry unless it was recorded in the Avogadori's locked-up parchment register. This was a radical departure from past practice and from the deeply ingrained legal principle that, as a woman's inheritance, her dowry was ultimately her property.[78] By holding it hostage to her family's conformity with official norms, the government forced families to choose between their matrimonial ambition and their desire to provide for their daughters. That the target of the sanction was the former rather than the latter emerges from another provision of the law, which echoed the act of August 1420 exempting a woman's nondowry inheritance from the limits on marriage settlements: as long as the surplus over 3,000 ducats was considered a legacy rather than an addition to the dowry, "it should be freely hers, as is honest."[79]

The Senate was reaffirming an important distinction. Parents were free to bequeath as much as they liked to their daughters; it was their lavish pursuit of desirable sons-in-law which must be restrained. Yet the son-in-law would be the beneficiary of the sanctions for noncompliance with the law. Not only would he or his estate be exonerated from restitution of a deceased wife's or a widow's dowry, but he would actually benefit doubly from his father-in-law's illegal extravagance, by gaining an exceptionally large dowry in the first place, then getting to keep it. The casualties of the transaction would be his widow, losing her inheritance, and her natal family, rewarded for their dowry generosity by forfeiting the beneficence they could normally expect in the will of a married daughter. By expressly permitting nondowry bequests to women while threatening their traditional rights to their dowries, the Senate was leveraging fathers' concern for their daughters as a way of discouraging dowry excess, and in the process distinguishing between women as daughters of generously affectionate parents and women as instruments of their families' matrimonial ambitions. The 1420 dowry law had also intruded the state into father-child relations, but only to the extent of levying retrospective penalties on profligate fathers. In 1505 the Senate took preemptive action to restrain them. Besides issuing new rules for daughters' inheritances, it authorized the other heirs of a man whose daughter's dowry exceeded the limit to receive "summarily" from their father's estate an amount equal to the excess over 3,000.

The state was dictating inheritance practice, with precisely calibrated sanctions. Its immediate goal was to force patrician fathers to discharge their responsibility for the transgenerational integrity of their family and its property, instead of alienating it in the quest for costly marriage alliances in the present. But as in 1420, the deeper objective was to protect the interests of the noble rank and file by restraining a rich minority from further concentrating wealth and influence among themselves by bidding up, beyond the reach of less well-to-do nobles, the dowries commanded by the most attractive marriage partners.[80] The dangers of such concentration were clearly recognized in legislative debates of the time. "In a well-ordered Republic," said an opponent of a 1511 proposal to give rich patricians special office-holding advantages, "equality should always be maintained so that all can share in the benefits and advantages it brings";[81] and the diarist Girolamo Priuli asserted that "those who wish to preserve and maintain a good republic must above all preserve and maintain equality."[82]

For the proponents of dowry limitation, good government in a well-instituted republic meant equality not just in the distribution of remunerative offices but in marriage possibilities, as well. Citing the constant vigilance of "our forefathers" (li mazor nostri) against all things that offended "our exalted Creator," they declared that excessive dowries not only impoverished noble families but also gave rise to "inconveniences of which every prudent person is aware" and which we may understand as the patrician majority's resentful frustration over the unreachable dowry levels of the rich. It was therefore "the responsibility of our well-instituted republic to enact a remedy for that immoderate and pernicious custom, out of reverence for God and for the benefit of our city."[83] Here was displayed the ideology of the early Cinquecento: the ruling class's fulfillment of its divinely ordained and historically proven mission of ensuring civil concord depended on political and social equality among its members. That required usurping the authority of *patresfamilias* over inheritance and marriage, with their volatile potential owing to the inherent economic rivalry between the sons who continued the family over time and the daughters who projected it outward in the present. In contrast to the struggle between libertarian and statist interests over the 1420 dowry law, the new measure swept the Senate, passing with 116 favorable votes, 3 opposed, and 1 abstention.

The dowry-limitation act of 1505 applied a new ideology to marriage regulation, tightening the relationship between government authority and the noble ideal in order to contain tensions between rich and poor nobles and between sons and daughters. Both regulation and ideology were elaborated thirty years later. Like their Quattrocento forebears, many fathers after 1505 embraced the official norm, demonstrating their nobility by obedience to the law and by meeting the dowry level deemed appropriate to patricians. In the first two years after the law's passage, forty-six—nearly two-thirds—of the seventy-two nobles who duly registered their daughters' marriage contracts acknowledged dowries of exactly 3,000 ducats, affirming "by their oaths that this is a true contract conforming in all respects to the law."[84] Yet other fathers blithely ignored the new limit, giving their daughters dowries that doubled and even tripled the new maximum, reaching 8,000 and even 10,000 ducats, which the diarist Sanudo reported as though they were common knowledge.[85] So in April 1535 the Senate responded with still more legislation, reaffirming its determination to restrain dowries but once again raising the ceiling, now to 4,000 ducats. In the process it gave dowry limitation a powerful new symbolic dignity, tying it to ideals of noble behavior, public and private, individual and familial, rooted in Venice's most cherished traditions.[86]

The senators blamed three categories of patricians for flouting the 1505 law. First were fathers who, "heedless of their responsibilities," persisted in amassing money in order to give their daughters "immoderate dowries." Then came young men, so "content to live off their wives' dowries" that they disdained "business in the city, in overseas commerce, or in any other worthy industry." Finally, even the officials entrusted with enforcing the law had fallen short of their duty.[87] Women's dowries thus led men to forsake their proper roles as nobles in the domestic realm, in economic life, and in the government itself. The Senate's response was to prescribe more precise rules for male conduct, with more carefully calibrated enforcement mechanisms, reinforced by the participation of the most exalted symbolic authority of the state—all revolving around the movement and the property of women.

Young men's abandonment of the patriciate's mercantile traditions was particularly distressing. Like other commentators of the time, the senators looked back with nostalgia to the robust adventurousness of bygone days, contrasting it with the languid luxury now spreading through the patriciate, which many blamed for the crisis that had gripped Venice during the traumatic war of Cambrai.[88] Especially galling was the economic effeminization displayed in men's dependence upon the wealth of their wives. This inversion of proper gender relations, negating domestic patriarchy, reinforced the current complaint that youths were losing their distinctive maleness, even to the extent of dressing like women, prompting sumptuary prohibitions of the fashion excesses of men as well as women.[89] To forestall further deviation from proper masculinity, the senators turned again to the corredo, the husband's proprietary share of the marriage portion. Ever since the law of 1420 had limited the corredo to one-third of the total settlement, that proportion had been the norm in marriage contracts, including those registered in keeping with the law of 1505.[90] Now in 1535 it changed. Although the maximum marital conveyance was increased to 4,000 ducats, the bride's family was not to "lose more than 1,000 ducats in the form of the husband's third [terzo]." The corredo third was reduced to a quarter. In addition, the husband was to be fined the equivalent of one-half of any excess over 4,000 ducats. The Senate was here taking aim at bridegrooms who, living off their wives' dowries, spurned a patrician masculine ideal that blended Venice's commercial traditions with the economic mastery of the domestic patriarch. Ironically, however, its action had the effect of further transferring wealth to women. Whereas a wife dowered in accordance with the 1505 law could expect a dotal inheritance of 2,000 ducats, after deduction of her husband's 1,000-ducat corredo, her counterpart after 1535 would receive 3,000 ducats, while the husband's share remained fixed at 1,000.

Overeager fathers also would pay a fine equal to one-half of any amount over the limit, but a new sanction menaced their immovable property as well. Evidently, many men had been including in their daughters' dowries real estate that they deliberately undervalued, to feign compliance with the 1505 law. To discourage this fraud, the senators now gave the fathers' kin the right to buy such properties at 15 percent, neighbors at 25 percent, over the value stated in the marriage contract. Even with the surcharges, such purchases would presumably entail the loss of the father's property for a price below its real value, a loss he could avoid by having real estate in dowries officially appraised under the supervision of the Avogadori di Comun. This feature was a clever ploy to discourage dowry cheating; it also marked a further incursion by the government into the management of private property by domestic patriarchs.

Two weeks later, on 12 May, the Senate took action to tighten supervision of the officials entrusted with enforcement of its dowry laws. In the process it raised the state's regulation of marriage to a new level of solemnity by instituting a ritual involving the most exalted authority in the Venetian state. A new law instructed the Avogadori di Comun, on pain of a 500-ducat fine, to have every contract read aloud on the Sunday morning following its registration, at a special session of the doge and the Ducal Council. After the reading, the doge and at least four of the six councilors were to countersign the contract. The senators underscored the importance of this procedure: "because the graciousness of the most serene prince will certainly lead him to want that morning dedicated to this [reading], his councilors are obliged, on their oath of office, not to take up any other matters that morning until they have expedited the Avogadori's business."[91]

The Senate could reach no higher in displaying the importance of marriage contracts in the state's business. With this action it completed the decades-long transformation of noble marriage from a private transaction to a matter of supreme governmental concern, endowed with the ritual dignity essential to the multiform program of *renovatio urbis* then being carried on under the reigning doge, Andrea Gritti (1523–38).[92] Manfredo Tafuri describes Gritti's program as a "radical renewal" of city and polity, pursued according to a "unitary design, an organic policy implemented in a variety of areas, representing a peaceful 'rebirth' " for Venice, the "recovery of identity and internal prestige" lost in the war of Cambrai a quarter century earlier.[93] In this context, the involvement of the charismatic Doge Gritti in the campaign to restrain dowries put the state's regulation of noble marriage on a new plane. No longer just an effort to protect family fortunes and to promote the marriage possibilities of all noble families, it was now part of Venice's recovery of its shattered glory. Hence the linkage between dowries, the standards to which they should conform, and the government's authority over them—and over marriage generally—and the behavior of patricians, men and women, in the increasingly overlapping public and private spheres. The "recovery of identity and internal prestige" was premised on a renewal of the *virtù* of the members of the ruling class, as manifested in their domestic conduct, their productive economic activity, and their discharge of their governmental duties. The surest guide to *virtù* in all these areas was Venice's traditions, which all came together in patrician marriage. It was therefore incumbent upon the Avogadori di Comun and the doge and his council to ensure, by means of rigorously enforced procedures and solemn state ritual, that every patrician marriage conform to the principles laid down by *i nostri maggiori*.

Hence it is not surprising that one of the authors of the act was the eminent Gasparo Contarini, at the time himself a ducal councilor.[94] May 1535 was a watershed moment in Contarini's career. He had completed his *De magistratibus et republica Venetorum* only two or three years earlier and within three weeks of the passage of the dowry act would receive the cardinal's hat that took him from Venice to Rome and the difficult campaign for Catholic reform.[95] Whether his treatise was an endorsement or a criticism of the Gritti *renovatio* is a matter of scholarly debate.[96] Yet there is no doubt that it underscored the crucial importance of the doge's authority in enforcing the proper behavior, public and private, of the nobles, on which the common good depended and for which "our forefathers," in their wisdom and goodness, provided institutional guidance.[97] It was this same conviction that wrote into the 1535 dowry law the doge's presiding over a procedure whose avowed purpose was to redirect patricians toward those traditional governmental, paternal, and mercantile habits that had contributed to the ancient greatness of Venice and its ruling class. The recognition of the need for government action to rehabilitate old traditions runs through the *De magistratibus:* thus, "ancient laws and customs endure even to our time, although certain young men, corrupted by ambition or luxury since the expansion of the empire, have neglected their country's institutions"—nearly an exact echo of the criticism in the dowry-limitation law of young men who lived off their wives' dowries.[98]

In his famous treatise, as in the dowry legislation that he shepherded through the Senate, Contarini saw as the key to his city's well-being a patriciate unified by disciplined adherence to time-honored tradition. Member of the most numerically imposing of the case vecchie, he scorned excessively rich parvenus ("huomini vili, iquali niente altro fanno, che guadagno"—pungently rendered in the 1599 English translation as "filthy and ill mannerd men sauouring of nothing but gaine"); but he praised the wise provision of Venice's founders "that all which were noble by birth, or enobled by vertue, or well deseruing of the commonwealth, did in the beginning obtain this right of gouernment: which hath likewise happened in these times of ours."[99] This varied ruling class, composed of Dolfins, Gabriels, and nobles from 142 other houses covering a wide range of antiquity and wealth, required governmental direction in its private and public activity to ensure the social equality that was essential to the patriciate's discharge of its venerable governmental vocation.[100]

Contarini brought to culmination, in ideological theory and legislative practice, a process begun in 1420. The *De magistratibus* and the dowry law of 1535 marked the convergence of three developments that had been coming together for a century: the state's growing direction of individual and familial activity in the domestic environment, in social relations, and in public life; the refinement of the composition, relationships, and ideology of a pluralistic ruling class; and the growing role of women as the symbol and medium of an articulated patrician culture. Marriage—who married, whom they married, and the terms and fruits of their marriages—was the terrain on which the government asserted its authority to regulate the delicate interactions of noble families, generations, and genders. The structure of patrician marriage fashioned by legislation between 1420 and 1535 was the rare fruit of shared interests between, on one hand, a majority increasingly hard pressed to meet standards of noble social conduct set by a wealthy minority and therefore eager to conform to an attainable standard validated by the government and, on the other, men of political weight concerned about the disruptive potential of the growing gap between the two.[101] According to Sanudo, Doge Gritti himself declared shortly after his election that "in this state [*terra*] there are rich, middling, and poor, and it is very fitting that the rich aid the middling and the middling the poor"; and there are indications that the Senate, the organ of dowry limitation, was regarded as the body representing the "middling," seeking to maintain a balance between the truly impoverished nobles and the wealthy elite, which dominated the increasingly powerful Council of Ten.[102] However, this is the place not to sort through the complicated politics of the early Cinquecento but rather to recognize the persistent importance of marriage legislation as a responsive and formative element in that sociopolitical environment, and in the long-term intersection of nobility, women, and the state in Renaissance Venice.

From Trousseau
to Groomgift

IN THEIR 1993 ARTICLE "Father of the Bride: Fathers, Daughters, and Dowries in Late Medieval and Early Renaissance Venice," Donald Queller and Thomas Madden explored the motivations of fathers and other kin in contributing to the dowries of young patrician women in late Trecento Venice. The crux of their analysis is a challenge to the widespread tendency in the scholarly literature to attribute rising dowries among the urban elites of late medieval and Renaissance Italy to the eager efforts of fathers of daughters to promote their family interest by investing in marriage alliances with wealthy, influential, or prestigious in-laws.[1] On the contrary, for Queller and Madden fathers in Venice "refuse[d] to engage in the competition" for advantageous marriages and "in fact steadily decreased their contributions to dowries."[2] The reason, they propose, was that fathers in fact expected little practical benefit from their sons-in-law. Rather, their chief interest was to avoid the dishonor of failing to provide suitable dowries for their daughters. But that paternal concern only kept dowries from falling. The driving force behind their rise was, instead, an accumulation of wealth in female hands, which women directed toward ever higher dowries for their daughters. For Queller and Madden, fathers and mothers thus complemented each other's contribution to dowry inflation: "The two worked together."[3]

"Father of the Bride" is rich in suggestion and ingenious in analysis. Its bold challenges to cherished views are based on original new twists it provides to the scholarship on marriage in the Italian cities. Especially valuable is the attention that Queller and Madden give to the interaction between, on one hand, the multiple resources and contrasting aims observable among the various relatives of marriageable girls and, on the

76

other, the convergence of these in a collective family interest in getting them married. The authors present their findings in forceful prose, inviting responses from holders of different views. The role of zestful debunker is one that Donald Queller productively played throughout his distinguished career, and Thomas Madden now joins him in a provocative rethinking of marriage strategies among the Italian urban elites. Catching their spirit of robust exchange, I want in this chapter to pay tribute to the generous collegiality that marked all of Queller's writing on Venice, by continuing the debate on marriage among Venetian patricians. I begin with brief comments on two points in his and Madden's analysis; then I take up an aspect of marriage arrangements briefly mentioned in their article, which has an important bearing on the purposes, components, and evolution of marriage settlements in Venice.

Underlying Queller and Madden's conclusion that fathers made only a limited contribution to dowry inflation is their finding that during the period they studied, 1370–89, "1,000 ducats seems to constitute a standard dowry level for nobles, which few exceeded, most could meet, and some could not afford."[4] The graph that illustrates that finding, however, shows that only five of the thirteen dowries in their sample met the 1,000-ducat standard; six were for smaller amounts and the remaining two far larger. This spread suggests the need for further discussion of their statement that Venetian daughters received "identical" dowries despite a wide range of wealth among their fathers. Some additional information can be found in the records of the notary Marino of San Tomà, who in the later Trecento served as a scribe for the Giudici del Proprio, civil court judges whose jurisdiction included the restitution of dowries to widows or to the heirs of wives who predeceased their husbands.[5] Between 1366 and 1390, Marino recorded 170 acts of dowry restitution (called diiudicatus acts) involving wives of nobles. Especially pertinent are 142 entries that indicate the year in which the dowry was originally conveyed to the husband. Seventy-eight of these recorded dowries were conveyed between 1361 and 1390, spanning the period from which Queller and Madden derived their sample. Table 1 presents the information on those seventy-eight, divided into quartiles by size. (Amounts are in ducats.)[6]

As in the Queller-Madden sample, the most frequent dowry was 1,000 ducats; but also as in their sample, it fell far short of a majority—indeed, much further short than in their case. Whereas the five 1,000-ducat dowries that they found are 38.4 percent of their sample, the fourteen 1,000-ducat dowries recorded by the notary Marino constitute only 17.9 percent

Table 1. Seventy-eight Dowries Conveyed, 1361–1390

	Range	Avg	Med	Mod	n
1–19	3,600–1,000	1,623	1,500	1,538/1,000	3 each
20–39	1,000–800	951	1,000	1,000	11
40–59	800–385	622	640/600	769	4
60–78	385–100	306	308	35	7
Totals	3,600–100	873	800	1,000	14

Source: Information from CI 114, Marino, S. Tomà, prot. 1366–91, unfoliated.

Key: Avg = average; Med = median; Mod = modal, or most frequent, dowry.

of his total. Indeed, the median of 800 ducats among the seventy-eight cases shows that at least half of the fathers supplied their daughters with dowries 20 percent smaller than 1,000 ducats. But the main revelation in the table is the wide range among dowry amounts. Forty-eight, three-fifths, of the fathers were either unable or unwilling to commit dowries of 1,000 ducats to their daughters' marriages but found noble sons-in-law all the same. Thus Secondo Barbarigo quondam *nobilis viri* Matteo received 400 ducats from his wife, Maria, in 1373; *nobilis vir* Pierpaolo Querini received the same amount from his wife, Filippa, in 1382; *nobilis vir* Dardi Grioni received 200 ducats at his marriage to Maddalena in 1369; and *nobilis vir* Fantin Bon 155 ducats from his wife, Benvenuta, at their marriage in 1367.[7] These dowries fell far short of the putative standard of 1,000 ducats. But they were truly dwarfed by the sixteen (more, it should be noted, than the fourteen that met the standard) which exceeded it—some by very large margins indeed. These include the 3,600 ducats that Lorenzo di Francesco Morosini received from his wife, Lucia, in 1376; the 2,700 ducats that Elena Soranzo brought when she married *nobilis vir* Marco Contarini in 1365; the 2,600 ducats conveyed to Bertuccio Contarini, whose father, Andrea Contarini, was the reigning doge when Bertuccio married his wife, Lucia, in 1370; and the 1,731 ducats that Beriola Falier brought to her marriage to Nicolò Giustinian in 1371.[8] Taken together, the forty-eight dowries below 1,000 ducats and the sixteen above that figure illustrate not "relative stability of dotal levels across the economic strata of the nobility"[9] but a wide range in the dotal arrangements that patrician fathers were able, or chose, to make for the their daughters' dowries in the later Trecento.

A second point emphasized by Queller and Madden is the reliance of dowry-building fathers on the contributions of other kin. Their consideration of this matter is triggered by a disparity that they observe between, on one hand, amounts destined for women's dowries by fathers and other contributors and, on the other, amounts actually conveyed to husbands.[10] The key to this perception is a statistical model that they constructed on the basis of thirty-one contributions to women's dowries (presumably from the 1370s and 1380s), of which roughly one-fourth came from the women's fathers, the remainder from other relatives. The paternal allocations averaged 966 ducats, to which Queller and Madden add three nonpaternal contributions, calculating a normal size of 100 ducats each.[11] Their model assumes that the largest nonpaternal contributions complemented the smallest paternal ones, thus producing the standard dowry total of 1,266 ducats. However, it is at least as likely that the daughters of rich fathers would benefit from the largesse of equally wealthy mothers, grandfathers, and so on, thus concentrating dowry wealth at the upper end of the range noted above, with the reverse concentration of smaller contributions at the lower end.

Their statistical model is nonetheless valuable in renewing attention to the importance of nonpaternal contributions to dowries. More particularly, it highlights the crux of their analysis, namely, the gap between what should be the total of all contributions, in their model 1,266 ducats, and the average of 963 that they found in their sample of thirteen dowries conveyed to husbands. Assessing this gap, they ask the question, what happened to the missing 300 ducats between benefactors' commitment and bridegrooms' receipt? They base their answer on a statute that they have brought to light. It authorized fathers of daughters to administer, and accrue interest on, bequests and inter vivos gifts toward their daughters' dowries.[12] From this important discovery they argue plausibly that in actual practice fathers received and invested those gifts, then incorporated them into their own provision for their daughters' dowries. Thus, they conclude, the 300 ducats contributed by nonparental kin to women's dowries were not missing at all; rather than being added to the 966 allocated by the fathers, they were absorbed into that paternal allocation.

This ingenious suggestion closes the gap between Queller and Madden's model of intended dowries and dowries actually received by husbands. However, it rests on three questionable assumptions: that the executors of nonpaternal donors' estates gave the bequests to the nubile beneficiaries' fathers immediately, rather than waiting until the girls were ready to marry; that fathers delayed making provision for their daughters' dowries until all the contributions of those others had been deposited with them; and, crucially, that fathers outlived their daughters' other benefactors. This last assumption is especially problematic in the case of the most generous nonpaternal contributors in Queller and Madden's sample, the daughters' mothers, who accounted for one-quarter of all contributions, paternal and nonpaternal.[13] The problem arises because the great majority of wives outlived their husbands. Of 142 entries in the notary Marino's *protocollo* in which one spouse was recorded as living, the other dead, widows were the survivors in 116 cases, more than four-fifths of the time.[14] Doubtless spouses sometimes joined together in assembling their daughters' dowries, the wives informing their husbands of their intended contribution. But in the often long years of widowhood, which might include remarriage, women often experienced marked changes in their economic circumstances and their circles of kin and family: changes that their husbands obviously could not take into account when calculating their daughters' marriage portions.[15]

The case of Beruzza Soranzo can serve as an illustration. In a will she wrote in 1388 while pregnant with her second child, she bequeathed 192 ducats toward the dowry of that child if a girl. It is possible that her husband, Marco Soranzo, whom she named as an executor of the will, took that bequest into account later on when calculating the dowry of the daughter, Caterina, who was the offspring of that pregnancy.[16] However, thirteen years later, in 1401, Beruzza wrote another will, in which she bequeathed the now thirteen-year-old but still unmarried Caterina not 192 but 1,000 ducats for her marriage portion. By then, however, Marco Soranzo had died, leaving the widowed Beruzza to make Caterina's marriage arrangements on her own. One way she did so was to alter her late husband's testamentary provisions for Caterina's dowry. Whereas he had left her a one-third share of the family palace, Beruzza, reckoning that cash was better than real estate for dowry purposes, arranged to have her son, Girolamo, add another 1,000 ducats to his sister's portion, making a handsome package of at least 2,000 ducats with which to launch Caterina onto the marriage market. In return, Beruzza would persuade Caterina to cede to Girolamo her share of the palace. Nor did she shrink from applying a bit of pressure to bend Caterina to her purpose. If the girl should refuse the arrangement, Beruzza would deduct 500 ducats from her own allocation to the girl's dowry. For Girolamo, on the other hand, the arrangement was attractive because, besides adding Caterina's one-third of the palace to the one-third their father had left him, it gave him the prospect of being its sole proprietor, since Beruzza bequeathed him the final one-third, which her late husband had left to her.[17]

It is not known what other provisions Marco Soranzo had made for Caterina's marriage portion besides a share in the family real estate.[18] But it is unlikely he was aware of the elaborate scheme his widow would devise to maximize their daughter's marriage prospects by altering his previous testamentary arrangements. This ignorance was shared by most other fathers, who died unaware of what their daughters would get from the most generous nonpaternal contributors to their dowries, their mothers. Therefore, the extent to which "paternal dowry contributions include both paternal and non-paternal donations" was probably minimal. The greater likelihood is that in most cases the amounts allocated by fathers toward their daughters' dowries reflected the fathers' own contribution, independent of outside assistance yet always hopeful of it.[19]

Queller and Madden's analysis compresses the variety in patrician dowries in late Trecento Venice and credits fathers with calculating dowry contributions that they could have been sure of in only a minority of cases. Nonetheless, their imaginative research has performed an important service by calling attention to the troubling disparity between amounts allocated by fathers and others toward marriage portions and the dowries actually conveyed to bridegrooms. The rest of this chapter will be devoted to exploring this disparity from another angle, that of the components of marriage portions and the connection between those components and the social purposes of marriage.

Central to the Queller-Madden interpretation is their rejection of the possibility that fathers bestowed large dowries to attract future in-laws who might provide political and economic benefits. They emphasize instead the profound fear, felt by "all but the wealthiest patrician fathers," of being dishonored by failing to keep up with the increases in dowry levels generated by, in Queller and Madden's view, other contributors—especially female ones—who "took much of the control over dowry size out of the father's hands."[20] This widespread concern was the motive, they argue, for the Senate's enactment in 1420 of the well-known measure that imposed a limit of 1,600 ducats on marriage settlements.[21] Their image of patrician fathers is thus one of men responding to ambivalent, not to say contradictory, impulses: gratefully incorporating nonpaternal contributions into their provision for their daughters' marriages yet seeking in legislative councils to arrest the inflationary effects of that blending.

This contradictory picture is surely a realistic one. Men, and women perhaps even more so, were pulled in different directions by a variety of principles, interests, and loyalties when launching their children into adulthood.[22] Moreover, the dowry-limiting law of 1420 reveals not only individual men torn by conflicting impulses but also different interests within the ruling class. The law's preamble depicted fathers as victims of dowry inflation but also as its villains. High dowry levels prevented them from getting their daughters married and "forced" them to immure un-marriageable girls in convents. Yet at the same time they eagerly strove to emerge as "victors" in the competition for good marriages. The beneficiaries of this self-destructive paternal striving, the preamble went on, were not the well-dowried daughters, for only a "minimal part" of those sumptuous marriage settlements ended up as dotal property of the brides. Rather, it was the bridegrooms who benefited most from the rising tide of dowries and upon whom the sanctions punishing violations of the new 1,600-ducat limit were to fall. A husband found to have received an excessive marriage settlement could lose half of his estate—to the very wife whose family had paid the abusive dowry. More draconian still, anyone in the groom's family who, unknown to him, received gifts from the bride's side which pushed the total conveyance beyond 1,600 ducats would have to pay *double* the value of those gifts to the bride at the end of the marriage.[23] These sanctions show that men seeking husbands for their daughters were indeed pouring large portions of their property into the effort to attract desirable in-laws.

Another aspect in the law also pointed in that direction. It addressed the relationship between the components of marriage settlements. This relationship is tied directly to the disparity, alertly observed by Queller and Madden, between marriage portions assembled and dowries conveyed. The law enjoined a division of marriage settlements into two parts, in a two-to-one ratio: respectively, the dowry and the *corredo*. The corredo provides the key to the disparity. It explains why the legislators of 1420 complained that married daughters were not benefiting from the dowry inflation and why they penalized the in-laws who received excessive settlements rather than the fathers who gave them. What was the corredo? Fundamentally, it was a marriage conveyance outside the rules and conventions that defined the dowry. How far outside is illustrated by the marriage portion of Franceschina Querini, whose dowry is one of the examples cited by Queller and Madden to show the prevalence of the 1,000-ducat standard.[24] As they report, in early May 1382 Franceschina brought a dowry in that amount to her new husband, Bernardo Giustinian. However, ten weeks earlier the executors of her father's estate had released to Franceschina, then *maritata set nondum transducta* (married but not yet cohabiting with Bernardo), 500 ducats for her corredo, which her father bequeathed for that purpose.[25] So although Marco Querini had indeed destined a dowry, strictly so called, of 1,000 ducats for Franceschina, his total marriage provision was 1,500 ducats, divided into two-thirds dowry and one-third corredo, a ratio he explicitly allocated to the portions of Franceschina's sisters: "For the marriages of each of my other daughters I bequeath 100 lire di grossi [equal to 1,000 ducats] for the dowry [*impromessa*] and 50 lire di grossi for the corredo."[26]

Citing another instance of disparity, the gap between the 1,500 ducats that Regina Molin's father had bequeathed for her marriage and the dowry of 1,100 ducats that she actually conveyed to her husband, Queller and Madden speculate that the unaccounted-for 400 ducats "went into Regina's personal wealth or, perhaps, her trousseau."[27] That second surmise is almost certainly the correct one. *Corredo* was the term used in Venice for the trousseau, and by the 1380s most women were marrying with dowries and corredi in roughly the ratio of Regina Molin's and Franceschina Querini's cases.[28] It was the ratio given legal force in the 1420 law. But was the corredo equivalent to our understanding of the term *trousseau*? The answer involves issues central to the evolution of patrician society in the late Trecento and early Quattrocento.[29] What follows only sketches an approach to these issues, but Queller and Madden's fruitful broaching of the content and purpose of marriage settlements encourages at least a sketch in response.

The crux is the distinction between dowry and corredo. The dowry was considered a daughter's share of her father's patrimony, conveyed to her husband as her contribution toward the maintenance of the new household.[30] From this principle flowed a critical aspect of the dowry in Venice: although it was under the administrative control of the husband during the marriage, once the marriage ended, normally at the death of either spouse, it returned to the wife or to heirs designated by her.[31] It was her inherited property, to dispose of as she wished. The decisions of the Giudici del Proprio recorded by the notary Marino of San Tomà in the examples discussed earlier were acts restoring dowries to widows or their heirs in keeping with this principle. The corredo, though also a part of the marriage settlement, was legally and practically distinct from the dowry. Rather than a contribution by the bride's family to the economic substance of the new marital household, the corredo in its original character consisted of clothing, jewels, and other personal items given to a bride for her own use.[32] The documents are rich with examples of the careful distinction that Venetians, public and private, drew between dowry and corredo. In 1353, acknowledging receipt of her marriage portion from the executors of her father's estate, Maria quondam Ermolao Lion noted that 405 ducats were "for my dowry" but that the nearly identical sum of 407 ducats was *pro meis coredis*. She specified further that of the corredo, "200 ducats are in gold, and the rest are my personal effects."[33]

As the example of Franceschina Querini discussed above showed, the distinction between dowry and corredo influenced the timing of their disbursal. Because the purpose of the dowry was to support the husband's management of the family economy, it was conveyed to him only when the marriage had been ratified and consummated and the bride *transducta* to the groom's residence. But the corredo, associated with the celebration of the marriage and especially with the bride's jewelry and apparel, had to be disbursed earlier. The examples of Maria Lion and Franceschina Querini illustrate the flexibility that the combination of dowry and corredo gave Trecento Venetians in designing the marriage portions of their daughters. Franceschina Querini's father had provided her with a substantial corredo of 500 ducats, equal to one-half of the amount separately allocated for her dowry; his will, written in 1375, thus anticipated exactly the ratio legislated in 1420. But Ermolao Lion in 1353 had bequeathed his daughter Maria equal amounts, roughly 400 ducats each, for her dowry and her corredo. Franceschina's and Maria's fathers weighted the elements of their daughters' marriage portions differently to achieve different objectives, and their reasons likely reflected different levels of prestige within the patriciate. As a member of one of Venice's most distinguished old houses, the so-called *case vecchie*, or *longhi*, Marco Querini was secure in his status.[34] The Lion, by contrast, had joined the ruling class only early in the Trecento; although by midcentury they had gained political prominence, their social ambitions still benefited from giving generous corredi.[35] Because information on corredi is more elusive in the records than that on dowries, any generalization is uncertain. But it appears that the corredo was the more useful instrument of social ambition, because unlike a dowry it offered immediate attractions both to the family of the bride, to whose prestige it gave visual display, and to the bridegroom, who gained, or retained, stature from a lavishly outfitted wife. Let us observe the distinction more closely.

A large dowry could certainly be attractive to a prospective husband, but his use of it was surrounded by restrictions. He could invest it and enjoy its fruits, but as the wife's inheritance it remained her property, carefully protected in her interest by the statutes.[36] So strong was the principle that most husbands, upon receiving their wives' dowry, ensured its restitution, either by obtaining pledges from their fathers or other kinsmen to make their property liable for the dowry if the husband's estate was not sufficient[37] or by securing it directly on the husband's own property.[38] In one way or another, the requirement that a woman's dowry be secured involved the transfer or encumbrance of a husband's or his family's property, or at least his incurring an obligation toward some other person. None of these restrictions attended the corredo.

The corredo of Maria quondam Ermolao Lion, cited above, was a combination of personal goods for the bride and cash. Those two components correspond to the two main purposes of the corredo: namely, to enhance the prestige of both the bride's family and the groom, by arraying the bride in clothing and jewelry; and to induce the groom to marry the bride by means of a gift.[39] The relationship between the two purposes changed toward the end of the Trecento, and the change bears directly on the evolving purposes of patrician marriage settlements as well as on the Senate law of 1420. Maria Lion's 200 ducats appear exceptional; throughout most of the Trecento the corredo consisted chiefly of the material possessions of brides. In 1372 Francesco Pollini arranged the marriage of his daughter Lucia with 2,000 ducats for her dowry and another 400 ducats "in gifts: namely, jewels, clothing, and other precious objects."[40] There was no reference to cash here, or to anything besides sumptuous raiment for Lucia. For Pollini, to adorn his daughter handsomely was a matter of honor, a way of asserting his family's dignity at the same time that he provided her and her husband with an exceptionally large dowry. The importance of sending daughters to their marriages with respectable accoutrements was something of which Venetians were articulately aware. Alessandro Morosini was revealingly conscious of this necessity when he provided in his will of 1331 that the daughters of his son Paolo should receive dowries from Alessandro's estate and also "be given corredi suitable for noblewomen."[41] Equally forthright was Piero di Marino Morosini four years later: he bequeathed his daughter Beta a dowry of 385 ducats and a corredo "as is customary for noblewomen of Venice."[42] So deeply ingrained was the practice that another Morosini, Marco quondam Gentile, simply instructed in 1359 that in addition to receiving a dowry of 500 ducats, his daughter Beriola was to "be given a good corredo in accordance with local custom."[43]

By then, however, local custom was becoming a source of concern to government officials. In 1334 the Senate, noting the prevailing practice ("ut moris est") of giving brides lavish wedding gifts, passed a law limiting to 200 ducats the value of the "clothing and any other corredo or furnishings of any sort" which a bride could take to the house of her new husband.[44] But the impulse elevating corredi was too strong among fathers of nubile girls. In the example noted earlier, Maria Lion's 200 ducats' worth of *fornimentis* in 1353 corresponded exactly to the Senate's limit, but the additional 200 gold ducats in cash raised her total corredo to twice the legal amount. Evidently, many other Venetians flouted the 1334 limit, as well, for in 1360 another law was enacted, which increased the limit on "corredi, gifts, or anything else serving as wedding gifts" to double that imposed in 1334, 400 ducats instead of 200.[45] This was a concession to "modern fashions [*modernas consuetudines*]" that were sending corredi to unprecedented heights as families displayed their magnificence or bade for status on the backs of their marrying daughters.

It is vital to recognize that the concern in both these pieces of legislation was with corredi, not dowries. The law of 1334 made no reference to dowries, and that of 1360 mentioned them only to require fathers who gave their daughters dowries of 300 ducats or more, and were therefore the likeliest candidates to provide extravagant corredi, to swear to the state attorneys, the Avogadori di Comun, that they had observed the new corredo limit of 400 ducats.[46] The legislators thus envisaged corredi larger than the dowries with which they were paired. The language of the act tranquilly accepted that some dowries would be larger than 300 ducats. What alarmed the sponsors of both laws was, instead, sumptuary excess, wasteful spending on jewels and clothing for women, specific items of which were described in detail in both measures.[47] But families were reluctant to give up their practice of providing material evidence of their dignity on the occasion of their daughters' marriages.

It may be that the senators, in the Trecento primarily members of well-established old houses, enacted these measures as a response to especially sumptuous displays by men from newer families, like Ermolao Lion in the example above, seeking to project themselves into prominence by furnishing their marrying daughters with lavish corredi.[48] Yet men from Venice's oldest houses, like Alessandro and Piero Morosini, also felt it important to advertise their dignity by giving their daughters corredi worthy of *nobiles dominas*. Some fathers, like Marino Lion in his will of 1374, adjusted to the legal limits, bequeathing his daughters dowries of 1,730 ducats and corredi "such as a lady should have, according to the law."[49] However, as we have seen, others exceeded the 400-ducat limit enacted in 1360. Giovanni Morosini, son of the late Doge Michele Morosini, instructed in 1388 that the marriage portions of 2,000 ducats which he was bequeathing to each of his daughters should be divided into dowries of 1,400 ducats and corredi of 600.[50] The most prominent and securely noble clans in Venice were just as caught up in the practice of giving illegally sumptuous corredi to their marrying daughters as were status-seeking nobles. It was a tendency that would only increase. When Nicolò Mudazzo wrote his will in 1411, he allocated 1,800 ducats for the *maridar* of each of his two nubile daughters, and he specified that of that sum 1,000 were for the dowry and 800 *per coriedi*.[51]

However, by the time Giovanni Morosini and Nicolò Mudazzo wrote their wills, the nature of the corredo was changing, reflecting changes in patrician social and economic relations after the great upheaval of the war of Chioggia, 1378–81, when a siege by the Genoese and other enemies of Venice provoked massive exactions by the government fisc. The resulting economic trauma devastated private wealth and transformed economic and social relations, between classes and within the patriciate.[52] In this atmosphere of upheaval, the desirability of marital alliances with influential families induced fathers to redouble their efforts to amass large marriage portions for their daughters, but with a new twist. It was the consequences of this intensification of groom courting which the Senate bill of 1420 sought to address. We can get a taste of the new character of the corredo in a notarized dowry receipt of 1403 from Giovanni Ghisi, son of *nobilis viri* Francesco, to his wife, Fiordelise, quondam *nobilis viri* Paolo da Canal. Acknowledging that he had received Fiordelise's dowry, which consisted of real property in Capodistria ("Justinopoli") and Venice and 1,000 ducats in shares of the state debt (*prestiti*), he added that "those 1,000 ducats in prestiti are understood to include 300 gold ducats of sound money promised to me as gifts and corredo."[53] He went on, with careful precision, "Be it noted that when the dowry is restored [i.e., at the end of the marriage], those 300 gold ducats of sound money promised and given to me, as indicated above, in gifts and corredo should be deducted from the 1,000 ducats in prestiti" which as dowry would become Fiordelise's property.[54]

That phrase, "promised to me as gifts and corredo," eloquently reveals that the corredo, which the sumptuary act of 1334 had associated with the accoutrements of the bride, was now becoming a gift of cash to the groom. Nor was the marriage contract between Giovanni Ghisi and Fiordelise da Canal an exception. In an instrument of 1413, Roberto Contarini noted that in the marriage contract that he had entered into with Micheletta Gradenigo, he had been promised all the property she possessed or which might come to her in any fashion. But the feature of the arrangement that he emphasized was that "the first 800 ducats of your money that I receive shall be mine to keep, as corredo and furnishings, with no obligation whatsoever on my part to restore it to you. Everything else is to be considered as your dowry."[55]

By 1420, when a majority of the Senate sought to limit the corredo to one-third of a new 1,600-ducat limit on marriage settlements, it had gone through a transformation from the clothing, jewelry, and other *arnesi* with which families of marrying daughters displayed their status and wealth, to a gift to the groom—as it were, a premium offered by his new in-laws for marrying their daughter. The transformation can be illustrated in a comparison of two marriage contracts, one from the mid-Trecento, the other from the early 1400s. No one document can capture the social practice, by definition varied, of any one time; much less can two documents from different periods chart precisely the social changes between them. But they can at least suggest the direction of change in the terms of noble marriage between the mid-fourteenth and the early fifteenth century.

In a contract of 1344, Marco Marion and Andrea Morosini, each pledging his wealth as a sign of good faith, arranged the terms of the marriage of Marco's grandson, Piero Sanudo, to Andrea's daughter Lucia, "who is underage" (i.e., was thirteen or younger).[56] They agreed that the couple would exchange vows and Piero, himself younger than eighteen, would *transducere* Lucia only when she came of legal age, two years hence. Andrea Morosini bound himself to give his daughter a dowry of 1,000 lire (equal to 313 or 385 ducats) but would invest it himself on young Piero's behalf for the intervening two years, with all profits or losses charged to Piero.[57] If Piero should die without heirs before turning twenty, the capital of 1,000 lire would, as dowry, become the property of Lucia, though in that case her father would himself incur the profits or losses of his investing. He also promised to give his daughter a corredo "as befits a noblewoman," and he specified that the corredo would be "from the Morosini *palazzo*, consisting of items belonging to Ca' Morosini [*coreda vero de domo Mauroceno, de bonis da [sic] ca Mauroceno*]." This corredo was to be treated differently than the dowry. If Piero should die intestate and without heirs before turning twenty, then the corredo would not, like the dowry, devolve upon Lucia but would instead return to her father.

It is evident from this that the corredo was a gift of clothing and household goods from the bride's family to the married couple, to be enjoyed by the groom only if the marriage was fully established, with children, to whom it presumably would eventually pass. Otherwise it returned to the bride's family, perhaps to be used in a second marriage for Lucia. In addition to making the gift of the corredo conditional, the contracting parties also carefully provided security for the dowry. Marco Marion (father of young Piero's deceased mother) undertook to give to Andrea Morosini 1,000 lire, which he originally had promised to bequeath to his grandson in his will but which instead he now conveyed to him on the occasion of the impending marriage. However, for the two years until Lucia was *transducta,* these 1,000 lire, like Lucia's dowry of the same amount, were to be invested by the young man's future father-in-law, Andrea, in commercial ventures ("debetis mercari et mitere ad mercatum, per marem et per terram"), with the profits, like those from Andrea's investment of Lucia's dowry, going to the young couple. Consequently, not only was Andrea Morosini assured that his future son-in-law would have the means of restoring Lucia's dowry at the end of the marriage, but he would himself have the capital that secured it in his own hands. But even that was not all the dowry security written into the contract. For in addition to temporarily entrusting to Piero's future father-in-law his 1,000-lire gift to his grandson, Marco Marion also pledged his own property for the restoration of Lucia's dowry.

The marriage contract of Lucia Morosini and Piero Sanudo was marked by sturdy protection of the interests of the bride and her father and by a corredo in the form of goods that in certain circumstances would revert to the possession of the bride's father. On both counts, it contrasts radically with the contract drawn up in 1401 between the prospective husband Nicolò Corner and Nicolò Foscolo, acting on behalf of his daughter Lucia. Even the form of the Corner-Foscolo contract was altogether different from that between Marco Marion and Andrea Morosini six decades earlier. In contrast to the dialogic document of 1344, in which the voices of Morosini and Marion alternated, each expressing his commitment in the first person singular, with young Piero Sanudo likewise binding himself to observe their agreed-upon terms, that of 1401 was a *diktat* issued by the bridegroom-to-be, to which the father of his future wife simply assented. More striking than differences in tone are the substantive terms that Corner demanded and obtained. His peremptory language deserves to be quoted in full:

> I, Nicolò Corner, want a dowry of 1,000 gold ducats, of which 300 ducats are to be reckoned as corredo. This corredo I want immediately in hard cash. Also, I want her [Lucia's] personal effects to be likewise reckoned as corredo. In addition, I want four years of living expenses for my wife and me. I also want messer Nicolò Foscolo to give me enough *denisado* of Flanders to fashion a *pelanda* for my wife, to be paid for from the 700 ducats remaining in the dowry. For the balance of the 700 ducats, I want messer Andrea Bembo to stand surety, so that if messer Nicolò has not paid upon the arrival of messer Andrea, I want the latter to pay it; and I want him to agree to a penalty of 25 percent in case of nonpayment. I further want messer Nicolò and his heirs to be obligated for all of these terms; and if, for valid reasons, none of his house is able to meet them [at once], I want to be paid sixty ducats annually until they are met. Moreover, if, after four years have elapsed, I elect to continue living with him [Nicolò Foscolo], I want him to pay my wife's and my living expenses at the rate of sixty ducats per annum.[58]

To this series of demands Nicolò Foscolo and Andrea Bembo, presumably Foscolo's friend or relative, gave their full assent.

In tone and substance this contract could not be more unlike that between Marco Marion and Andrea Morosini. Where in 1344 Marion provided a double security for Lucia Morosini's dowry—his own property as well as the 1,000 lire he was giving to his grandson Piero Sanudo—the burden of pledging in 1401 fell to the bride's side: to ensure that Andrea Bembo would supply any of the dowry, corredo, and living expenses to her and her demanding new husband should her father and his heirs be unable to do so. Especially worthy of note is that of the total expenditure that Nicolò Foscolo agreed to disburse, little more than one-half would qualify as his daughter's dowry in the strict sense of the term. For to the total marriage portion of 1,000 ducats, which included the 300-ducat corredo in cash which Corner wanted immediately, must be added the 240 ducats that Foscolo would pay for four years' living expenses for the newly married couple, at 60 ducats per year, as well as the undetermined value of the personal goods that Lucia would bring as her real trousseau. Moreover, the 700 ducats remaining after the deduction of the cash corredo would be further depleted by the purchase of the Flemish fabric for the "pelanda," or large-sleeved cloak, which Corner obliged Foscolo to have fashioned for his daughter. This was an expensive article of apparel, usually trimmed in fur, which the Senate had only the year before restricted owing to its excessive luxuriousness.[59]

Although no dowry receipt has been found, it is certain that upon receiving the dowry, Nicolò Corner would have had one drawn up for Lucia, binding himself to return it to her and securing it upon his own property or that of a kinsman. Whether he would have deducted the cost of the *pelanda* is uncertain; but even if it was included in the dowry, Lucia Foscolo would be entitled to at most 700 ducats of the 1,250 or more that her father had agreed to spend on her marriage. Like the examples mentioned earlier of Giovanni Ghisi in 1403 and Roberto Contarini in 1413, as a bridegroom in the early Quattrocento Nicolò Corner benefited from the transformation of the corredo, from the personal effects of the bride into a cash gift to the groom, for which he incurred "no obligation whatsoever"—as Roberto Contarini expressed it—to his wife or her family. It was his to keep.

The change in the nature of the corredo represented, however exaggeratedly, by these two contracts is an indication of the increased importance of marriage alliances among patricians in the years around 1400. It was a moment when, economically pressed and worried about retaining their status, a large part of the ruling class supported the erection of new legal barriers between themselves and the populace, dramatically advancing the process toward noble exclusivism begun a century earlier in the so-called Serrata del Maggior Consiglio. By thus spelling out more precisely the patriciate's distinctiveness, new legislation imposed a leveling template upon its membership. It applied to all nobles, from ancient as well as recently ennobled houses, wealthy as well as impoverished families, a specific new definition of patrician status, which was implemented in practice by new procedures that all nobles were now required to undergo in order to prove their credentials. In the face of this procedural leveling, marriage grew in importance as a means of gaining or retaining distinction, influence, or patronage within the legally undifferentiated ruling class.[60] At the center of this alliance strategy was the quest for government posts. In a century when large numbers of nobles—the majority, according to official statements—came to depend for their livelihood on what Donald Queller aptly called "welfare jobs" in the government, the importance of marital kin influential (or numerous) enough to drum up votes in the job-dispensing Great Council pressed on nobles with unprecedented urgency.[61]

That was the chief motivation behind the competition for bridegrooms sternly censured in the preamble to the 1420 act. The same motives that led patricians to give overwhelming approval to laws that strengthened their monopoly over the status and practical benefits of nobility also urged the forging of ties with the most influential, prestigious, and numerically abundant allies within the closed class. For families of the patriciate's second or third tier in terms of antiquity, wealth, or political prominence, the most effective way to do so was to induce young men from prominent families to marry their daughters. The most direct inducement was a compelling corredo. That was the tactic employed by Nicolò Foscolo in acceding to the terms dictated by his future son-in-law, Nicolò Corner, scion of one of the great case vecchie. To be sure, the total marriage settlement negotiated by Foscolo and Corner, 1,000 ducats plus living expenses of 60 ducats annually for an indeterminate period, was modest when compared with the gargantuan dowry of 5,000 ducats, accompanied by an unknown but probably equally thunderous corredo, commanded by the son of a reigning doge, Nicolò di Doge Antonio Venier, in the 1390s.[62] Nicolò Corner, however lustrous his genealogy, was not the son of a doge and had to set his sights lower. But an immediate and permanent gift of 300 ducats in cash was attractive enough to command in the peremptory tones of the pursued bridegroom from a historically prestigious house. Yet he might have commanded a larger corredo if he had been willing to marry a woman with a more conspicuous liability than the modest place of Lucia Foscolo's family among the patriciate. Luca Falier, like Corner a member of a casa vecchia, was willing to do so, marrying in 1410 the illegitimate daughter of Moretto Bragadin in return for a corredo of 1,000 gold ducats together with a dowry of 1,500 ducats.[63]

The marriage was a good deal for Luca Falier despite Isabetta Bragadin's bastardy. Even prescinding from any sexual or emotional attraction she might have exercised upon him—not to be excluded—Luca's arrangement with her father brought him a well-dowered wife, a handsome corredo, and in the end a noble father-in-law gratified by the match that he had arranged for his daughter. For his part, Moretto Bragadin's success in finding his daughter a husband of illustrious lineage doubtless evoked the "combination of pride, sorrow, and a firm belief that they had done the best they could to provide for them in their new adult lives"

which, as Queller and Madden persuasively argue, motivated most patrician fathers of nubile daughters. Isabetta's illegitimacy made arranging
her marriage more costly than if she had been legitimate. But in the end,
for Bragadin, just as for the fathers-in-law who gave large cash corredi to
Nicolò Corner, Roberto Contarini, Giovanni Ghisi, Nicolò di Doge Antonio Venier, and countless other patrician bridegrooms, settling upon
their daughters, legitimate or not, marriage portions consisting of generous dowries and corredi had a double benefit that made it worth the
expense. For it was not the antithesis but rather the means of a father's
achieving "his own benefit and that of his patriline."[64] The best provision
an attentive father could make for a daughter was a dowry that secured
her personal future and a corredo that would attract a husband who could
give her, her brothers, and indeed her patriline the benefit of cooperation
and prestige in the closed but differentiated and competitive environment
of the patriciate.

In the early Quattrocento, that meant above all finding a noble husband. The 1427 will of Andrea Arimondo captures the motivation at work
on fathers of daughters—highlighting the shaping effect of the legislation
of 1420. Andrea instructed his executors—who included "my beloved
consort, Maddaluzza," her mother, father, and brother from the patrician
Capello clan, as well as Andrea's own mother and two brothers—to marry
his daughter Marietta "to a Venetian noble [a uno zentilomo de Veniesia]";
moreover, if Maddaluzza gave birth to any other daughters, they, too, he
reiterated, should marry uno zentilomo de Veniesia.[65] He gave the executors authority to decide on the amount of the marriage portions, but if his
estate proved insufficient to provide them with 1,600 ducats each (the
maximum allowed in the law passed seven years earlier), the executors
would be free to put the girls in convents. Arimondo was here displaying
in detail patrician matrimonial strategy, adapted to the new legally chartered parameters. He was enlisting the participation of his own in-laws to
help procure in-laws for his son, Simone, by means of the marriage of
Simone's sister (or sisters). But these in-laws must be noble themselves,
and that required a proper patrician marriage portion of 1,600 ducats;
anything less would fail to attract a suitable bridegroom for Marietta, a
suitable brother-in-law for Simone. The convent was a better alternative
than a bad—that is, inadequately dowered and corredoed—marriage.

As Queller and Madden argue, nobles like Andrea Arimondo were indeed concerned with their daughters' futures. But they did their best to
combine that solicitude with attention to the benefits that their male heirs,

equal objects of parental concern, would derive from being brothers-in-law of the men their sisters married.[66] That double motivation, fatherly and familial, for finding husbands from the noble ranks for their daughters was the principal force driving up dowries for daughters and corredi for sons-in-law in the later Trecento and early Quattrocento. Despite the wide range of men's provisions for their daughters' marriages, they nonetheless had one thing in common: at all levels of prestige, wealth, power, and antiquity, they sought husbands for their daughters (and wives for their sons) who would be both socially, economically, and emotionally satisfactory mates for their children and collaborators for their family. The ingenuity and risk taking that many of them displayed in binding these in-laws to themselves elude easy generalization. Queller and Madden remind us that fathers had every reason to welcome the assistance of wives and kin in assembling marriage portions for their daughters, both before and, with hopeful anticipation, after they made their own provision. In the political, social, and economic environment of the early Quattrocento patriciate, every resource was precious when fathers dug deep both to provide decent dowries for their daughters and to bestow gifts, in hard cash, to the patrician grooms who married them.

㊀

Getting Back the Dowry

NO SUBJECT has been as fruitful for studying the condition of elite women in late medieval and Renaissance Italy as the dowry.[1] Dowries have provided a gauge for assessing women's share of private wealth, their relations with their families of birth and marriage, the determination of their adult vocations, and their status vis-à-vis legal institutions, public authority, and prevailing cultural principles. Scholarship on Florence has been especially productive in exploring the dowry system's effects on the family orientation and economic resources of married women, but it has produced a mixed verdict. One influential tendency in that scholarship, led by Christiane Klapisch-Zuber and Isabelle Chabot, has been to view the dowry regime as inflicting economic and social distress upon women. In this body of writing, private and official spheres appear as collaborators in fashioning dowry practices that were detrimental to wives. Patrilineal imperatives led the families that sent their daughters into marriage to treat the dowry as a way of honoring the girls' inheritance rights in appearance but denying them in substance; family needs led men to make instrumental use of women to advance the interests of the patriline, and to deprive them of a secure membership in either natal or marital family. Simultaneously, Florence's government enacted statutes that severely limited women's rights to enjoy or dispose of their dowries.[2] Yet, another body of scholarship, to which Giulia Calvi and Thomas Kuehn have contributed prominently, reaches a more nuanced conclusion, emphasizing adaptations in practice which attenuated or undermined the patriarchal structure of the dowry regime. To proponents of this interpretation, women appear not merely as instruments of patriarchal policy but also as objects of concern on the part of their families, freely disposing of their property,

95

administering their deceased husbands' estates, exercising guardianship over their children, and retaining enduring ties to their families of birth and marriage.[3]

In an effort to broaden the perspective on Italian women during this period and to provide a larger context for the Florentine case, I want to discuss the relationship of upper-class Venetian women to their dowries, especially the ways in which dowries connected women with their families of birth and marriage, with the wealth of those families, and with the institutional environment of gender relations in Venice. Exploring that relationship reveals a more unambiguously positive picture than the Florentine one. From the beginning to the end of marriage and beyond, the Venetian dowry regime gave women a broad and long-lived set of relationships and economic influence within them. Isabelle Chabot has shown how the relationships mobilized in a marriage lasted for its entire duration and how the final disposition of the property whose transfer marked its beginning—the dowry and its satellite elements—mapped the kinship terrain around a marriage at its end.[4] The location of a wife or widow on that terrain was tied to her continued stake in her dowry. In Venice it was women, either acting personally as widows or by designating agents to act for them, who managed the outcome of a marriage already ended or whose end was being anticipated. In this they were supported by two powerful patriarchal structures, their families and government institutions.

Our route into the subject is through the end of marriage. Much of the writing on dowries has been concentrated on the efforts of families to provide dowries or of governments to regulate or facilitate dowry giving.[5] But the purposes of families in providing dowries and the attitudes of the young brides whom they accompanied had little bearing on the interests of widows or their heirs over the course of the ensuing years and decades. Marriage was a long and evolving experience, and the women who passed through the uxorial cycle from young bride to mature wife and mother to widow inevitably formed and re-formed many times over the meaningful attachments and loyalties in their lives. Their relationship to their dowries underwent similar evolutions, especially as, with age, they contemplated the ends of their marriages. To have a fuller sense of the social and economic meaning of wifehood it is therefore useful to balance discussions of its beginnings with consideration of how it ended, who got the dowries, how they got them, and who participated in the getting of them.

To begin with, let us review some information about dowry restitution in Venice. Incomplete records from the period 1366–90 provide information on 168 cases of dowry restitution to widows of nobles, whose counterparts in Florence have been the main objects of study there.[6] For the fifteenth century the court records are more complete. Here I use 139 cases regarding noble marriages from 1466 to 1477.[7] I was unable to complete a systematic study of dowry restitution in the early Cinquecento, when the records are even more abundant, but I will make some anecdotal reference to them. These restitution acts, called in Venice *diiudicatus* or *de giudicato*, are useful in the first place for tracking the steady increase in marriage settlements from the mid-Trecento through the early Cinquecento. Between 1331 and 1360, wives conveyed to noble husbands dowries averaging 500 ducats; during the period 1361–90, the average grew to 873 ducats.[8] The upward pressure continued all through the Quattrocento. Among 122 noble dowries repaid from 1466 to 1477 in which the amounts are noted, the average was 1,230 ducats—a nearly 50 percent increase from 1361–90.[9] And they still kept going up. In 72 noble marriage contracts from November 1505 to November 1507, the average dowry had risen to 1,732 ducats.[10] Altogether, average noble dowries grew by 350 percent over 180 years. It is important to note that these sums represent the amount technically designated as dowry, exclusive of the personal goods brought by the bride to her marriage and, more important, of the part of the settlement which remained as the property of the husband. By the early Quattrocento this gift to the bridegroom, labeled the *corredo* (*corredum*), constituted one-third of the entire settlement. Thus, the amounts returned to widows were normally the remaining two-thirds.[11] Dowry inflation in Italy has been much discussed and well documented.[12] Equally important is that the increase meant that the Venetian Giudici del Proprio, who had jurisdiction over dowry matters, were awarding to widows a steadily growing portion of private wealth in the dowry-restitution procedure. That procedure and the roles of the government and private interests in it are the focus of this chapter.

The government's regulations for dowry recovery were set in the statutes of 1242, and except for occasional refinements they remained constant through the period under discussion. Once a marriage ended, if the widow had not already recovered her dowry from her husband's estate, she, or the executors or heirs designated by deceased wives, reclaimed it in a two-stage process: the *vadimonium*, in which the widow or her heirs presented documentation of the dowry to the Giudici del Proprio, and the diiudicatus, in which the same judges authorized payment of it from her husband's estate and, when that was insufficient, from the property of the persons who had guaranteed the dowry.[13] A widow was required to notify the court of her intention to claim the dowry (*dare vadimonium comprobandi*) within a year and a day after the death of her husband, or her executors or heirs within a year and a day after her death; the claim then had to be documented within thirty days after that.[14] Once this initial flurry was completed, the widow had thirty years to request actual restitution of the dowry by means of a diiudicatus decree from the Giudici del Proprio. All the while she could continue to live at the expense of her husband's estate. Although once she had received her diiudicatus she could no longer claim a living allowance, she could still remain in his house "until she has received full repayment of her dowry."[15] A statutory correction of 1343 added a further clarification to the effect that, unless a husband had specifically bequeathed his widow *statio*, she must vacate his house within two months if she received her dowry without having to go through the vadimonium procedure.[16] This provision indicates that some husbands facilitated their widows' recovery of their dowries, enabling them to dispense with the courts.

Widows' entitlement to support from their husband's property until they claimed their dowries gave them considerable latitude. This had widespread significance because the overwhelming majority of marriages ended with the death of the husband. Table 2 breaks down 454 fourteenth- and fifteenth-century vadimonium and diiudicatus cases involving nobles. The most striking information is that nearly three-quarters of the claims were filed by or on behalf of a living widow; the others were filed by her heirs or executors after her death. In reality, however, wives survived their husbands at an even higher rate than that. The table shows that in nearly three-fifths of the claims involving dead wives, the husbands also were deceased. In an indeterminate but undoubtedly large number of those cases, the widow had chosen not to claim her dowry but instead to live in her late husband's house, raising their children with her expenses paid by his estate.

In so doing she acted in conformity with the wishes of many, if not most, husbands. Like their counterparts in Florence and elsewhere, Venetian men offered their wives economic inducements not to remarry.[17] In a will of 1420, Nicolò Mudazzo bequeathed to his wife, Elena, over and above her dowry of 1,100 ducats, the income from 1,000 ducats in shares in the state's funded debt (Monte) as well as food and clothing expenses for the rest of her life. Those bequests were unconditional. But if she was willing to remain with their children, "in the interest of greater love and

Table 2. Spouse Survival at Vadimonium or Diiudicatus

	Cases	%
Wife survives	333	73.3
Husband survives	49	10.8
Both deceased	72	15.9
Total	454	100

Source: Information from CI 114, Marino, prot. 1366–91; De Giudicato 1, 2; Vadimoni 1, 4, 5, 8, 9; Proprio, Testimoni, Reg. 4; and Proprio, Parentelle, Reg. 1.

Note: The 454 cases include only those vadimonium or diiudicatus procedures in which the vital status of both spouses is clearly indicated.

peace," she would receive from his estate an additional 50 ducats a year, two beds, and all her clothing.[18] Mudazzo, like the countless men who imitated him, was supplementing his widow's statutory right to perpetual residence in the husband's house with additional material advantages, as long as she did not remarry. The reason was the conviction of such husbands that it was in the best interests of their children that their widows see to the children's upbringing. Equally important in the calculations of husbands was the desirability of inducing their widows to preserve their dowry wealth for the children rather than wresting it away and applying it to a remarriage, which in Florence occurred among one-third of women widowed in their twenties.[19]

It is critical to note, however, that the Venetian statutes also explicitly stated that in choosing to remain a widow a woman did not jeopardize her right to her dowry.[20] Many husbands acknowledged that their wives would eventually claim its restitution, but asked them to defer it until the children were grown. Bartolomeo Grimani in 1469 acknowledged his wife's dowry of 1,066 ducats and 16 grossi but added, "I pray her that she be willing to delay requesting repayment of it [*indusiarse a pagar*]." Leonardo Priuli in 1477 was more precise, entreating his wife not to reclaim her dowry until five years after his death.[21] The text of his request conveys the concern of fathers and the strong position of mothers: "To my most beloved wife, Maria, I leave the entire dowry of 3,000 ducats which I had from her; however, I beseech [*oro*] her that it please her to leave the dowry in my estate for five years, or as long as she requires cash for the benefit of our children. In addition, I bequeath to her all the clothing and personal effects she received from her father, which she should freely possess together with all the items that I have had made for her, except for my jewels, which should be calculated as part of my residuary bequest. Item, I also leave her expenses for food and clothing for as long as she remains a widow, as my executors deem suitable for her status; but she should have more if she requires it and my estate can supply it. I commend to my most beloved wife our dear son, Zaccaria, and all other sons or daughters who might be born to us, that she be both departed father and mother to them, and take the place of a father in seeing to their care."[22]

Despite all these inducements, Maria rejected Leonardo's request. She claimed her dowry one month after his will was probated and married the widower Piero Loredan within the year, undoubtedly making effective use of her handsome dowry and the trousseau to which both her father and her late husband had contributed. In that regard, she fits Klapisch-Zuber's typology of the "cruel mother," the young widow quickly remarried by her male kin—all the more so because she must have been quite young, having married Leonardo Priuli only two years before he wrote his will.[23] Yet her remarriage did not entail abandonment of Zaccaria, her son from the Priuli marriage; fifteen years after marrying her second husband, she launched Zaccaria on his political career by personally registering him for the Barbarella, the lottery for young patricians whose winners could enter the Great Council early, at age twenty.[24]

In reality, remarriage of widows like Maria Priuli was exceptional, accounting for fewer than 9 percent of women's marriages.[25] Most widows remained in their marital residence for many years, claiming their dowry only decades after its conveyance to their husbands. In 138 fifteenth-century vadimonium claims that indicate the date of the marriage contract or dowry receipt (in effect, when the marriage began), the average length of time between that and the vadimonium filing was 23.5 years, the median interval 21 years.[26] But that tells only part of the story. More widows or their heirs reclaimed the dowries at least three decades after their conveyance than did so after ten years or less of marriage. The information is displayed in table 3.

Brief marriages and young widows like Maria Priuli were thus the exception, accounting for just a bit over one-quarter of the vadimonium claims. Many and probably most widows, old and young, took advantage of statutory rights and husbands' inducements to refuse remarriage, staying in their marital residence and delaying claiming their dowry for years or even decades. Vadimonium filings frequently failed to meet the statutory deadline of a year and a day after the husband's death; in those cases,

Table 3. Intervals from Dowry to Vadimonium

	Cases	%
<1–10 years	38	27.5
11–20 years	25	18.1
21–30 years	29	21
31–40 years	22	15.9
>40 years	24	17.4
Total	138	99.9

Source: Information from Vadimoni 1, 4, 5, 8, 9; Proprio, Testimoni, Reg. 4; Proprio, Parentelle, Reg. 1; CI 126, Buosi, parchments.

the women or their heirs made use of a loophole in the statutes extending the deadline to the full thirty years for those "ignorant of the law."[27] Those dilatory women enjoyed the best of both worlds, dwelling in the marital residence, raising their children at their late husband's expense, and then, when mothering—or life itself—was over, finally taking possession of their dowries or bestowing their dowry wealth on the heirs of their choice.

When eventually they did file, they did so in person. The statute outlining the vadimonium procedure required that "the woman . . . must go before the doge and the *giudici* or send another person on her behalf."[28] Most took the first option: only 12.4 percent of the Quattrocento vadimoniums involving living widows were filed by proctors; in the rest the women themselves appeared in court.[29] They made use of varied documentation to prove their claims. The preferred proof was the husband's notarized acknowledgment that he had received the full dowry (the *securatis dotis carta* or the *instrumentum dotis*). Eighty-five (53.8 percent) of 158 vadimonium claims that identify the documentation presented were based on such receipts, a preference supported by the Maggior Consiglio, which in 1449 passed legislation requiring notaries to submit copies of all dowry receipts to the chancery office, in order that widows might claim their dowries without "labore magno."[30] Another 22 percent were documented by means of marriage contracts; even though a contract is an undertaking to give a dowry rather than proof that it was actually given, the judges did make diiudicatus awards to widows on the basis of them.[31] Eleven percent offered entries in the husband's account book as proof of dowry payment, and 5 percent presented the husband's acknowledgment in his will, as in the case of Leonardo Priuli cited earlier. The remaining 8

Table 4. Heirs Acting in Vadimoniums and Diiudicatus

		%
Sons	22	45.8
Daughters	8	16.7
Sons and daughters	13	27.1
Brothers and sisters	5	10.4
Total	48	100

Source: From Proprio, Testimoni, Reg. 4; Vadimoni 1, 4, 5, 8, 9; Proprio, Parentelle, Reg. 1; De Giudicato 2.
Note: The information represents those instances among the 85 fifteenth-century vadimoniums and diiudicatus of deceased women in which the relationship between them and the filing beneficiaries is certain.

percent used miscellaneous evidence, such as entries in the account books of the wife's or husband's father or brother, or the testimony of witnesses.

When women were deceased, their vadimonium claims and diiudicatus authorizations were managed by the executors or the beneficiaries they had designated in their wills.[32] The identities of these persons reveal much about the familial orientation of married women and how much—or how little—it evolved during the course of the uxorial cycle. Broadly speaking, the wife's executors (*commissarii*) filed the vadimonium or claimed the diiudicatus when the marriage was briefer and the children were not old enough to make their own claims; the reverse was true in cases of long marriages or delayed claims; then, it was the heirs who managed the transaction. The difference is evident in the vadimonium filings, in which the interval from dowry receipt or marriage contract to vadimonium when executors filed was 24 years but when heirs filed was 38.4 years.[33] As table 4 shows, the overwhelming majority of beneficiaries acting in these cases, just under 90 percent, were the woman's children. Beneficence toward her children is what might be expected in a mother's will; the statutes themselves dictated that the property of intestate women was to be shared by all their children. This included their married daughters.[34] The statutes thus differentiated between mothers' property relations with their children, based on personal familial relations, and those of fathers, shaped by the imperatives of the male patriline; the rules governing succession to intestate fathers excluded their married daughters, who had presumably received their share in the form of their dowries.[35]

Table 5. Executors Acting in Vadimoniums and Diiudicatus

		%
Sons	11	32.4
Daughters	2	5.9
Husbands	2	5.9
Brothers	13	38.2
Fathers	3	8.8
Mother	1	2.9
Son-in-law	1	2.9
Daughter-in-law	1	2.9
Total	34	99.9

Source: From Proprio, Testimoni, Reg. 4; Vadimoni 1, 4, 5, 8, 9; Proprio, Parentelle, Reg. 1; De Giudicato 2.
Note: The information represents those instances among the 85 fifteenth-century vadimoniums and diiudicatus of deceased women in which the relationship between them and the filing executors is certain.

When women nominated their executors, however, they looked to their natal as well as their marital families, as displayed in table 5.

The complexity and variety of the family orientations of young married women are revealed by the near parity between the natal and marital family members they chose to administer their estates: 44.2 percent of the executors who filed vadimonium claims were the women's husbands or children; but 49.9 percent were their parents or siblings. (Note that these figures apply only to the individual executor who filed the vadimonium claim; most testators entrusted their testaments to several executors.) Most revealing, and indeed startling, is that the largest category of the filing executors was the women's brothers, who constituted 38 percent of executors; that compares with women's sons, who were 32 percent. It really is not surprising that a woman would enlist adult men from her family of birth to ensure that her property, including (but not limited to) her dowry, would be yielded up by her husband after her death; nor is it surprising that those designated executors would comply, since in addition to sentiments of fraternal loyalty they had expectations of their sister's grateful beneficence as an inducement.[36] What is noteworthy is the enduring trust, sometimes spanning decades, between married women and their brothers. It is exemplified in the tie between Zanetta Trevisan and her brother, Nicolò, who in 1458 filed the vadimonium for the dowry that Zanetta had brought to Tolomeo Donà thirty-four years earlier, in 1424.[37] Equally revealing is the infrequency with which women named their husbands as executors; widowers made up less than 6 percent of executors filing vadimonium claims, the same percentage as the women's daughters and a smaller one than that of their fathers. No husbands appear as their wives' beneficiaries in the vadimonium and diiudicatus cases studied. This small representation of husbands, however, may result from the practice, discussed above, of widows forgoing restitution of their dowries and living instead on their husbands' estates, then leaving their dowry wealth to their heirs; the husbands of such women would be unavailable as executors. But even when their husbands were alive, it made good sense for wives to designate executors other than their husbands to procure the restitution of their dowries from those same husbands or their estates.[38]

In filing their claims, widows or their executors were able to rely on government institutions mobilized to protect women's economic interests. According to the statutes, a widow's right to her dowry took precedence over all other claims on her husband's property, even those of his creditors, a principle reaffirmed by the Maggior Consiglio in 1403; and the estate of a man who died without a will had to repay his widow's dowry even before his children got their share.[39] The statutes also decreed that if a husband wished to sell property pledged for his wife's dowry, she could require him either to replace it with other real estate of equal value or to turn the sale price over to a government agency, which would invest it in the wife's name.[40] The diiudicatus judgments that formally awarded widows their dowries put these principles into practice. The procedure called for the widow to present proof of the amount of her dowry. The statutes imply that the process began with the filing of the vadimonium, but only one-third of the Quattrocento diiudicatus judgments studied cite a previous vadimonium to document the dowry.[41] The others refer, to the evident satisfaction of the judges, to marriage contracts, husbands' wills and ledger entries, and above all notarized dowry receipts. Thus some women evidently bypassed the vadimonium step, proceeding directly to the diiudicatus. In any event, after the proof of the dowry was presented, the judges subtracted from that sum four types of deduction: the value of any property already deeded by the husband to his wife; any part of the dowry which she might have given him, for example, in the form of a bequest; any partial repayment that his estate might have already made to her; and, I believe, any contributions that she might have made from her dowry toward those of her already married daughters.[42] The remainder was hers, and the judges authorized her to appropriate it—as well as 12½ lire a grossi (equal to just under 5 ducats) "for her widow's apparel [*pro sua veste viduali*]"—from her husband's entire estate, both movables and immovables.[43]

In many instances, however, the judges, doubtless at the urging of the widow or her executors, made provision for the possibility that her husband's estate would be insufficient to repay the dowry, a prospect discussed by Julius Kirshner.[44] They therefore authorized her to sequester (*intromittere*) the remainder from the property of some other person, who at the time of its conveyance had stood as surety for the dowry's restitution.[45] This brings us to the question of dowry security, and I would like to devote the rest of this chapter to it because, like the presence of brothers and fathers in vadimonium and diiudicatus proceedings, the practice of providing guarantees reveals how the dowry system made women participants in complex, evolving, but also durable social networks.

Venetians contrived a wide variety of dowry guarantees, but no contract was without some guarantee.[46] In most cases, the husband, if he was emancipated, pledged all his goods for the dowry's return. To cite one example, from 1424, among many: "Ser Zorzi [Dolfin] promises to have a dowry receipt notarized [*carta de segurta de inpromessa*] for dona Barbarella [Contarini] . . . obligating all his goods, movable and immovable, present and future."[47] A husband's sense of obligation led Nicolò Arimondo in 1422 to describe himself as "my wife's debtor."[48] That was in conformity with the statutory provision that all of a husband's property was obligated for the return of his wife's dowry from the moment of her *transductio* to his house; to clear up any uncertainty, the Great Council in 1413 reaffirmed that her precedence extended to both the movable and the immovable property.[49] Normally, the husband's promise in the contract to *meter in carta* his wife's dowry was fulfilled after its conveyance, when he acknowledged it in the notarized *securitatis dotis carta* or *instrumentum dotis*, pledging all his goods toward its restitution.[50]

Many families of prospective brides, however, were not satisfied with their future son-in-law's pledge; they insisted on more tangible assurance of his ability to repay the dowry. Husbands often complied by following the Florentine practice of assigning shares in the state's funded debt (Monte) or other government investment vehicles for the dowry's restitution.[51] Frequently, part of the dowry itself was invested in government funds, earmarked explicitly for its restitution. In such arrangements, the husband usually, though not always, was to enjoy the income from the investment but had no control over the capital. Marcantonio Priuli agreed in his marriage contract of 1530 that "the capital of 2,000 ducats is always to remain as a dowry fund or security [*per fondo dotal o pro caucione*] for the dowry of madona Morosina," his wife.[52] Of the immense marriage portion of 7,600 ducats which Maria Morosini conveyed to her bride-groom in 1435, 6,000 were to be registered, in Maria's name, at the Monte office, the Camera degli Imprestiti.[53] Negotiating his daughter's marriage in 1453, Girolamo Dandolo prevailed on his new son-in-law to agree that she could require him, "at any time," to put 1,000 ducats in Monte shares in her name as dowry security.[54] To be on the safe side, fathers contracting their daughters' marriages took pains to ensure that changes in the market value of such shares would not erode dowry investments, by spelling out precisely their equivalent in gold ducats, so that the dowry would be repaid "danari per danari, monte per monte" [money for money, fund for fund], as a contract of 1532 had it.[55] The government itself periodically enacted legislation affirming that when such investments were redeemed at the time of dowry restitution, they were to be calculated not according to the current market value of the shares but to their real value at the time of purchase.[56]

Government investments were an attractive repository for dowry security, but in contrast with Florentine practice, Venetians were not hesitant to negotiate real estate, as well, both as components of dowries and as security for their repayment.[57] The designation of immovables as dowry security was so normal that the statutes instructed that diiudicatus judgments must award widows contiguous properties, or at least "the ones most useful for the women [*utiliores pro mulieribus*]" in their husbands' estates.[58] The statutes also required husbands who sold real estate pledged toward repayment of dowries to file with the government, "in the wife's name," title to any property purchased with the proceeds of such a sale; or if the proceeds were kept in cash, it was to be deposited with the Procuratori di San Marco, also "in the name of the wives."[59] Those rules were enforced. In 1398 one of Gasparino Contarini's kinsmen sold real estate that had been partially obligated for the dowry of Gasparino's wife, Marina, whereupon the Giudici di Petizion ordered Gasparino either to secure the dowry on his own property or to deposit its cash value, 1,000 ducats, with the government's grain office, "as is customary," where it would earn interest. Gasparino was to carry out this order within one month "in order that the said domina Marina will have her dowry effectively secured and bonded."[60]

The judges' pressure on Gasparino reflected the determination of brides' families to ensure that their dowry investment would be protected. In a contract of 1531, Gian Francesco Bondumier prevailed on his sister's future husband to agree to turn over the 1,500-ducat cash portion of Ludovica's dowry to the Procuratori di San Marco, to be invested by them in "real estate . . . , which investments are to be obligated for the dowry."[61] Other husbands pledged their own real estate. In 1365, Marco Ruzzini "gave and assigned" to his wife two apartments, appraised at exactly the amount of her dowry (30 lire di grossi, equal to 300 ducats), in the family palace (*domus maior*) of one of his kinsmen; she would henceforth have "full power to delegate, have, hold, give, donate, sell, commit, and possess [the property] as your own, or to do anything else with it that might please you."[62] Giovanni Querini "gave, assigned, and transacted" to his wife the "the entire house [*tota domus a stacio*]" in which he was living.[63] These were residential properties, but husbands also assigned their wives income-producing investments. Jacopo Morosini gave to his wife, Lucia, four rental properties at Rialto, valued at 500 ducats, "as security for her dowry," and Luca Falier obligated to his wife, Maria, among other real estate, five rental properties in San Luca.[64] Paolo Contarini signed over to his wife eighty-eight *campi* in Camponogara which he had received as part of the dowry.[65]

Husbands earmarked real estate, or Monte shares, or investments in the government's grain office as guarantees in order to satisfy their affines' demand for assurance of the dowry's restitution. But other husbands with insufficient property of their own had to call upon relatives or friends to back them up. In 1462, Francesco Morosini's three brothers had to pledge all their property to ensure repayment of his bride's dowry, unenthusiastically it seems: they stipulated that "if Francesco should purchase real estate or Monte shares [*prestiti*] for his wife's security, they wanted ipso facto to be freed from their pledge."[66] They had good reason to worry, since guarantors were in fact called upon to honor their pledges. Because the estate of Francesco de Mezzo's late brother was insufficient, Francesco was forced to commit all his future prestiti income and all his profits from merchant ventures to repay his sister-in-law's dowry, of which he had been co-guarantor.[67]

Not only brothers but other relatives stood surety for dowries, and their involvement maps the range of kin mobilized to protect women's

Table 6. Co-guarantees of Dowries (by Relatives of Husbands)

	Cases	%
Fathers	15	32.6
Brothers	12	26.1
Mothers or grandmothers	18	39.1
Unknown relationship	1	2.2
Total	46	100

Sources: Proprio, Testimoni, Reg. 4; Proprio, Parentelle, Reg. 1; Vadimoni 1, 4, 5, 8; CI 62, Buosi; Contratti di nozze 140/1 and 142/3.

Note: Information from contracts and dowry receipts. These 46 do not include the cases in which husbands pledged their own property without co-guarantors.

economic interests. A sample of forty-six guarantors who joined with husbands to secure dowries from the 1420s to the 1530s, though small, can give an idea of the categories of pledges (see table 6).

As with Francesco Morosini's contract just discussed, brothers took an active part in backing up a husband's capacity to repay the dowry. However, for most families of brides, one brother's pledge was not enough, and in nine of the twelve fraternal co-guarantees, two, three, and even four brothers pledged their goods.[68] It was more usual for fathers to counterpledge for their daughter-in-law's dowry or, in the case of unemancipated sons, to assume primary responsibility for its restitution. Fathers acted as guarantors one-third of the time, in fifteen of the forty-six cases; in fact, the practice and the principle were so well established that the priority of a woman's dowry among claims on her father-in-law's estate was written into the statutes, which mandated that if a man died intestate with his daughter-in-law's dowry in his possession, it was to be consigned to her husband before the estate was divided among the heirs.[69] Individual fathers made the same provision in their wills, allocating additional property to their unmarried sons in order to enable them to demonstrate to prospective in-laws the same dowry backing from their father's estate which their married brothers had received.[70] The economic resources of the fathers of bridegrooms loomed large in marriage bargaining, and not just as fallback dowry security. In 1412, Nicolò Coppo accepted his daughter-in-law and her dowry with the customary formula, "over all his goods [*in su i suo beni*]." He stated his willingness to emancipate his son, Agostino, but, like other fathers, also held out the reassuring alternative of housing and feeding the newly married couple and their children "as long as his son desires."[71] Although emancipation could be a way of disclaiming responsibility for repayment of a daughter-in-law's dowry, as Thomas Kuehn has pointed out, convention weighed heavily on the side of the father-in-law's liability.[72] Even doges assumed their fatherly responsibility. In 1393 Doge Antonio Venier secured his daughter-in-law's dowry upon all his property.[73]

It's only to be expected that in the patrilineal environment of the Venetian patriciate fathers and brothers would act as co-guarantors, as they did in nearly three-fifths of the cases examined, twenty-seven of forty-six (58.7%). They stood to benefit most from the infusion into the family's collective resources of a daughter- or sister-in-law's dowry, so they had the best motive to encourage prospective in-laws by obligating their property as security for its restitution. For that reason it is remarkable that the mothers and grandmothers of husbands secured the dowry upon their property in nearly two-fifths of the cases. The frequency of their appearances in contracts provides powerful evidence both of women's loyalty to family and kin and of the substantial economic resources they were able to deploy in demonstrating it. Women's wealth was an element in guaranteeing dowries in indirect ways, as well. In the case just mentioned of Nicolò Coppo pledging for the dowry of 1,500 ducats received by his son, Agostino, he carefully pointed out that Agostino also possessed, in his own name, 1,500 ducats in inheritance from his mother and grandmother.[74]

This was doubtless reassuring to Agostino's future parents-in-law, but living women also negotiated their wealth directly in dowry negotiations. To back up Domenico Barbaro's pledge of his own goods for his wife's dowry, his maternal grandmother promised that she would bequeath him "a large residential house [chaxa granda da stacio], a courtyard of houses, and other houses," and his mother promised that at her death he would get one-third of her property in San Paternian, "freely and without any contradiction." In addition, the two women signed over to Domenico, "free and clear [senza alguna eception]," 420 ducats that they had received in a civil judgment against one of their male relatives, as well as 200 ducats in prestiti.[75] Finally, they agreed jointly (chadauna de lor insolidum) to receive Domenico's bride's dowry, pledging all their property for its restitution. For the reasons already discussed, these women were far from unusual in possessing enough real estate to satisfy the families of prospective brides.[76] But other kinds of female wealth served just as effectively as dowry security. In a contract of 1428, the bridegroom's mother and grandmother promised to bequeath him half of their prestiti holdings of 5,000 ducats.[77] Their commitment of their imposing wealth was a necessary (and, in the event, sufficient) condition of the dowry offer. How important it was, and how scrupulously the families of brides sought assurance of the security of the dowries they were bestowing, are conveyed in a contract of 1462. Maria Davanzago pledged two-thirds of her wealth, "movable and immovable," to secure the dowry of her daughter-in-law; to reinforce the credibility of the pledge, her two sons-in-law, acting for themselves and on behalf of their wives and heirs, "renounce[d] any gifts [that Maria might have promised them]; in sum [intuto], the donation that the above-mentioned madona Maria is making to her son Marino Davanzago is understood to have the primary claim [on her goods]."[78]

The wealth of these women came from their own dowries, as some stated explicitly. Cristina Renier in 1479 pledged "all her goods, whether dotal or present and future," to secure the dowry of her daughter-in-law, and Gabriella Barbo in 1528 likewise obligated "all her dotal goods and all other goods of whatever sort she has or may have, present and future," for the same purpose.[79] Both of these women possessed nondotal property, but by far the largest portion of the wealth upon which they and the many other female pledges could credibly secure the dowries received by their sons and grandsons came from their own dowries.[80] The key to women's prominence among co-guarantors of dowries is thus to be found in the very credibility of their guarantees, conclusive evidence that women got back those carefully secured dowries.

Female guarantors of dowries demonstrate the importance of women in nourishing the dowry system that procured their own marriages and those of their sons and daughters. Their marriage portions gave them the economic substance necessary to reassure anxious parents of the next generation of brides that their investments in their daughters' marriages would be available in turn to those women when they were widowed. That actually represented an enlargement of mothers' role in their children's marriages. At the same time that they guaranteed the dowries of their daughters-in-law, they also made important contributions to the dowries of their daughters.[81] Isabetta Corner's three sons-in-law acknowledged in notarized declarations in 1476 that each had received from her 500 ducats in partial payment of their wives' dowries. Of the 6,600-ducat marriage portion that Laura Bragadin brought to Nicolò Querini in 1533, 4,500 were contributions from her mother, including Monte shares, furnishings and clothing (mobeli et vestimenti) for the bride, and rental property.[82] Similar instances appear regularly in the records, and it is not rare to encounter a marriage contract with women making contributions to both sides. In the contract, noted earlier, of Agostino Coppo, whose mother and grandmother bequeathed him the 1,500 ducats needed to secure his bride's dowry, that dowry itself was enriched by 500 ducats in Monte shares contributed by the bride's grandmother and aunt.[83] In 1477, part of the dowry that Giovanni Dolfin's mother guaranteed with her own property was money that the mother of Giovanni's bride had won in a judgment against the estate of her late husband. That case is a demonstration of women's involvement in the complete dowry cycle: its assembling, its conveyance, and its repayment—here, as usual, assured by the authority of Venice's judicial system.

The dowry system was the means of its own continuity and expansion, owing in no small measure to the active participation of dowered women at all stages. It was in the interest of men to keep strong their connections with their married sisters, daughters, aunts, wives, and mothers even over the course of decades, to keep up their membership in the evolving social networks of these women of substance. It was the stake of such men in the wealth and benevolence of their married womenfolk which demanded the guarantees that secured dowries and which sustained the government institutions that ensured their restitution. Families may have dreaded the dowry inflation that forced them to invest ever larger amounts of family wealth in their daughters' dowries. But the support with which they, in collaboration with the institutional structure of Venice's government, enabled their women to get back their dowries nourished their own ability to find places in the marriage market for the next generation of daughters and sons.

PART TWO

Women, Marriage, and Motherhood

Patrician Women

in Early Renaissance

Venice

ALMOST A CENTURY AGO, the Venetian archivist and historian
Bartolomeo Cecchetti undertook to discover what he called "the general
concept that Venetians had of women." Although he called his study "La
donna nel medioevo" (Woman in the Middle Ages in Venice), nearly all of
his documentation came from the fourteenth and fifteenth centuries, the
early Renaissance. His conclusions after a long and wide-ranging survey
of aspects of women's experience during the period were forthright. "Neither works of imagination nor high intellectual attainments, nor flights of
poetry adorn the figure of woman in Venice's earliest epoch. Modest,
domestic [*casalinga*]," he declared, "she is swept up in the great whirlwind
of life; and she appears to us only in her weaknesses, or in the splendor of
her beauty, or in the context of one of the high offices of her mission—her
children, her family."[1]

Cecchetti's characterization contrasts with some other earlier writers'
pictures of women in the Middle Ages. Nearly fifty years ago, Eileen
Power concluded that "taking the rough with the smooth and balancing
theory against practice, the medieval woman played an active and dignified part in the society of her age." More recently David Herlihy observed
that "woman comes to play an extraordinary role in the management of
family property in the early Middle Ages, and social customs as well as
economic life were influenced by her prominence."[2] Perhaps the contrast
between these writers and Cecchetti can be explained chronologically.
Power and Herlihy were dealing with the early and high Middle Ages,
while the early Renaissance that Cecchetti focused on has been viewed as
witnessing, in another writer's words, "a slow and steady deterioration of
the wife's position in the household" in Europe.[3] Yet this idea, too, has

been challenged. Richard Goldthwaite, writing on Florence, perceives an actual increase in the effective role of women in the household in the early Renaissance.[4]

This chapter is an attempt to examine some of the conflicting ideas and to confront Cecchetti's view of Venetian women during the early Renaissance. My scope is more modest than his was. While he sought to discover Venetians' "general concept" of women, I consider only patrician women during the fourteenth and fifteenth centuries. Moreover, my focus is limited to one aspect of women's role in society, their influence on interfamilial relations. Within these limits, however, I shall argue that Cecchetti's dismissal of women was inaccurate. Women did have an important influence on economic and social relations within the patriciate. Not only that: because of that influence, they contributed much to the relative intraclass harmony and stability that constituted one of the hallmarks of the patriciate during the Renaissance. The sources of this significant female role are threefold: (1) the social principles that governed Venetian society; (2) the status of women and of their property under the law; and (3) certain social and economic developments that increased women's economic importance during the period. I propose to consider these three things in turn, then to look at the ways in which they increased the importance of women in patrician society.

THERE ARE TWO THINGS about the organization of Venetian society which bear on the situation of patrician women, one deeply embedded in the legal and cultural traditions to which Venice belonged, the other a more recent phenomenon. The first is that complex of attitudes, legal principles, and succession rules which for convenience's sake we can call the patriarchal regime. Like other European societies, Venetian society was male-dominated. Both of the traditions from which Venice drew its laws and customs, the Roman and the Germanic, were patriarchal, and Venice inevitably followed their lead.[5] Descent, for example, was reckoned patrilineally (i.e., through the male line), and agnates (male-line kin) were favored in the succession to intestate individuals.[6] The most important monument of this male dominance, however, the one that gave significance to the others, was the *fraterna*, the shared patrimony among brothers.[7] By its provisions, the sons of a family were locked together in the joint inheritance of their father's estate. And their sisters were excluded, possessing only the right to their dowries.[8] On the face of it, the

Venetian social order was founded on juridical principles that put women in a secondary position as far as the long-term interests of the kin group were concerned.

The second feature of Venetian social organization that had an impact on the role of patrician women was the peculiarity of aristocratic status in Venice. In contrast to the situation elsewhere in Italy, Venice had a defined, hereditary aristocracy. A series of legislative measures at the end of the thirteenth and beginning of the fourteenth century had effectively closed the patriciate to all but the members of those families already represented in the government in the 1290s. There is debate on the short- and long-term significance of these measures, collectively known as the Serrata, or closing, of the Great Council, but it is clear that they laid a juridical basis for some two hundred clans and families to regard themselves with self-conscious assurance as Venice's ruling class.[9] In the context of our subject, however, the Serrata had two main effects. It gave added importance to the patrilineal orientation of society. Now patrician status itself depended on the ability to prove one's descent from patrician stock—through the male line.[10] Consequently, patricians had a stronger motive than ever to entertain a sense of the lineage in which only the masculine chain of descent mattered.

At the same time, the Serrata gave patricians a strong motive to pay strict attention to their social connections. The emphasis on pedigree which their hereditary status gave rise to, the political associations that they were involved in as monopolists of political activity, and the impulses toward internal differentiation within the class all led patricians to view marriage ties as alliances of considerable significance for the family's interests and status. Whom their sisters and daughters married meant a great deal to patrician men. When, for example, the patrician Gasparino Morosini, in a will of 1401, bequeathed some money for the dowry of a daughter of his dead son, he instructed that the husband she eventually should marry had first to be acceptable to Gasparino's surviving sons and to certain of his cousins in the male line.[11] The reason was that the young suitor who met the test would be a potential business associate, will executor, legal representative, political colleague—would in short carry into the marriage associations with and potential benefits for Gasparino's line. So it was appropriate that members of the line, the potential beneficiaries of the relationship, should pass on the suitability of their niece's future husband.

This combination of social principles gave women a curious status in patrician society. On one hand, the patrilineal and patrimonial character of society excluded them from full and enduring membership in the lineage, which they nominally left upon marriage. On the other, they figured prominently in their family's social strategy, representing an important means of improvement, or at least maintenance, of their family's social and economic status through marriage ties. This distinctive social identity gave women a kinship orientation that contrasted with that of men; at the same time it provided them with a particular kind of social leverage outside the natal lineage.

We can get some idea of the difference between men's and women's kinship orientation from the bequests that they wrote into their wills. For this purpose, I looked at fifty married men's wills and fifty married women's wills from the period 1305–1450.[12] To simplify the analysis, I considered only bequests to first- and second-degree natal and marital kin. That is, for the natal kin, to parents and siblings, grandparents, uncles and aunts, first cousins, nieces and nephews, and for the marital kin, to spouses, children, and grandchildren. The most striking information from the analysis is that while men directed the largest portion of their bequests, two-thirds, to their marital kin, women divided their bequests just about evenly—half to natal kin, 45 percent to marital kin. (In both cases, 5 to 6 percent went to affines.)[13]

Like all figures, these are tricky. The trickiness is especially true in this case because the figures here gloss over differences in the life cycles of testators and the developmental cycles of their families. For example, men may have been older when they made their wills than women were when they made theirs. (In the absence of precise demographic data it is very hard to know dates of birth or of other vital events.) Nineteen of the fifty women mentioned living parents, while only five of the men did; moreover, the men mentioned twice as many children as women did, by 124 to 62. Both of these differences, fewer parents and more children, are strong indicators that male testators were older; and this, rather than differences in kinship orientation, might account for the greater percentage of bequests to marital kin in men's wills: they simply had fewer living natal kin when they wrote their wills. However, other considerations soften this impression.

For one thing, the presence or absence of names in a will may or may not indicate the existence of individuals; all that they do indicate with certainty is that an individual was named as a beneficiary or an executor.

This point becomes a matter of significance when we note that the women in the sample tended more than men did to make blanket bequests to their children without indicating either their numbers or their names; only three of the men made such blanket bequests, while eleven of the women did.[14] This difference partially accounts for the greater number of individual children mentioned in the men's wills. Secondly, the patrimonial regime itself may explain in part the lower number of parents and siblings appearing in men's wills. A man's economic relationship to his father and brothers was governed by the rules of the patrimony, particularly the principle that a father's estate was to be shared equally and jointly by brothers, united in the fraterna.[15] Under these circumstances, a man may have regarded it as redundant—or generous beyond the call of fraternal and filial duty—to put his brothers and father in his will. Finally, the impression that men wrote their wills at a more advanced age than women did—or at least at a further stage in their natal and marital families' developmental cycles—is mitigated by the facts that just as many women as men, eight, mentioned grandchildren and that more of the women were widowed than men—by twenty-two to thirteen.[16]

So while the differences in men's and women's bequest patterns may stem from the different points in their life cycles and their families' developmental cycles, the evidence is not conclusive that this was in fact the case.[17] A better explanation, I think, is that men simply took more responsibility for the economic fortunes of their marital families than women did. It seems likely that men, with their economic relationships to their natal families clearly established by law, concentrated their own efforts on their wives and children, whose contribution to the enduring prosperity of the lineage depended largely upon paternal provisional.[18] Women, on the other hand, not so deeply involved in the meshes of the patrimonial and lineage system, made their bequests on the basis of other considerations, including those of sentiment.[19]

This last consideration leads to another aspect of female bequest patterns, and it also raises a puzzling question. If, as noted earlier, women participated only instrumentally in the affairs of the lineage (as the currency with which families established marital alliances), why is it that they maintained the close ties to their families of origin which their bequests reveal? A suggestion toward an answer may be found in the writings of social anthropologists. Meyer Fortes, for example, using categories derived from the study of African societies, notes the differences between two kinds of social interest that individuals may have. On one hand are those interests that have, in Fortes's words, "the sanction of law and other public institutions"; on the other hand are those "that rely on religion, morality, conscience and sentiment for good observance."[20] He goes on to observe that where corporate descent groups exist and constitute a framework within which individuals take their places in the larger society, as in the case of the Venetian patrician lineage, they are governed by formal law. But in those same societies, Fortes maintains, less formally institutionalized sanctions, such as sentiment and morality, govern the relations within what he calls "the complementary line of filiation," in effect the tie that exists among husband, wife, and children by reason of their collective involvement in the family's fortunes.[21] Because in a patrilineal society mothers normally come from outside, the mutual attitudes and expectations of family members are different than among lineage members, who are born into and brought up in the lineage.

Applying these ideas to the Venetian patrician environment, men, because of their necessary lineage orientation as hereditary patricians, concentrated on promoting the interests of the lineage. In this connection, it is worth noting that the one category of natal kin which men favored in their wills more than women did was secondary male natal kin—grandfathers, uncles, cousins, and nephews of the same surname—in other words, those men who were linked to the testator by a common lineage interest but in a relationship not covered by the legal rules of the fraterna among brothers.[22] Women, on the other hand, were comparatively free of these lineage restrictions. Their kinship orientation was based more on the ties of sentiment and morality to which Fortes referred. A good indication of this attitude can be seen in the differences by sex between men's and women's bequests. The female testators in the sample clearly favored the women among their natal kin over the men, and this is true of both primary relatives, mothers and sisters, and secondary relatives, grandmothers, aunts, cousins, and nieces.[23] Since those female relatives, like the women writing the wills themselves, took formal leave of the natal lineage when they married, bequests to them represented gestures of personal, rather than lineage, loyalty.

Pulling all these considerations together, we can make the general observation that while old traditions and recent political developments fastened upon male patricians a concern for the patrilineage, women's more tenuous and temporary role in the lineage resulted in a freer, more flexible kinship orientation. As we shall see, the difference had important implications for patrician social relations. But before turning to that it is important to take a look at Venetian women's position under the law.

IF VENETIAN WOMEN were different from their menfolk by reason of their freer, less lineage-structured social orientation, they also enjoyed, and suffered, distinctive treatment by the law. A good deal of the difference between men's and women's legal status derived from the patrilineal system of descent and succession. For example, a girl's only claim upon the family patrimony was for her dowry. However, although on its face this rule would seem to favor men, in fact it cut both ways. A large literature accumulated among medieval commentators on Roman law, who argued that a woman's dowry not only had to be "congruent" with her family's status but should roughly equal a full share of the patrimony.[24] Moreover, when fathers died without providing adequate dowries for their daughters, the same commentators maintained, the girls' brothers were obliged to take up the burden.[25] Another difference arising from patrimonial considerations had to do with succession to mothers and to fathers. A married, and thus dowered, daughter of a man who died intestate had no further claim on his estate. This is consistent with the idea that a woman's dowry was her entire inheritance. But when a woman died intestate, all her children—sons, unmarried daughters, and married daughters—entered equally into the inheritance.[26] The reason was that women's property was not part of the patrimony but, like women themselves in this patriarchal society, responded to the impulses of filiation, a thing of sons and daughters both, rather than to those of the descent group, which favored the males.[27]

The distinctive position of women before the law went deeper than just the implications of the patrilineal system. It reflected Venetian society's conception of a fundamental difference between maleness and femaleness. The difference comes through with disturbing clarity in the criminal statutes. One section prescribed a series of corporal punishments for theft, varying in degree of gruesomeness with the value of the stolen goods. However, where a man lost an eye, a woman lost her nose; where a man lost an eye and a hand, a woman lost her nose and one lip; and so on ad nauseam.[28] These penalties were imposed in practice. In 1356, Jacopa, wife of Piero Alessandri, was sentenced to have her nose and both lips amputated and to be whipped for stealing a neighbor's tunic. Seven years later Maria, wife of Nicolò de Foremillio, was sentenced to the loss of her nose and one lip, a whipping, and a branding for theft.[29] Why this difference in penalties according to sex? The likeliest reason is that punishments for men were designed to deprive them of the means of earning a livelihood (or its perversion, stealing); but those for women were designed to deprive them of the means of attracting men.[30]

In the civil courts, too, the view of women as different in fundamental ways influenced official action. For one thing, courts and legislators felt a responsibility to protect women. The Great Council said as much in the preamble to an act of 1352 regulating inheritance rights: "In legal matters involving men and women," the preamble reads, "upon whom nature bestows equal affection, we want not to introduce prejudicial differences but, rather, humanely to take into account the fragility of women."[31] The statute went on, however, to reaffirm that men were to be preferred as heirs to immovable property over women of the same degree of kinship to the deceased, though both shared equally in the succession to movable goods. But other than privileging male succession to real property, a principle universally observed in Italian society, Venetian institutions did offer protection to women.[32]

A good indication is in the sphere of the respective rights of husbands and wives. Given the patriarchal cast of Venetian law and custom, one might expect men to enjoy unrestrained dominion over their wives.[33] The reality was quite different. A measure of 1374, for example, asserted the right of a woman to sue for separate maintenance if she lived apart from her husband because of some grievance against him.[34] Nor was this an empty legalism. In 1317, and probably earlier, the courts had made separate maintenance awards.[35] A case before the Giudici del Procurator in 1343 illustrates the kind of domestic situation in which women received official support. The noblewoman Caterina Morosini sued for separate maintenance, alleging that "the cruelty, harshness, and wickedness of . . . Micheletto Morosini, her husband, were such that he threw the said Caterina, his wife, out of his house. Nor," Caterina's complaint continued, "does she want to live with the said Micheletto," preferring to remain removed from his "cruelty and wickedness."[36] Micheletto defended himself by claiming that "his wife, Caterina, would never live with him, that he would never take her into his home."[37] Unfortunately for his case, his testimony consisted of these and other "verba iniqua et dolosa" [wicked and deceitful words]. In the event, the judges found for Caterina, awarding her 30 ducats a year, which Micheletto was obliged to pay, under pain of imprisonment, as long as the marriage should last. By way of epilogue, the spouses may have reconciled: in his will of 1348 Micheletto made provision for the eventuality that Caterina was pregnant.[38]

This case shows that the tutelage of husbands over their wives was limited, that husbands had to conform to certain standards of behavior vis-à-vis their wives, and that judges, though likely married men themselves, could respond to a wife's complaint against an abusive husband. In a wider context, the judgment here indicates that patrician men looked after the daughters they married off in the interests of the lineage. Paternal and fraternal solicitude doubtless entered into such protection. But more material considerations, focused most likely on the bequest tendencies noted earlier in women's wills, played their part, too. It was in the interest of men to be loyal to their married daughters and sisters because they stood to benefit from the loyalty that the women reciprocated.

The same consideration is even more clearly at work in the laws protecting women's property. Married women possessed two kinds of property: outright possessions, generally derived from legacies, and dowries.[39] In Venice there were no restrictions on a married woman's use of property she owned outright. She could enter into any transaction that she pleased with it, the statutes asserted, "even without her husband's consent."[40] Despite the principle that a girl had the right only to a dowry, it was fairly common for women to possess nondowry property as well. In a will of 1397, for example, Giovanni di Marino Morosini, who had already furnished his married daughter with a dowry of 1,000 ducats, bequeathed to her an additional 10,000 ducats' worth of shares in the funded state debt, or Monte.[41] Although the daughter was not to sell the shares and could not dispose of them in her will, since Giovanni made other disposition for them after her death, she could count during her lifetime on an annual interest of 300 to 400 ducats from the legacy, a very substantial income and potential investment capital.[42] His bequest was exceptional only in its amount, for men frequently remembered their married daughters and sisters in their wills.[43] It comes as no surprise that women showed an even stronger disposition to make bequests to their married female kin. Among the Morosini women's wills forty married daughters are mentioned, of whom twenty-eight received bequests from their mothers.[44] This is consistent with the statutory provision, noted earlier, which admitted married women to the inheritance of their intestate mothers. All of this shows that women had the means of getting property over and above their dowries. The statute affirming a married woman's right to the free employment of her nondowry property was therefore not just an empty formality but was addressed to concrete situations.

However, by far the greatest part of a woman's economic substance, and thus her most important source of economic influence upon kin and associates, was her dowry. Because the dowry was regarded as a contribution to meeting the economic burdens of marriage, a wife could not invest or otherwise use it without her husband's consent.[45] Yet it was still regarded as her property.[46] I was unable to find in the Venetian statutes anything limiting the husband's use of the dowry, but in Italy generally such limits did exist, and in any case there is Venetian evidence of husbands rendering to their wives some of the profits they made investing their dowries.[47] Moreover, the statutes were precise in defining the safeguards protecting a woman's dowry from her husband's maladministration.

In the first place, a husband's entire estate was put under obligation toward repayment of his wife's dowry, and he was required to deposit with the Procuratori di San Marco an amount sufficient to guarantee repayment to his wife upon his death or her heirs upon hers.[48] But either because the rule was not always observed or because husbands did not always possess sufficient property for such a deposit, other safeguards also were employed. One was the practice of having a guarantor of the dowry cosign the receipt along with the husband.[49] Even more sweeping was the principle that the male kin of a deceased husband had to supply whatever was lacking in the husband's estate for full restitution of his widow's dowry. Usually, responsibility fell to the husband's father, or his father's estate, and this was true even when the married son had been emancipated from the father's *patria potestas*.[50] But on occasion other agnatic kin of the husband also were held responsible; in an odd reversal, one emancipated son was required to contribute toward the restitution of the dowry of his father's widow.[51] Finally, the statutes stated clearly, "in order that from this time forward no question should arise," that the repayment of his wife's dowry took precedence over all other obligations a man might have incurred on his estate.[52] When he died, his heirs and creditors had to wait until his widow had secured restitution of her dowry; and she even had the statutory right to choose from among the goods in her husband's estate.[53]

Venetian law thus went to considerable lengths to guarantee women's dowry rights, and for that matter their property rights in general. There seem to be two reasons for this solicitude. One is that a widow had to have the means of supporting herself, and especially of furnishing herself with a second husband. At a time when girls married in their early teens and when wives generally outlived their husbands, young or middle-aged widows simply had to possess basic material resources.[54] The second and more interesting reason is a seeming paradox: male society protected the interests of women, secondary and temporary members of the lineage though they were, out of concern for the well-being of the lineage. It was in the interest of Venetian men to ensure that the dowries and other donations that they gave their daughters and sisters would not be permanently alienated from the patrimony out of which these provisions had been carved. Seen from the perspective of the lineage, protecting a woman's right to the restitution of her dowry meant, in effect, protecting her capacity to return it, or at least part of it, to her natal kin by means of testamentary legacies—something that, as we saw earlier, women did in half of their bequests.

In fact, the testamentary legacy was not the only way in which a married daughter could use her dowry for the economic benefit of her natal kin. Widows also made their property available to their kinsmen for business purposes. Tomasina, widow of Albano Zane, invested 1,000 ducats in a business venture her father was undertaking in 1380; in her will of 1394, Beria, widow of Martino Morosini, noted that her brother and her nephew, Bernardo and Zanino Contarini, had borrowed 1,000 and 100 ducats, respectively, from her for business purposes.[55] It is this kind of economic choice which reveals the extent to which the laws guaranteeing women's property rights also protected families' investments in their daughters' dowries.

Yet we must not lose sight of the fact that a widow's natal kin shared her largesse with her marital kin, her children and grandchildren above all.[56] It is this division of social and economic allegiance between two families, two lineages, which gives the role of women in patrician society its significance. That role, formulated in response to women's position in the patriarchal regime and defined by law, became even more important as a consequence of social and economic developments in the fourteenth and fifteenth centuries.

THE MOST IMPORTANT of these developments was the inflationary trend in dowries during the period, in Venice as elsewhere in Italy.[57] In the mid-fourteenth century an average patrician dowry was about 650 ducats; by the 1370s and 1380s it had risen to 1,000 ducats.[58] The rise continued at an alarming rate, inducing the Senate to pass a law in 1420 imposing a fine on all parties to dowry transactions exceeding 1,600 ducats, an indication that many dowries were larger than that.[59] The reasons for the rise are complex; although this is not the place to go into them in detail, it is worth noting that dowry inflation is an important wedge into major social and economic issues in late medieval Italy. Some writers have observed that higher dowries reflected a rising cost of living; prospective husbands demanded higher dowries to help them make ends meet, which, after all, was the purpose of the dowry.[60] Another cause in Venice was intraclass differentiation between the oldest noble clans and newer ones that had gained noble status in the aftermath of the Serrata of the late thirteenth and early fourteenth centuries. Relative patrician newcomers sought status by marrying upward with higher dowries, and more ancient families preserved theirs by the same means.[61] Still another cause may have been the loss of other investment opportunities in the wake of fourteenth-century economic dislocation.[62]

Once dowry inflation took off, the most important force pushing dowries upward was large dowries themselves. As the first and second generations of richly endowed wives observed their daughters approaching marriageable age, they hastened to make their own increasingly weighty contributions to the girls' marriage portions. Among 305 wills of the Morosini clan written in the fourteenth and fifteenth centuries, the involvement of women in the dowry accumulation of their daughters increased significantly. In the period 1331–70, dowry bequests from fathers outnumbered those from mothers by a ratio of 6 to 1; during 1371–1410, fathers' bequests outnumbered mothers' by only 2.2 to 1; but in the period 1411–50, dowry bequests of mothers had come to outnumber those of fathers, by 1.5 to 1.[63]

The explanation for this increase in maternal beneficence is not just that women had more wealth as a result of dowry inflation, although it certainly was an important factor. Nor was it only that women's consciousness of the importance of good dowries for their own daughters had been raised, although that also was likely in the circumstances. Equally important, more women were writing wills. To cite the Morosini wills again by way of illustration, from 1331 to 1370 women accounted for 56 percent of the wills; from 1371 to 1410 their share was 66.9 percent; and from 1411 to 1450 it had risen to 71.7 percent.[64] In part, this striking increase in female testation can be explained by the fact of larger dowries; with larger estates, women had a greater reason to exercise care regarding their disposition. Since legally the inheritance of intestate women belonged to their children alone, a woman who wanted to make bequests to her natal kin (which most women did want to do) would have to be sure to draw up a will. Still another reason for the increase in women's wills can be found in the plague that struck Venice repeatedly in the century after 1348.[65]

The vivid acquaintance with unexpected mortality which characterized the generations of the Black Death and its repeated sequels persuaded all Venetians to write more wills, and to write them earlier in life. Although this was true of both sexes, women's wills accounted for the great bulk of the increase. Among the Morosini wills, during the period 1311–50 there were 16 men's wills and 19 women's wills, a ratio of 1.2 in favor of women. During 1351–90, women's wills outnumbered men's by 54 to 33, a female ratio of 1.6. From 1391 to 1430 there were, again, 33 men's wills, but now no fewer than 87 written by women, a female ratio of 2.6. Female testation outstripped that of men chiefly because women had, and now took, more opportunities to write wills than men did. They married younger than men did, and they tended to outlive their husbands and thus to witness more changes in the life cycles of their potential beneficiaries, in response to which they altered their bequests.[66]

In view of the larger estates that they now possessed by reason of their larger dowries, and in view of the always present possibility that the plague might suddenly snatch them away, Venetian patrician wives took occasion to write several wills in the course of their adult lifetime.[67] That they did so, taking pains to determine for themselves the destiny of their estates instead of letting the statutory regulations take effect, indicates that women had a clear sense of their legal prerogatives and their economic significance and were determined to exercise them on behalf of the kin that they felt most responsibility for or sympathy with, without regard for lineage.

Up to now we have considered several aspects of patrician women's position in early Renaissance Venice. We noted, first, that in the patrimonial and patrilineal society to which they belonged, women demonstrated a distinctive social orientation, different in important ways from that of their menfolk. Less concerned with the interests of the lineage, they appear to have responded more to impulses of personal sentiment than of collective descent-group interest. We observed that this distinctive social sense expressed itself in the economic choices they made in their wills and business investments. Secondly, we saw that Venetian law, and Italian law generally, responded institutionally to women's position in society. Particularly important was the protection that the law and its representatives gave to women and their property. Although during marriage wives were denied control over the use of their greatest asset, their dowries, nevertheless their ultimate dominion over the dowries and their right to dispose of them in wills and during their widowed lifetime were assured. Finally, we noted that during the late Middle Ages women's economic substance increased—largely a result of dowry inflation—and that their determination to keep control of this enlarged wealth also increased. The overall impression that this configuration of women's position conveys is that they had the means of producing a sizable impact on society. Did they in fact do so? In at least three areas they did.

The first is one we have already touched on, women's economic activity. Disposing as they did of ever larger estates, women were now in a position to have a substantial economic impact on their kinsmen and other associates. As it happens, Venetian women, like their sisters elsewhere, had a history of business enterprise.[68] It took many forms: making loans to businessmen;[69] investing in manufacturing concerns;[70] and putting money into the state-run galley voyages to distant ports of call.[71] Sometimes these investments were made outside the web of kinship, but the most substantial sums seem to have been committed to kinsmen. Now, with larger amounts to work with, women were capable of making large-scale capital investments of as much as 1,000 ducats at a time.[72] There can be little doubt that the possibility of such economic cooperation from widowed daughters and sisters eased the minds of fathers and brothers as they contemplated the dowry inflation. But these substantial female investments went to marital kin as well as to the natal kin who had footed the dowry bill. For example, in her will of 1398 Chiara, widow of Marco Morosini, noted that her son-in-law, Francesco Zen, owed her the hefty sum of 3,000 ducats, which he had borrowed from her.[73] Like the sizable bequests that such widows of substance now made, their business capital gave them influence over both natal and marital kin—a sort of Venetian instance of the proverbial rich aunt—and consequently made them formidable figures on the economic and social scene.[74]

The second effect of patrician women's position in early Renaissance Venice is connected with their economic strength. It is the psychological leverage that they came to exercise over their male kinsmen. Assessing the position of women in modern rural Greece, Ernestine Friedl notes that women there have considerable "informal power over household economic decisions and over the economic and marital future of their sons and daughters" because of their contribution, through their dowries, to the household economy.[75] In Venice, women were able to influence the course of family, and kin group, affairs in the same way, for example, by attaching conditions to their bequests. This is something that their husbands traditionally had done, but for the typically male purpose of promoting the lineage. Male testators regularly bequeathed to their wives a yearly income, or some property, or both, on condition that the wives not remarry, instead devoting their widowhood to the upbringing of their children.[76] The purpose was to ensure that the testator's offspring would not become stepchildren of another husband, from another lineage.

Now women could use the same kind of pressure, but for purposes of their own, which were more behavioral than lineage-centered. Beruzza, wife of Marco Soranzo, threatened to cut her bequest to her husband in half if he did not free a female slave named Anna upon Beruzza's death.[77] This was not a trivial whim: her reason was her concern, as she wrote, "for the salvation of his soul and mine"; there is here the strong suggestion that Marco was using Anna for purposes other than just domestic service, an illicit liaison to which Beruzza wanted to put an end.[78] In another example, Agnesina, widow of Lodovico Morosini, gave the bulk of her estate to her son Vittore only on condition that he first free himself from his debts.[79] The economic leverage that women were able to exercise upon men's behavior is a large matter with large cultural implications. In the present context we can at least make the general observation that Venetian men had reason to stay on the good side of their kinswomen, especially their wives, and this gave women a means of influencing male activity.[80]

The final effect of women's position which I want to mention is related to the first two, but in the larger political context it is the most important of all. Because of their social, legal, and economic position, Venetian women contributed to the strengthening and stabilizing of ties among patrician lineages and within the patriciate generally. It has been frequently remarked that in Venice, unlike, say, Florence, patrician kinship ties beyond the elementary family remained strong well into the sixteenth century; this is usually attributed to the institutional endurance of the fraterna, which lasted for two generations.[81] But equally well known is the Venetian patriciate's unusual degree of intraclass cooperation and collective political discipline—at least as compared with other Italian ruling elites of the time.[82] Social anthropologists, among others, have observed that a strong sense of lineage and a well-defined commitment to a state usually do not coincide; they are, rather, alternative modes of sociopolitical organization.[83] Yet in Venice they coexisted. One of the chief reasons was married women's importance to the economic interests of both their own lineages and those of their husbands.

As ever larger portions of the patrimony became earmarked for dowries, men sought to maintain ties to their married sisters which could yield economic benefits in the forms of legacies and investments, as we have seen. Husbands and sons for their part could also entertain expectations of a share of their wives' and mothers' wealth. Given the strength of lineage solidarity among males, demonstrated in the endurance of the fraterna and the high incidence of men's bequests to secondary male natal kin, the benefits that these various natal and marital familiars received from their womenfolk radiated outward to a wider circle of kinsmen of both lineages. As a consequence, a married woman became a link between the separate economic destinies of two lineages, pulling them together into a sort of suprafamilial, supralineage economic association. The complexity of associations of this type is illustrated in the 1431 will of Ingoldise, widow of Simone Morosini, whose bequests ranged over a web of kinship including three different patrician clans.[84] She bequeathed 200 ducats to the daughter of her sister Nicoletta, wife of Dragono Zen; 1,000 ducats to her granddaughter Maria, the wife of Marco Zane, as well as 100 ducats to Marco Zane himself; and 100 ducats to each of Maria and Marco's sons. The *residuum* of her estate she left to her grandson Giovanni Morosini, son of her late son Piero. Just to spin the web even more densely, she named her brother, Antonio Contarini, and his sons among her executors, along with her grandson, her married granddaughter, and the latter's husband.

Nor were these large clusters of kinsmen on both sides of the marriage link simply competitors for women's largesse. The rise in dowry levels was accompanied, naturally enough, by a rise in the importance attached to the alliance dimension of marriage ties.[85] The expectations from a son-in-law to whom a father sent not only his daughter but a conspicuous dowry were high. The return on the investment might be political benefits, as Frederic Lane observed in the case of the Pisani and Vendramin families.[86] In any case the family of the bride naturally hoped for economic advantages. The same Gasparino Morosini whose intentions regarding the marriage of his granddaughter were mentioned earlier is a case in point. The ties that he forged with the father and brothers of the first of his three wives remained strong well after the wife's death. In his will of 1374 he bequeathed 50 ducats to each of his late wife's brothers, "because," he stated, "of the great love and interest I have always felt for their house."[87] Just as he was behaving toward his late wife's kinsmen exactly as a good brother-in-law should, on the other side of the affinal equation he expected as much from his own sisters' husbands: in the same will he named one of them, Piero Venier, as his principal executor.

Gasparino's example is only one of many; associations among affines, political and especially economic, were a regular feature of patrician society. The influence of women on the conduct and on the economic direction of such associations was often considerable, as we have seen.[88] In these circumstances a dense and complex network of associations was woven throughout the patrician class. In the first half of the fifteenth century, for example, the Morosini entered into 240 marriages with 70 different clans; the Balbi contracted 31 marriages with 24 different clans; the Da Canal had 40 marriages with 29 different clans.[89]

This wide range of spouse selection within the patriciate and the close interlineage ties that resulted created an overlapping system of horizontal ties among patrician clans which complemented the vertical ties of lineage within the clans. The role of women in reinforcing this cross-lineage association, by means of their wealth and their flexible and unprejudiced social orientation, constituted their most significant function in early Renaissance Venetian society. How important it was among all the other factors that contributed to the patriciate's relative stability is a vast question that cannot be dealt with here. But it safe to say that women's economic strength, legal status, and distinctive kinship orientation had considerable importance in achieving the celebrated integration of Venetian patrician society in the Renaissance.

Dowries and Kinsmen

IN THE FIFTEENTH CANTO of the *Paradiso* (ll. 103–5), Dante wistfully observed that in contrast to his own time, the epoch of his great-great-grandfather Cacciaguida did not see fathers taking fright at the birth of daughters. In those good old days, dowries had not yet "fled all limitation." Dante may have been indulging in a familiar kind of romanticizing; certainly twelfth-century Florentine fathers also had to face responsibility for their daughters' dowries. But his laments about the rise in dowries had plenty of echoes. In fact, the problems that the dowry institution itself, and especially dowry inflation, posed in the early Renaissance (fourteenth and fifteenth centuries) are a familiar theme in the historical literature on the period.[1]

The fact of dowry inflation is well documented. An example from Venice can give a sense of the trend. In a sample of fifty mid-Trecento patrician dowries, the average was about 650 ducats and the largest about 1,540 ducats.[2] By the fifteenth century, however, it was a rare patrician dowry that fell below 1,000 ducats, and there was a strong tendency to go much higher.[3] This tendency was alarming enough to induce the Venetian Senate in 1420 to place a limit of 1,600 ducats on patrician dowries, a good indication that many dowries were larger. But such measures did no good. There are many instances of larger dowries in the years after 1420; and at the beginning of the sixteenth century the Senate passed another law reaffirming the principle of dowry restraint—but resignedly raising the ceiling to 3,000 ducats.[4]

It would be valuable to know whether the rise in dowries was greater, smaller, or about the same as price movements generally in the period. Were Dante and the Venetian senators alarmed because dowries were soaring out of all proportion to other expenses—and to incomes? Or were their laments over dowries just symptomatic of a general concern over a rising cost of living? Sketchy data, great variations year to year in the availability of articles of consumption, and a complex monetary system that fluctuated dizzily during the period make it impossible to plot with any precision general movements in prices or, on a broader level, in the overall cost of living—even without getting into the delicate and complex question of different levels of wealth in the consuming, and dowry-raising, population.[5]

In general, there seems to have been a rise both in prices, particularly in manufactured goods, and in the standard of living.[6] However, not much research has been devoted to this question in the Italian context. As a center of exchange Venice certainly escaped the worst of the "price scissors" that afflicted the agrarian sector. Yet wheat prices appear to have risen during the period. In 1342–43, a *staio* (2.3 bushels) of wheat cost a Venetian householder 22 silver grossi, equal at the time to just under 1 ducat. By 1390 importers were selling wheat to the Venetian government's grain office at about 1.7 ducats per *staio*—a wholesale price that still prevailed, however, in 1432.[7] But wheat prices are a notoriously unrepresentative index of prices generally. Although other isolated bits of evidence testify to a rise in the cost of living, they do not add up to a clear enough picture against which we can gauge the relative impact of the dowry rise. Yet the leading authority on medieval Italian dowries speculated that the increase in dowry levels could be attributed in large part to prospective bridegrooms' growing dowry pretensions in the face of the rise in the cost of living.[8]

But if we cannot be sure whether the increase in dowries was greater than general increases in the cost of living, there is good documentation of a development that helps to explain the concern of fathers in the fourteenth and fifteenth centuries. It is the great squeeze that governmental exactions, especially in the form of forced loans (*prestiti*), put on private wealth. This important question cannot be dealt with in detail here (studies by Luzzatto and others have treated it thoroughly), but its bearing on the rise in dowries can be stated briefly.[9]

Military expenses throughout the third quarter of the fourteenth century put a mammoth burden on the nobles and citizens of Venice—the assessable part of the population. At their worst, during the years of the desperate war of Chioggia with the Genoese, the fisc's levies in two years, 1379–81, drained away about one-quarter of the private wealth in Venice.[10] It is true that the impost-paying public gained interest-bearing shares of the state debt (Monte) for most of these exactions. It is also true that Monte shares could be negotiated for various purposes, including dowry transactions. But by this time the government had given up its former practice of making amortization payments in addition to interest payments; moreover, after 1382, interest payments effectively dropped from 5 to 4 (and for some even 3) percent—considerably lower than the return on commercial or real estate investments; and the market price of Monte shares, at its low point of 18 percent of face value in 1382, had risen only to 63 percent of face value by 1400, despite governmental efforts to shore up the Monte by buying shares through a sinking fund.[11] So dowry payments in Monte shares, whether computed at the market price or at face value, were not a one-for-one solution to the squeeze on private wealth which endless prestiti levies had effected.

Considering the effect of these fiscal burdens on private wealth, the growth of dowry standards must have been particularly painful for Venetian patricians—"insupportable" in the words of the Senate act of 1420.[12] It is probable that dowries came to demand a much larger chunk of the family patrimony than had earlier been the case. For these reasons, the rise in dowries had important ramifications for Venetian economic life. However, we are primarily concerned here with effects rather than with causes. Specifically, we shall deal with the way in which these ever larger dowries were assembled. It happens that, at least in Venice, at the same time that dowry inflation was straining the resources of Dante's frightened fathers, the fathers were in fact getting a good deal of help to meet the challenge. This nonpaternal involvement in the raising of dowries is a little-known fact of Venetian social history during the early Renaissance. Yet it has importance not just for the dowry as an institution but for the family and kinship system of Venice's ruling class. Stated briefly, a widening circle of dowry contributors encouraged a patrician social orientation in which the traditional emphasis on lineage was increasingly complemented by nonlineage ties of affection and interest.

ACCORDING TO ROMAN dowry practice, the main purpose of the dowry was to help the groom bear the burden of matrimony (*sustinere onera matrimonii*).[13] In its medieval Italian version, however, the Roman *dos* had a special twist. Unlike original Roman practice, the Italian dowry came to be regarded as the girl's share of the patrimony. From this principle flowed several important effects. One was that girls were excluded from a share in the patrimony (the *exclusio propter dotem*). The *fraterna*, or enduring joint inheritance, was for brothers alone. Sisters, provided with dowries, had no further legal part to play in their paternal family's economic life. Another effect was that dowries were supposed to be "congruent"—to equal a full share in the patrimony. It was, Pertile observes, to guarantee that dowries would not exceed an equal share under the pressure of dowry inflation that Venice and other cities legislated against excessive dowries.[14] Finally, and most fundamentally, the view that a girl's dowry represented her rightful share of the patrimony meant that she had an indisputable right to a dowry. This was the source of the fathers' fright.[15]

Of course not all girls received marriage portions, no matter what the legal principles demanded. Closeting them in convents was a regular practice and at its worst led to the scandalous situation in which convents, it was said, were little better than brothels. The 1342 will of the patrician Leone Morosini illustrates why the practice was widespread.[16] He bequeathed to his daughter Lucia a dowry of 576 ducats, along with a *corredo* (in effect, a trousseau of movable goods—personal effects, household items, etc.) of 346 ducats. But his wife was then pregnant and might give birth to another daughter. Rather than divide Lucia's portion between two girls, which would have led to two undistinguished marriages, Leone simply instructed that the second daughter be placed in a convent and given an annuity of 10 ducats—quite a saving over Lucia's marriage portion.

Leone proposed the convent for his unborn daughter—in fact, the child turned out to be a son—because it was cheaper than an adequate marriage dowry. But his motive was not simply to rid himself of the burdens of daughters. If two girls were too much to deal with, Leone, like other fathers, still viewed a well-dowered daughter as a social asset. In the same will he provided that if the unborn child was a boy, then Lucia was still to have a dowry "of the right amount for a patrician girl." It was the fathers' interest in effecting favorable matrimonial alliances which kept the marriage market booming and contributed to the rise in dowries—and gave concrete application to the legal principles governing families' responsibilities for their daughters' dowries.

But if, according to law, fathers bore primary responsibility for their girls' marriage portions, the responsibility did not stop with them. Contemporary commentators on Roman law and the Venetian statutes asserted that when a man died or became feeble minded (*mentecaptus*) without providing for his daughters' dowries, his sons, the girls' brothers, took on the charge. This was consistent with the principle of the fraterna. The sons who assumed joint proprietorship of their deceased father's estate also assumed his obligations. The same principle further dictated that when male descendants were lacking, dowry responsibility went to the deceased father's male ascendants.[17]

Even more interesting, and usually unremarked in discussions of the early Renaissance dowry, is the principle that mothers were sometimes obliged to provide dowries, specifically when the father was too poor to do the girl justice. Since mothers were not part of the lineage (they had no membership in their husbands' and sons' patrimonial group), this responsibility signifies that dowries were not exclusively the concern of the patriline. But this slight hint of economic matriliny in a society usually regarded as stoutly patrilineal may have gone even further. If an unmarried and undowered girl lacked parents, brothers, and paternal ascendants, then, according to one authority, responsibility passed to her maternal grandfather and other maternal ascendants.[18]

What this indicates is that the jurists considered dowry provision important enough to commit a fairly wide kinship web to participation in it. And even though in medieval practice the dowry took on the appearance of a share in the patrimony, which was the classic patrilineal institution, the maternal line also figured in this central fact of the family's social and economic life. But although the confluence of paternal and maternal kin around dowry raising seems by itself to caution against overemphasizing the patriarchal character of Venetian upper-class society, what we have seen so far is only legal prescription. Did it correspond to actual practice? More specifically, did hard-pressed Venetian fathers receive the help in dowering their daughters which the legal prescriptions promised?

The evidence indicates that they did, and more. In the fourteenth and fifteenth centuries, patricians showed a strong and increasing disposition to contribute to the dowries of their young kinswomen. These conclusions are based on the testimony of 305 patrician wills, all but 7 from the period 1300–1450. The wills were written by members of the sprawling Morosini clan or by wives of Morosini. Although one clan cannot be regarded as representative of the entire patriciate, the Morosini wills do offer something of a cross section. The clan was a large one, spread over the city; there were at least fifty property-owning Morosini males in 1379, at all levels of wealth; and nearly half of the wills, 140, were written

Table 7. Dowry Bequests (%)

Beneficiaries	Male Testators	Female Testators	Totals
Daughters	50 (61.7)	31 (38.3)	81
Granddaughters	7 (46.7)	8 (53.3)	15
Nieces	11 (52.4)	10 (47.6)	21
Sisters	4[a](80)	1 (20)	5
Cousins	—	3 (100)	3
Total	72	53	125

Source: NT, CI, PSMC. *Note:* [a]Includes one sister-in-law.

by women from other families who married into the Morosini clan.[19] It should be acknowledged at the outset that testamentary bequests for dowries are not the same as actual contributions; Venetians frequently rewrote their wills, thus canceling their original bequests. However, each bequest indicates an intention valid at the time made, even though sometimes later revised. So the evidence of these wills can provide some indication of Venetian patricians' involvement with young girls' dowries.

There are in the wills many bequests to unmarried girls, and in view of the principle that a girl's dowry represented her share of the patrimony, most of them probably amounted to contributions to the legatees' dowries.[20] Nevertheless, to avoid ambiguity the analysis is limited to 125 bequests, in seventy-nine wills, which the testators destined explicitly for the dowry purpose. Forty-two of the wills were drawn up by men, the remaining thirty-seven by women. Table 7 gives the distribution of the bequests among the various recipients.

Table 7 shows that although they were about equally generous to granddaughters and nieces, men outdid women in bequests to daughters by a ratio of 5 to 3. That ratio is only slightly larger than that of about 3 to 2 between the total number of children named in the forty-two men's wills and those in the thirty-seven women's wills.[21] Thus, part of the reason that men gave more in dowry bequests lies in the apparent fact that they had more children than women when they wrote their wills. How can this be explained? For one thing, women had a tendency, as we shall see below, to draw up wills during their first pregnancies. Men generally testated after their families were already born. However, we should not make too much of this difference; only four of the thirty-seven wills in the sample were written by women apparently in their first

Table 8. Paternal and Nonpaternal Dowry Bequests

	To 1330	1331–70	1371–1410	1411–50
Largest bequest				
p[a]	769[b] (1)[c]	1,000 (5)	2,300 (22)	4,500 (9)
n	4[b] (1)[c]	769 (6)	2,000 (27)	2,000 (26)
Smallest bequest				
p	269	382	1,000	1,000
n	4	4	1	10
Median bequest				
p	509	576	1,350	2,000
n	4	634.5	200	500
Average bequest				
p	535	606.4	1,340.9	2,244.4
n	4	500	589.6	569.2
Total amounts bequeathed				
p	3,214 (99.9%)	3,032 (50.3%)	29,500 (65.7%)	20,200 (57.7%)
n	4 (0.1%)	3,000 (49.7%)	15,379 (34.3%)	14,800 (42.3%)
Total	3,218 (100%)	6,032 (100%)	44,879 (100%)	35,000 (100%)

Source: NT, CI, PSMC.

Notes: [a]p = paternal; n = nonpaternal. [b]All amounts are in ducats. [c]The number of bequests in this category, during this period.

pregnancies, and, more generally, women, like men, wrote wills at all points throughout their adult lives and at all points in their families' developmental cycles.[22]

A better explanation is that men on the whole named their children individually and made specific provision for their respective legacies. Women, by contrast, tended to make blanket bequests to their offspring, with equal shares to boys and girls alike. In this connection it is worth noting that young married women in their first pregnancies, like other female testators in later pregnancies, did make generalized bequests for their daughters' dowries. All four of the women in their first pregnancies provided for the dowries of their unborn children, should they be girls.[23] Thus, the appearance—to judge from dowry bequests—that men had more children may be illusory, a result of different habits of testation by men and by women.

In fact, the primacy of paternal involvement in dowry raising which the figures in table 7 reveal—50 percent of the total—is even more clearly reflected in the amounts of dowry bequests.[24] Table 8 shows that through-out the period fathers continued to discharge their patrimonial respon-sibilities as leading contributors to their daughters' dowries and that the size of the contributions rose with the inflationary trend in dowries. But the table also shows that though nonpaternal bequests did not increase in size to the same extent, they did increase in numbers—to the point that in the fifteenth century they outstripped bequests of fathers. The effect was to give nonpaternal bequests, small in average, considerable aggregate importance in the total amounts bequeathed for dowry purposes, as indi-cated in the bottom row of the table.

This substantial, and growing, involvement of kin other than fathers in the accumulation of dowries, coinciding as it did with an alarming rise in dowry levels, must have been welcome to hard-pressed fathers of daughters. But it raises an important question in the general context of family and kinship relations. The compensation that fathers and brothers traditionally had received for dowry expenditures was the acquisition of economic, social, and even political allies in the persons of their new sons- and brothers-in-law.[25] Did the growing involvement in dowry raising of kin from outside the patrimonial group—or, in its identity over time, the lineage—now attenuate the lineage's expectations from the marriage alli-ance? The answer to the question requires a closer look at the kinsmen who contributed to girls' dowries.

SINCE WE WANT to discover whether the patrimonial group's concern in girls' marriages diminished as the pool of dowry contributors increased, it makes sense to divide contributors into those who belonged to the en-dowed girl's lineage and those who did not. What this means in practice, since we are concerned with dowry bequests from kinsmen, is a division between the legatee's paternal and maternal kin. With that in mind, a nice parallel emerges with table 7: just as fathers dominated among contribu-tors within the lineage, mothers were the foremost contributors from outside the lineage, accounting for nearly one-quarter (24.8 percent) of all dowry bequests.

It is a disputed point whether a married woman belonged to her husband's lineage.[26] For our purposes, however, differences on the one hand between statutory regulations governing succession to intestate fathers and those governing succession to intestate mothers and, on the other hand, between men's and women's general bequest patterns indi-cate that married women did not demonstrate the same patrimonial and

Table 9. Men's and Women's Wills

	To 1330			1331–70			1371–1410			1411–50		
	No.	%	Ratio	No.	%	Ratio	No.	%	Ratio	No.	%	Ratio
Men	8	57.1	1.3	22	44.0	1	40	33.1	1	34	28.3	1
Women	6	42.9	1	28	56.0	1.3	81	66.9	2	86	71.7	2.5
Total	14	100		50	100		121	100		120	100	

Source: NT, CI, PSMC.

patrilineal concern that characterized their menfolk.[27] So their participation in the dowry-raising process lay outside the interests of the lineage. Why, then, did women contribute to their daughters' dowries? There was an obligation attached to dowries which required wives to benefit their children with them; some jurists even held that a woman enjoyed only the usufruct of her dowry, its real proprietors being her children. Venetian law seems to have stopped short of that view, but statutory provision for succession to the estates of intestate women was completely in favor of their children.[28] Those maternal bequests are interesting less because they were made (there are, after all, cultural as well as legal reasons for that) than because of their size and importance and the timing of their appearance as an important element in the assembling of dowries.

Women, in general, were at first slow in contributing to dowries, but in the course of our period they gradually came to represent an increasingly important source of dowry money. In part this can be attributed to a constant rise in the ratio of women's wills to men's (see table 9). The relative stabilization in the number of men's wills is curious. It could be simply an accident of documentary survival, although why should women's wills have survived more than men's? There is, however, another explanation. The most dramatic increase in the number of wills of both sexes occurred in the decades after the Black Death.[29] It is probable that the experience of the great mortality that accompanied the plague in 1348 induced survivors, and especially their descendants, to look to their own estates with greater attention. One result would be more will making. Another would be more will making by younger people, with the specific effects of (1) more multiple wills—that is, several wills written by the same individual over a number of years; and (2) more women's wills, as pregnant wives, concerned over intestacy, drew up their first wills during first pregnancies, modifying the intentions contained therein in later wills, also written during pregnancy.

The evidence of the 305 wills examined here documents both these effects. Eighty-seven, or 28.5 percent, were written by thirty-six individuals. Moreover, 77 of these multiple wills were bunched between 1371 and 1450, constituting 32 percent of all wills written during those years. In fact, among the Morosini no series of wills by a single individual was begun before 1360—close enough to 1348 to suggest the influence of that year's events, and long enough after it for an institutionalized reaction to have taken hold.

Women dominated among the multiple testators. Twenty-eight of the thirty-six individuals who wrote more than one will were women. This fact adds credibility to the hypothesis about increased will making following the Black Death. Women in Venice had a greater opportunity to write multiple wills than did men, by reason of their earlier entry into adulthood. In the fourteenth and fifteenth centuries, the preferred nuptial age for patrician girls was thirteen to fifteen, and, as far as their elders were concerned, marriage meant that they became mistresses of their own affairs.[30] A young wife's first occasion to exercise this mastery would present itself during her first pregnancy; if she survived that and subsequent pregnancies, she would have occasion to write a number of wills as her intentions regarding her bequests changed with changes in the life cycles of her kin.[31] As it happens, 28 of the 202 women's wills in our group were written, by the testatresses' own explicit affirmation, during pregnancy; and another 31 were written by wives who may well have been pregnant but did not say so in their wills.[32]

This statistic is even more impressive in view of the fact that only 120 of the women's wills were written by wives; of the rest, 76 were by widows and 6 by single women or nuns. One of the pregnant testatresses was, in fact, a widow, but her example seems unique in the sample.[33] So the representation of pregnant women among married testatresses was at least 23.3 percent (28 out of 120) and, considering also those possibly pregnant, may have been as high as 49.2 percent. Moreover, this pronounced tendency to draw up wills during pregnancy was a development of the later fourteenth century. In the period 1331–70, pregnant women wrote one of twenty-eight women's wills (3.6%); in 1371–1410, thirteen of eighty-one (16.4%); and in 1411–50, fourteen of eighty-six (16.3%).[34] There are grounds, then, for arguing that the shock of the Black Death—

and the successive visitations of the plague—induced Venetians to concern themselves more regularly than before with the disposition of their property by testation. The fact that the increase in women's wills outstripped that of men's simply reflects women's more numerous encounters with the prospect of death because of pregnancy.[35]

But a more compelling acquaintance with mortality during the plague years only partially explains the increase in women's wills. Equally important is that in the second half of the fourteenth century, and especially during its last quarter, they had more property to dispose of. Here we are brought back to dowry inflation. Once women started bringing larger dowries to their marriages, by that fact they became more economically substantial persons, with a greater capacity to influence the economic fortunes of those around them. Once begun, dowry inflation was a self-accelerating process.[36] When wives who had brought large dowries to their own marriages thought of disposing of their own estates (and, as we have noted, they started thinking of it sooner and more frequently in the later fourteenth century), they naturally thought of their own daughters. We shall see that they also thought of others; but their own knowledge of the importance of large dowries inclined them to look after their daughters. The existence of their dowry money, protected by law from husbandly rapacity and, often, enlarged through fruitful real estate and commercial investment, added a further impulse to well-considered testamentary disposition in favor of daughters.[37]

There was thus a self-reinforcing spur built into dowry inflation, derived from a woman's right to dispose of her own property, her concern for daughters, and the increased dowries that she was bringing to marriage. To illustrate the extent of this important dimension of dowry inflation—of which women were not only the objects but the effective agents, as well—we can compare paternal and maternal dowry bequests in tabular form.

Table 10 reveals three things with clarity. First, mothers began bequeathing money toward their daughters' dowries only after the middle of the fourteenth century; but from then on, the frequency of their contributions grew rapidly, both in absolute terms and relative to fathers' dowry bequests. Second, the size of the maternal bequests was also on the rise, in keeping with the general trend in dowries. Finally, until the middle of the fourteenth century, mothers' dowry bequests had little impact on the total amounts bequeathed for dowries; but starting in the last third of that century, they accounted for an increasing share of parental contribu-

Table 10. Paternal and Maternal Dowry Bequests

	To 1330	1331–70	1371–1410	1411–50
Largest bequest				
p[a]	769[b] (6)[c]	1,000 (5)	2,300 (22)	4,500 (9)
m	—	200 (1)	1,500 (8)	2,000 (12)
Smallest bequest				
p	269	382	1,000	1,000
m	—	200	200	400
Median bequest				
p	509	576	1,350	2,000
m	—	200	891	900
Average bequest				
p	535	606.4	1,340.9	2,244.4
m	—	200	897.8	991.7
Total amounts bequeathed				
p	3,214 (100%)	3,032 (93.8%)	29,500 (84.1%)	20,200 (62.9%)
m	— —	200 (6.2%)	5,582 (15.9%)	11,900 (37.1%)
Total	3,214 (100%)	3,232 (100%)	35,082 (100%)	32,100 (100%)

Source: NT, CI, PSMC.

Notes: [a]p = paternal; m = maternal. [b]All amounts are in ducats. [c]The number of bequests in this category, during this period.

tions—more than one-third in 1411–50. So from all three standpoints, frequency, size, and relative importance, mothers' dowry bequests were enabling their daughters to meet the challenge of dowry inflation—an inflation to which the mothers, as dowry recipients themselves, were contributing.

The importance of this maternal involvement in providing relief for Dante's frightened fathers is obvious. But it has considerable social significance as well. It means that an increasingly larger role in the critical (and to some, central) social fact—marriage—was being played by individuals whose commitment to the brides' paternal lineage was much less intense than that of the brides' fathers. It is a question of lineage orientation. In the patrilineal order of Venice, fathers never left their lineages, and they could attend materially to the interests of a wide range of kinsmen without this attention ever exceeding the realm of lineage interest.[38] Their bequests to members of their natal families and to those of their marital families alike remained within the lineage. As we have seen, men were tied to both by the fraterna, and the hereditary nature of patrician status in Venice only strengthened their commitment to the male line. In this context, a bequest to a daughter or sister was not essentially less beneficial to the interests of the lineage than one to a son or brother. In the latter case, the lineage benefited directly; in the former, it stood to benefit indirectly from the matrimonial alliance thus established.

With mothers the case was different. They were members of two conjugal families, usually from two different lineages, and the result was a freer, less lineage-centered social orientation. The statutes, for example, did not exclude married daughters from succession to intestate women; women's property, lacking the patrimonial quality of men's, could more readily be diffused into the families of sons-in-law.[39] And women's habits themselves attest to a more flexible social attitude. The general pattern of their bequests reveals a nearly equal regard for their natal kinsmen, and thus for two distinct lineages.[40]

It would be valuable to know whether the increased maternal role in dowry accumulation equipped women with a greater voice in the choice of husbands for their daughters, as is the case, for example, in modern rural Greece.[41] Although there is some evidence of general motherly interest in whom their daughters married, the documentation does not reveal the extent to which mothers actually participated in matrimonial decisions. It seems reasonable to conjecture, however, that the concern that mothers demonstrated in the form of dowry bequests and the impact of their increasingly weighty contributions at a time of dowry-raising difficulty were negotiated into greater influence in the arrangement of their daughters' marriages.

More fundamentally, the contributions of mothers to their daughters' dowries may have helped to alter the social posture of the elementary conjugal family. In a widely held view, the Italian family during the twelfth and thirteenth centuries was subsumed under and in important social matters subordinate to the larger kinship group—clan, consortery, and so on.[42] With mothers now counting for more in marriage—the most socially involving family enterprise of all—the importance of the larger kinship group, to which intermarrying women demonstrated a relatively weak allegiance, may have diminished. To see if this was the case, we can now turn to the dowry contributions of kinsmen other than parents.

WHATEVER THE long-range impact on dowry standards of mothers' growing contributions, in the short run fathers must have welcomed them. But fathers had additional cause for happiness in the dowry contributions from a wide variety of other kinsmen, as well. On the whole, women contributed to the dowries of girls other than their own daughters at a higher rate than did men: 41.5 percent of women's dowry bequests were external to the marital family, as against 30.6 percent of the men's. This is consistent with what we observed about wives' enduring attachment to their natal families. But, in fact, all Venetians, regardless of sex or marital status, were stimulated to help their nubile kin. Altogether 44 of the 125 dowry bequests, more than one-third, were to girls other than the testators' daughters. And nowhere is the complexity of Venetian kinship patterns and of the bonds existing among kinsmen better illustrated than in the wide variety of relationships between girls receiving dowry bequests and their benefactors and benefactresses. One group of nonparental dowry bequests was consistent both with the spirit of Roman law and with general patrimonial principles: bequests from paternal grandfathers and uncles. Eighteen of the sample's twenty-two nonparental bequests from men were of this relationship. In the context of the undivided fraternal patrimony, such bequests made good sense. A father's contribution to the dowry of his son's unmarried daughter, a type of bequest encountered seven times in the sample, amounted to a farsighted arrangement for money that would have gone to the son anyway, probably ultimately serving him for his daughter's dowry. But the concern that grandfathers manifested in these bequests suggests that granddaughters' dowry prospects had a more than casual importance to them. For example, Alessandro di Michele Morosini, in his will of 1331, bequeathed his entire estate, less pious and charitable bequests, to his only child, Paolo. According to the instructions in the will, Paolo was not to come into his inheritance until age twenty, except for one eventuality: if he should marry and have a daughter before his twentieth birthday, he was to make a will and in it provide for the girl's dowry in the amount of 653 ducats along with a corredo "worthy of a noble woman"— all from Alessandro's estate. Seventy years later, Gasparino di Bellello Morosini added 800 ducats to the dowry left to his granddaughter, Franceschina, by her late father, and this at a time when Gasparino had three living sons of his own, at least one a minor.[43]

There is a clue to the reasons for such grandfatherly concern in Gasparino's will. He declared that he wanted Franceschina to marry a "Venetian gentleman worthy of her status and acceptable to my sons." Gasparino and, presumably, Alessandro, and other grandfathers like them, were willing to cut into the property of the male line—the jealous preservation of which was a toughly held principle in many wills[44]—and to alienate wealth by sending it into other men's families because such expenses were investments that promoted the interest of the lineage in two ways. First, it ensured that the line would not lose status through unworthy marriages. Second, it provided the direct male heirs with affinal connections that, precisely because they were expensive to come by, promised social and economic benefits to the lineage.

This transgenerational solicitude for the well-being of the lineage, as expressed in dowry bequests to granddaughters, is even more striking in the case of men who had unmarried daughters of their own. An example of such a man is Andreasio di Michele Morosini, brother of the Alessandro whose will we have just considered. In his will of 1348, Andreasio left his own unmarried daughters dowries of 692 and 382 ducats, respectively, at the same time as he willed a dowry of 616 ducats to any of his sons' daughters who should be her father's sole heir.[45] In such cases, the testators appear to slight their own daughters in the interest of their granddaughters. That they did so indicates Venetian patricians' sense of lineage as a superpersonal abstraction that would live on after the testator but the well-being of which was nevertheless in his interest and deserving of his efforts on its behalf. It also shows that they viewed its well-being not only in narrow terms of retaining wealth among males but also in a more sophisticated sense of social and economic alliances of the kind built up through marriage.[46]

The same sense is evident in the dowry bequests of uncles to nieces. There are eleven such legacies in our sample, and eight of them were bequeathed to brothers' daughters.[47] Of the testators, five had children of their own to provide for, including, in three cases, unmarried daughters. Yet the avuncular providence could be impressive: in 1413 Giovanni di Piero Morosini willed 1,200 ducats toward the dowry of his late brother's daughter, while bequeathing his own daughter a dowry of 2,000 ducats.[48] The reasons for such generosity were twofold. The continued existence of the fraterna long after the father's death meant that the dowries of all daughters of a group of brothers came, to some extent at least, from the same common estate. But along with the common dowry burden went common advantages—the second reason. The economic and social benefits that a bride's father might harvest from a good marriage—at the price of a large dowry—were shared by his brothers. These were the considerations underlying Gasparino Morosini's instructions that any husband of his granddaughter Franceschina had to be approved by his surviving sons, the girl's uncles.[49]

The mutual involvement of brothers in the marital destinies of each other's daughters was complemented by their collective involvement in the marital destinies of their sisters. It is not too much to say that the brothers of endowed girls bore the brunt of the entire dowry system, and especially of its inflationary trend. The inheritance theoretically devolving upon them, as continuers of the lineage and of the patrimony, was diminished by each dowry that accompanied a sister to her marriage. It was probably recognition of this potential clash of interests which prompted the legislators to guarantee the inheritance rights of daughters vis-à-vis their brothers. On the other hand, Pertile observed that it was to protect brothers from the effects of dowry inflation that governments such as Venice's attempted to put restraints on dowry amounts.[50] Yet despite the grounds for brother-sister rivalry, brothers helped their sisters' marriage prospects from a sense of family advantage that extended beyond a narrow, and self-serving, emphasis on male inheritance. In the 1374 will in which he bequeathed 1,500 ducats to his newborn daughter, Gasparino Morosini gave 100 ducats to each of his nubile sisters.[51] In 1416, Nicolò di Giovanni Morosini, with no children of his own but with two living brothers and a sister, wrote in his will some instructions that testify to the broad view that men held of the lineage interest. After making some pious bequests, he willed the rest of his estate to his two living brothers, under two conditions. One was that from that inheritance the two brothers were to add enough to the 1,400 ducats that their father had bequeathed for their sister's dowry so that "she may marry in a way that befits the condition of my house and brings honor to it."[52] The other condition was that some of the money was to augment the dowries that their late brother had left to his daughters, Nicolò's and his brothers' nieces.

The case of solicitous brothers, like that of grandfathers and uncles, demonstrates a commitment to the continuing interests of the patrilineage. That much is consistent with the patrilineal traditions of medieval European society.[53] Even if Venetian patricians extended the range of lineage-promoting tactics to include investment in good marriages for social and economic reasons, the orientation was toward the lineage. If an occasional patrician bequeathed something toward the dowry of his wife's sister, as Fantin di Giovanni Morosini did in 1413, that was a remarkable exception.[54] The dominant impulse among men making dowry bequests, whether to daughters, granddaughters, nieces, or sisters, was to bring honor and profit to the male line to which they belonged and which they regarded as their duty to preserve. When hard-pressed fathers were helped in meeting the challenge of dowry inflation by their own fathers, brothers, or sons, this help had its roots in a long tradition of male kinship solidarity.

But among women the pattern was different. In the context of women's increasing prominence in dowry raising, the differences are important for an understanding not only of how this major aspect of the familial experience developed but of changes in the family's place in the larger kinship system and in society. In certain respects, of course, women did resemble men in their dowry bequests. We have already seen the priority they gave to their daughters. But they also resembled men in some of their express motivations in making such bequests. Like men, they regarded social suitability, marrying according to one's station, as a major desideratum for their daughters. Lucia, wife of Roberto Contarini, made a forthright statement of this sentiment in her will of 1413. If at her death her daughters did not have dowries adequate to permit them "to marry well, according to their station," then they were to get more from her estate, "in order to marry better."[55] Superficially, women also resembled men in their dowry bequests to girls other than their own daughters. Against seven bequests to granddaughters by men, there were eight by women; against eleven bequests to nieces by men, there were ten by women.

It is among these nonfilial bequests, however, that differences occur. A closer look at the bequests to grandchildren reveals that both women and men divided their bequests evenly between sons' daughters and daughters' daughters. But the three men who made bequests to their daughters' daughters had no sons,[56] whereas in three of the four cases of male bequests to sons' daughters, the testators also had daughters of their own (in two instances, married daughters) for whose living and prospective female offspring no dowry provision was made in the wills. The eight women's bequests to granddaughters make an interesting contrast. In three cases, the testatress had only one child. But of the remaining five, only one made a bequest to the granddaughter by one child without also remembering the granddaughters by her other children of both sexes. The wills of Giovanni, son of the doge Michele Morosini, and of his widow, Novella, illustrate the difference more clearly. Giovanni bequeathed

2,000 ducats to any of his sons' daughters who might be her father's only child. Novella also made a bequest to daughters, giving 500 ducats toward the dowries of her son Marino's daughters. But at the same time, and unlike her husband, she bequeathed the same amount to the daughter of her daughter.[57]

The implication is clear. In their nonfilial bequests men showed a prejudice in favor of the lineage, which benefited from dowry assistance given to the daughters of its male members. Where male testators helped their daughters' daughters—and thus, indirectly, the lineages of their sons-in-law—they did so only when they had no sons to carry on their own lineages. Women, however, demonstrated no such prejudice. Their contributions to their granddaughters' dowries were not governed by consideration either of lineage or of the sex of the child whose daughter was benefiting.

But does that mean that married women substituted loyalty to their natal families' lineages for that of their husbands'? Certainly they maintained close ties to their natal families. The wills reveal that nearly half of the testamentary executors chosen by married women were primary natal kin (parents and siblings); and this was true both of women with living husbands and of widows.[58] But such continued rapport makes sense in the context we are considering. A family investing a substantial dowry in a socially and economically desirable marital alliance could be expected to keep in touch with its son- and brother-in-law; *a fortiori*, they would maintain contact with his wife. Moreover, the wife herself, as a propertied person with the capacity to make testamentary disposition of and, provided her husband consented, to invest her property, could be expected to maintain economic ties to the family that had been the source of her property.[59]

However, women's social and economic contact with their natal families is not the same as identification with the continued interests of the natal family's lineage. In this connection, a comparison between men's dowry bequests to their nieces, already discussed, and those of women to their nieces discloses a significant difference. We noted that of eleven male bequests to nieces, eight specified the girls' precise relationship to their benefactors, and in each of these eight cases she was the daughter of the benefactor's brother. By contrast, only two of the ten women's dowry bequests to nieces went to daughters of brothers; three are unclear about the relationship, and five went to daughters of the testatresses' sisters. If we regard a bequest of this kind as helping a lineage, the lineage to benefit was neither that of the benefactress nor that of her husband but that of her sister's husband. So although women were relatively more active than men in making dowry bequests to consanguines other than their own daughters, their motives were different from those of men. Where men emphasized their own lineages, women did not share this priority. For them, considerations of the lineage, whether natal or marital, seem to have been relatively unimportant. But family ties, whether male or female, natal or marital, represented an important imperative.

WHAT CONCLUSIONS can we draw from these differences between men's and women's dowry bequests? The most important is that a distinctive female social impulse was coming to have considerable influence in patrician social relations. The aspect of this orientation which set it apart from that of men was a weaker sense of lineage. This did not mean indifference to kinsmen. It did mean, however, that the principle of selection governing women's testamentary beneficence—in the context of our discussion, their dowry beneficence—was different from the commitment to kingroup interest that characterized men. It was, instead, "religion, morality, conscience and sentiment," the sanctions that govern relations not of the kin group but of the family.[60] Of these, in the case of Venetian patrician women, personal regard—sentiment—seems to have been the decisive one.

It can be seen in a special bond that existed among women. This point must not be exaggerated. Women did demonstrate concern and responsibility for their male kin, sometimes even attaching greater importance to them than to the females.[61] But the attachment between women was both different and, in important ways, stronger than the attachment between a woman and her male kin. We can see this by taking another look at the wills, this time focusing on bequests in general. A group of ninety-seven wills of wives and widows contains a total of 415 individual bequests to primary and secondary kin.[62] Of these, 218 (52.5%) went to women and only slightly fewer, 197 (47.5%), to men: on the face of it not a great difference. But if they are divided into bequests to primary and to secondary kin, the results indicate more clearly the special relationship among women. In the 302 bequests to primary kin (parents, siblings, husbands, and children), males and females benefited almost equally, receiving 154 and 148 bequests, respectively. But among the secondary-kin beneficiaries (aunts and uncles, nieces and nephews, cousins, grandparents, grandchildren, and first-degree affinal kin: children-, siblings-, and parents-in-law), females outnumbered males by a considerable margin, receiving 70 bequests compared with 43 to males, or 61.9 percent to 38.1 percent.

The discrepancy between the sex ratio in women's primary-kin bequests and that in their secondary-kin bequests is revealing about the motives behind women's choices of beneficiaries. When they bestowed equal testamentary largesse on the men and women of their primary kin, they were acting under the natural impulses of loyalty and affection that domestic proximity stimulated. Young wives, married at age thirteen or fourteen, naturally held tightly to the reassuring ties to their parents and siblings regardless of sex.[63] Mothers naturally felt affection for both sons and daughters. But though the preferences for females among more distant kin also reflects affection, it is of a more discriminating kind, resulting from association by choice, not by biological chance. Those preferences are in keeping with the indications of women's relative indifference to considerations of lineage. Women left property to their female relatives not to advance the interests of the lineage but because they felt affection for these relatives. There may have been a sense of kinship responsibility at work, for example, toward aged grandmothers; and the apparent tendency of women to outlive their husbands may have provided testatresses with a number of elderly widowed kin toward whom they could discharge that responsibility. But such gestures are still not sufficient to account for the 5-to-3 ratio of females to males among women's secondary-kin beneficiaries. Moreover, even the type of motivation in bequests to aged female relatives is different from lineage allegiance, because it has a personal rather than institutional object.

In light of the growing importance of women's property, organized in wills and, particularly, directed toward dowries, the impulse of personal affection apparent in the pattern of their bequests has a special significance. It means that a richer and more complex set of social forces was at work within the Venetian patriciate in the later fourteenth century and especially the fifteenth than had been the case earlier. The male commitment to the lineage still persisted, as indeed the endurance of the patrimonial system and the hereditary nature of the ruling class dictated that it would. But alongside the lineage orientation of men, and complementary to it, there was appearing—in a position of social influence—the more personal attitude of women. This may have bearing on the old but recently rekindled discussion of a more intense family consciousness among fifteenth-century Italians.[64] The heightened personal affection that, as some writers have argued, constituted the hallmark of the resurgent elementary family may have its origin in the enlarged role of women. Yet, in Venice at least, women's increased influence and distinctive social orientation did not replace attention to lineage; it simply blended with it another set of values.

The dowry inflation that caused Venetian and other Italian fathers such anxiety can be seen as contributing to a reordering and an enrichment of the social relationships within the Venetian patriciate.[65] It strengthened the traditional kinship bonds by inducing kinsmen to aid beleaguered fathers of marriageable daughters. It created stronger interlineage ties by increasing the expectations that families of effortfully endowed girls entertained vis-à-vis the girls' husbands. And by encouraging women themselves to take a substantial part in the accumulation of their daughters' and other kinswomen's dowries, it created a condition in which impulses of personal regard, both within and between families and lineages, assumed a larger place among the principles governing patrician social relations.

The Power of Love:

Wives and Husbands

IN DECEMBER 1445 Valerio Zeno and Vittoria Vitturi, a Venetian patrician husband and wife, summoned a notary to draw up their wills.[1] In his, written 2 December, Valerio designated Vittoria as his sole executor and, acknowledging his obligation to return her dowry of 2,400 ducats to her, instructed that she was to inherit all his other goods, as well, whether she remarried or not. He made a point of underscoring this intention, anticipating "impediments or opposition" to Vittoria's inheritance from his agnatic kinsmen, who would be reluctant to see his property escape them, especially if Vittoria should remarry (as, in the event, she did, twice).[2] Still, that he favored his wife over kin did not signal alienation from his lineage, for he asked to be buried "in our tomb of Ca' Zeno at SS. Giovanni e Paolo." In her will nineteen days later, Vittoria reciprocated by making Valerio her sole executor and universal heir—except for one other bequest, a 400-ducat dowry contribution to a daughter of Valerio's late brother, Basilio Zeno. This generous bequest surprisingly shows Vittoria more beneficent toward her husband's kin than he himself was and indeed more than she was to her own natal family, which then included one brother with a son just entering adulthood.[3] Yet although, like Valerio, she favored her spouse over her kinsmen in tangible bequests, also like him she wanted to be buried "in the tomb where my father, *dominus* Andrea [Vitturi], and my mother are buried."[4]

The wills of Valerio and Vittoria Zeno, fairly typical examples of the genre, expose the rich complexity of social relations among married patricians in late medieval Venice. They show married people's enduring loyalty to family and lineage of origin, expressed here in the symbolically weighty choice of burial sites, but they also show deep trust and gener-

osity between husband and wife. Such strong bonds between spouses had
the potential to subvert other, older loyalties, notably those to the natal
family and lineage.[5] The Zeno wills, and others like them, however, reveal
that married patricians did not always face a sharp either/or choice between natal and marital family. Rather, they inhabited a dense interwoven thicket of social and psychological relationships, through which
they navigated in a variety of ways, limited by the constraints of individual circumstance but also following the urgings of individual desires.
Family and lineage ties were important, as was calculation of personal
interest, but affection also figured in married people's choices in bestowing loyalty and largesse. In the following pages I make an initial foray
into the uncharted realm of affection between spouses, with special concern for its place in patricians' overall social orientation.[6] I pay particular
attention to husbands' regard for their wives, for there are signs that
husbandly affection deepened in the fifteenth century. This development
appears to have been influenced by an increase in the status and power of
women. At the same time, it contributed toward expanding still further
women's influence in the economy, in society, and in the psychological
culture of the patriciate.

On the whole, the literature on marriage among the late medieval and
Renaissance Italian elites has tended to emphasize, properly and profit-
ably, its alliance aspect, viewing marriage as an instrument of family and
lineage strategy, a means of promoting the family's status and advancing
its interests.[7] Although less concerned with the strictly social dimensions
of family history than scholars working on other cities, historians of
Venice also have studied patrician marriage, emphasizing the political
and economic stakes in families' matrimonial strategies.[8] Such family-
centered concerns were manifestly important, but emphasis on alliances
can give the impression that marriage had little to do with the person-
alities or even identities of the spouses, who figure in this picture chiefly
as instruments of family interest, especially the teenage brides (grooms,
in contrast, often took part in marriage negotiation).[9] When we stress
alliances, too, we take a perspective that shows all parties—contracting
families, spouses, even children—operating chiefly, if not solely, from
calculated interest.

Although marriage was an important vehicle of patricians' family and
individual interest, attention to alliances did not necessarily preclude intense relations between spouses. Indeed, it would be surprising if close
bonds did not often develop. As instruments of family strategy, spouses

might be drawn to each other by mutual sympathy. For that matter, family strategy encouraged good relations between the two joined links as a guarantee of the alliance's enduring success. Over the course of years and decades of proximity and intimacy, during which the contours of their families were constantly being reshaped and their shared experiences accumulating in scope and complexity, husbands and wives could develop feelings of companionship, loyalty, and affection for each other. A full picture of marriage must consequently consider husband-wife relations over time. The interfamilial dimension is important, but so are the years after the bride and groom were thrown together, often willy-nilly, by the interests of their families, the long postnuptial period when spouses had the opportunity to forge a relationship of their own.

Special attention should be given the experience of wives over the uxorial cycle, the long evolution that saw them change, in many cases, from terror-stricken child brides into mature wives and mothers and finally into widows who often commanded formidable resources. Because each of these phases has its own dense and busy reality, distinct from those of other phases, no one moment in the wifely experience captures its essence. Nor can a "typical" wife be found. Different women went through the uxorial cycle in different ways. Some had many children; some had few or none. Some kept close ties to their natal families; others forged warm affinal associations. Some built relationships of loyal tenderness with their husbands; others suffered through marriages marked by strain and alienation. Some predeceased their husbands; others lived into long widowhoods and, like Vittoria Vitturi Zeno, contracted second and even third marriages.

Sparse documentation makes it difficult to reconstruct married persons' concerns and sentiments in detail, but one type of source offers abundant insights into the attitudes of patricians at moments of social and economic assessment. The source is wills. Wills, or testaments, allow us to observe women, and men, as well, confronting the last things, taking careful stock of the contents of their lives, and expressing their ultimate preferences and hopes. Because the concerns of Venetian testators emerge with remarkable clarity from the thick undergrowth of formulas that often mark wills, these documents are a rich mine of information about husbands' and wives' opinions of each other. Accordingly, the principal documentation in this chapter is a group of 361 wills drawn up between 1290 and 1520 by patricians with living spouses.[10]

Fourteenth- and fifteenth-century wills reflect changing attitudes during the period. We must be wary of assigning neat dates or precise causes to attitudes and especially of devising too clear-cut a chronology of sentiment. Whether historical conditions trigger new kinds of emotional relationships among people is a hugely delicate and complex question and a controversial one.[11] Nevertheless, evidence is strong that the fifteenth century saw the emergence among Venetian patricians of a higher regard for women and a deepening of husband-wife affection. These tendencies appear tied to certain general developments in patrician marriage during the period.

In his will, Valerio Zeno acknowledged the large dowry of 2,400 ducats which his wife, Vittoria, had brought to their marriage. He declared that half of it had come in the form of real estate that he treated as his own while he was alive but which should be returned to her at his death.[12] Vittoria's family, the Vitturis, had thus considered her marriage to Valerio worth a substantial investment of movable and immovable Vitturi wealth. As Vittoria's will showed, such marriage portions could take permanent flight from the wife's lineage. Had Valerio outlived his wife, her bequest to him would have given him the real estate her family had put into her dowry. The construction of patrician marriages on big and growing dowries is a phenomenon that Venice shared with other Italian cities during this period.[13] One of the strongest reasons for it in Venice was the increased importance of marriage in patrician family strategy and a consequent willingness to invest heavily in it. The emphasis on marriage increased women's influence in patrician society by increasing their wealth. This is a vast, many-sided question, but the main points can be stated briefly.

Contributing strongly to women's enhanced power in patrician society were changes in the nature of the patriciate during the decades around 1400. Briefly, members of the class became at this time more dependent on government support for their economic well-being and more jealous of their status and the prestige and privileges it brought them. The two tendencies led to the erection in the early fifteenth century of a barricade of exclusivist legislation around the ruling class.[14] The officially enforced patrician self-consciousness set a higher premium on the choice of marriage partners, specifically on the prestige and influence of brides' and grooms' families. In the early fifteenth century, Venetian legislators were already raising the status requirements for patrician wives, and the patrician humanist Francesco Barbaro was attaching at least as much importance to a mother's birth as to that of a father in the breeding of worthy patricians.[15] In these circumstances, matchmaking was a serious business indeed.

The currency of matchmaking was dowries, which climbed steadily throughout the period, as families invested ever larger portions of their substance in marriages that brought prestige and cemented valued friendships.[16] So important to family strategy were advantageous marriages that in the fifteenth century girls' dowries sometimes outstripped their brothers' patrimonies—something occasionally noted by will-writing parents, such as the father who excluded his married daughter because she had already received "much more than all her brothers will get."[17] By the sixteenth the impact of the dowry on male-female relations had reached such a point that legislators were blaming Venice's declining commercial enterprise on the tendency of husbands to live off their wives' dowries.[18]

Still, for all the dowry's importance as a tool of family strategy, in the end it belonged to the daughter whom it accompanied to marriage. It was in fact her *patrimonium*, to be returned to her or transferred to her chosen heirs at the end of the marriage.[19] For this reason a testating father would bid his married daughters to "be well content with their dowries and have no reason for complaint" when they were denied further bequests. Yet although some fathers (and mothers) were concerned about the deep bite that dowries were taking out of family wealth, others compounded the effect by leaving additional bequests to their already dowered daughters.[20] These contrasting attitudes alert us to the variety of patrician family situations and the broad range of personal choice open to individuals. They also signal that fathers benefited their daughters in a number of ways over and above dowry provision—benefits that added further to women's disposable wealth. This wealth, rising *pari passu* with dowry levels, gave married women new power in their social relations. For one thing, they were now in a position to help their own daughters meet the rising dowry standards—in the process contributing to their further rise.[21] They could extend their largesse to others as well. The result of the swelling of married women's actual and potential benefactions was to exalt their importance and influence within their social worlds. A wife's or widow's family and kin had compelling practical reason to keep in her good graces by showing her every affectionate consideration.

These circumstances magnified the influence of married women upon those near them, above all, their husbands. The material expression of a wife's regard could now literally change her husband's life—as no doubt

Valerio Zeno's life would have changed if, instead of bequeathing him her 2,400-ducat dowry, his wife, Vittoria, had exercised her legal right to have him restore it to her estate, for the benefit of other kin. Some wives followed Vittoria in selecting their husbands as prime beneficiary.[22] Others made different choices, however, and favored natal kin, so that they returned the dowry to the family from which it had come in the first place.[23] It was the capacity to dispose of their wealth as they liked—on the basis of calculation but also of inclination—as much as the wealth itself, which gave married women their potent new presence in patrician society. A constellation of potential beneficiaries, most prominent among them fathers hoping that their daughters would return at least some of the dowry wealth to their natal families and husbands desirous of lodging it permanently in their own family, was anxious to earn the favor of these increasingly rich benefactresses.[24] The parental bequests to already married daughters, mentioned above, were probably stimulated at least in part by the desire to retain the daughters' continued benevolence and the economic generosity in which it might find expression.

The heightened importance of women affected men in a variety of ways. One was in their attitude toward women's fashions in clothing. This complex subject, on which I can touch only glancingly here, involves important aspects not only of women's economic autonomy but also of individual psychology and the relations between private and collective interests, as well.[25] Female fashion, like male fashion, grew increasingly splendid in the fifteenth century and elicited ambivalent responses. Public concern centered on costly attire that proponents of sumptuary legislation saw as unproductive waste, an attitude fully displayed in the preambles to the sumptuary laws that proliferated in the fifteenth century. They express endless agonizing over women's "excessive expenditures on wicked and impractical [*inutilem*]" apparel that "consumes their husbands and sons" or, again, leads to the "ruin of their husbands and fathers."[26] Many individual men shared this concern, their votes passing the laws, but others took pride in their handsomely decked-out womenfolk, even encouraging their expenditures. In the sixteenth century, we are informed, family and friends saw brides-to-be display their elaborate trousseaux at betrothal parties, and husbands themselves engaged tailors and mercers to clothe their brides in up-to-date splendor.[27]

Yet the wearing of sumptuous clothing may also have been a way for women with wealth but few opportunities for productive economic (let alone political) outlets to make a gesture of self-assertion. In a culture that narrowly limited women's activities in the public sphere, heavy spending on lavish dress could be viewed as doubly assertive, calling visual attention to individual identity and demonstrating the autonomous possession of wealth.[28] That it might be detrimental to men may have been incidental—or for some it may have been a gesture, with available means, protesting institutional or individual male domination. The significance of female fashion in male-dominated societies is a rich subject, with the erotic as well as the sumptuary aspects touching relations between men and women at several different levels. Whether women wore splendid attire to attract or to challenge men (or without regard to men at all), whether men took pride in their wives' appearance or were sexually or economically threatened by its public display, whether expenditures on dress were regarded as wasteful or as investments in status— these questions deserve extended consideration. Although the answers are incomplete, the Venetian legislation makes it clear that women were spending money on fashion, that men were thought to be suffering as a result, and that neither government nor private male society was able to curb their expenditures.

Women's wealth and their autonomy in using it, even in ways that were potentially harmful for men, made women figures of consequence. Their power inspired a complex variety of responses. Here we venture into psychological waters ill charted in the sources and the literature. The first fruits of research, however, strongly suggest that the increase in married women's wealth led the menfolk to take their mates more seriously and to court their favor more assiduously. This development in turn seems to have produced a deeper bond between spouses, with implications for the whole patrician culture and specifically for the articulation of both male and female gender identity.[29]

The new regard that women gained found varied expression. One form was an increased tendency in the fifteenth century for husbands to name their wives as executors (*commissari*) of their wills. The wills of 104 patricians with living wives give a crude overall idea of the trend. Fifty-five were from the fourteenth century; in these, wives were named as executors by 35 of the testating husbands, or 64 percent. Of the 49 husbands who wrote their wills in the fifteenth century, however, 43, or 88 percent, elected their wives—a striking increase. Moreover, a few, such as Valerio Zeno, made the wives their only *commissari*, while others instructed that, in disputes among executors, the wife would hold the deciding vote. None of the Trecento husbands' wills that I have seen gave such authority to wives.[30]

Practically speaking, these appointments made good sense. Well-dowered wives would acquire substantial personal wealth upon becoming widows; as noted, many also had other wealth, from legacies not encumbered with dowry restrictions, to enjoy during their marriage. The practical skills or expert help they used managing their own resources might fruitfully be applied to the benefit of their husbands' estates and especially to that of their common offspring. A family-conscious patrician had every reason to deepen his widow's involvement—and possibly that of her wealth and her brothers—in his sons' grooming for adulthood.[31] To be sure, in entrusting his estate to his wife, a husband effectively removed it from the control of his agnatic kin. The short-term alienation, however, could be counterbalanced by the lineage's potential longer-term benefit from his sons' improved chances for a generous inheritance from their mother and also for the support of her natal familiars, especially the sons' maternal uncles. At any rate, a husband entrusting his estate to his wife's care was likely to be pretty sure of her benevolence toward their children and even (as with Valerio Zeno) toward his other kinsmen. Yet apart from these hardheaded reasons, that husbands placed their wealth in the care of their wives, alone or with others, signifies trust and a sense of shared interest, impulses that marital intimacy could easily blend into strong emotional attachment.

Another sign of men's personal regard for women can be found in fathers' attitudes toward their daughters' vocational preferences. We must tread cautiously here. Family interest weighed heavily on fathers, and marriage was one of the chief weapons in the arsenal of family strategy. An attractive, intelligent daughter and adequate dowry resources added up to a combination of family-enhancing assets a father would only reluctantly avoid using. Alternatively, scant dowry capital might make the convent unavoidable for the daughter.[32] It was a rare father who would or could go against the perceived family interest to satisfy a daughter's choice of adult life. And indeed, most testating fathers left instructions about their daughters' futures with no regard for the girls' thoughts on the matter; the governing principle apparently was that as many daughters should marry as family resources permitted.[33] Yet despite the powerful imperative of family economic and social needs and interests, we do find the occasional father giving weight in his will to his daughters' "intentions" or "desires" when providing for them. Such cases appear more frequently in the fifteenth century than in the fourteenth.[34]

The apparent new fatherly concern for daughters' vocational preferences coincides with a rise during the fifteenth century in the age at which testating parents wanted their daughters married. Indeed, the two tendencies appear to be related manifestations of an increased attention to the timing and substance of female adulthood.[35] Fathers according their daughters greater participation in the choice of their vocations would want the choice delayed until the girls gained greater maturity. Alternatively, a general delaying of the female marriage age, and with it the presumption of adult status, would incline fathers to view their married daughters as more mature persons. These signs of an evolving notion of female adulthood have important implications for changes in Venetian ideas about female, and particularly wifely, gender; they require fuller treatment than is possible here. In the context of the present discussion, it is important to note that fathers' new solicitude for their daughters' preferences may have been encouraged by the example of their wives, who when writing their wills appear even more inclined to offer their daughters the choice between the convent and marriage.[36] Indeed, an emerging maternal tendency to allow daughters complete freedom of vocational choice, including even lay spinsterhood, represented a challenge to traditional male conceptions of family honor, seen as threatened by unmarried daughters' exposure to secular temptation.[37] I have seen no evidence that fathers permitted women to choose a single life, but the willingness of even a few of them to entertain their daughters' preferences in a choice between marriage and the convent suggests that the increased importance that wives derived from their wealth was spilling over into influence on their husbands' cultural attitudes as well as on family strategy.

The more influential presence of women in the patrician family seems to have stimulated not only men's regard and solicitude but their affection, as well. Affection arises from many things, and it would be simplistic to attribute it to the wealth or power of the loved one, even more so to assume that Venetian spouses had not loved each other before the rise in dowries. Nevertheless, men in fifteenth-century Venice were more eloquent than their grandfathers in expressing their affection for the women in their lives. Nowhere is the change more apparent than in the language of wills, in which terms of endearment became steadily more frequent and more elaborate during the fifteenth century. A preliminary sense of the trend emerges from sixty-seven husbands' wills written between 1322 and 1511.[38] Of the thirty-three from before 1400, only eight went beyond simple references to *uxor* or *moier* (or sometimes *muier*), and these eight all used the conventional adjective *dilecta*, as in "uxorem meam dilectam." In the thirty-four written between 1402 and 1511, however, twenty-two of the husbands, almost two-thirds, added an affectionate adjective when they mentioned their wives. The tendency accelerated as the Quattrocento advanced: twenty of the twenty-six wills written after 1425, more than three-quarters, include a term of affection for the wife. Moreover—and more important than the numerical evidence from this tiny sample—although most fifteenth-century husbands still favored *dilecta* when referring to their wives, growing numbers resorted to such tender terms as "mia molier charissima," "mia chara e dileta chonsorte," or "mia dilectissima consorte."[39] (The new application to spouses of the old kinship term *consorte*, literally, "destiny sharer," shows the use of terminology once reserved for kinship to describe matrimonial loyalties— sign of the growing importance of marriage in family strategy.)[40]

The new articulateness in affection did not belong only to husbands and wives but extended to other relations, as well. We find in the Quattrocento, for example, a daughter called "dilectissima et dulcissima," a son "mio fio dilectissimo," a "carissimum" brother, and even—revealingly— "dilectissimos" brothers-in-law.[41] Still, men had applied similar (though less effusive) terms to natal kinsmen in the previous century, too. The big change was their application to wives. The new language of husbandly love is remarkable not just because of its warmth but because of its flexible variety, its individuality. Testators chose the exact terms they wanted, supplying their own nuances; superlatives, for example, seem to have been chosen expressly to convey an exceptionally close bond. Sometimes husbands used different terms in different passages of a single will, showing that each instance was an act of personal choice.[42] The contrast with the narrow vocabulary and perfunctoriness of such usage in fourteenth-century wills could not be sharper.

The change owes much to increased literacy and verbal confidence, evident in the greater incidence of wills written not by notaries but by the testators themselves, in the vernacular—although Latin wills from the late Quattrocento also contain far more terms of affection than Latin wills of a century earlier. Especially noteworthy (and worthy of more systematic investigation), women as well as men drafted their wills by hand more frequently in the fifteenth century than they had earlier. The personal language in these handwritten wills gives even more weight to their expressions of affection as well as showing women's increased control of language as a means of asserting themselves. While this new expressiveness in conveying marital affection suggests development in literacy and linguistic facility, however, it also shows that new feelings were stimulating a new articulateness. The language of affection was so widespread in wills of the later Quattrocento that it appears to have become a convention, raising the question of whether its use is a valid gauge of individual feeling behind the words—although even its adoption as a cultural convention would suggest that affection between spouses was becoming normative. There is also evidence, however, that the affectionate expressions in fifteenth-century wills were not empty formulas.

The wills reveal still more about sentiment in the testators' descriptions of the relationships that they reward or ignore in their bequests. It is telling, for example, to read a man's instruction that his wife and children not come to his funeral "in order not to add pain to their pain" at losing him.[43] However much pain his death actually did cause them, such bereavement seemed to him likely or at least natural and his instruction a touching last thoughtful gesture to his loved ones. Another testating husband declared that he wanted his wife to be aware of "the love I have always borne her."[44] Disarmingly candid was Jacopo Morosini, who in 1448 praised "Cristina, *mia molier charissima*, to whom I am altogether too obliged, for her admirable conduct, and also for all the cash—over and above her dowry—that I have received from her family." In gratitude he made her his universal heir.[45] Such expressions of sentiment, rarely found in fourteenth-century wills, crop up regularly in the fifteenth, displaying a greater male concern with the feelings of wives and children and more openness about sentiment in general.

By leaving his whole estate to his wife, Jacopo Morosini, like Valerio Zeno three years earlier and like other fifteenth-century husbands, backed up his fond words with deeds. By one deed with symbolic weight, husbands associated themselves with their wives in acts of piety and penance—together in the prayers of the priest as they had been in life.[46] Another, weightier still, was making joint burial arrangements. In 1499 Donato Arimondo ordered the construction of a tomb, complete with carved inscription, for himself and his "chara chonsorte," madona Bianca—despite Bianca's own wish, nine years earlier, to be buried with her natal relatives from the Dolfin clan. Here we sense an emotional tug-of-war, Donato doing his best to steal Bianca's ultimate allegiance away from her natal family and attach it to himself.[47] Not all husbands provided for joint burial with their wives; even the uxorious Valerio Zeno preferred entombment in the lineage crypt and made no mention of his wife's posthumous companionship. Those who did, however, reveal a powerful desire to preserve symbolically their closeness to their wives.

The complexity and implications of husbands' affection are even more apparent in their bequests to their wives. Again, variety is the rule. Some husbands bequeathed nothing, some just their wife's dowry—although that was not really a bequest at all, for a widow's legal right to her dowry did not depend on any action by her husband. Indeed, her entitlement to its restitution was so strong that it took precedence over all other claims on her husband's estate. Nevertheless, a husband's acknowledgment of the dowry in his will helped his widow by supplying quick and sure documentation for the *vadimonium*, the legal action by which a widow (or her heirs) established the fact and amount of her dowry, thus taking the indispensable first step toward the *diiudicatum*, or dowry-recovery procedure.[48] Men, however, characteristically went beyond the dowry in providing for their wives, adding a few hundred ducats, a life annuity, very frequently food and lodging, and sometimes, like Valerio Zeno or Jacopo Morosini, their entire estate. To be sure, motives of interest were not absent from these husbandly bequests. Generous bequests to wives, like their selection as testamentary executors, could stimulate wifely reciprocity, to the benefit of the husband's family and lineage. Moreover, husbands normally made bequests to their wives conditional on the latter's willingness to renounce remarriage and stay with the children. Will-writing husbands were considerate of their wives, but they also thought hard about their children's reduced prospects of inheritance from a remarried mother.[49]

Yet tender feelings are unmistakably evident in husbands' bequests. Even childless husbands sometimes offered economic inducements for their widows to forgo remarriage; Donato Arimondo did so, and so did his uncle, Marino. Marino, who was very generous to his wife as long as she remained a widow, instructed his kinsmen to treat her "as if she were my own self."[50] Disturbed at the prospect that their wives might desert their memories for other husbands, these men made it worth the wives' while to preserve in death the lifelong marital bond, in Marino's case forged forty-five years earlier, in Donato's, thirty-seven.[51] Yet others, including Valerio Zeno, benevolently encouraged, or at least accepted, their wives' remarriage, explicitly granting the wives benefits whether they married again or not.[52] All these gestures show husbands committed to caring for their companions of many years. The variety in their approaches, however—acknowledging the dowry or not, making outright bequests or not, encouraging widowly celibacy or cheerfully contemplating their wives' remarriage—shows men acting individually, tailoring their bequests to the distinctive qualities of their particular marital relationships. This male behavior can be seen as one of the transforming cultural effects of women's changed place in patrician society. Men did not abandon lineage loyalty in their affection for their wives; on the contrary, one form taken by husbandly love was the association of their wives with the lineage, its fortunes, and its symbols. Indeed, for success, marriage strategies, on which families staked large chunks of their resources in the hope of benefits from matrimonial alliances, required at least tolerable relations between spouses. Nevertheless, the testimony of fifteenth-century patrician wills reveals a new element in men's social orientation, rooted in a new respect and affection for their wives, which was now taking an influential place alongside lineage loyalties. It was a more personal response to the peculiarities of individual relationships. To the extent that a man with finite resources exhibited this responsiveness in concrete ways, as in a bequest to his wife, he necessarily reduced his tangible expression of lineage loyalty. That consequence, however, was offset by the hope that, by being loving and generous to their wives, men could encourage wifely love and generosity in return, to the benefit of family and lineage.

Yet calculations of interest, personal and lineage, did not alone determine these men's choices. The new husbandly attitude is also evident in changed emotional relations between the sexes. The validation that women's wealth gave to the sentimental ties that connected men to them—validation from the material standpoint of the lineage—enabled men to complement with more personal kinds of loyalty the lineage-based discipline that had traditionally dictated their social behavior. Thanks to the enhanced importance of marriage in patrician society and the increased stature it gave to well-dowered women, husbands could more closely approach the freer, less circumscribed, less lineage-determined orientation of women, in which individual responses to the contingencies of personal relationships, responses such as gratitude, respect, and affection, were allowed wider scope. Men could respond more fully, more reciprocally, to their wives' personal gestures, and in their wills they appear to have been more inclined to do so. Maddaluzza da Canal made her husband her universal heir, in the event of childlessness, as a reward for his "excellent companionship," which she hoped would grow even better.[53] Maddaluzza had her dowry and no particular economic ax to grind; she simply wanted to show her pleasure in her husband's company. The same kindly affection probably led Lucrezia Priuli in 1503 to bequeath her husband, Sebastiano, a dwelling and 1,000 ducats in state securities, along with instructions that, as with Valerio Zeno's strictures regarding his wife Vittoria's legacy, Sebastiano was not to be subjected to "any molestation" in enjoying his legacy from her.[54]

When well-dowered wives voluntarily bestowed their affection in these ways, their husbands were now able and willing to respond in kind. Marco Loredan in 1441, for example, admonished his kin not to be surprised that he was making his wife his sole executor and universal heir, for he was obliged to her more than to "any [other] creature in the world" for her ministrations, costly to her own health, during his protracted illness— ministrations that he likened more to the labors of a slave than to the attentions of a wife.[55] Less touching but still full of tender gratitude is the statement of another Loredan, Francesco, who after allocating his wife's dowry repayment regretted that "I lack the capital to give her what she merits for all her benefits to me."[56] These cases and others like them illustrate how, gradually and always within the limits of family and lineage obligations, men, under the influence of their wives, were now enriching their social culture with a new responsiveness in word and deed to the claims of emotion. The change in women's wealth and influence thus had a larger significance beyond men's more respectful and solicitous, more affectionate and generous behavior toward women. Women, with their economic weight and their traditionally less lineage-encumbered model of social relationships, were also providing a pattern for male culture and a stimulus toward modifying it and making it more flexible. Women's gender identity was changing with the growth in the power and influence of the wifely state, but men's gender identity was being transformed, too, as male society's changing attitudes toward marriage and wives modified husbandhood.[57] In apportioning bequests in response to personal as well as lineage urgings, in choosing interment with a wife rather than a father, in respecting the convent or marriage preferences of a "dulcissima e charissima" daughter, in thoughtfully apportioning bequests to brothers, nephews, sons, daughters, and also the "dilectissima consorte"—in carving out a structure of bequests that reflected the peculiarities of individual social geographies and the diverse loyalties they evoked, men were modifying their social personas under the influence of their formidable, substantial wives and in a manner more congruent with female patterns of social relations.

Three principal results of women's influence are apparent. One was to perpetuate and enlarge women's influence still further, as the men in their families courted them with ever larger bequests, gifts, and dowry settlements. This swelling of female wealth alarmed patrician legislators as a group, but individual patricians continued to find, in the importance of marriage in patrician relations, compelling reason to assemble large dowries for their daughters. Once under way, the transfer of family resources into female hands was carried along by its own momentum. The second result followed. With so much invested in marriages, patrician families sought to gain more from them. In consequence, patterns of social relations were altered throughout the patriciate. Lineage remained the principal framework of social orientation, but the desire to capitalize on the investment in marriage led to greater emphasis on affinal ties and the support and prestige they could offer. In this dense blending of kinship and marital association, the mediating role of propertied women, objects of both natal and marital kinsmen's interest, had large and growing significance.[58]

Third and most important, women's large and growing share of patrician wealth and the influence it brought could find expression in an approach to social relations less restricted by lineage obligations than that of men. It is ironic that the heavily patriarchal structure of Venetian lineage patterns made women freer of enforceable lineage discipline. A man was bound to his lineage by an array of legal constraints and economic inducements. A woman, at least a married woman, shared in two lineages and was thus bound tightly to neither except by moral ties that themselves pulled in two directions. In this freer female social space, personal loyalties and sentiments and tangible expressions of them took their place alongside the defined patterns of lineage loyalty and the more adjustable but no less strategically rooted expectations of marriage alliances. Women were the chief proponents of this more individualized approach to social relations, but their impact, on patrician society generally and especially on their own husbands, stimulated a response in kind.

Husbands were obliged, by self-interest and lineage interest, and specifically by the centrality in family strategy of favorable marriage alliances, to pay more attention to their well-dowered wives and daughters. To do so they had to devote greater efforts to gaining and keeping the women's tangible favor. Women's favor, however, owing to their position outside the strict confines of kinship discipline, responded more to personal loyalties than to family or lineage loyalties and thus had to be earned in personal ways, so that men had a powerful inducement to adapt their male culture to the affective culture of women. This tendency, offered here only as a hypothesis, needs further study, as do a host of related questions such as the coincidence of increased women's wealth and a rising marriage age, the patriciate's remarkable sociability in the sixteenth century, and the frank sensuality of Venetian art and social behavior in that century.[59] Even at this early point, however, there is reason to believe that changes in the relations between the sexes, in the function and nature of marriage, and, fundamentally, in the status and influence of women had a powerful transforming effect on the culture of Renaissance Venice.

"The Most Serious Duty":
Motherhood, Gender,
and Patrician Culture

"Educatio liberorum, pars uxorii muneris fructuosa et longe
gravissima" [the upbringing of children, which is surely a rewarding and
by far the most serious of a wife's duties].[1] When the young Venetian
patrician Francesco Barbaro wrote these words in his erudite treatise on
marriage of 1415–16, he likely did not have in mind the complex implications they would have over the next century for the private and public
culture of the ruling elite to which he belonged. Although convinced of
the importance for family well-being of a wife's breeding and character,
Barbaro fully shared Venice's time-honored subscription to the patriarchal principles of Roman law, encapsulated in the *patria potestas*.[2] For
him, as for most commentators then and later, mothers contributed but
fathers commanded; as Barbaro wrote, "Let the husband give the orders
and let the wife carry them out with a cheerful temper."[3] Indeed, for the
Venetian patriciate the patriarchal ideal covered both private and public
life. Husbandly dominion within the palazzo paralleled the central place
of fathers in the functioning of the patrician regime. A man's membership
in the elite rested on his documented descent from generations of patrician fathers, and the benefits he gained from patrician status depended on
his paternal legacy: not just material assets but also the friendships, es-
teem, and social and political credit acquired by his father through involvement in the activity of his class.[4]

These traits made up the gender triptych of patriarchal, patrilineal, and
patrimonial principles that formally governed family and regime. They
give the strong impression that if any women had a Renaissance, it was not
patrician women in Renaissance Venice. Yet gender and the relations
between the sexes are complex matters with many dimensions and em-

bracing both precept and practice. For a historian the insights offered by attention to gender come not just from ascertaining society's gender principles but also from exploring the relationship between these and the practical activity of men acting as men and women acting as women. It is in this dialectical dynamic between gender norms and gender-interpretable behavior that much of what we think of as cultural change takes place—change of the kind implied in the complex question of a Renaissance for women.[5] Gender as an analytical concept is still in lively evolution, with no fixed consensus about its dimensions yet in place. This encourages exploration of varied configurations, mining its many rich veins in the interest of achieving an enhanced, more nuanced historical discourse.[6]

In this chapter I would like to venture such an exploration, taking as my point of departure a configuration of gender as involving two sets of relationships, one between men and women, and one between individuals of each sex and the cultural norms governing gender. It seems to me helpful to picture these relationships as played out along the sides of a triangle, with reciprocal dynamics going on along each side. Along the horizontal base, men at one corner and women at the other interact under the influence of various cultural norms, chiefly that of patriarchy but also according to the peculiar contingencies of individual circumstance, allowing or forcing greater or lesser conformity with those norms. The contingencies also figure in the other two dynamics. Individual men, grouped in this image at one of the bottom corners, and individual women, grouped at the other, both interact with the prevailing gender norms (or culture, or ideology: any term will do), which sit at the apex of the triangle. The action is reciprocal on all sides, for the subordination of individual women to patriarchal dominance depends on, as well as influences, their relationships with men. With individual men the situation is the same, but in reverse: their conformity with the patriarchal model is expressed in, but in practice also depends on, their relationships with women. And gender ideology itself is subject to change on the basis of large-scale nonconformity with it in individual experience.

Among Venetian patricians, to ease away from such abstract schemes, the relationship between gender principles, gender in practice, and the direction of change may be observed concretely along three axes. One is influence within the family, and we may pose a focusing question about it: How closely did the legal endurance of the *patria potestas* correspond to a reality of paternal dominance in the home? The second axis runs through gender roles in patrician society at large: To what extent did deeply rooted

patrilineal and patrimonial imperatives give rise in practice to male privilege and centrality, female subordination and marginality in the identities, activities, and relationships that made up patrician society? The third
axis arrives at the symbolic forms in which patrician culture expressed
itself at its broadest: Did the patriciate convey its dominant ideals in a
symbolic vocabulary that is recognizably patriarchal? These are big questions, the interrelatedness of which draws attention to the linkage between manifestations of gender in the domestic setting and in the broader
social, political, and cultural arenas, and to the dynamic friction of that
linkage as it affected individual lives and identities.[7] They are too vast to
be fully posed, let alone satisfactorily answered, here.[8] But it is possible to
pick at them in a limited way. This chapter inquires into patriarchy by
looking at patrician mothers and specifically their involvement in the
shaping of their children's adult identities.

Just as gender elucidates its social and cultural context, so context is
essential to understanding gender. Two matters of context must be kept in
view when assessing gender in Venetian patrician culture. One is the
paramount place of marriage.[9] From the late fourteenth century, nobles
deepened their class's exclusivism, enacting a steady stream of laws that
built an iron curtain of pedigree between themselves and the populace,
with the patrician antecedents of a man's mother coming to be regarded as
almost as important as those of his father in making valid his claim to
patrician status.[10] This increased the stakes of matrimonial choice, making
it more desirable than ever to marry within the class but also to marry
well within it, leading patricians to seek the richest, most influential and
socially lustrous spouses possible for their children.[11] The concern with
status was inseparable from practical interest. The material advantages of
membership in the elite were of pressing concern to patricians, and an
elaborate business of patron-client relations, friendship cultivating, favor
exchange, alliance forging, and bloc voting, all directed toward gaining or
apportioning the remunerative government jobs and other privileges on
which patrician families depended, was the main stuff of patrician politics.[12] In this high-stakes social world matrimony was the chief means of
forging the associations through which families ensured their status and
promoted their interests. Matrimony involved marriage portions, good
marriages required big portions, and assembling these entailed the commitment of great chunks of family resources.[13]

The zeal for good marriages is tied to the second component of the
context of patrician gender. Dowries, the currency of matrimony, were the

property of the women whose marriages they brought about. Husbands could invest their wives' dowries, and in fifteenth-century Venice one-third of the total marriage portion normally became the husband's property to keep.[14] But the bulk of these growing marriage portions belonged to the wives themselves, to spend, save, or distribute as they pleased during widowhood, and to bequeath to the heirs of their choice, whether they predeceased their husbands or not.[15] Wifely dowry wealth, growing in lockstep with families' matrimonial ambitions and safeguarded by statute and court, is central to gender in patrician society and culture. It is the key to the way women discharged their "most serious duty," the launching of their children into the complex world of patrician adulthood.

Formally and prescriptively, fathers as *patresfamilias* had the principal responsibility for and authority over family strategy, including the planning of the children's destinies.[16] In the pedigree-conscious climate of the fifteenth century, fathers exercising this authority merged the interests of family with those of lineage, the matrix of membership in patrician society and the operating environment of the patriarchal triptych. The influence and motivations of fathers in the concentric settings of family and lineage are illustrated in the 1401 will of Gasparino Morosini.[17] Widowed three times, Gasparino had, among other kin, three living sons and a married daughter, a widowed daughter-in-law with two sons (Gasparino's grandsons), and an orphaned granddaughter by another deceased son. To each of these persons he had something to give, but he commanded as he gave. Setting up a generous investment fund for his youngest, underage son, Antonio, he declared that his two adult sons (Antonio's half brothers) were not to complain, because they had already been provided for; indeed, of one of them, Nicolò, Gasparino said, "non digo niente" [I say nothing], because Nicolò had been so well set up at his emancipation.[18] Gasparino's strictures had added force because, beyond his own wealth, he had administrative control over the legacies that the elder sons had received from their respective mothers. And he flatly asserted that if they failed to treat the underage Antonio well, they would lose half of their bequest from him, which would then go to Antonio.

Gasparino's authoritative largesse extended beyond his sons to the women in his life. To his widowed daughter-in-law, Maria, he bequeathed several properties, including the house where she was living, and he declared that his estate should bear the expenses of the upbringing of his two grandsons, who were also to share one-quarter of Gasparino's residuary estate (the other three-quarters going to his sons). He even bequeathed 200 ducats toward Maria's dowry, should she decide to remarry. That is remarkable, since a remarriage might produce children who would compete for Maria's beneficence with her present offspring, Gasparino's grandsons. He further declared that if any of his sons should oppose his generosity toward Maria, he was to be disinherited.[19] Finally, to his orphaned granddaughter Franceschina he left the conspicuous sum of 2,000 ducats in state securities, to be used for her marriage, at age thirteen, to a "Venetian patrician worthy of her rank and acceptable to my sons Nicolò, Benedetto, and Antonio, and also to my cousins Bernardo and Barbon Morosini and my cousin-german Zanin Morosini."[20]

He enlisted the involvement of his sisters, as well. One, a nun, he asked to care for Franceschina, keeping her in the convent until the girl was eleven, at which point his other, married sister was to take over, presumably to prepare Franceschina for her marriage. Gasparino also provided for Franceschina's living expenses; but despite his wide-ranging generosity in substance, the tone of the will, in this as in its other arrangements, is one of command. He was head of the extended family, mobilizer of its human resources, committed molder of the lineage's destiny. In short, he was the very model of a patriarch, solicitous of his living kin, mindful of the dead, but especially concerned with the young, both children and grandchildren, whose upbringing and future prospects he attended to in detail, applying moral and material leverage to ensure equity among his heirs, especially his sons by different mothers.[21] And as he made explicit in his instructions for his granddaughter, his authoritative concern extended to the enduring dignity of his lineage, to be secured by "worthy" marriages in which an array of agnatic kinsmen were to interest themselves. Gasparino resembles the patriarch ruling over what F. W. Kent calls in a Florentine context the "grand family."[22] As such he fills a quintessentially conventional male role. Yet virtually every one of his will's provisions (and those of other patrician patriarchs) can be found, though with significant differences, in the wills of wealthy, influential, self-confident patrician mothers.

Gasparino's solicitude over the needs of individual kin is a useful reminder that men did not mechanically follow a blinkered lineage interest. Nevertheless, male patricians were constantly reminded that their very social identity, to say nothing of their enjoyment of the benefits of elite status, was rooted in a title tied to the male line of descent. From the ritual at age eighteen which ascertained and registered their paternal descent to the mobilization of lineage loyalties and associations that gained

them remunerative government posts and other privileges, men of the
patriciate were labeled as their fathers' sons and indeed had every reason
to brandish the label and, like Gasparino, to transfer it, and the lineage
orientation to which it was the key, to their own progeny.[23]

The case of patrician women was different. As Christiane Klapisch-
Zuber, Diane Owen Hughes, and Sharon Strocchia have emphasized,
women's membership in the patrilineage was tenuous and temporary.[24]
All married women belonged to two families, and most to two lineages, in
some respects sequentially, moving from the natal to the marital *casa*, but
in another sense simultaneously, retaining ties to each.[25] The complementary, countervailing, complexly interwoven lineage ties of married
patrician women affected their relations with their variously aligned kin.
Especially toward their children and grandchildren, dowry-possessing
women projected influences that intersected the lineage orientation of
men, alloying it with the values of what the anthropologist Meyer Fortes
termed the "complementary line of filiation."[26] It is the exercise of the
moderating influence of mothers in the discharge of "their most serious
duty" of raising children to adulthood which is of interest for our understanding of patrician gender roles. For the participation of mothers, with
their distinctive social orientation, in ostensibly patriarchal prerogatives
affected the gender identities of their children.

Male identity in patrician culture was essentially public. No sooner
did a young man reach age eighteen than he was presented to public
officials for an induction ritual, the so-called Balla d'Oro, which began his
gradual passage into full adulthood, which was reckoned in terms of
governmental activity.[27] The public nature of men's vocational activity
and the economic dependence of, as officials noted, a "majority" of patrician families on government programs reinforced lineage discipline.[28]
Fathers hurried sons into public life, and young manhood was a period of
apprenticeship under the guidance of fathers and male kinsmen, whose
political direction and economic support emphasized the benefits to be
derived from cultivation of collective virtues: of the family, the lineage,
the patriciate as a whole. Personal relations between fathers and sons in so
highly structured a family culture make a fascinating subject requiring
more study. But they were in any case enfolded within an ideology of
mutually advantageous conformity to the requirements of lineage and
regime. From this structure it was psychologically and materially difficult
for either generation to extricate itself, with the result that the public gave
form and substance to the personal, leading fathers to cultivate in their

sons a conformist ideal of male adulthood, a male gender model in which, paradoxically, patriarchy dictated a narrow range of individual identity for men.[29]

Fathers' relationships with their daughters were inevitably different from those with their sons. The exclusion of women from the public life where fathers and sons consorted, and the convention that ushered daughters out of the natal household to marry in their midteens, make fathers seem remote figures in their daughters' lives. That helps to explain the apparent coldness with which fathers, or grandfathers such as Gasparino Morosini, negotiated marriages that took girls from the family hearth at a tender age and sent them, likely with little choice, into the households and beds of male strangers.[30] It is wise not to universalize paternal stoniness: statements by fathers of warm affection for daughters do appear in the sources.[31] Moreover, fathers were under considerable pressure to forge advantageous family alliances by means of marriage; gathering a competitive dowry and bestowing a young daughter in marriage were two sacrifices that even tender-hearted patriarchs might be obliged to make. Nor were married daughters written off by their fathers or other family members. On the contrary, a father had a powerful practical reason for maintaining close ties to his daughter: the hope that she would return some of her dowry wealth to the natal family that had assembled it. For their part, young wives showed lingering ties to their fathers, for example, by making them executors and legatees of their wills, thereby attesting the endurance of father-daughter bonds beyond the wedding day.[32]

Nevertheless, practical interest blended with cultural principles to make daughters instruments of the family strategies pursued by their fathers. Prevailing values tied men's honor to control over their womenfolk's sexuality; in practice, that limited women's approved gender roles to wifehood or enclosure in a convent.[33] Even that restricted vocational choice generally seems to have been made by the father, not the daughter. The large dowries that families were obliged to commit to favorable marriages, and the tender age at which women's vocations were decided, meant that factors other than a girl's preference dominated in her father's assessment of prospective sons-in-law; at the same time, many families simply lacked the wealth to arrange marriages for all their daughters, requiring fathers to force some into convents amid, as the preamble to one legislative act put it, "tears and wailing."[34] The evidence in fathers' wills shows that Gasparino Morosini was following custom in decreeing that the "gentleman" to whom his granddaughter Franceschina was to be married at age thirteen should be chosen by her male kinsmen.[35]

Mothers writing their wills applied the influence of their wealth in ways that both contrasted with and complemented the intentions of fathers, but with the ultimate effect of broadening the range of gender identity for both sons and daughters. Owing to their distinctive placement overlapping two lineages and families, women had greater flexibility in their family and kinship orientation than did men; indeed, such variety is a hallmark of women's wills. Women wrote more wills than men—in a sampling of 614 patrician wills more than twice as many, 431 to 183.[36] This seems chiefly a result of adjustment to the sharp social and thus affective changes in a woman's life as she proceeded through the uxorial cycle from young bridehood to mature wife- and motherhood to widowhood. But it also reflects a woman's broader range of choice among potential recipients of her beneficence, a consequence of her more complex network of family ties, and it contrasts with the determinism apparent in men's wills, whose provisions followed a narrower path of family and lineage responsibility.[37] Whereas men's wills usually added a few special touches to the statutory conventions, sticking mainly to the male line, those of women included both greater variety among beneficiaries and less conventional—that is, less masculinely lineage-bound—patterns of bequests to children and others. These different approaches to testation, revealing concrete differences in gender characteristics and showing women's confidence in institutional responsiveness to their intentions, enlarged the impact of women's dowry wealth beyond the economic to the social and cultural.[38]

To their sons, women offered a more ample social context for lineage affiliation. Husbands themselves frequently recognized the capacity of their wives to contribute to the lineage, enlisting them as collaborators in family strategy, naming them as executors of their estates, and committing to them, with inducements, the upbringing of the children, including control over their children's patrimonies—a mirror image of Gasparino Morosini's administration of the estates of his wives.[39] For their part, mothers appreciated the inseparability of their sons' well-being from the matrix of the lineage. When, as often happened, widows sponsored their eighteen-year-old sons' patrician credentialing, they joined with their husbands' paternal kinsmen in seeing the young men through the ritual.[40] Women recognized the symbolic as well as the practical importance of lineage, for example, with regard to real estate. In 1401 the widow

Beruzza Soranzo urged her son Girolamo to add 1,000 ducats to the dowry of his sister Caterina, in return for which Beruzza would prevail on the girl to consign to Girolamo the share of the family palace that their father had left her. That is a wonderfully neat and revealing arrangement. It fattened the dowry that would enhance Caterina's social placement and, ultimately, her personal wealth, while at the same time giving Girolamo sole possession of the palace that identified him with his father's line. It also displays the contrast between fixed, locked-in male property, literally "immovable," and the more liquid, flexible, "movable" wealth that gave women's social relations greater agility.[41]

Mothers also supplemented their sons' lineage affiliation by strengthening the sons' ties to the mothers' kinsmen. Maternal uncles frequently joined with their widowed sisters in ushering nephews into official patrician adulthood. This practice served both parties. For young men it enlarged the web of friends and patrons whose support was necessary for success in the adult patrician world. To the uncles it offered a friendly vote in the council chamber as well as the prospect of economic cooperation, and through that some tangible benefit from the investment they had committed to their sister's dowry.[42] Young men who entered adulthood in these circumstances had a broader range of social options with which to fashion their identities, enlarging the basic lineage orientation, with the guidance of mothers serving as a key to flexible social placement and the vocational advantages that it promised.[43] Encouraging that filial attitude was mothers' wealth and the capacity it gave them to smooth their sons' way, for example, by providing business capital and—interesting irony here—by pledging their own wealth for the safe restitution of the dowries of their daughters-in-law.[44]

Such mother-son associations softened the edges of patriarchy by giving mothers a role in guiding their sons into successful adulthood. This urges nuance in categorizing parental roles by gender, showing as it does that mothers could be directive, not merely supportive, in discharging their upbringing duties—even vis-à-vis their patriarchally privileged male offspring. For patrician social organization, it shows mothers enriching the basic kinship structure, interlacing formal patriliny with practical bilaterality. But dowry wealth had another effect on male gender identity, one with deep cultural and psychological as well as social significance: it narrowed men's chances to fulfill the patriarchal ideal of becoming husbands and fathers. The heavy commitment of family wealth to daughters' dowries effectively deprived many of their brothers of the chance to marry: men from less influential or prestigious families, or members of fraternal groups that lacked the resources to guarantee the dowries of wives for all the brothers, or simply men into whose sisters' dowries had gone the wherewithal for taking on the responsibilities of patrician husbandhood. In the fifteenth century fewer than three in five adult patrician men married.[45] Other reasons contributed, but the premium that high dowries placed on worthy husbands was an important one. In an indirect way, then, wealthy mothers fostered a schism in male gender identity, separating those who would assume the mantle of patriarchy from those who neither ruled families nor propagated their lineage (at least legitimately) nor presided over the integration of sons into patrician government and society. But mothers also had a more direct effect on the options of their sons by way of their concern for their daughters.

As I have noted, fathers by preference or necessity generally treated daughters as prime instruments of family strategy. But, as if in compensation, mothers gave them concern, wealth, and latitude of vocation. A couple of examples convey the texture of this maternal influence. In 1415 Barbarella Contarini declared that her imminent marriage had been made possible by "her most benign and generous mother," who had provided the entire dowry: a good thing, she went on, "because of the meagerness [*carentium*] of my inheritance from my father."[46] In thus providing for her daughter's vocational destiny, Barbarella's mother was discharging an essential patriarchal responsibility. By supplying the material means that spelled the difference between Barbarella's being able to marry or not, she was also influencing—or, instead and significantly, giving Barbarella herself the chance to shape—the young woman's gender identity.

A second case further displays this maternal power, here generationally doubled. In 1464 Petronella Falier, wife of Zilio Morosini, ordered in her will that as soon as her daughter Paolina turned fourteen, she was to be immediately married to a patrician ("subito in un zentilom"), to be chosen by her husband and her executors, the Procuratori di San Marco. Paolina's dowry was to consist of a one-third share of Petronella's estate (the other two-thirds to be divided between her son and her unborn child) and 1,000 ducats that Paolina's maternal grandmother had bequeathed the girl. Yet, worried that Zilio might prove dilatory or even resistant, Petronella gave primary authority for the marriage arrangements to the Procuratori, who were to carry out her intentions for Paolina whether Zilio liked it or not.[47] Remarkably, Petronella was asserting that a mother with enough wealth could prevail over her husband in deciding their daughter's marital future. It is impossible to know who would have won in litigation, but in the event, Paolina did get married two years later, at age fifteen or less, to a member of Petronella's natal lineage.[48]

Petronella Falier's influence came from female wealth, specifically her own and her mother's large contributions to her daughter's dowry, which it would have pained her husband to do without. But the dowry wealth of other mothers enabled them to influence their daughters' destinies in even more elaborate ways, by letting them choose their vocations. The 1479 will of Maria Bembo, wife of Girolamo Zane, illustrates this point. Toward the marriage portion of each of her three daughters Maria allocated 600 ducats.[49] But she also allocated bequests to them if they should decide not to marry but instead elect the religious life ("nolent maritare, sed monacare"). That was not the end of it, however, for she offered them an even broader range of choice. If the girls chose neither marriage nor the convent ("nolent maritare nec monacare") but instead wished to remain spinsters, living with their father and brothers, then Maria's estate was to provide their expenses for food and clothing for as long as they lived. Moreover, if for some reason they could not live with their brothers, then each was to get an additional 40 ducats yearly for housing expenses, and each who lived to age twenty-four under these circumstances would be able to dispose freely of an additional 100 in her will.

Maria Bembo effectively underwrote for her daughters three different vocational choices, involving three different social situations and gender identities. Nor was she unique. Increasingly in the fifteenth century, mothers were offering daughters vocational choice and the economic means to exercise it.[50] Fathers were restrained from opposing these maternal intentions because to make the good marriage alliances that served family interest, they needed the mothers' contributions to their daughters' marriage portions, many of which were paid out to husbands while the mothers, like Petronella Falier, were still alive. Indeed, in a remarkable development, which I believe shows the influence of wives on their husbands' attitudes toward their families, by the late fifteenth century fathers, too, were beginning to follow their wives' lead and themselves offer their daughters the choice between marriage and the convent, although, not surprisingly, they do not appear to have followed them into an acceptance of lay spinsterhood.[51]

Addressing the issue of female identity in early modern France, Natalie Zemon Davis suggests that giving oneself away in marriage, consciously accepting the imposed vocation, was a means by which women could attain a certain psychological autonomy, could carve out a personal identity, in a patriarchal society.[52] In the case of Venice, the wealth of mothers was permitting some women to go even further, to elect the adult vocational and sexual identity of their choice. To be sure, even young women who could choose marriage rather than be thrust into it still had their husbands selected for them, with family interest, not psychological compatibility, the paramount consideration. Yet the growing attention to female choice in the matter of marriage, by mothers above all but also by some fathers, is reflected in a gradual rise in the preferred marriage age for women. The evidence is sparse, but by the later Quattrocento the age at which parents wanted their daughters to marry had risen from the early teens—the fourteenth-century fashion—to the middle or late teens.[53] This delay may have been encouraged by fathers, for whom a married daughter's greater maturity made likelier a capacity to resist the influence of husband and father-in-law, thus enabling her to demonstrate tangible loyalty to the natal family. But mothers, as well, were influential in pushing back their daughters' marriage age.[54] The later a girl married, the more maturely considered her choice of vocation. And we may speculate that mothers may also have eagerly used their influence to spare their daughters the psychological distress, even terror, of coercive youthful marriage to a stranger.

A trend toward later marriage for women, toward a more considered measure of female adulthood and its implications, is one notable effect of the influence that propertied women were having on the upbringing and the adult identities of their children. Later marriages, larger dowries, and the choice of vocations altered the gender balance in patrician society, giving each successive generation of wives greater means of influencing the culture of the ruling class. But the modification of male gender models through the direct and indirect action of mothers was equally significant for patrician culture. Alongside the patriarchal figure shaping the interests of family and lineage, his authority in the household mirroring his patrician entitlement to participate in Venice's government, the irreversible commitment to ever larger dowries was now producing in increasing numbers alternative male types, notably the patrician bachelor, equally active in political affairs but lacking the titular family authority of his married brothers. As Guido Ruggiero has suggested, these bachelors may also have produced alternative sexual cultures, or subcultures, both heterosexual and homosexual.[55]

Indeed, for all male patricians the broad-ranging social orientation of influential mothers complemented and even displaced the narrow lineage configuration with strong loyalties to and involvements with a broad range of kin, maternal as well as paternal. Young men whose mothers forged close ties between them and their maternal uncles grew into full adulthood with an ampler kinship orientation, embracing a range of close, trusted associations beyond the boundaries of lineage. I have argued that this elaborate network of loyalties combined with shared exclusivism to promote the solidarity for which Venice's patrician regime was noted; I believe that this adds up to an important female impact on patrician politics, the public sphere putatively monopolized by men.[56]

In a sociopolitical elite such as Venice's patriciate the private and public spheres can be only artificially separated. It is therefore no surprise that the influence on patrician society at large of propertied women with clear intentions found parallel expression within the private sphere of the conjugal family, as well, in ways that caution against easy assumptions about patriarchal authority in practice. An act of the Venetian senate in 1535 noted that many men were no longer engaging in productive economic activity but were instead living off their wives' dowries.[57] Such men were adapting to the fact that patrician liquid wealth was gravitating into female hands, a consequence of steadily increasing dowries, the commitment by families of large portions of their wealth to their daughters' marriage prospects, and the provision by wealthy mothers for their daughters' adulthood. Without knowing more about individual marriages dominated by wifely wealth, one cannot conclude either that such husbands exploited their wives or, alternatively, that wives called the connubial tune. In either case, however, the inescapable fact is that these husbands were apatriarchally making a vocation of marriage.

Yet the nonconformity of individual men, whether bachelors or husbands, to a generalized mold of the authoritative, directive patriarch does not mitigate the wholesale formal dominion of patriarchal institutions in Venice. However dependent on or even subject to this or that woman an individual male patrician might have been in practical matters, his sex gave him a share of the formal stature and prescriptive dominance that belonged exclusively to men as men. Michelle Rosaldo noted some time ago that female *power* does not undermine male *authority*; no matter what leverage patrician mothers might have been able to exert on their families, the institutional and discursive framework of Venetian society accorded authority only to men—authority that no amount of female influence, wealth, and power could ever dislodge.[58] The asymmetry between firmly lodged principle and fluid, contingent practice reminds us how complex gender was in Venice, and remains in historical discourse about Venice and elsewhere. Indeed, it is the conceptual plasticity of gender, its potential to provide a coherent pattern connecting deeply ingrained patriarchal conventions with the Brownian movement of quotidian social relations guided by but also deviating from these conventions, which makes gender so valuable for a nuanced historical discourse embracing public and private life.

The anecdotal evidence presented here shows Venetian patrician society as lacking absolute patterns of either patriarchal power or female subversion of it; of either exclusively patrilineal or effectively bilateral kinship orientation; of either paternal or maternal inheritance as the critical element in a child's future. Indicating above all that both sides of each pair constitute essential elements of the picture, the lack of compelling evidence either of sweeping patriarchy or of its absence reveals that patterns of gender identity in the Venetian patriciate were flexible, offering at least a range of choice, for women and for men. Although the possibilities of alternative gender identities were contained within the formal boundaries of patriarchy, their expression in the practical world of patrician adulthood owed much to—and therefore reveals the cultural importance of—propertied, socially influential, self-confident patrician mothers performing their most serious duty.

PART THREE

Varieties of Masculinity

Measuring Adulthood:
Adolescence and Gender

IN 1474, Agnesina da Mula Loredan, a Venetian noblewoman
pregnant with her fourth child, took pen in hand to write her will. As her
residuary heirs she named her three children and "the creature I am making," but she ordered that none of them were to get their bequests "until
they become their own masters, that is, my sons at twenty and my daughters at sixteen; at that point they may dispose of their shares as they see
fit."[1] Those instructions call attention to two fault lines running through
the culture of Venice's patriciate during the Renaissance, one separating adolescence from full-scale adulthood, the other distinguishing men
from women. But they are overlapping fault lines with twists and turns,
mapped by individual circumstances and personal choices, some of which
are illustrated in the will of another patrician mother, written thirteen
years before Agnesina Loredan's. Bianca Morosini Giustinian also instructed that her residuary bequests to her children be withheld until the
sons were twenty, the daughters sixteen, but she added a specifying condition: "The daughters, *veramente*, should each receive their shares upon
turning sixteen, *if married;* if they are not married I want them to have
nothing until they reach age twenty" (emphasis added).[2] For this mother
and, I wish to suggest, for patrician society in general, it was marriage
that made a woman economically capable at sixteen rather than twenty.
Among Venetian nobles marriage meant adulthood—but only for women
and, as Bianca Giustinian contemplated, only for some women. Moreover, even for them the marriage-adulthood equation was true only in a
partial sense. It is these "onlys" that signal the interest of patrician adulthoods and adolescences in early Renaissance Venice.

This chapter considers these distinctions and through them the criss-

185

crossing paths along which nobles negotiated their varied ways into adulthood. Exploring this complexly veined terrain permits us to see how ideas of women's and men's adulthood were interwoven and how gendered notions of adulthood affected adolescence.[3] It also helps bring into view the connection between enduring patterns of behavior and forces pushing toward cultural change. Finally, it provides a good vantage point for scrutinizing the newly raised issue of individual identity, or at least particularity, as manifested in personal (and familial) nonconformity with cultural norms, through choice or circumstance.[4]

Observing the end of adolescence permits us to trace evolving parameters of culture as these appear in changing ideas of male and female adulthood in the culture of Venice's ruling class. The entry into adulthood is the volatile crossroads where a society's expectations of mature adults meet its deepest convictions about relations between the sexes and where both of these abut against the vagaries of individual experience. Consequently, in the same measure that adulthood implicates gender, so changing ideas about adulthood go hand in hand with changes in gender relations. In the concrete historical setting, both contingencies vibrate with the tense forces working on society and with society's uncertain capacity to enforce its rules on its individual members.[5] Moreover, nobles' concern with status constituted a third element in the definition of adulthood. As the determinants of patrician status evolved over the fourteenth and fifteenth centuries, so too did the requirements that individual nobles satisfied in order to enter adulthood. Taking note of all these chronological, cultural, and individual variables, we shall investigate the distinctive institutions of female and male adulthood, observing the varieties in patricians' concrete experience of adolescence, adulthood, gender relations, and the possibilities of individual adult identity.

A FUNDAMENTAL FACT about adulthood in Venice is that although legal majority was reckoned the same for men and women, in practice, as the wills mentioned above show, the age and substance of adulthood were located differently for the two sexes. The statutes of 1262 put majority at twelve for all children "whether male or female [*sive masculos sive foeminas*]," but as early as 1299 the Great Council specified that "a woman of thirteen or younger is not to be reckoned a woman unless married," indicating that married women even younger than twelve could be deemed adults. In contrast, the act went on to state, "any man twenty or younger is not to be held a man."[6] Girls became women much earlier than boys became men, not necessarily because of more rapid maturation but because of two essential cultural facts: the centrality of marriage in female adulthood, and women's earlier marriage age. Together, they evoke Arnold van Gennep's distinction between physiological and social puberty.[7] By and large, patrician culture keyed female adulthood to reproduction, male adulthood to other "social" functions. As a consequence men had a longer period of adolescence than women—if, indeed, child brides of thirteen can be said to have had an adolescence at all. In practice, however, these tidy principles gave way to a wide range of experience on both sides of the gender divide.

Commentators of the time counseled marriage in late adolescence for girls. Paolino di Venezia, a Franciscan writing in the early fourteenth century, warned that girls who married too young gave birth to wicked children; they should marry no sooner than age eighteen. A century later, the young patrician humanist Francesco Barbaro made the same recommendation, adding the authority of Lycurgus's prescriptions for Sparta. But Barbaro was also mindful of arguments for youth in brides, who, he argued, should be made from fresh, not hardened, wax, the better to receive their husbands' stamp.[8] On the evidence, patrician parents were more impressed by the fresh-wax argument than the wicked-children one. In a group of 614 wills drawn up by nobles between the late thirteenth and the early sixteenth century, most parents indicated that they wanted their daughters married when they reached "legitimate" or "suitable" age. But thirty-four specified what those terms meant. Their preferences ranged from eleven or twelve (one father's instruction) all the way to twenty. Seventeen of the parents clustered their choices in the years from fourteen to sixteen, making a sort of critical mass, but the range was broad enough, spanning the entire teenage decade, to resist statistical simplification. With marriage the mark of female adulthood, this range warrants a closer look.[9]

For many parents, the operative principle regarding daughters' marriage ages was haste. Giovanni Morosini urged in 1414 that his daughter be married "as soon as possible," words echoed by Marino Pisani in 1476 and by many others. Piero Morosini, more precise, instructed in 1335 that his executors arrange for his daughter to marry between thirteen and fifteen, "not permitting her to exceed [*transire*] age fifteen" without wedding. In 1464, Petronella Falier Morosini's worry that her husband might delay their daughter's marriage beyond age fourteen led her to order that if he did so he should be removed from the administration of her estate, leaving her other executors to see to the daughter's marriage, for which Petronella was bequeathing a handsome marriage portion. Orsa Soranzo da Canal, testating in 1440, was willing to let her daughters wait until their seventeenth birthday, but if at that point they had not yet married, they would forfeit their bequests from her.[10]

In seeing their daughters married in their midteens, Venetian patrician parents resembled their counterparts elsewhere, notably in Florence, whose historians have in recent years suggested a variety of parental reasons for hurrying girls into wedlock. David Herlihy and Christiane Klapisch-Zuber emphasize the substantial age gap between spouses, which produced an excess of prospective brides over grooms, prompting parents to arrange their daughters' marriages as quickly as possible, a practice that only exacerbated the problem. Klapisch-Zuber elsewhere stresses the functional use made of daughters in their families' social strategies, sending them into marriage at an early age in the interests of their natal households. An emphasis on the instrumentalization of women by their families also characterizes the interpretation, extended to Mediterranean Europe generally, of Diane Owen Hughes. Julius Kirshner and Anthony Molho explain early female marriage by noting men's concern with the danger that unmarried women posed to androcentric family honor.[11]

All these interpretations have as a common denominator the hurrying of immature, heretofore sheltered, and therefore, we must assume, psychologically vulnerable girls into marriage for male purposes, whether of individual men or of the patriarchal family or patrilineal kin group. Indeed, the motives were complementary and could all come into play simultaneously, among different families and even within the same family, in Venice as well as Florence. So could the eagerness of the families of nubile girls to establish links to substantial, prestigious, and influential sons-in-law. Whichever motive dominated, however, the effect was the same: to deny daughters a full prenuptial adolescence—or in some cases any adolescence at all—instead rushing them, mature only physiologically and even that barely, into what the Great Council in 1299 reckoned as the key to female adulthood: wifehood. It would be revealing to know how these early to mid-teenage brides were prepared for the social and sexual encounters that awaited them upon their transfers, once married, to the houses of their husbands or, more likely, of their fathers-in-law. We get a hint from the 1401 will of a solicitous noble named Gasparino Morosini. Providing his orphaned granddaughter with a dowry for her marriage at age thirteen, apparently some years in the future, he instructed that she was to dwell in a convent with Gasparino's sister, a nun, until she turned eleven. Thereupon she was to begin residing with his older, married sister, who presumably would instruct her in wifely duties during the two years until her marriage.[12]

The young girl may have benefited from her great-aunt's prenuptial counsel, but the fact remains that she was destined to be given over to a husband at a tender age, likely becoming pregnant soon afterward. Evidence shows that despite Fra Paolino's warnings, patrician child brides conceived soon after their weddings.[13] The image of the patrician bride is thus the poignant one of a girl in her early to middle teens thrust by her family of origin into the household of male strangers, one of whom, considerably older than she, would sexually initiate her, whereupon she would begin childbearing. For such women, prenuptial adolescence came early and passed so quickly as to be nonexistent, seemingly giving way to a precipitate adulthood limited to domestic or even merely biological functioning.

Yet, accurate as far as it goes, this image is not a universal or complete one. For Venetian patrician women did not fit into a single model, either by age or by vocation—or, we may add, by family context. Their varied experiences reflect alternative female adulthoods and therefore adolescences. Alongside parents hurrying their daughters into wedlock there were others counseling delay. Silvestro Morosini in 1432 bequeathed a generous 2,500 ducats for the marriage portion of each of his daughters. But he instructed that they were not to marry before age fifteen, and he added 200 ducats to the dowry for each year they waited after fifteen before marrying. Vida Valaresso Loredan wanted 300 ducats invested in state bonds for the marriage of her daughter, then no more than six years old. These investments were to accrue interest until the girl was twenty, at which point she could marry.[14] Such parents may have sought to maximize dowries by giving them time to grow, reckoning the benefits of that to be greater than those from early marriage. But they may also have had in mind the psychological advantages that a girl could derive from marrying at a later age, prolonging adolescence and gaining maturity. Whatever their motives, they show a variety of ways of marrying daughters, cautioning against too neat generalization about brides' ages or parental attitudes toward daughters.

Although wills show that both mothers and fathers encouraged sometimes early, sometimes late marriage for their daughters, two trends are discernible which invite gender-sensitive attention to parents as well as to their children: a rising marriage age and increasing vocational choice for women. Regarding marriage ages, our small sample gives only a tentative indication that must be controlled by broader sampling. But the evidence at least suggests a change between the mid-fourteenth and the later fifteenth century in parents' preferences, from the early to the late teenage years.[15] In attempting to explain this very gradual change, one must add to the economic and psychological motives just mentioned the effects of increasing governmental regulation of marriage, especially dowries, and, intricately bound up with that, more intense concern by nobles in the fifteenth century with the social implications of marriage alignments. But it is important also to note the increased importance of the dowry-based wealth of mothers in the economic fortunes of their children. Mothers, themselves former child brides and very often still in their teens, appear to have used their wealth and the influence it gave them to delay their daughters' marriages. The growing influence of mothers on family culture may also have encouraged greater concern with daughters' psychological well-being on the part of their husbands.[16] In view of the sparseness of the data and Venetians' taciturnity about motives, one can only speculate about reasons. Moreover, different motives and combinations of motives operated on different parents. Nonetheless, while it would be quixotic and reductive to ascribe precise reasons for so gradual an evolution, hints of changes in affective family culture help explain the trend toward delaying daughters' marriages.

The second tendency, giving daughters a choice of vocation, is related. For patrician girls traditionally there were only two acceptable vocations, marriage and religious profession. The third alternative, the unmarried lay state, apparently struck fear into individual men and institutional male society because of the threat that female sexuality unregulated by conventual or marital authority was seen to pose to male honor.[17] In general, to judge from parents' intentions in wills, it was they who decided their daughters' fate, usually giving preference to marriage, if family wealth was sufficient for marriage portions. When it was not, the convent loomed as a dumping ground, in Venice as elsewhere.[18] The problem was that over time even the religious alternative became problematic. As more and more parents used it as an expedient, convent dowries rose, posing still more excruciating difficulties for desperate parents. Historians of Venice and other cities are unanimous in emphasizing that family wealth and social aims had a determining effect on women's careers, just as they did on men's.[19] But the restricted vocational possibilities available for women and the well-defined price levels set by the marriage and convent markets give force to the idea that a young woman's destiny, unlike that of a young man, rested almost wholly with forces beyond her control. Moreover, these considerations strengthened the rationale for deciding young women's vocations at an early age, and certainly before they had matured to the point of muddying family strategy with clear ideas of their own. Physiological puberty would be quite enough, and less troublesome than social puberty.

Therefore, the emergence of a parental tendency to let young women choose among their limited vocations marks a significant cultural development. Even in the fourteenth century an occasional father might be found offering his daughter the option of marriage or the convent. Marino Morosini provided in his will of 1380 that his daughter Agnesina could choose at the tender age of thirteen.[20] But he was exceptional. Most parents of the time, fathers and mothers alike, decided their daughters' fates for them, usually providing dowries until the money ran out, then consigning any remaining daughters to monasteries.[21] There seems to have been little thought of the girls' preference (let alone of their aptitude) for one state or the other. David Herlihy suggests that in a plague-filled period powerful demographic instincts may have swept aside other considerations before the need to repopulate, thus urging early marriage for women.[22] But whatever the specific reasons influencing individual parents, the effect was to ignore the sensibilities of the girls thus married and to deny them the expression of their own desires, fears, and expectations in the determination of their vocational and sexual identity.

By the later fifteenth century, however, the situation was changing. A growing number of parents and others appear offering young girls the choice between marriage and the religious life. Francesco Navagero in 1484 provided enough for his daughter's dowry to allow her to marry "in keeping with my status [*segondo la condizion mie*]," indicating that like many other parents he viewed her marriage as implicating his family's well-being and prestige. Yet that did not stop him from also instructing that if instead she chose to become a nun, "of her own free will [*de volonta soa*]," she was to be settled in an observant convent. Other fathers of the period gave their daughters the same "libertade," as one put it.[23] Mothers and other female relatives appear even more frequently offering young girls vocational choice. Married young themselves by male kin likely to be concerned more with patrilineal family interest than the women's wishes, wives with property and influence might well want to use it to spare their daughters and kinswomen the heedless instrumentalization that had been their lot. Such a motive would explain the unprecedented fifteenth-century phenomenon of women offering their young female relations the choice not just between marriage and the religious life but even between those two and the unmarried lay state. In 1435 Fantina Contarini Morosini instructed her executors to provide whatever was needed for the marriage portion of her daughter, Lucia. But if the girl "should not want a husband [*sela no volese mario*]," they were to provide her with adequate living expenses ("che la posa ben viver"). Only after that provision did Fantina allocate 100 ducats for the possibility that Lucia might choose the convent ("volese andar munega"). Here was a mother consciously making specific provision for three possible vocations for her daughter, with the choice explicitly left to the girl.[24]

By the later decades of the century women were even more articulate. Franceschina Loredan Capello in 1473 bequeathed 400 ducats to each of her daughters, but "this condition should be understood to regard my daughters who shall marry. Those on the other hand who become nuns or live chastely at home [*starent honeste in domo*] are to have 300 ducats." Isabetta Gritti da Lezze made similar provision for her daughters who might decline marriage or the convent and "wish to live chastely in the world [*vellet honeste vivere in seculo*]," as, in 1450, did Isabetta Morosini for her granddaughter, "who might wish to remain in the world without either marrying or entering a convent [*vuol star in nel mondo sença maridarse o munegarse*]."[25]

How representative such cases are is difficult to gauge; even in the late fifteenth century most families probably decided their daughters' vocations for them. There were plenty of mothers who said nothing about choice for their daughters, simply expecting them to marry; and undoubtedly some of the daughters offered alternative options by their mothers were forced regardless by their fathers into marriage or the convent. Nevertheless, that women now subsidized such choices in their wills indicates confidence that their intentions would, or at least could, be respected. This marks a frontal female assault on the principle that male honor required female sexuality to be under the command of men. Taken together with the rise in the preferred marriage age of women, these instances indicate that parents and others were increasingly regarding young women as individual personages deserving the time and opportunity to participate in the charting of their adult destinies.

Rather than marriage being the sole determinant of a woman's adulthood, a measure of maturity was now considered a prerequisite for choosing between marriage or an alternative vocation. In van Gennep's terms, social, not just physiological, puberty was coming to be seen as a measure of young women's adulthood. This appears tied to the concurrent rise in dowries and the increasingly important role that dowried wives played in the economic and social fortunes of their natal and marital families. The responsibilities, even pressures, of wifehood—in particular the concern of a bride's parents that she be capable of resisting the influence of her husband's family and demonstrate loyalty to the natal family that was investing heavily in her marriage portion—now stimulated an uncertain but in any event unprecedented number of parents to defer their daughters' marriages and ensure that they were psychologically suited to the wedded state.

Marriage remained the principal gauge of adulthood for patrician women; even in the late fifteenth century women were still expected to marry at tender ages. The enduring association of female adulthood with wifehood kept the scope of female maturity largely, though not exclusively, focused on the domestic sphere. Nevertheless, approaching 1500, patrician society tentatively began to accept that its daughters might be destined for, or might elect, alternative vocations. It showed a growing disposition to let them mature a bit—to experience a longer and presumably more enriching adolescence—before assuming their adult station. We shall discuss further this graduated approach to female adulthood, but we can observe at this point that tendencies in the later fifteenth century make the measure of women's adulthood resemble a bit more that of men, to which we now turn.

IF THE PRINCIPAL (though evolving) measure of women's adulthood lay in the quintessentially private sphere of wife and motherhood, that of male nobles was largely in the public sphere of business and government.[26] The differences between the two gendered spheres produced profound differences in the adolescent experiences of the sexes with regard to age, activity, and supervision by constituted authority. Yet as with women, men's emergence into adulthood displays variety in individual experience and evolution over time. Like that of women, the measure of patrician male adulthood is not reducible to a universally applicable typology. A result is that alongside the sharp gender differences can be found odd similarities between the sexes as they emerged out of adolescence. Nevertheless, one glaring contrast did distinguish male from female adulthood in the patriciate: for men, unlike women, marriage did not begin but rather completed the passage to adulthood, coming at the end of a long, elaborately punctuated process carried out in the public sphere.

In his treatise on marriage Francesco Barbaro wanted brides to be of tender, malleable wax. But grooms were expected to have the mature experience to mold their lives and more broadly to direct the family's inward and outward functioning.[27] Venetian husbands were expected to be patriarchal, and the role of the paterfamilias at home reflected the organization of patrician society around the gender triptych of patriarchy, patrimony, and patriliny. The welding of public to private male adulthood is evident in the confluence of age expectations for husbandhood and for responsible office holding. Men became husbands at ten or more years older than women became wives. Table 11 tracks the trend in male age at first marriage through the fifteenth century.[28] It shows a tendency to push back the marriage age, suggestively paralleling that for women; but more fundamental is the general (though not universal) dislike of youth in husbands. By and large the late twenties to early thirties were the age at which men were judged ready to take on the responsibilities of husbandhood.

Unlike their sisters and wives, men were deemed fit for marriage only long after the onset of their physiological puberty; it was social puberty that was required of both husbands and full-fledged participants in government. In the fifteenth century the great majority of nobles took part in government, some because it was the basis and expression of their families' prominence, a much larger number because they depended on it for their livelihoods.[29] Attaining political adulthood required a long period of apprenticeship, for the patriarchal impulses densely threaded through the fabric of patrician culture reserved access to positions of significant responsibility in government to men at least in their thirties, veterans of a *cursus honorum* that began with minor posts in the governmental apparatus for those under twenty-five and gradually escalated to positions of increasing importance for men in their late twenties.[30] David Herlihy for Florence and Guido Ruggiero for Venice have commented on the personal tensions and public disorders produced by this delay in finding legitimate sexual outlets, domestic autonomy, and desirable government offices. Certainly the exuberance of young Venetian nobles accounted for its share of disturbances, on the streets and even in the councils of government, though it is difficult to gauge how widespread youthful unruliness really was.[31]

Table 11. Patrician Men's Marriage Ages, 1408–1490
(511 cases from 16 clans)

Period	No. of Cases	Average Age	Median Age
1408–20	38	26.6	25
1421–30	64	27.2	25.5
1431–40	72	30.1	29
1441–50	61	30.1	30
1451–60	53	31.7	30.5
1461–70	74	32.1	30.5
1471–80	79	33.3	32
1481–90	70	33.5	33

Source: From BO 162, 163, 164; Barbaro Nozze.

Venetian governmental institutions and cultural patterns were in place to control and direct this lengthy sociopolitical pubescence.[32] Young men were introduced to their governmental apprenticeship at age eighteen in a ceremony with many of the trappings of a rite of passage, the so-called Barbarella (or Balla d'Oro), at which they documented before government officials their age and their hereditary entitlement to patrician status, with the right to political participation which lay at the center of it. Soon thereafter, between ages twenty and twenty-five, they took their places in the patrician Great Council and also began their service, in low-level positions, in the organs of government. The early channeling of young nobles into a governmental frame did not crush their youthful spirits or even tamp out their unruly manifestations. But it did tether them to the patrician political culture from which they and their families derived status and tangible benefits.[33]

The conformist structuring of male late adolescence was reinforced in spheres not themselves strictly governmental but bearing the stamp of the regime's provision for, and enveloping influence upon, the members of the ruling order. For young nobles from the families of modest means which by the early fifteenth century probably constituted the bulk of the patriciate, the government provided appointment as crossbowmen on state-run merchant vessels. These posts, carrying respectable stipends and offering incumbents free passage to ports of call along the Venetian trade routes where they could buy and sell, became the object of intense competition among patricians, as Donald Queller has shown in the most thorough account of the institution.[34] A sort of welfare measure for needy nobles, the institution of state-appointed bowmen was viewed also as providing young patricians with the training in the seafaring ways of their ancestors upon which, so the official line had it, the continued welfare of Venice itself depended. The targeted participants were youths of eighteen or twenty, young men, that is, of the same age as neophytes in government office.[35] Still in their adolescence, they were being guided toward a social puberty in which hewing to the regime's line appeared the way to economic well-being, the criterion of status, and an indispensable requirement for attracting the interest of dowry-assembling parents of nubile patrician women.

A somewhat different set of lures attracted young men from wealthier families into conformity with the aims of the patrician collective, the leading figures in which, the men whose domination of government allowed them to define the regime's aims, likely came from the same wealthy families. These lures took the form of participation in the glamorous activities of the state's ceremonial apparatus, through membership in the *compagnie della calza*, chic dining clubs of patrician youths which were commissioned by the government to add festive splendor to the visits of foreign dignitaries and other ceremonial occasions.[36] The *calza* companies, so called because the members of each wore its distinctive, elaborately patterned hose and other gorgeous raiment, deserve a full-scale modern study. But enough is known about them to establish that they represented a wealthy elite among patrician youth. The statutes of one of them, the Modesti, chartered in 1487, for example, obliged each member to acquire and maintain in good condition a set of the company's official embroidered hose and jacket of colored silk, on pain of a 100-ducat fine; at the time of his wedding to host two dinners for the entire membership, one at his own house, the other at that of his bride; and to deposit 50 ducats (the yearly stipend, incidentally, of a galley bowman) with the elected master of the company's revels as a guarantee of participation in festive occasions.[37]

Youths who could foot the bill for membership in these societies were a far cry from the young men hustling their way into the crossbow contests that led to selection as galley bowmen. Disparity in wealth between the two groups provides further evidence of the heterogeneity of Venice's patriciate. But although richer than those who vied for the bowman posts, members of the *calza* companies were about the same age; the eleven of the sixteen charter members of the Modesti whose ages can be determined were all seventeen or younger at the time of the company's constitution.[38] The two groups resemble each other in other ways, as well. Both had reason to identify their interests with the regime: the bowmen because the economic benefits they gained were a direct consequence of their participation in state-organized commercial activity; the *calza* companions by their governmentally invited participation as audience-delighting features of public rituals and festivals—a participation that, giving official validation to the expenses of membership, set them substantially apart from their poorer fellow nobles.

Nevertheless, bowmen posts and *calza* membership alike gave men too young to take an active hand in government the opportunity for prestige or profit from publicly supervised paragovernmental activity. They may thus both be seen as elements in a carefully designed structure of public experience which filled out the liminal period of early adulthood for patrician men, between the Barbarella registration, which ritually separated them from underage youths, and their assumption into the official activity of fully qualified adulthood.[39] Moreover, the public aspect of their activity was reinforced by the guiding presence of their fathers. For, in apparent contrast with the contemporary situation in Florence, Venetians in their late teens and early twenties were likely to have living fathers who had every reason to direct their sons into conformity with the regime's practices on which they and their families depended for their status and the material benefits that went with it.[40]

Summing up, male nobles in their late teens and early twenties went through very different experiences than their marrying sisters. While the latter were spending their teenage years bearing children and adapting to a life at least officially private, men were being gradually and systematically exposed, for an additional decade at least, to the public arenas of patrician manhood, getting trained in the skills needed to take a productive part in it and, by reason of that exposure and training, preparing to take on the patriarchal role of a noble husband with the qualities requisite to attracting the interest of fathers of dowry-bearing daughters. By all appearances, then, patrician husbandhood blended seamlessly with adult male participation in the activities of the regime, public and private spheres converging in the model of the patriarch, devoted to promoting the harmonized interests of family, lineage, and regime in the council chamber and the other arenas of public life, while at home commanding and cultivating family resources, prominent among these the access of his sons to similar prerogatives and the prospects of his daughters for alliance-cementing marriages.

The reality, however, was not nearly so tidy or universal. Just as circumstance and choice forced or invited some patrician girls into alternative careers to that of child bride, so many male nobles deviated from the patriarchal model of male adulthood just sketched, rejecting or falling short of the criteria of social puberty which marked the ideal patriarchal type. The varieties of both male and female adult experience displayed in the documents caution against too neat a definition of either patrician manhood or womanhood. They also direct attention to the effect of different social circumstances on the measure of adulthood and on the adolescent experience that led to it.

Many young men were unable to afford the expenses of membership in the *compagnie della calza* or to penetrate the social circles from which the companies drew their membership; many also failed to gain bowmen posts.[41] It is thus possible to trace at least three conspicuous categories of male patrician youth, according to participation in or exclusion from state programs. Such socioeconomic distinctions within the patriciate at the level of semipublic institutions for liminal youth should be studied alongside the distinctions based on differential access to governmental power which historians have in recent years illuminated, for they form an important element of patrician politics. In the present discussion they may be seen as a parallel to the dowry poverty that forced some families to consign their unmarriageable daughters to convents, "amid tears and wailing," as an official act put it.[42] Moreover, as was true of young women, the age of vocational choice for men was changing in the fifteenth century. Earlier we noted the receding age of men at marriage during the course of the century: a gradual delaying, like that expressed in parents' preferences for their daughters' marriages. A counterpart in the public sphere is a change legislated in 1497 in the age of registration for the Barbarella. It was eighteen until 1497, then raised to twenty.[43] The causes and circumstances are obscure, but the effect was to extend male adolescence. For patrician culture at large, it represents another example, alongside that of a rising marriage age for men and women, of change over time in this formative early Renaissance period.

Another, even closer parallel exists between young men and women, lying in a distinction among male nobles which separated not only the wealthy and prestigious from the lesser ranks of the ruling order but brother from brother: the distinction between husband and bachelor. Just as with patrician daughters, not all sons married. Indeed, a remarkably large percentage of adult males remained permanent bachelors. Out of 952 men from sixteen clans who went through the Barbarella ritual between 1410 and 1490 documenting their patrician birth and entering the threshold of adulthood, only a bit more than half, 540 (56.7%), eventually married.[44] The reasons for this widespread bachelorhood have been discussed for the sixteenth century by James C. Davis, although their variants in the fifteenth merit extended treatment.[45] Essentially, they are the same ones that limited female marriages: a family's inability both to provide all its sons with the means of heading a household and to have anything left to pass on to the next generation. Indeed, the pressure for large dowries, which forced many girls out of the marriage market, ironically forced many men out as well, because cobbling together suitable dowries for its daughters sometimes forced a family to deprive its sons of the property that would make them attractive catches for similarly endowed girls.[46] More directly, a dowry-receiving husband was obliged to pledge, or have kinsmen or other associates pledge for him, an equivalent amount of property to ensure the dowry's ultimate restitution to his wife or her designated heirs. Some parents responded by allocating "dowries" to their sons as well as their daughters; in any event someone on the husband's side had to make a commitment of property to protect the wife's right to her dowry at the marriage's end.[47] In a patriciate increasingly hard pressed economically and burdened with heavy expenses for their daughters' marriages, such liens on the family estate were not obligations entered into lightly, whether on behalf of sons, brothers, or friends.

For these and other reasons, which must be treated more fully elsewhere, a large portion of the male patriciate did not meet the basic requirement of patriarchal male adulthood: husbandhood. Guido Ruggiero has argued that others elected for themselves a homosexual cultural identity that veered away from the husbandly model or which in any case led them willingly to accommodate permanent bachelorhood.[48] And we should also note the case, the typicality of which remains to be fully explored, of the humanist Ermolao Barbaro, whose passionate rejection of the burdens of patriarchy is an eloquent critique of the loss of individual freedom entailed in membership in a patrician family, in the patrician regime.[49] Whether imposed or chosen, the varieties of male identity in the domestic microsphere, paralleling the range of youthful experience in the public and semipublic macrosphere, caution against defining too precisely a model of youthful experience, male identity, or masculine gender characteristics for nobles.[50] As with women, the measure of adulthood for men had many gradations, and these wash back upon adolescence in patrician culture.

THE VARIETIES of adulthood reveal that the preparation for it, adolescence, carried a range of possibilities and expectations for both men and women. During this period of many directions, the inclinations of individual adolescents, the purposes and resources of their families, and the principles and requirements of patrician society all interacted in a complex dynamic, not without conflict, to produce the individual adult noble.[51] Moreover, despite the vast differences between male and female adolescence, there is another parallel between them, in addition to the variety characteristic of both: women and men alike underwent a graduated entry into full adulthood, a series of phases marked by changing responsibilities vis-à-vis widening circles of society.

The phases are more sharply visible in the case of men because they were played out in the public arena monopolized by men and were thus more systematically documented. We noted at the beginning that most parents expected their sons to become economically responsible, "to be their own *signori*," at about age twenty. That followed by two years the age at which, until 1497, they could register their patrician status in the Barbarella rite, and it coincided exactly with the minimum age for entering the Great Council, serving in minor governmental offices explicitly destined for young patricians, or setting out with the merchant fleet as a galley bowman. The gradual process of becoming a male adult, then, began for most of the period under discussion around age twenty, which after 1497 became the official exordium age. But it did not reach a plateau of acknowledged maturity until nearly a decade later, when, after having already moved on to offices of escalating public responsibility at age twenty-five (at which age all hereditarily entitled nobles could enter the Great Council), men were deemed ready for major offices and the responsibilities of husbandhood at around age thirty. As we have seen, not all men qualified for the rewards of this culminating maturity, and many of the disqualified—those denied remunerative or prestigious office, for example, or those forced into permanent bachelorhood—must have been doubly embittered by reason of having themselves gone through the steps that paved the way for better-endowed contemporaries to attainments that these less fortunate men could never claim. But although not all chose to, were able to, or did follow the process of phased male adulthood to its culmination, it was nonetheless a process that for many served the needs of family and regime and offered influence, prestige, and the fulfillment of patriarchal identity.[52]

Women had no publicly institutionalized phases of adulthood. Indeed, many women appear superficially to have experienced neither adolescence (understood as a time of training for mature responsibilities) nor adulthood itself (understood as a state of acknowledged capacity for responsible action affecting others). Yet such an appearance is misleading, for it relies too heavily upon the testimony of public institutions, which in a patriarchal society inevitably carry an androcentric prejudice. From another perspective, which seeks to counterbalance the official documentation of men's experience with indications from more private sources of that of women, female adulthood was less definitively tied to marriage than the wills of Agnesina Loredan and Bianca Giustinian and the Great Council act of 1299 would suggest. Fundamental to this alternative perspective is the view that teenage brides were only technically adults, made to appear as such in order to come into their inheritance, so that they might marry, since the dowry was their inheritance.[53] Underlying, and largely belying, this impression of early female adulthood, with marriage the quick, definitive passage, was a phased process paralleling that undergone by young men. The phases made up what may be called the uxorial cycle, from bridehood to mature wife and motherhood, to widowhood. Young wives reveal themselves in their wills as still reliant upon their parents, even when pregnant, although some appear to have struck up warm ties with their husbands right from the start.[54] Although the physical removal from natal to marital household imposed a difficult, and doubtless often cruel, adjustment on young brides by forcing them to mature rapidly and develop a psychological toughness, as well as to endure the physical stress of childbearing, the first years of marriage still saw them as unformed and limited. But those early teenage years of wifehood were only the first phase of the uxorial cycle. The experience of wifehood traversed a variety of ages and circumstances, and over the course of the decade or so following their weddings, patrician wives moved into the second phase, that of mature wives and mothers.

In a process symmetrical with the gradual introduction into adult activities undergone by male patricians in their twenties, wives of the same age reshaped their social orientation in rhythm with the changes in their natal and marital families. The children born to them in the earliest years of marriage, tended in infancy and early childhood by nurses, became the mother's responsibility in the years of later childhood and early youth, the years, that is, when mothers were in their twenties.[55] By the time mothers turned thirty, their own firstborn daughters were entering the marriage market or had already chosen, or been forced into, the religious life; by thirty-five many saw their sons taking their first step into adulthood by registering for the Barbarella.

These wives in their twenties and thirties were not just witnesses but also shapers of the passages of their children. We earlier encountered Petronella Falier Morosini, who instructed in her will of 1464 that her husband was to be overridden by her other executors if he delayed the marriage of their daughter beyond age fourteen. When she asserted this intention, Petronella had been married for fourteen years, putting her in her late twenties (her husband, Zilio Morosini, was about thirty-nine at the time). Yet she apparently got her way in the matter, for her daughter was married two years later, at no more than fifteen years of age, to a member of Petronella's natal Falier clan.[56] Michela Zane married in 1491 under the tutelage of her widowed mother, Cecilia, as urged in her father's will. Cecilia, probably then in her early thirties, likely arranged her daughter's marriage. Another husband, Filippo Priuli, was even more explicit in his will of 1485. Appointing his wife, then probably nearing forty, as his sole executor, he instructed that their five daughters were to marry only "when it was deemed appropriate by Cristina, their mother."[57]

Cristina Priuli was a mature woman when her husband left her in charge of their family's fortunes. But the other examples show younger wives playing an important role in their daughters' future. And that of their sons, as well, although the wait until age eighteen or twenty before men took the first step into adulthood meant that mothers guiding them were inevitably older, certainly in their mid-thirties. Thus when Maddaluzza Capello, widow of Andrea Arimondo, presented their son Simone to the Barbarella in 1444, she was probably about thirty-six years old, as was Caterina Morosini Zane when she presented her son Antonio in 1481; Elena Mocenigo Balbi may have been only thirty-five when she presented her son Jacopo in 1458.[58] Such women had progressed far beyond the stage of frightened teenage brides. Socialized by family and broader culture, they were discharging what by one reckoning was the father's role in this essential ritual of patriarchal-patrilineal-patrimonial society, the inauguration of men's passage into adulthood. Indeed, some mothers guided their sons through further stages of the passage. When Antonio Zulian entered the Great Council in 1457, his proof of requisite age was given by his mother, Maddaluzza Dolfin, as was that of Lorenzo Morosini by his mother, Bianca Priuli Morosini, in 1461. Bianca appears, in fact, to have internalized so thoroughly the family interest that she swore falsely, since Lorenzo appears to have been underage.[59]

Mothers such as these were active players in the family's public enterprise as in the private side.[60] To reach that point they had been obliged to learn the rules of patrician culture in the sociopolitical as well as the domestic sphere as these affected the well-being of their families. This process of education, more hidden than that guiding young men, was nevertheless just as complex and intense as for the men. Indeed, it was probably more intense, and certainly more complex, owing to the bilateral impulses playing upon married women's loyalties, from both natal and marital family and kin. Considered in this way, marriage for women was not the diploma of adulthood but rather the tuition beginning the passage to it, equivalent in its way to the Barbarella for young male nobles and running the course of the same biological stages. It is likely that recognition of the heavy responsibilities that a mother might have to assume contributed to the gradual rise in the preferred marriage age for women. In the patrician society of the fifteenth century, with so much staked economically on marriage and so much hoped for in social and even political return, a prenuptial period stretching further into the teenage years, during which the natal interest could be inculcated to an increasingly mature female consciousness, must have struck many parents as desirable for their daughters.

To RETURN to the question raised at the outset, the evidence of patrician adulthood in Venice points in several different directions that, however, cross and converge in unexpected ways. In general, male adolescents appear to have been gradually weaned away from rambunctious youth into conformist adulthood through a careful, gradual process with publicly ordered phases marked by ritual observance. In seemingly glaring contrast, women were directed early, definitively, and unconsultedly into the private sphere, there to bear the children and follow the authority of husbands considerably older and sanctioned in their domestic patriarchy by groomed participation in the government of the Venetian state. However, concrete experience shows surprising bends in these ostensibly parallel tracks. For men, adulthood and even adolescence held variety, owing to wide gaps in wealth and prestige between sectors of the patriciate and even between brothers. This variety appears in the public life of adoles-

cents, with the privileged accorded celebrity in Venice's elaborately serious public ritual activity, the less wealthy vying for welfare opportunities
overseas. It appears also in the profound divergence between men who
married, blending thereby the public status of their hereditary patrician
title with private status as domestic patriarchs and legitimate generators
of the next levy of continuators of the patrician regime, and their brothers
who remained bachelors, denied or rejecting family headship and patrician generativity.

Variety is similarly evident in the experience of women. Although
bridehood came early, seemingly robbing women of a youthful growing
period by thrusting upon them burdens of wife- and motherhood, there
are signs of a developing sensitivity to women's need for prenuptial youth
in a trend toward later female marriage. More subtly, the fact of wifehood
did not end women's development as adults; the changing phases of the
uxorial cycle found women discovering new capacities and taking on new,
putatively fatherly, responsibilities, to which male society, from their
husbands to government officials, unblinkingly accommodated them.
Unlike men, married women did not undergo a patterned process of acquiring the skills of patrician adulthood; they learned on the job. But we
may wonder whether precisely that absence of a publicly structured adolescent experience, together with the tempering experience of coping at a
tender age with the uncertainties and even terrors of transplantation
as brides into strange households, may have given patrician women a
greater capacity than men for fashioning individual adult personality.
Women, at the margins of the male lineage, regarded by at least some
men primarily as instruments of lineage interest, and most assuredly
prohibited from participating in the governmental activity at the heart of
the status with which the men of a patrician lineage were endowed—such
women ironically were thereby freed of the discipline of the natal lineage
that sent them to their marriages, as of the marital lineage to which they
were transferred.

It may even be the case that the choice between marriage and celibacy
was more available to women than to men. Many girls were married with
little thought of their preferences, of vocation or of mate. But at least
some parents, mothers foremost, allowed their adolescent daughters to
make the vocational choice. It is less clear that lineage-promoting marriage was an obligation that a male patrician could decline—or an opportunity that a man from a poorer family, or a brother with less political or
economic promise to fathers of nubile girls, could enjoy. Mothers, pos-

sessors of wealth, used the influence it gave them to offer their daughters individual choice. The wills are silent about matrimonial options for sons.

In conclusion—provisional rather than firm in this scarcely tilled field—the normative gauges of adult status for men and women may have resembled only incompletely and may have influenced only partially the complex and varied reality of the entry into patrician adulthood. For many male youths adolescence probably led to frustration over the ultimate elusiveness of the goals of the careful training they had undergone. To others, unwilling to conform to a prevailing model of disciplined patrician manhood, limited opportunities for men to marry and to play an influential role in government may instead have brought relief, a chance to forge an alternative identity. For many women, on the other hand, the brusque interruption of adolescence by the uncertainties of youthful marriage could lead, through the twists and turns of individual experience, to a confident, influential, self-defining wifehood. For others, the choice of vocational and sexual identity offered at least a few the possibility of electing an adult life in a community of women or, more rarely, in unmarried secular privacy. Neither for men nor for women were the mainstream models of patrician adulthood universally valid. The outcome and therefore the experience of adolescence, for men and women alike, was crisscrossed by the varieties of circumstance and experience. This variegated panorama counsels caution in characterizing patrician adolescence and adulthood. By displaying the varied possibilities of vocational, sexual, and familial experience among both men and women as they came of age, it also urges a complex, nuanced configuration of gender in the patriciate. Together, the varieties of adulthood and gender reveal the wide diversity of individual responses to the normative measures of the full-fledged male and female patrician types. The result is to signal the range of individual identity in a sociopolitical elite that, distinctive vis-à-vis the great multifarious majority of Venetian commoners, was itself a multifarious community.

Kinship Ties
and Young Patricians

REGIMES AND FAMILIES: historians have recently enriched our understanding of the patrician regimes of late medieval and Renaissance Italy by analyzing relations among their component social units.[1] This chapter seeks to contribute to this literature by throwing light on the social structure and practices of the ruling class of fifteenth-century Venice. For a long time, but with quickening rhythm in the last decade or so, historians of Venice have been charting currents that ran through the Venetian patriciate. On the whole, they have preferred to concentrate on political and economic groupings, less on the family and kinship patterns that fascinate investigators of other cities, notably Florence.[2] But in a patrician regime such as Venice's, society, economy, and politics cannot be separated. Exclusive, hereditary, and in the Quattrocento increasingly self-conscious, Venice's patricians (or nobles, as they called themselves) focused their political and economic aims within their own social class, whose contours inevitably reflected, and in turn influenced, economic and political trends. Studying the patriciate's social structure, interesting in its own right, can thus enlarge understanding of Venice's regime in the Renaissance.

The following pages approach these matters by developing one main point: the fifteenth-century patriciate's avid attention to patrilineal descent, the operating principle of the class's hereditary exclusivism, was only one aspect of a denser, more intricate kinship system. Blood relationships and marriage ties blended with surprising intimacy in one of the patrician family's most important concerns, the formal entry of its young men into adulthood. The significance of this blending becomes clearer with the help of the distinction ethnographers draw between descent and

206

kinship. It is pertinent because their strictly enforced hereditary exclusivism gave Venetian nobles a powerful inducement to center their loyalties
on the male descent line, raising the question whether other social connections—other types of kinship—counted for much. Briefly and roughly,
descent rules are jural constructs that divide society into groups with legal
characteristics, such as inheritance rights, which bind their members together and distinguish them from other, similar groups. At bottom, such
rules promote orderly relationships between the groups that make up
society. Kinship cuts a wider swath. Where descent rules configure an
individual's legal personality by locating him or her in a particular group,
kinship is concerned with the whole array of a person's relationships,
within and outside the descent group; rather than pigeonholing people,
kinship traces the outward radiations of their individual social worlds.[3]
The distinction is central to understanding how Venetian nobles and their
families dealt with the larger society of their class.

Patrilineal descent had a special, political significance in Venice. At the
moment of its legal definition around 1300, the patriciate made descent
from male nobles the essential qualification for class membership.[4] Tin-
kering in subsequent decades refined the principle but left it untouched in
essence; in the fifteenth century, it got added force from legislation deepening the gulf between patricians and the populace.[5] Thus patrilineal
descent not only located persons in their society past and present but
served as the basis for the entire patrician social and political regime. Not
surprisingly, the offspring of patrician descent groups had a strong sense
of lineage, displayed in such practices as preferential inheritance for patrilineal kin and burial in family crypts.[6] Lineage consciousness was also
reinforced by status consciousness, as descent from past nobles built up in
each successive generation a stronger sense of differentiation from those
Venetians unable to claim such descent.[7]

But a strong sense of lineage does not mean a narrow, vertical sense of
kinship; it can mean just the opposite. A lineage's fortunes, like those of
its members, are tied to relations with the outside. The classic way of establishing such relations is through marriage. The connections forged by
marriage can blossom into an elaborate kinship orientation for the offspring, whose commitment to their patrilineal kinsmen fuses with links
to their mothers' relatives.[8] So it was with Venetian patricians. In the
fifteenth century, marriage created powerful bonds between families and
lineages, leading to a bilateral kinship orientation that complemented patrilineal descent and created widespread social networks through the class.

This expansive sense of kinship is displayed in the records of the Balla
d'Oro. This exercise, also called the Barbarella, after Saint Barbara, on
whose feast day (4 December) it was held, was a lottery in which a certain
portion of the entrants, who had to be at least eighteen years old, won the
privilege of taking their seats in the exclusively patrician Great Council
at age twenty instead of the normal twenty-five. Set up as early as 1319,
the Balla d'Oro became an important rite of passage for the newly self-
conscious patriciate only in the Quattrocento.[9] But by midcentury it had
become the most frequently followed route to full adult patrician status,
with patrician families flocking to enroll their sons.[10] The Barbarella's
boom in popularity is explained by Quattrocento nobles' reliance on the
state, which in that century became an increasingly important source of
economic succor, notably in the form of government posts.[11] Getting sons
quickly into government service, or in any case into the Great Council,
where they could join in the electoral maneuvering that allocated jobs,
became in these circumstances sound family strategy.

Because the Balla d'Oro touched the very core of patrician family
interest, the way young men were enrolled reveals a good deal about
nobles' ties to lineage, larger kinship networks, and patrician society as a
whole. In the following pages, we examine the registrations of 1,065 men
from sixteen patrician clans between 1408 and 1497, looking for the social
ties that were important enough for patricians to call upon at a moment of
supreme family interest.[12]

THE PRINCIPAL GAINERS from a Balla d'Oro winner's early catapult into
political adulthood were his family: especially his father and brothers,
sharing with him the perquisites of full class membership, and his sisters,
whose marriage prospects were brightened by their brother's contributions to the family's well-being (to the extent, that is, that patrician girls
as distinct from their families may be said to have benefited from their
marriage prospects). Mothers had a more complex social orientation, embracing both their family of origin and their marital family. But they, too,
were not indifferent to their sons' prospects as mature men. All this
makes it natural that young men's family members would do the lion's
share of Barbarella enrolling: all the more so because the benefits a Barbarella winner could bring his family as an adult patrician—remunerative
political office, economic opportunities, eventually a chance for a favorable marriage with a handsome dowry—were coveted by other patrician

families pushing their own sons' candidacies. At a time of narrowing economic opportunities and apparently widespread economic need among patricians, there was competition in the pursuit of available opportunities.[13] Legislation on office holding from the late Trecento onward reveals heavy competition for available political posts, and the same was true of economic prospects.[14]

But although it might pursue its interests in competition with others like it, the patrician conjugal family was not isolated. An adult noble with wife and children kept close ties with his brothers, often bound to him by the legal force of the *fraterna*, or collective patrimony.[15] Spreading the circle still wider, the Quattrocento patriciate's deeper concern with status and birth lengthened genealogical memories, stretching lineage consciousness beyond near relatives.[16] Finally, and crucially, legislation during those decades which made mothers' status as well as fathers' a criterion of Great Council eligibility signals the growing importance of marriage in patrician families' social strategies, as does the steep rise in dowries then taking place.[17]

The Balla d'Oro records trace the geography of this complex kinship system. Enrolling a candidate involved at least three and sometimes four or five people: the registrant's sponsor or presenter (sometimes there was more than one) and normally two or three others, here called guarantors, who stood surety for payment of fines—200 lire if investigation found the registrant younger than eighteen, 500 if he turned out not of legitimate patrician birth.[18] It was a sizable group, though certainly recruitable among the near kinsmen of most young patricians. Family members were the likeliest participants because they knew better than anyone else whether a candidate's credentials were in order—or because they stood to gain most from risking fines if the claims were shaky. *A fortiori*, outsiders' knowledgeability about a candidate's credentials or willingness to risk fines on his behalf indicates strong ties to his family.

Candidates were usually enrolled by their fathers. Fathers directed the family interest served by their sons' entry into adulthood, and the 1414 Balla d'Oro law expressly preferred them as presenters.[19] Yet although they dominated as sponsors, their domination was not overwhelming. Fifty-six percent of the candidates, 597 out of the 1,065 studied, were presented by their fathers: a majority but not a crushing one. Most of the others were fatherless, but by no means all. Many fathers were out of town on government or private business when their sons registered, a

Table 12. All Balla d'Oro Sponsors

	No.	%
Fathers	597	53.9
Brothers	55	4.9
Paternal kin	163	14.7
Mothers	158	14.3
Maternal kin	42	3.8
Others	93	8.4
Total	1,108	100

Source: BO 162, 163, 164.

contingency explicitly provided for in the 1414 law, which authorized near kinsmen to fill in.[20] All told, nearly two-thirds of the young men sampled (678, or 63.7%) had living fathers when they enrolled in the Balla d'Oro.

So if fathers were not always present at their sons' Balla d'Oro registrations, in the great majority of cases they at least had a hand in determining who the sponsors might be. This put them in a strong position to promote their version of the family interest. Moreover, the odds are that in their time these same fathers had been enrolled as nobles and had had their own patrician adulthood shaped under the family-interested direction of their fathers. So when it was time for them to work for the wellbeing of the families they had come to head, their operating notion of family strategy was likely to fit snugly into a chain of patrilineally defined policy that stayed unbroken for generations.[21] The continuity of family interest made possible by the overlapping of adult male generations—by authoritative fathers living into their sons' young manhood—is a notable characteristic of the Venetian patriciate which gives a special concreteness to patrilineality and bears on the relative stability of the regime.[22]

But fathers' weighty influence notwithstanding, it remains the case that of 1,108 persons who acted as sponsors in our sample of Barbarella registrations, 46 percent were not the candidates' fathers.[23] Who, then, were they? First, a breakdown of all the sponsors, including, for a complete perspective, the fathers already discussed. Table 12 shows fathers' dominance. But it also makes clear that their place was often taken by a wide range of others connected in a variety of ways with the young registrants. The great majority of these others were patrilineal kin or at least members of the candidate's clan.[24] But there were a lot of others

Table 13. Sponsors other than Fathers

	No.	%
Brothers	55	10.8
Other paternal kin	163	31.9
Total paternal kin	218	42.7
Mothers	158	30.9
Other maternal kin	42	8.2
Total maternal kin	200	39.1
Other	93	18.2
Total	511	100

Source: BO 162, 163, 164.

Table 14. Parental-Kin Sponsors other than Fathers

	No.	%
Brothers	55	13.2
Other paternal kin	163	39
Total paternal kin	218	52.1
Mothers	158	37.8
Other maternal kin	42	10
Total maternal kin	200	47.9
Total	418	100

Source: BO 162, 163, 164.

from outside the lineage as well. We can get a clearer picture by looking at the registrations in which fathers did not take part.

It is likely that the "Other" category consists mainly of affines, marital kin; we shall get back to them later. But on the hypothesis that a young man's strongest social bonds were his kinship links through his parents, let us get a clearer picture of Balla d'Oro sponsorship in fathers' absence by eliminating the "Other" category.

Table 14's most striking feature is its revelation that when fathers were out of the picture, sponsorship of Balla d'Oro registrations was almost perfectly divided between matrilineal and patrilineal kin. In a patrilineally defined elite such as Venice's, especially at a time when gene-alogical consciousness was encouraged by the patriciate's growing ex-clusivism, such a weighty presence from the mother's side in a matter so important to family and lineage fortunes urges careful attention to the balance between the ties that grew out of the patrilineal descent principle and those created by the lineage's matrimonial outreach. A closer look at the different sponsors reveals more of the details of this orientation.

It is not surprising to see brothers taking the place of absent fathers. The economically united fraternal group gained if each of its members exploited the benefits of patrician status. That prompted first- or second-born sons to make sure their fatherless younger brothers got into the Great Council as quickly as possible. It prompted Nicolò and Girolamo quondam (qd) Giovanni da Mula, for example, to register their brothers Alvise in 1464 and Giacomo in 1469. A fifth brother, Cristoforo, was enrolled in 1465 under different sponsorship, but with Nicolò and Girolamo acting as guarantors for the false-credential fines.[25] Nevertheless, despite the inducements that such examples reflect, brothers accounted for little more than one in ten of sponsors substituting for fathers. The reason is probably that in most cases they were themselves only in their twenties or early thirties and still learning their way around patrician adult life when their younger brothers came of Barbarella registration age at eighteen.[26] Guiding young men into adulthood was a job better left to more practiced hands.

There were plenty of other kinsmen's hands around. Table 12 showed that patrilineal kinsmen from outside the family made up the biggest group of sponsors after fathers; Table 13 showed that they were nearly one-third of all sponsors, fathers absent. Many and probably most of them were candidates' paternal uncles, since the legal ties of the fraterna lasted into the generation of the brothers' sons.[27] Thus Giovanni qd Nicolò da Mula, whose sons Nicolò and Girolamo we just saw sponsoring their brothers' registrations in the 1460s, had himself been presented for registration in October 1431 by two of his late father's brothers. The Barbarella registration records are crowded with such cases.[28] Uncles also stepped in when the candidate's father was living but unavailable,[29] but most of them were substituting for dead fathers, motivated by the same shared interest that prompted men to sponsor their younger brothers.

Patrilineal sponsors also came from further afield in the kinship geography. Some relationships are hard to pin down.[30] But occasionally we run across a figure such as Piero qd Alvise Balbi, who in 1490 sponsored his young cousin, Nicoletto qd Marco Balbi. Sponsor and candidate were the sons of brothers but were far separated in age, Piero himself having registered for the Balla d'Oro back in 1463.[31] The genealogical links were stretched even thinner in the case of Piero qd Giovanni Lando, who in 1493 presented his cousin's son, Girolamo di Piero Lando, to whom he was related only through a common ancestor already dead nearly six decades earlier.[32]

What led patricians to sponsor their young relatives in Balla d'Oro registrations? Shared economic interest was, of course, part of it. The two Lando second cousins involved in the registration of 1493 were probably too far removed from each other to have fraternal property in common (although Piero, the sponsor, and his registrant's late father were the sons of two brothers and could thus have shared in their fathers' undissolved fraterna). The two Balbi cousins in the 1490 registration were more likely, as sons of two brothers, to have had property in common. But even without economic connections, kinsmen in the Great Council were a valuable resource in the booming business of office seeking. Office required election, and election required votes. Patron-client relations helped, and reciprocal favors seem to have been the rule in elections.[33] The office seeker with many patrilineal kinsmen could hope for votes from their extraclan associates as well as from his own; this advantage helped compensate for the legal ineligibility of members of his clan to take part in balloting when he was a nominee.[34] So enrolling a young nephew or second cousin in the Barbarella could earn the grateful loyalty of his other kinsmen and their friends—the latter eagerly hoping that the young registrant would win the lottery and lend his fresh Great Council vote to their own office-seeking ambitions. A new addition to its Great Council delegation could promote a lineage's interest more directly, of course, by providing an additional potential officeholder to tap into the state's salary system.[35]

We can see the process at work in the Lando lineage just mentioned. When Piero qd Giovanni Lando enrolled his young second cousin, Girolamo qd Piero Lando, in 1493, it fit into a tight, elaborate pattern of agnatic kin involvement in Lando Barbarella registrations. At Piero's own registration in 1480, his father's brother, Alvise qd Marino Lando, had been a guarantor, a service this same Alvise had rendered also at the 1475 registration of his nephew Francesco Lando, son of another brother, Vitale qd Marino. A decade earlier, in 1465, this Vitale had done his part by sponsoring the registration of his nephew Piero, son of still another brother, Girolamo, and the father of that younger Girolamo with whose 1493 registration we started out. Vitale's avuncular service in 1465 can in turn be seen as repayment for the brotherly intervention of Piero's father, Girolamo qd Marino, who had been a guarantor when Vitale himself was enrolled in 1439. Finally—just to show that none of these lineage members escaped service—the 1465 registrant, Piero di Girolamo, made his contribution by acting as a guarantor at the 1474 registration of his cousin Francesco di Alvise Lando, whose father we just saw doing similar service at nephews' registrations in 1475 and 1480.[36]

This thicket of reciprocal Barbarella aid is hard to detach from the Landos' office-holding records. Piero qd Giovanni, the sponsor of 1493, had begun his career at age twenty-three or twenty-four when in 1482 he was elected an advocate in the civil courts of the Ducal Palace, a job frequently given to younger patricians. By 1496 he had qualifications sufficient to get elected *podestà* and captain at Bassano, and five years later he won the post of *patronus* of the Arsenal, Venice's shipyard.[37] These last two offices indicate a measure of prominence, thus displaying in operation the friendships—cemented in marriage alliances, as we shall see— that his politically enrolled Lando kinsmen enjoyed with wide circles of the patrician electorate, whose votes got him the posts. He probably benefited also from the influence of his illustrious uncle, Vitale qd Marino, who had a prestigious military and political career as well as enjoying some distinction as a humanist.[38] As just noted, Vitale sponsored the 1465 Balla d'Oro registration of his nephew, Piero di Girolamo Lando, whose son Girolamo would be sponsored in 1493 by Piero qd Giovanni. The latter Piero's political career probably was enhanced also by the prominence of another uncle, Vitale's brother Alvise qd Marino, who was an *avogadore di comun* at the very time he was serving as a guarantor at Piero's registration in 1480.[39] All of these things probably came into play in Piero qd Giovanni Lando's political career, which was crowned by his election to the dogeship in 1539.

Its ducal climax apart, the Lando story could be repeated for all the clans in the sample. Its theme is continued lineage involvement, across generations and degrees of kinship, in the rite of passage that officially signaled young men's readiness for patrician adulthood and thus strengthened their families' presence and resources within patrician society. But all things considered, there really is no surprise in that. A genealogically fixed ruling class, especially one that in the fifteenth century was exhibiting keener concern with pedigree, would naturally display lineage loyalty. What makes the Lando case and that of the other sample clans— and by implication that of the entire patriciate—more interestingly complex is the Balla d'Oro involvement of people from outside the patri-lineage and the wider clan.

TAKING ANOTHER look at Table 13 we see that close behind the patrilineal kinsmen who made up the largest group of father-substituting sponsors (i.e., brothers and other paternal kin: 42.7%) was a second group, made up of mothers and maternal kinsmen—39.1 percent. The striking facts are that mothers and their kinsmen contributed one of every five Balla d'Oro sponsors, even taking fathers into account, as in Table 12, and two of every five when fathers were out of the picture. The very least that can be said of these people is that as members of other clans they felt other loyalties, often stronger ones, than just to the lineages of the candidates they registered. So their prominence in the Balla d'Oro gives the strong-est indication yet seen of a patrician kinship orientation far more complex than just solidarity within the patrilineage, no matter how strongly gene-alogical consciousness and concrete interest were urging such solidarity. A closer look bears this impression out.

In the first place, mothers themselves were four out of every five of these maternal-kin sponsors. Mothers usually came from other clans and conserved ties to their families of origin.[40] But by the time their sons were ready for the Balla d'Oro, they had spent a good eighteen years or more rubbing elbows with their husbands' families, especially the brothers whose economic fortunes were bound up with those of the mothers' husbands. Concern for their sons' fortunes drew mothers closer to their marital lineages, as no doubt also did the cool recognition that their own material well-being was tied to that of the families into which they had married.[41] We can get an idea of mothers' Barbarella coopera-tion with their husbands' lineages by looking more closely to the guaran-tors for payment of false credential fines. Table 15 breaks down guaran-tors' participation when fathers and when mothers sponsored their sons' registrations.

Table 15 shows that sponsoring mothers worked with their sons' male kinsmen in roughly the same proportion as did sponsoring fathers. The larger number of "other" guarantors, most of unknown or uncertain relationship with their candidates, makes this information rather soft. But it is clear that women actively cooperated with their husbands' kins-men in an activity that strengthened the patrilineage. This gives concrete effect to the heightened importance that fifteenth-century legislation at-tached to mothers in their sons' pedigree.[42] The point to emphasize here,

Table 15. Balla d'Oro Guarantors

	Father Presents		Mother Presents		Total	
	No.	%	No.	%	No.	%
Paternal kin	243	23.3	75	25.2	318	23.7
Maternal kin	108	10.3	43	14.4	151	11.3
Others	693	66.4	180	60.4	873	65
Total	1,044	100	298	100	1,342	100

Source: BO 162, 163, 164.

Note: Guarantors from 755 parentally sponsored registrations.

though, is that mothers' Balla d'Oro sponsorships did not weaken the patrilineal stake but on the contrary fortified it.

One way they did it was by collaborating with their older sons in the registrations of younger ones.[43] These joint efforts reflect the Balla d'Oro's appeal as an instrument of family interest. But cooperation between women and their husbands' lineages ranged beyond the nuclear family. When Contarina, widow of Antonio qd Daniele Loredan, signed up her son Federico in 1473, one of the guarantors was Francesco qd Giovanni Loredan, a son of her late husband's brother, also deceased, and thus young Federico's first cousin.[44] This example reminds us once again of the continuing ties between the offspring of brothers in the transgenerational fraterna. Given the fraterna, indeed, it was natural for uncles to cooperate with their widowed sisters-in-law, and such cases abound in the Barbarella records, drawing attention to the complex interweaving of interests, focused on young men, which connected patricians' widows with their husbands' kin.[45] All potential beneficiaries of the young man's emergence as a patrician adult, they were at the same time competitors for the economic substance he inherited—uncles promoting the collective lineage interest, mothers hoping for a secure widowhood at their sons' hands. The Barbarella prominence of mothers, cooperating with their husbands' kinsmen in an enterprise of deep concern to the lineage despite their ambivalent stake in its fortunes, makes the whole fabric of kinship orientation in the patriciate especially intriguing.[46]

Widows' relations with their husbands' kinsmen were complicated by the women's enduring ties to their own families of origin. The figures in table 15 show that sponsoring fathers occasionally recruited their wives' kinsmen into their sons' Balla d'Oro registrations. But mothers were almost half again as likely to call upon their natal relatives when they enrolled their sons. If patrician wives and widows had ambivalent feelings about their husbands' lineages, their ties to their own natal families remained strong, even after eighteen or more years in their husband's family palace. The way they demonstrated those enduring bonds is the most remarkable part of their active involvement in their sons' passage to adulthood. In a mirror image of the paternal kin involvement already discussed, mothers favored their own brothers as guarantors when registering their sons. When Delfina, widow of Antonio qd Cristoforo da Canal, signed up her son Paolo in February 1479/80, her late husband's brother Luca guaranteed Paolo's credentials. But when, seven years later, she registered her younger son Bernardo, this time it was with the guarantee of her own brother, Andrea qd Giacomo Dolfin, and no da Canals in sight.[47] Even several decades of marriage failed to weaken women's ties to their brothers. In 1459 Ambrogio qd Federico Contarini guaranteed the registration of his widowed sister's son, Piero qd Francesco Ruzzini; it had been at least thirty-five years since the sponsoring mother, Vida, had left home to marry Francesco Ruzzini, yet she still called upon her brother—as indeed she had also done eleven years earlier, in 1448.[48]

Nor did mothers turn to their brothers only when their husbands' kinsmen were in short supply. Just five months before Delfina da Canal entered her younger son Bernardo in the lottery in December 1487, her late husband's brother Francesco qd Cristoforo da Canal had registered the son of yet a third brother, Giovanni qd Cristoforo, and was thus probably available to assist at the presentation of his nephew Bernardo, Delfina's son.[49] And when Vida Ruzzini presented her son Giorgio with the backing of her brother Ambrogio Contarini in 1448, it was just ten days after her late husband's brother, Marco qd Ruggero Ruzzini, had registered his own son.[50] In some of these cases, and the many others like them, there may have been little love lost between the widows and their husbands' kin. A widow's efforts to recover her dowry could easily trigger bad feeling between them, since they sometimes occasioned economic hardship for her affines as they labored to come up with liquid wealth in order to forestall her dowry-restitution claims upon the family real estate.[51] So it is not completely mystifying to find a Vida Ruzzini even after thirty-five years of married life calling upon a brother instead of a brother-in-law to assist at her son's Balla d'Oro registration.

Yet it would be a mistake to treat choices such as these women made as necessarily signs of bad blood between them and their marital kin. The cold fact of the matter, as table 15 shows, is that mothers bringing their sons to the Balla d'Oro cooperated nearly twice as often with their husbands' relatives as with their own natal kinsmen. But viewing it that way implies competition, even tension, between a woman's natal and marital kin. No doubt there was plenty of it, but it was hardly the rule. Indeed, the most important thing about mothers' sponsorship of their sons' registrations was that it offered them occasion not only to choose between natal- and marital-kin guarantors but also to invite cooperation between the two sides. The sources are silent on the ways individual families made their Balla d'Oro arrangements. We should not exclude the possibility that orphaned young registrants themselves had a say in the planning; and they may have had attachments of affection and interest to maternal and paternal uncles alike, both of whom were blood relatives. The point to be stressed, however, is that mothers played a pivotal role in recruiting both paternal- and maternal-kin patrons for their sons' arrival at patrician adulthood, in that fashion complementing other ways in which women mediated between the families and lineages that they linked by marriage.[52]

The records are full of examples. To mention just four cases among many, the aptly named Barbarella Vitturi in 1438, Maddaluzza Arimondo in 1444, Agnesina Loredan in 1468, and Elisabetta Mudazzo in 1477 all were widows who, registering their sons, enlisted both their own and their husbands' brothers as guarantors.[53] Men's participation in the Balla d'Oro registrations of their sisters' sons is an intriguing indication of lasting bonds between adult brothers and sisters, meriting further study. More important, the merging of paternal and maternal kin around a young noble's adulthood which these cases illustrate makes clear the importance of married women, and marriage generally, as the connective tissue in patrician society. These cases show, moreover, that the interfamilial, interlineage ties forged by marriage lasted into the next generation, linking brothers-in-law in a network of cooperation anchored by women. The focus of this cooperation was the young man whose introduction into patrician manhood thus drove home a bilateral socialization that gave him a heritage of gratitude and loyalty to both his patrilineal and his matrilineal kinsmen.

THE PRACTICAL STRENGTH of marriage ties stands out even more vividly when parents were not on hand to sponsor Balla d'Oro registrations. Glancing back at table 13, we see that more than one-quarter (26.4%) of all the sponsors who substituted for dead or absent fathers came from outside their registrant's family and lineage; that is, they were people other than brothers, mothers, or paternal kinsmen.[54] As noted earlier, many are hard to track down, so only part of them have been pinpointed. But the identities of these show that they, too—and probably also the sponsors whose relationships have not been established—were connected by marriage with the young men whom they ushered into adult patrician life.

The clearest evidence once again concerns maternal uncles, now not just as guarantors but as their nephews' sponsors. A nephew's relationship with his uncle, whether father's or mother's brother, is a consanguineal one. But a Venetian patrician's interactions with his mother's brother fell outside the genealogical membrane and the fraterna-based property sharing that formally united lineage members in the promotion of common status and interest. Yet Barbarella sponsorships by maternal uncles reveal how the ties of marriage could intersect or even supplant those of lineage.[55] In one twenty-two-year period, to give an example, three young Landos were registered by their mothers' brothers, each from a different clan and none ever again a sponsor for any of his sister's sons.[56] What makes these cases and others like them especially revealing is that in none of them was the maternal uncle stepping in to fill a void in the patrilineage. There were plenty of other Landos around to do the job, and in fact brothers of all three of these candidates had been or would be sponsored by Lando kinsmen.[57] Nevertheless, men from other clans were deemed suitable substitutes to preside over this crucial moment in the family experience—at a time when evidence shows that the Balla d'Oro was looming ever more important in family calculations.[58]

In the overall picture, of course, maternal uncles—maternal kinsmen in general—were far from elbowing paternal kin out of the picture. We have seen the overwhelming predominance of lineage members in the Balla d'Oro; in any case maternal kinsmen make up only 8.2 percent of father-substituting sponsors. Nevertheless, by taking on the principal Barbarella role even when candidates' paternal kinsmen were available, they show that at an event of major importance for the family, matrilineal consanguinity could serve just as effectively, and be called upon just as readily, as the presumably more interested membership of the lineage. And the calculation was reciprocal. By shepherding young men from other lineages into the political world of the patriciate, these sponsoring uncles were in effect enlarging the field of competitors for office which their own lineage mates had to confront. Thus they demonstrate that from their angle, too, lineage loyalty could yield to matrimonial ties. All of this illustrates how complex were the ties that wound densely through the patriciate. Based on constant and overlapping marriage connections, the deeply rooted and widely ramifying work of generations, they were bound to encourage in the young patrician at the center of the process a notion of kinship loyalty and cooperation which embraced his mother's family as well as the men of his own lineage.

Significant as maternal uncles were in Barbarella registrations, however, they were much less active than the persons who make up the category of "Other" in table 13, which accounts for nearly one-fifth of all sponsors in the absence of fathers. Most of these are elusive, but those whose connections have come to light give the strong suggestion that their ties to the candidates also were grounded in interlineage marriage. Once again, a Lando experience tells the tale. When Alvise qd Marino Lando registered in 1438, his sponsor was Marco qd Albano Capello, who two years earlier had married one of Alvise's sisters. This Marco Capello's good relations with his wife's family lasted into the next generation: in 1465 he registered the son of another of her (living) brothers, Piero di Girolamo Lando.[59] Marco Capello was far from unique. Even though systematic tracing of all marriage connections is not yet complete, enough instances have appeared to give the impression that taking a hand in his young brother-in-law's Barbarella registration was becoming a regular means by which a husband could justify the dowry he had received from his wife's family. In this way, brothers-in-law joined maternal uncles in demonstrating the concrete results of a lineage's matrimonial strategy over two generations: in 1474, Francesco Lando (son of the Alvise who had been registered in 1438 by his brother-in-law Marco Capello, above) was sponsored by both his sister's husband, Jacopo Bembo, and his mother's brother, Antonio Valier.[60]

The interventions of brothers-in-law and maternal uncles both center on a noblewoman's serving as a knot tying her brothers to her new marital family. But the marital connections that came to bear in the Balla d'Oro registrations went further and lasted longer than just ties between brothers-in-law or uncles and nephews. Showing that the good interfamilial relations created by marriage could have the same transgenerational staying power as the ties between paternal uncles and nephews, the husbands of young men's aunts (their fathers' sisters) sometimes stood in as Barbarella sponsors. Triadano Gritti, for example, had married the sister of Filippo qd Piero da Canal in 1417, yet he remained closely enough involved in his wife's family's affairs to sponsor Filippo's son Francesco two decades later. Daniele Bragadin showed even more endurance as a loyal affine: when he sponsored the registration of Lorenzo qd Marco Loredan in 1484, it was twenty-six years after he had married a sister of the young man's father.[61]

More impressive still as testimony to the durability of these matrimonial ties are cases of Barbarella cooperation continuing across several generations removed from the married principals. Marco qd Piero Lando was registered in 1496 by his mother's brother, Giorgio Corner—not an uncommon thing, as we have seen—but also by Andrea qd Marco Soranzo, whose relationship to young Marco was the distant one that his mother was a sister of young Marco's paternal grandfather.[62] An even more drawn-out connection through women involves families in the Morosini and da Mula clans. In 1412, Paolo qd Francesco Morosini married Franceschina, daughter of Antonio da Mula. Three decades later, in 1442, when Paolo registered their son Piero, one of the guarantors was Franceschina's brother Benedetto.[63] Two years after that, in 1444, Paolo returned the favor indirectly by sponsoring the registration of young Andrea di Francesco da Mula, grandson of another of his wife's brothers, Giovanni.[64] But the favors did not stop there. When this Andrea's younger brother Domenico signed up in 1470, his sponsor was Lorenzo Morosini, another of Paolo's sons and related to Domenico only as the son of a sister (Franceschina) of the young man's grandfather.[65] Yet that frail connection, radiating in another direction, lasted at least another sixteen years. In 1486, this same Lorenzo qd Paolo Morosini cosponsored—along with the candidate's maternal uncle—the registration of Girolamo di Piero qd Benedetto da Mula. Young Girolamo was the grandson of another of Lorenzo Morosini's da Mula maternal uncles, Benedetto qd Antonio—who, we just saw, had in turn guaranteed the 1442 Barbarella registration of Lorenzo's brother Piero Morosini.[66]

The Balla d'Oro records show how many more such remote marital connections were reinforced in registrations.[67] But the cases reported above should be enough to show how strong and long lasting the associations established in patrician marriages could be. They point to a couple of other conclusions, as well. Bonds such as those forged between the Morosini and da Mula families at the marriage of 1412 were not dusted off only at Barbarella time. They were strengthened and deepened by constant use, as both families sought to benefit from the alliance the marriage had cemented, notably in business and office holding.[68] Marriage alliances were made out of interest: they existed to be exploited, and their coming up in such an important matter as young men's entry into adulthood reflects the confidence in each other that years of cooperation had given the two sets of affines.

The Barbarella records attest to the enduring strength of marriage ties and make clearer the main characteristics of the patrician social system. They trace an image of individual nobles at the center of extended kinship networks, in which men and women from the same lineage intermingled with a vast array of people from other lineages, some freshly introduced into a family's affairs through recent marriages, but others more solidly grafted on by the blood ties with offspring which gave depth and permanence to marital associations. Moreover, growing patrician exclusivism in the Quattrocento gave marital ties a still deeper significance. Their class's membership now stabilized, patricians tended to marry less outside it— not surprising in view of the kinds of the exclusively patrician benefits they expected from their matrimonial alliances.[69] This growing class endogamy only strengthened the process by which, over the course of several generations of marriages, a noble lineage would find itself connected to a sizable chunk of the entire patriciate. Take the example of one Balbi lineage, the three generations that sprang from Lodovico (or Alvise) di Bernardo Balbi, who lived early in the Quattrocento. Lodovico's children, grandchildren, and great-grandchildren contracted among them forty-five marriages, and the spouses came from no fewer than thirty other noble clans, plus one from another Balbi branch. The four generations of progeny of Fantin di Nicolò Arimondo followed the same pattern: in fifty marriages, the spouses bore thirty-five different patrician surnames.[70]

This panoply of affines is interesting to observe in its own right as evidence of the thick webbing of ties developing throughout the patriciate. But the webbing became thicker still as those matrimonial connections fed on one another at Balla d'Oro registrations. When brothers, uncles, and even remote cousins got involved in their young kinsmen's Barbarellas, they often brought along their marital kinsmen, as well. Thus, when Antonio qd Donato Arimondo sponsored the registration of his younger brother Paolo in 1427, he persuaded his wife's brother to stand in as a guarantor. Paolo qd Nicolò Morosini did the same thing in 1446 when he registered Francesco, son of his late brother Giacomo.[71] In

1467, Giovanni qd Piero Pisani got an even more distant marital alliance involved when he enrolled his late brother's son: one of the guarantors backing him up was his own son-in-law, Cristoforo Duodo.[72] In each of these cases, the young registrant entering adult patrician society fell heir to a doubly enriched network of associations anchored in his family of origin: in the form of enduring ties to several degrees of his own kinship group and also to newer associations that his kinsmen extended to him from their own strong and active marital connections. The picture that emerges is of the young patrician at the center of a social solar system, his kinsmen revolving around him at different distances, each in turn surrounded by his marital satellites and all these bodies gravitating toward support of the young man's entry into adulthood.

So strong were the bonds created by marriage that they often entered, so to speak, their own independent orbit around a young registrant and his family. We have already seen plenty of cases of this sort of thing: maternal and affinal kin acting as sponsors and guarantors in seeming independence of direction from their candidate's own lineage. It is the active involvement of these persons from other lineages, bringing into play on their candidate's behalf the social ties built up in their own families' matrimonial activity, which documents most vividly the intricate density of patrician social relations in the Quattrocento.

A couple of examples illustrate the range of these connections. Cristoforo qd Giovanni da Canal was registered in 1487 by his father's brother Francesco da Canal and his mother's brother Francesco Priuli. Such cooperation by now seems normal enough. What gives it a special twist, however, is that the Canal-Priuli connection led to still another clan's involvement. For Francesco Priuli, the maternal uncle, brought in as a guarantor *his* maternal cousin, Alvise qd Bertuccio qd Piero Bondumier, a son of Priuli's mother's brother.[73] Thus one affinal relationship established by the Canal family—the one with the Priulis—opened onto another, through the Priulis to the Bondumiers, who felt comfortable enough with the arrangement to risk paying the fines for false information and who now, as a likely consequence, became part of the social network of young Cristoforo da Canal, his uncle Francesco da Canal, and their families. The same interlocking of matrimonial ties was probably taking place when Giorgio Corner registered his sister's son Marco qd Piero Lando in 1496. One of the guarantors was Vettor Soranzo. This Vettor's connection with the Landos, if any, is uncertain, but in that same year his son married Giorgio Corner's daughter.[74] Corner was likely more earnestly concerned with his daughter's marriage than with the fortunes of his sister's family. Yet thanks to his brotherly loyalty, which led him somehow to pull his verging Soranzo marriage connection into his Lando nephew's Balla d'Oro, the nephew's family also found itself in a position to knit the Soranzos into their own social fabric.

EXAMPLES SUCH AS THESE help to pry open the social world of the patriciate, a thickly grown jungle of social ties spreading between, around, and through families until in time most clans must somehow have been tied to almost all others. Such dense reticulation was probably inevitable in an exclusive society of little more than 150 clans, jealous of their dignity, doing their best to fend off intruders, and increasingly inclined to marry among themselves. But it was not just the marriage ties, in the course of generations of class endogamy renewed again and again, which knit the patriciate together. It was their combination with strong lineage consciousness. It was as members of the lineage, and through it of the more vaguely gathered clan, that patricians staked their claims to membership in their class. Hence the genealogies and records of marriages which public and private recorders were compiling by the early Cinquecento.[75] Kinsmen's mutual reliance for economic and political well-being also fortified the ties of blood, probably with a persuasiveness even more compelling than genealogical memory. Marriage connections and the maternal kinship ties that grew out of them merged with this lineage consciousness, deepening and extending the importance of both for the noble carving out his place in society.

The blend of lineage consciousness and a bilateral kinship orientation is a widely met consequence of the lineage's efforts to assert itself in society through beneficial contact with other lineages.[76] The two had gone hand in hand in Venetian noble practice for decades, maybe even centuries. Even before the class-defining legislation around 1300 formally emphasized patrilineal descent, near kinsmen were officially recognized as including maternal and affinal as well as paternal relations.[77] But developments in the late fourteenth and early fifteenth centuries raised the stakes of both and in the process welded them together even more tightly in the patrician social consciousness.[78] Governmental action, specifically acts of the Great Council, made it harder to prove patrician status; the Balla d'Oro law of 1414 is one example. This weeded out dubious claimants, but it had the larger effect of finally fixing the patriciate's composition. The families that met the tougher standards were consequently more jealous of their status. Indeed, these were the very families whose members legislated the standards, thus proclaiming their distinctiveness but also maximizing for themselves the practical benefits of noble status by restricting it to a small, descent-specified segment of Venetian society: themselves.

Three results of this tightening should be summarized in the present context. One was the heightened sense of lineage, already discussed, as the fixed class membership came to be reckoned in terms of the clans then extant and the lineages into which they were divided.[79] The second was the greater care, also noted earlier, which families took in their marriage strategy. The status-consciousness that exclusionary legislation sharpened made the pedigree of mothers more important than ever before. Thus, recording the maiden names of Balla d'Oro candidates' mothers— precisely the sort of thing to discourage marriage with nonpatrician women—began only in the early 1430s.[80] But considerations of status dovetailed into more concrete calculations in matrimonial decision making: in a noble-dominated social and political order, prosperity—even economic survival—required the support of other nobles, in the business arena of the Rialto and, ever more insistently in the Quattrocento, in the office-seeking, privilege-gaining politics of the Ducal Palace, where success was measured in the votes of cooperative fellow patricians. As we have observed at length, marital kin were a dependable resource; and in the circumstances of the fifteenth century special care was taken, as soaring dowry levels show, to procure the most influential and substantial ones available and then to harness them as tightly as possible to the family interest.

Finally, the third consequence of the patriciate's restrictive actions turns us away from kinship and toward a broader aspect of the patrician regime. It is the ruling class's governmental orientation. The patriciate had affirmed its essentially political character a century earlier, when Great Council membership was made the substance of hereditary noble status. But the governmental action of the decades around 1400 bound nobles more tightly than ever to the government that was the key to their exclusive status and the benefits, notably that of lucrative government service, which it conferred. In this environment, the primary significance of lineage and kinship ties lay in the support that patricians got from their kinsmen in securing the now more urgently sought political advantages of their status.[81] The Balla d'Oro is the perfect symbol and a focal institution of this quintessentially political patrician order. It gave a formal stamp to nobles' patrician identity. It demonstrated the government's determining role in bestowing that identity. It led directly to the Great Council membership that gave nobles their political franchise. And it summoned and reinforced the wide-ranging kinship ties that underlay the patriciate's fundamental political coherence.

Political Adulthood

IN AUGUST 1482, a sixty-one-year-old Venetian patrician named Piero Priuli climaxed more than three decades in the government of his city by gaining election as a *procuratore di San Marco,* an office in Venice's hierarchy of distinctions second only to the highest office, the dogeship itself. Even though Piero was not the most prominent of patricians (or nobles, as they called themselves), he had earned this honor after a career marked by numerous posts of responsibility. Specializing in fiscal matters, he had served a term as one of the three Avogadori di Comun, or state attorneys, and had sat on the Forty, Venice's highest court. His abilities (or connections) were strong enough to get him elected to the Forty when he was only twenty-nine years old, necessitating a six-month wait until he reached the statutory age of thirty before he could take his place on the bench.[1] But Piero Priuli's political distinctions, especially his election as an *avogadore di comun,* have an ironic twist that directs attention to some important but little-noted features of the patrician regime of Renaissance Venice. For his start in government was decidedly inauspicious. On 26 August 1442, when Piero was only twenty-one, he and twenty-six other young nobles shocked the Great Council, seat of government and preserve of the hereditary patriciate, by bursting out of the chamber and rushing down the stairs outside, sweeping along with them an *avogadore di comun* who had been guarding the council door. The "insolence and temerity" of these riotous young men, all but one under the age of thirty and three-quarters twenty-six or younger, clearly merited punishment. At the insistence of the offended *avogadore,* normal criminal procedures were suspended and the young "delinquents" tried and sentenced on the spot. For the "ignominy" their behavior had brought to the government and particularly to the Avogaria di Comun, Piero and his exuberant young companions were banished from council meetings for six months and given fines of 50 lire each.[2]

The coupling of Piero Priuli's involvement in the fracas of 1442 with his later political career, distinguished as it was by the Avogaria di Comun and the Procuratia di San Marco, raises questions about the vaunted patrician political discipline that contemporaries and many writers since have seen as the key to the remarkable governmental stability that set Venice apart from the more turbulent states of Renaissance Italy and which forms the substance of the famous "myth of Venice."[3] This apparent anomaly calls for an explanation of the practical efforts by the regime to make such discipline last, beginning with the conditions under which young nobles were integrated into the governmental activity of their class and educated in its political principles. An inquiry into the politics of Renaissance Venice, specifically, an investigation of the process by which young patricians reached political adulthood in the fifteenth century, can help to elucidate certain connections that remain unexplored in our picture of Venetian politics: the connections between Venice's reputation for orderly government and the youthful unruliness in the council chamber; between the marked favor the regime gave to age and experience and the persistent and sometimes prominent presence of young men on the political scene; and, fundamentally, between the turbulent antics of the young and legislation in the fifteenth century which spelled out the political ideology of the regime. Investigation of these issues reveals the influential presence in Venetian politics of that ethnographic staple, the rite of passage. It also reveals in Venice, as other research has discovered elsewhere in late medieval and early modern Europe, the importance of the symbolic and monitory role of the young in reinforcing the values of a society. And, in a special way, it casts light on the significance of the liminal, or threshold, period of young adulthood in the articulation of the patrician political ideology.[4]

The melee of 1442 was far from the only episode of youthful shenanigans in the Great Council. Four years later, another group of patricians— eleven this time, all but two of them younger than twenty-five—threw the council into an uproar with another hasty departure. In 1460, forty-one "nobiles juvenes" burst out of the chamber, once again buffeting, with "maximum impetum," the *avogadore* guarding the door. These clamorous events, in their "violent fury" (as the indictment of 1460 put it), offended the government's dignity.[5] But though the most spectacular, they were not the only youthful floutings of orderly procedure. In 1443, the year after the unseemly flight of Piero Priuli and company, "a multitude of noble boys" who had no business being in the chamber disrupted elections by chatting with voting members. Invasion of the council by underage nobles was a perennial problem; in 1449, they even presumed to cast electoral ballots. The chronic misbehavior of youngsters was so serious that in 1474 the council doubled the penalties levied on "noble youths" who brazenly flouted their suspensions for previous misdeeds and "disobediently and presumptuously" attended sessions.[6]

These episodes leave no doubt about the presence of youths in the fifteenth-century Great Council, the records of which speak plainly of the "noble youths" or even "noble boys" whose antics disrupted sessions.[7] Closer examination underscores how young they were. It is possible to determine the ages of sixty-one of the seventy-nine nobles who fled the council chamber in the eruptions of 1442, 1446, and 1460. Unlike the bothersome underage visitors, these nobles were all qualified members of the council. Yet fifty were twenty-eight years of age or younger and fully half were still in their early twenties.[8] In a political class famous for favoring age and experience in its officials, a large cohort of young men nevertheless took part in the affairs of government. For example, when the Great Council met to elect a new doge, an exercise from which members under thirty were excluded, voting totals dropped by about 12 percent, an indication that one of every eight of the active council members was in his twenties.[9]

The political participation of young men was not limited to meetings of the Great Council. Though suspended from government business for six months, Piero Priuli and his disorderly mates returned to plunge into active involvement in affairs of state. Two years after joining in the uproar of 1442, the young patrician Paolo Zane was elected to the high court of the Forty (Quarantia); the same honor went to Luca Pisani two years after he fled the chamber in the disturbance of 1446. Piero Balbi, one of the fugitives of 1460, was given in 1462 the frontline assignment of captain of the Venetian garrison at Brescia.[10] These three were not exceptional. In a group of fifteen young men involved in the three episodes (members of a sample of 1,065 men from sixteen patrician houses who entered adulthood in the fifteenth century and whose political careers I am analyzing in detail),[11] twelve went on to hold elective office, eight gaining election to the Forty, among other important offices.[12] Six had already held minor posts before their flight, in most cases, civil court advocacies earmarked for men in their early twenties.[13]

Participation of youths in government is a seldom noted but intriguing feature of the Venetian patrician regime. Why, given young men's "scant sense of the Great Council's dignity," as the indictment of 1442 read, were men under thirty not simply excluded from the council altogether and disqualified from the responsible posts that many later filled? The idea had precedent and support. The council barred members in their twenties from ducal elections, and at least one commentator, the bilious Domenico Morosini, proposed in the 1490s shutting men under forty out of governmental deliberations.[14] Yet far from closing the doors to the young, the patrician regime continued to welcome even twenty-year-olds into the council and thus into political life and gave its youthful members, even ones recently guilty of bringing "ignominy to the regime," important jobs in governmental service. To understand the forgiving nature of the regime and assess the place of young men in patrician politics, one must keep in mind that the patriciate was a multiform structure. It possessed several parts: a public governmental dimension (the patriciate as a political class); a scattered, multifamilial, multilineage social dimension; and a cultural dimension of values and symbols that gave it unity and coherence. All three of these were molded by a fourth dimension, the chronological, in which the patriciate reached a major turning point toward the end of the fourteenth century and beginning of the fifteenth.[15] The integration of young nobles into political adulthood illuminates each of these dimensions and cannot be fully understood without reference to them all.

FIRST, THE PERSPECTIVE of government can be understood partly as a result of its huge growth in this period. From the late fourteenth century, the state was involving itself in an ever widening range of political, economic, and, especially, social concerns. Among examples of social concerns were policies to regulate marriage, dowries, and display; to tighten control over corporate bodies such as the *scuole*, or religious confraternities; and to oversee the activities of the *compagnie della calza*, young patrician social groups that were just beginning to form in the fifteenth century.[16] Since fewer and fewer areas of social activity escaped state intervention, it is not surprising that the government wanted young nobles in the council chamber, where authorities could keep an eye on them and, when necessary, discipline them for their excesses. Youthful misbehavior in the council was tiresome, even outrageous, but it was preferable to having young men turn their energies to still more disruptive or even sinister purposes away from increasingly sharp-eyed official scrutiny.

Young patricians were swept up in another aspect of state growth: a massive increase in governmental activity by nobles. By the mid-fifteenth century, the number of offices in the state administration had swollen to more than twice that of a century earlier: 286 posts in the 1450s against 141 in the 1350s.[17] According to the diarist Marino Sanudo, writing in the 1490s, out of a population of 2,600 male nobles, close to one-third, some 800, were serving in government posts at any one time.[18] The increased opportunities for government service pleased many individual patricians whose interests were served. But, inevitably, some of the new jobs held little appeal. The result was a recurrent problem of men avoiding onerous or unrewarding posts, however necessary the offices may have been as cogs in the expanding bureaucratic machinery. Among the government's solutions were the carrot of bigger stipends and the stick of sanctions for electees unwilling to serve.[19] A third and more appealing solution was to name younger members of the Great Council to these low-level jobs, an arrangement that also served practical and ideological ends. These young men would hold apprenticeships in government and take their socializing first steps up the political *cursus honorum*—or, as we shall see, *lucrorum*.[20]

In practice, young nobles were not always willing to serve their time patiently at the bottom of the ladder. Most perforce did so, but some hankered after better-paying, more influential, or more prestigious posts. In 1433, for instance, this ambition spawned a clandestine caucus of thirty-four young patricians who organized into a voting bloc to elect themselves to desirable offices. Complaints about young men usurping posts reserved for their elders run like a bright thread through fifteenth-century legislation, as the council strove perennially to tighten the enforcement of age requirements for different offices.[21] The impatience of young patricians to get beyond tiresome, poorly paid posts and their frustration at being confined to them may have triggered the eruptions out of the council chamber by Piero Priuli and other youths. Although patricians in their twenties may not have liked the role reserved to them in the government, this service did have one important effect: it taught them to direct their ambitions toward the formal political arena that gave the patrician regime its structure.

The tug-of-war between older and younger rivals for choice offices shows that, for adult patricians of all ages, governmental expansion was less a burden to be borne than an opportunity to be ardently and competitively grasped. In this aspect of government, the patrician monopoly of political activity intersected with the private interest of family and lineage. If the state had its reasons for patiently and tolerantly easing young men into political life, the families also had theirs. From the late fourteenth century, the families came increasingly to depend on the tangible benefits of membership in the ruling class. Economic strains from the mid-fourteenth century onward had caused hardship for nobles, as for other Venetians. But hardship became desperation under the economic impact of the war of Chioggia against Genoa and its allies (1378–81). To sustain the war effort and fight off the Genoese besiegers at the very edge of the Venetian lagoon, the government remorselessly raided the holdings of nobles and citizens alike with forced loans throughout the war years. These exactions had a devastating effect, producing, in Gino Luzzatto's phrase, an upheaval in private—including patrician—wealth.[22] Even worse, long-term pressures choking off traditional economic activities, especially in the Levantine trade, deprived beleaguered nobles of opportunities to recover in the marketplace. The economic distress produced two important results: a governmental policy of providing economic assistance to needy patricians and patrician selfishness about sharing that assistance.

In the 1380s, the government instituted a welfare state for hardpressed nobles. One component directly addressing the fiscal woes pressing on many patrician families was leniency for truly needy men who fell behind in their impost payments. Nobles who proved genuine insolvency could spare themselves the loss, mandated by earlier legislation, of their noble privileges.[23] The government increased the opportunities for nobles to gain appointments as crossbowmen on state-run merchant vessels, posts that offered the poorer young nobles free passage to distant ports of call where they could make a little money by trading.[24] But the principal form of governmental succor, serving patricians of all ages, was political office. Most scholarly discussion of government posts as noble poor relief has focused on the late fifteenth century.[25] But as early as the 1380s, the Great Council wished to spread the benefits of office throughout the class and asserted its responsibility to provide for needy nobles by giving them political jobs.[26] It even frankly accepted that some minor posts were the monopoly of "our poorer nobles," who depended on them to support their families; the council therefore raised the stipends of these offices to make them adequate to family needs.[27] From the late fourteenth century on, patrician reliance on political office was an abiding concern of government, which throughout the fifteenth century responded with legislation that expanded office-holding opportunities for nobles.[28]

The combination of noble dependence on political office and the increased readiness of the government to provide positions marked a new stage for Venice's ruling class. The implications of a large dependent nobility extend to wide areas of Venice's history in the fifteenth century, not least to the expansionist push that made Venice a mainland power.[29] But a more immediate effect appeared in the beginnings of a new exclusivism, which was expressed in new measures to fix the patriciate's membership and give new precision to patrician status. In the decades around 1400, a wave of legislation completed the definition of the Venetian ruling elite which had been outlined a century earlier in the so-called Serrata, or closing, of the Great Council.[30] The new measures now spelled out in detail what patrician status was, who had it, and how it was to be demonstrated. In addition to meeting the basic patrilineal qualification put in place shortly after 1300, claimants to noble status had to satisfy government investigators about the legitimacy of their birth and even the social standing of their mothers.[31] The council devised elaborate new procedures for presenting noble credentials and increased fines for would-be nobles who failed the tests.[32] Reflecting the new rigor, the Avogadori di Comun, who had the principal responsibility for testing claims to patrician status, began in the 1380s to investigate these claims more assiduously and to deny accreditation more frequently than before.[33] The tightening continued throughout the fifteenth century, culminating in the early 1500s in laws requiring registration of noble births and marriages in what were known as the Golden Books, the Libri d'Oro, of the patriciate.[34] Exclusivism was a consequence of nobles' increased dependence on the benefits that their status brought them. Eager to limit the roster of potential competitors, they undertook to limit the size of the patriciate.[35] At the same time, they sought to dignify their entitlement to benefits by tightening the pedigree requirements of noble status, as in the legislation disqualifying sons of lowborn women. Raising the barriers against interlopers, these measures also contributed to the emergence of a caste mentality. Men whose economic shakiness made them rely on public welfare in the form of public office asserted their special genealogical qualifications for office, thus giving their dependence a cloak of dignity.[36]

Young patricians became the focus of this sharpened sense of status and the instruments of their families' enjoyment of its advantages. On the practical level, having sons in the Great Council added to the voting power of a family, enhancing its position in the electoral exchange of favors which, as Robert Finlay has recently illustrated, occupied ambitious adult patricians.[37] Once in the council, the young men themselves became candidates for office, potential conduits between their families and the government's paymaster. Young council members also strengthened the social position of their families by the appeal their political enfranchisement gave them as prospective sons-in-law.[38] If the government encouraged young nobles to enter political life in order to oversee them, socialize them, and place them in low-level posts, the families had a complementary material interest in ensuring that the young men qualified for political office. The bread-and-butter motives that united government and family in promoting the political adulthood of young patricians are only part of the story, however. In the fifteenth century, the role of young nobles transcended practical considerations, as they became the principal focal point of the new self-consciousness that marked the increasingly castelike patriciate. Cogs in the state machinery and instruments of family strategy, patrician youths were also the symbols of a new patrician culture that found its quintessential expression in an elaborate ritual of passage into political adulthood.

Like the classic rite of passage first outlined by Arnold van Gennep, the ascent of Venetian nobles into full adulthood was made up of three stages.[39] Starting with separation from adolescence and ending with incorporation into full-fledged political adulthood, young nobles spent an intermediate period corresponding to what van Gennep and his followers call the "liminal" or "threshold" phase. The peculiar characteristics of the liminal phase help put into perspective the antics of Piero Priuli and other young patricians in the Great Council and make clearer the part played by the young in the sharpening of the patrician ideology. The role of young men in reminding society of its basic values is a theme dealt with from a variety of perspectives in recent writing. For Victor Turner, liminal youths, collectively denied the attributes of full membership in society while undergoing education in its most sacred values, become, in their liminal purity, in their very incapacity to partake of the divisive concerns of their elders, the beacons of those values.[40] In the European context, Natalie Davis observes French youths, detached from the marital and occupational circumstances that led their elders to violate cultural norms, restating those norms in their ceremonial processions and charivaris, reaffirming rule by misrule.[41] Most closely related to the Venetian case, Florentine youths are seen by Richard Trexler as "ritual objects" on whose liminal innocence Florentines reposed their hopes for the "preservation, even salvation, of the natural and civil order."[42] These insights help put Venetian coming-of-age practices into a broader historical and ethnographic perspective. But the elaboration of those practices and the attitudes they reflect find their greatest significance in the context of the evolving patrician political and social order in the early Renaissance.

The passage to adulthood began with an exercise that formally took a young man out of the ranks of the *adolescentes* and established his legitimate noble birth.[43] This exercise was his registration for the Balla d'Oro, or Barbarella. A lottery for young nobles who had reached age eighteen, the Barbarella enabled winners to take their hereditary places in the Great Council at twenty instead of waiting until they turned twenty-five, the age at which all men with approved credentials could enter the council.[44] The Barbarella's original purpose, as stated in the instituting act of 1319, was to provide an orderly alternative to elections as the means of selecting council members; this act, together with another of 1323, established patrilineal heredity as the keystone of the patrician regime.[45] We do not know much about the Balla d'Oro in the fourteenth century, as it was not important enough for presiding officials to keep records of it. A decree of 1356 calling for a fine of 200 lire for registrants under eighteen nonetheless indicates the eagerness at this time of some families to hurry sons into the council.[46] Only after 1400, however, did individual and collective concerns merge to make the Barbarella the principal point of departure for the passage to patrician adulthood. The new collective interest in the Balla d'Oro was proclaimed in a Great Council act of 1414 which dressed it up with elaborate registration procedures and prescribed for the first time careful record keeping of registrations. The rationale for the new rigor was stated in the preamble. Membership in the patriciate was a "most solemn benefit," so solemn that unworthy men who "blemished" the patriciate by entering the Great Council under false pretenses endangered the "conservation of the state and the honor of the regime." Therefore, in view of recent episodes of encroachment, the adoption of new remedies to safeguard the purity of the patriciate was imperative.[47] The language and the vote tally (286 in favor, 22 against, with 13 abstentions) show patrician self-consciousness at a new level of intensity, with governmental mechanisms set in motion as the means of keeping unworthy persons out.

The Balla d'Oro registration procedure became in the fifteenth century the principal checkpoint for protecting patrician status, because fathers, more eager than ever to speed their sons into political life, hastened to sign them up for early admission. The sharpened interest of families in the Barbarella is apparent in the registration trends of 1,065 young men who signed up for the lottery between 1408 and 1497.[48] Between 1408 and 1450, 417 registered; but between 1451 and 1497, the number leaped to 648—an increase of 55 percent. The swelling desire to hurry young men into government shows up even more vividly in a comparison of the periods 1411–30 and 1471–90: during the former, 158 young men signed up; during the latter, nearly twice as many—292 (a 185 percent increase).[49] So powerful a hold did the Barbarella gain on the patriciate that, by midcentury, 85 percent of all nobles who entered the Great Council by whatever means had registered for the lottery, a percentage even more striking considering that the Balla d'Oro was closed to men whose fathers, though eligible, had themselves never joined the council.[50]

The fullest description of the Balla d'Oro is supplied by Marino Sanudo, who wrote about the ceremony in the 1490s.[51] Every 4 December— Saint Barbara's Day, hence "Barbarella"—slips of paper bearing the names of all young men who had proved to the Avogadori di Comun their legitimate patrician birth and attainment of age eighteen were placed into a voting urn (capello). Into a second urn were put a corresponding number of ballot balls, of which one-fifth were gilded. The two urns were set up in the Sala del Collegio of the Ducal Palace, where the doge himself extracted one by one the slips with the names of the registrants while a young boy (ballottino) simultaneously pulled out ballot balls.[52] The young men whose names were called as a golden ball emerged were winners and could enter the council when they turned twenty. The others would try again on subsequent Saint Barbara's Days, until they drew the golden ball, or were elected to one of twenty posts as advocates in the civil courts of the Ducal Palace (which also bestowed council membership on twenty-year-olds), or until they took their hereditary places at age twenty-five.[53] The Balla d'Oro drawing was a solemn occasion, dignified by the participation of the doge, whose charismatic presence signaled its importance among the Venetian civic rituals analyzed with great insight by Edward Muir.[54] The stakes were high for the young participants and their families; on the luck

237 ▸ Political Adulthood

of the draw rode their hopes of quickly expanding the presence of their family in government and adult society. But the deep solemnity of the proceedings—the fixed date, the location in the chamber where the supreme executive body of Venice, the doge and his council, deliberated affairs of state, the presiding presence of the Venetian polity's most august symbol—also had a powerful socializing effect on young men.[55]

The ceremony stimulated the desire of young men to be among the favored one-fifth and surrounded the prize of Great Council membership with a special aura. Testimony from the seventeenth century tells of family festivities celebrating Barbarella victories. In view of the eagerness of fifteenth-century parents to enroll their sons, it is likely that good fortune on 4 December triggered celebrations in that era as well.[56] For those who lost, especially those whose hopes were dashed year after year, a sense of great disappointment stimulated even greater eagerness to gain the prize.[57] The luster that these ritual acts imparted to membership in the Great Council helps to explain the otherwise puzzling spectacle of underage nobles flocking to council meetings. The special aura of early entry also explains why, as Sanudo relates, those forced to wait until age twenty-five to join the council were called the *tristi*.[58] They and their families suffered a diminution of noble dignity by being lumped together with sons of men who, never in the Great Council, had not formally participated in patrician political life. Failure in the Balla d'Oro implied by association a second-class patrician status.[59]

The significance of the Balla d'Oro extended beyond the youthful competitors and their immediate families as well as the solemn lottery of 4 December. The transition ritual actually began with registration in front of the Avogadori di Comun, at which a young man, establishing his legitimate patrician birth and producing evidence that he was eighteen years old, detached himself from youthful society. The procedure was fixed by the regulating act of 1414. Registrants were to be presented by their fathers or, in their absence, by near kinsmen, who were to swear to the *avogadori*, under penalty of fine, that the young men were indeed eighteen years old and legitimately born of patrician fathers.[60] The act says nothing about other participants, but two and sometimes three additional persons normally acted as pledges for payment of possible fines.[61] Although many of these guarantors belonged to the lineage of the candidate's father or mother, nearly two-thirds were members of other patrician houses, indicating that a widening circle of friends, neighbors, patrons, and clients were joining kinsmen in the ritual that officially solemnized the emergence of an adult noble.[62] By the time young patricians turned twenty, then, they had participated in two rituals detaching them from the ranks of adolescents, rituals that impressed on them the desirable dignity of political adulthood and deepened their awareness of and dependence on the community of elders, kinsmen, and others, who guided them into full adult patrician status. It was during the period of liminality inaugurated by these ritual moments that young men gave themselves over to boisterous episodes. The connection between these facts brings us closer to the role of young men in the patrician regime.

THE YOUTHFUL DISORDERS in the Great Council provoked indignant retribution. But once the heat of the moment cooled, the mature majority of members followed a benign policy toward liminal youths, continuing to admit men in their early twenties to council membership and, as noted, fully rehabilitating the disorderly among them. The patriciate, as a collective regime and as individual families, willingly endured bumptious youthful outbursts in order to inculcate in the young the centrality of politics for the ruling class and, specifically, the disposition toward government service.[63] The youthful excesses exceeded in the right direction— toward the institutional politics centered in the Great Council, politics that gave the ruling class its distinctive identity and apportioned the advantages in it. The toleration shown to unruly young members of the Great Council contrasts with the fierce reaction to the bloc-voting plot of 1433, as a comparison of penalties makes clear: Piero Priuli and the other youths who burst out of the chamber in 1442 were each fined 50 lire and deprived of council membership for six months, the same penalty that fell on their counterparts of 1446, while those of 1460 were simply given the six-month suspension and the threat of a 100-lire fine for each time they showed up during that period.[64] Though mild, the penalty of exclusion from council business is an additional indication that council membership had value for young men. The conspirators of 1433, in contrast, received sentences ranging from three-year suspensions of membership in the Great Council to outright banishment from Venice for ten years and perpetual loss of the right to hold office.[65] The difference is striking. Misbehavior in the council chamber was offensive, even disgraceful. But it was far less heinous than electoral conspiracies by the young away from official scrutiny—away, that is, from the socializing arena of the Great Council, where the adult majority was able, for its various purposes public and private, to orchestrate the process of political coming-of-age.

Once having turned twenty-five, young men, whether or not they had been unruly, were quickly drawn into governmental responsibilities. In the great majority of cases studied, nobles in politics won their first elective posts before turning thirty.[66] Indeed, the careers of men under thirty give the impression that pent-up expectations propelled them into government service as soon as they had overcome the age barrier, with many men winning their first elections at twenty-five.[67] Just as the long, elaborate transition to adulthood began with the ritual of registration for the Balla d'Oro, so it ended with a formal ceremony at which the electee provided evidence, often in the form of testimony by other nobles, that he had reached office-holding age and could assume his new post.[68] These proofs of eligibility for office, like Balla d'Oro registrations, were only ordered into careful procedures and recorded by the presiding officials in the early fifteenth century, another sign of the new concern with age, birth, and office which was giving a fixed shape to the political ideology of the nobility.[69] Although the proofs marked the act of incorporation into formal political adulthood and the completion of the liminal period, they did not end age-based political restrictions. Robert Finlay has discussed in detail the higher age requirements for higher posts (also documented in the proof-of-age registers).[70] The presence of men older than twenty-five among the conspirators of 1433 and the disrupters of 1442, 1446, and 1460 shows that frustration over limits on the political opportunities for patricians under thirty could galvanize energies on both sides of the twenty-five-year-old age divide. Efforts of nobles over twenty-five to falsify their ages to gain higher office—sometimes by picturesquely devious ruses—also testify to frustrated aspirations for office lasting beyond the liminal period.[71]

A graduated liminality was built into the Venetian political system, as it is in all systems with different age requirements along the *cursus honorum*. The principal aims of the government in reserving certain posts for experienced officeholders were to ensure competence in officials and to direct office stipends to the fathers of families who had special need of them.[72] At the same time, by introducing men into office holding while still denying them positions of prestige, power, or remuneration, the government kept alive an impatience that bore some resemblance to the rambunctious eagerness of the young men in the liminal period between Balla d'Oro registration and the first governmental post.

But eagerness for preferred posts is fundamentally different from restiveness over the complete denial of office-holding eligibility. Ambition among men qualified for office, even those between twenty-five and thirty, belongs more to the steady rumble of electioneering that lay at the heart of noble politics than to the liminal cohort's enforced wait for office. Once having crossed the barrier to eligibility for election, members of politically ambitious or economically needy families were inevitably drawn into competing family strategies and factional maneuvering.[73] Although the exuberance of men in their late twenties gave a lively aspect to their contribution to family striving, and their exclusion from ducal elections reminded them of the limits on their role in the political process, once elected to their first office, they became part of the governmental structure and lost the sense of shared anomaly which united men still short of their twenty-fifth birthday, men who could participate in the political process by voting for officials but were denied the full political status of the men for whom they cast ballots.

The contrast between the solidarity that characterizes members of liminal groups and the divisions that run through adult society figures prominently in recent writing on rites of passage, notably that of Victor Turner. The essential trait of liminal groups, for Turner, is their lack of clear status, their ambiguous passage through "a cultural realm with few or none of the attributes of the past or coming state."[74] Though held back from full membership, neophytes are nevertheless expected to spend the liminal period learning the principles of the mature state into which they will ultimately pass. Lacking a precise status and constantly reminded of their inferiority to their elders, liminal youths develop a strong sense of community, marked by "intense comradeship and egalitarianism."[75] Two qualities, internal solidarity and exclusion from full membership in the culture whose principles the youths are learning, are for Turner the basis of the liminal group's special character and function.

It is precisely the freedom of liminal youths from, in S. N. Eisenstadt's words, the "compromises inherent in daily participation in adult life" which, paradoxically, equips them to serve, as the "purest manifestation and repository of ultimate cultural and societal values."[76] To see how this pattern fits Venetian young men on the threshold, it is important to take note of the tendency of recent writers on patrician politics to view the patriciate as being divided on many levels.[77] On the level of daily life and elementary interests, competition for offices occupied government councils throughout the fifteenth and sixteenth centuries. It led to a steady stream of acts aimed at eliminating fraudulent devices by which officials clung to their posts (and continued to draw their stipends) beyond their legal term, impeding the equitable distribution of offices throughout the class.[78] Recent scholarship has taken an increasingly sophisticated approach to the connection between this general desire for government posts and the maneuverings of interest groups and power blocs within the patriciate, stressing the crucial role of a restricted political and economic oligarchy at the center and the relations of its members with one another and with their clients among the less wealthy and influential nobles on the fringes.[79] The precise geology of these divisions remains to be plotted, especially the crucial question of whether a family's membership in the dominant group lasted over generations. An answer will require patient research of great ingenuity. But enough is now known to reject the old characterization of the patriciate as monolithic. In the present state of knowledge, it is not possible to gauge precisely the degree to which common liminality created solidarity among young men which might have overcome the divisions among their fathers. That measurement would require a comparison of the interactions of the young men with the relations among their elders in the adult patriciate, a task impossible at present because of the lack of systematic prosopographical research that could reveal which families were powerful and rich, which were needy and ripe for clientism or manipulation.[80]

But there is one test that can be applied, a test based on distinctions of antiquity, which asks whether young members of Venice's oldest noble houses, the *case vecchie*, mingled in liminal fellowship with their contemporaries from houses of more recent nobility, the *case nuove*. In the fifteenth century, the two groups were engaged in a tense, sometimes conflict-marked struggle over preeminence in the government, symbolized by the dogeship.[81] The importance of these alignments should not be overstated; they did not carve a deep fissure through the patriciate. Like other intraclass distinctions, they marked off for certain issues antagonists who consorted amicably in other equally important contexts.[82] Yet, since the distinction between the case vecchie and the case nuove (or, alternatively, between the *longhi* and the *curti*) was one recognized by contemporaries as a source of tension within the class, it permits a test of the communitarian spirit of liminal young men. The test reveals that disrupters of the Great Council, office-seeking conspirators, and even members of the youthful social fraternities known as the *compagnie della calza* came from all points on the genealogical spectrum, from the most ancient of noble families to those accorded patrician status as recently as 1381.[83]

Young patricians, forbidden to trespass onto the adult battlefields on which were mobilized snobberies, resentments, and conflicting interests, were able to find in one another's company, if not solidarity, at least a fellowship of youthful patterns of behavior with which they responded collectively to the restrictions placed on their adulthood—restrictions based not on antiquity, wealth, or family prominence but on the age they had in common. Indeed, it is tempting to see in the restrictions of the threshold period a desire on the part of the elders to keep the young unsullied by the conflicts that animated the patriciate. But, equally likely, limitations reflected an adult consensus that young men, if permitted active participation in the political give-and-take, threatened to go beyond acceptable limits of political activity—to organize office-seeking cabals such as that of 1433.[84] Young men needed the socialization into patrician politics acquired in a period "on the threshold," observing the process, competing for prizes such as the Barbarella victory, swallowing disappointment at missing them and at having to wait still longer, even—like Piero Priuli and his comrades—taking out their frustrations in boisterous antics in the council chamber. They needed, in short, a period of directing their youthful energies toward the increasingly clearly focused public and private vocations of patrician politics.

The role of the young in the political culture of the patriciate encompassed more than the socializing transition to political manhood. As protagonists of the ritual process that elucidated the stages and nature of patrician adulthood, young men served as symbolic embodiments of the patriciate's evolving definition of itself as a ruling class. Rivalries and antagonisms continued, inevitably, to cause tensions within the fifteenth-century patriciate, but they faded in the light of the newly articulated, collective commitment of the class to preserving an exclusive hold on the political vocation, with its duties and benefits. The tests the young men of the fifteenth-century patriciate were obliged to pass, the restrictions they had to endure, the prizes now more systematically bestowed on them, and the satisfying conclusion of their long transition to full noble status expressed for the patriciate a clear, new, and precise definition of itself.

THE TWO ELEMENTS at the core of patrician status in the fifteenth century were public office and exclusivism—public office to satisfy practical needs both governmental and private, exclusivism to prevent diffusion of the benefits of office and to make enjoyment of them the prerogative of a genealogically specific caste. All these aims found institutional expression in the lengthy process by which male patricians passed from youth to adulthood. It was by means of the increasingly elaborate set of rituals that began, enlivened, and ended the liminal period that men established their identity as nobles and gained the political orientation essential to that identity. In articulating the steps to patrician adulthood, the rituals crafted by legislation after 1400 gave the patriciate as a whole its first opportunity to state its ideology. The punishments meted out to Piero Priuli and the other young disturbers of the council and their swift re-habilitation into patrician political life can be seen as opportunities pro-vided by the peculiar impulses of liminal youths for the patriciate to assert the dimensions of its status. Decorum, respect for officialdom, bow-ing to procedure, observing the limitations on different age levels, and, above all, blending individual interest with the collective purpose—these now emerged as the elements of a patrician ideology that served both public and private needs. A breach of these rules had to be punished. But the punishment itself and the necessity to impose it clarified, for the offending youths and offended adults alike, the principles flouted. At its highest levels, the patrician regime was indeed a gerontocracy, as Robert Finlay has argued. Piero Priuli's election at age sixty-one as a *procuratore di San Marco* exemplifies the predilection for steadiness, gravity, and maturity which characterized Venetian government.[85] But from the per-spective of the development of the patrician regime, Piero's contribution to Venetian government was not limited to his successful conformity to the ideal of mature steadiness. It had its paradoxical beginning forty years earlier, when he and his young companions, in their rowdy fellowship, gave vivid focus to the role of liminal patricians in shaping the political ideology of Renaissance Venice.

Subaltern Patriarchs:
Patrician Bachelors

IN A LANDMARK article of the mid-1970s, Natalie Zemon Davis observed that "[historians] should be interested in the history of both women and men. . . . Our goal is to discover the range in sex roles and in sexual symbolism in different societies and periods, to find out what meaning they had and how they functioned to maintain the social order or to promote its change."[1] Endorsing Davis's suggestion, this chapter explores the connection between two aspects of sex-role relationships in the governing patriciate of fifteenth-century Venice. The first aspect concerns the impact on gender roles of changes in the "social order," specifically in the patriciate's social and political structures, which early in the Quattrocento were modified in ways that implicated gender differentiation among patricians (or nobles). The other aspect concerns the relationship between the "range in sex roles and in sexual symbolism" among the women and that among the men of the patriciate. The hypothesis advanced is that the two aspects are closely connected: that changes in the social order led to changes in the range of gender identity among both women and men.

The principal focus of the investigation is upon differentiation among men, specifically between those who married and those who did not. Out of this focus emerge the two points advanced in the chapter. The first is that patriarchal principles refined during the early Quattrocento as part of the self-definition of the ruling class underscored the anomalous masculine position of bachelors. The second is that the position thus occupied by bachelors overlapped in social practice with that of their married sisters—though within a structure that clearly favored men of whatever marital status. The ambiguous gender placement of unmarried male patricians illustrates the nuance and plasticity to be found along the "range in sex roles and in sexual symbolism" in concrete, evolving historical contexts.[2]

It is important to mention at the outset some ideas that inform the discussion. A critical one is the relativity (or "relationality") of gender: the status and roles of women cannot be understood without concurrent attention to those of men, and the reverse; they are constructed vis-à-vis each other.[3] Those reciprocal influences work on two levels, the institutional and the personal; they can be configured in terms of the dynamic between structure and practice.[4] In the view advanced here, men and women tailor their practical actions with reference not only to structural definitions of gender behavior but also to their particular flesh-and-blood experience of the opposite sex. Laws and customs officially prescribed the elements of masculine and feminine identity in Venice. In practice, however, conformity with those prescriptions was mediated by the manifold contingencies in the interactions of individual men and women, with each other and with the laws and customs. It was through this double experience of gender that Venetian patricians constituted, or had constituted for them, their gender identities.[5]

Because both the institutional and the personal dimensions of gender were shaped by the circumstances of a specific historical context, they were subject to change as the context evolved over time. The laws and customs that prescribe how men and women are to act are constantly being revised in response to changes in the political, economic, social, and religious environment.[6] The revisions in turn lead men and women to adapt their actions and relationships to the altered gender structures—whether in conformity with them or in deviation from them.[7] This sequence seems likely to occur most dramatically in moments of major cultural change, such as the Renaissance is traditionally considered to be. Historians are still in the early stages of formulating a periodization of gender principles and relations in European history, and there is much disagreement among them. But that the status of women, the touchstone of gender, went through different stages from the Middle Ages through the early modern period is a matter of consensus.[8] In this chronological exploration, the Renaissance, not surprisingly, is actively contested terrain, with the question first posed in 1976 by Joan Kelly, whether women had a Renaissance, still the pivot of discussion.[9] A useful approach to that encompassing question is to inquire, in inseparable complement to investigation of the experiences of women, whether, which, and how men had a Renaissance.

EARLY RENAISSANCE VENICE is an auspicious context for probing these conceptual and historiographical issues. During the first half of the fifteenth century, a body of legislation was enacted which elaborated with unprecedented precision the structures that defined the ruling class's political and social identity. Those laws profoundly affected sex roles and sexual symbolism by prescribing new behavior and qualifications for both the men and the women of the class.[10] Central to this new articulation of patrician culture was reinforcement of the formal dominance of the father in public and private life. The roles and relationships of all the age and gender groups in noble society were reconstituted on the basis of officially enhanced paternal authority over wives and children. Space limitations permit only a few samples of this legislation, but they convey its flavor. Fathers were now expressly preferred as sponsors of their sons' formal introduction into political life, specifically charged with responsibility for their sons' behavior in public forums, and officially recognized as the parties responsible for providing dowries for daughters.[11] Men elected to office were to be identified with their patronymic.[12] Fathers and husbands were held responsible for restraining sumptuary excesses by their daughters and wives.[13]

The intensification of formal paternal authority in the fifteenth century built on a centuries-old tradition.[14] Yet, although they were the supreme figures in public and private life, fathers were only the most prominent participants in a broader structure of patriarchy which encompassed all patrician men, whose privileges as hereditary nobles were inseparable from those that accrued from their maleness.[15] The two dimensions of privilege were integral to each other. Nearly every aspect of patrician status celebrated masculinity, starting with its essential entitlement, that of participating in government, an activity reserved to men. Membership in the political class thus entitled depended legally upon one's birth to a father who possessed the same privilege, inherited in turn from his father. Locking it all together was the blending of the paternal legacy and paternal direction in public life with the *patria potestas* in the domestic environment. The dynamic driving patrician culture from generation to generation can thus be seen as the fusion of patriarchal, patrilineal, and patrimonial objectives into a triptych of gender principles which guided, by blending, the domestic and official worlds of the governing class.

The pivotal role of fathers in this dynamic had been crucial to patrician politics and society from the first official articulation of the hereditary principle in 1323.[16] However, the enforcement of the principle in administrative practice appears to have occurred only gradually, in response to changing historical circumstances and reaching maturity only around 1400.[17] The definitive steps in the functional implementation of heredity were laws enacted in 1414 and 1430, which instituted procedures for checking the genealogical credentials of claimants to noble status and enjoined the officials charged with conducting the procedures thenceforward to keep careful records of them. From those laws, which expressly required that young men claiming noble status be presented by their fathers for the official scrutiny, derive the first official lists of the patriciate's membership, based on uniform tests of qualification and inscribing the father-son link in the public documentation of the regime.[18]

The laws also mandated notation of the names of the mothers of the young claimants to noble status, as part of a campaign against liaisons between patrician men and women from the lowest classes. Indeed, mothers are identified, by given name and natal surname, in the records from this time forward. The emphasis on the status of mothers shows that married noblewomen also were acquiring a new symbolic importance as part of their class's effort to achieve a castelike distinctiveness in the early Quattrocento.[19] The formal effect, however, was to reinforce the status of their husbands and sons. Wellborn wives and mothers were means of enhancing the dignity of the men entitled to govern Venice today and those who would inherit the government tomorrow, by patrimonial and patrilineal succession. Thus, the institutional reformulation of the patriciate's public status was achieved by increased governmental direction of private behavior, by means of the enlarged authority officially bestowed on fathers to enforce the conformity of their womenfolk and children to the requirements of the class regime.

All these elements made the patriarchal husband and father the ideal type in patrician culture. The symbolic grandeur of patrician husbandhood was vividly displayed every year on Ascension Day in the feast of the Sensa. With lavish pageantry, the doge renewed Venice's "eternal dominion" over the Adriatic by ritually marrying it, thereby underscoring the authority of the patriarchal father in the blending of public and private life which was the essence of patrician culture.[20] The redoubtable image of the patrician father is beautifully rendered in the treatise *De re uxoria*, written in 1415–16 by the young patrician humanist Francesco

Barbaro and recently elucidated by Margaret King.[21] In brief, Barbaro held that the ultimate purpose of marriage among nobles was the continuance and prosperity of the regime. The excellence of the individual patrician, what gave him, or her, moral identity as a noble, lay in the integration of individual pursuits and family purpose into the broader aims of the nobility as a whole. Both fathers and mothers played important roles in the lofty enterprise of raising their children into this ideal, but it was the father specifically who, in Barbaro's words, should command and his wife who should cheerfully obey.[22] Barbaro thus invested patriarchal authority with a moral dignity carrying powerful sociopolitical resonance, which paralleled and complemented the legislation then refining the public culture of the noble regime. Fatherly primacy in public and private life was conveyed with special pointedness to the young men whose disciplining in the present and whose preparation for the patriarchal responsibilities of the next generation constituted one of the foremost duties of paternal authority.

The symmetry between Francesco Barbaro's ideal formulation of fatherhood and the principles of official patrician culture is attested in reverse in a treatise written six decades later by his grandson, Ermolao Barbaro. Consciously written as a mirror image of Francesco's *De re uxoria,* Ermolao's *De coelibatu* praised not the married state that merged with public duty but rather an ideal of bachelorhood which rejected it.[23] Ermolao preferred bachelorhood—strict celibacy, in fact—in the first instance because family responsibilities distracted the scholar from his learning. But equally important was his recognition, like that of his uxorious grandfather, that husbandhood and fatherhood in patrician reality entailed the relentless demands of public service as part of the seamless structure of patriarchal duty.

ERMOLAO BARBARO'S unwillingness to conform to the ideal of the male noble ultimately led him to put his personal conviction on the score into practice by casting off his Venetian birthright. His dissent directs us to the matter of an alternative masculine identity among nobles.[24] Ermolao dramatized his choice by associating an apatriarchal manhood with a non-Venetian manhood. But there were other patrician men who, like Ermolao, did not marry, head households, or propagate and educate the next generation of noble patriarchs but who, unlike him, remained in Venice living active lives as nobles. What was the relationship of those bachelors to the patriarchal paradigm? Were they denied it? Did they themselves deny its dignity by rejecting it? Or were they able to break the Barbaros' linkage by taking a productive part in the public and private life of the noble regime? These questions have implications for more than just the matter of masculine gender identity in a culture that celebrated the integrated private and public roles of the patriarch. Assessing the male periphery of patriarchy inevitably carries over into the significance of female identity in the unified structure of patrician gender relations. The pages that follow make a start in grappling with the seeming paradox of patriarchal bachelorhood by exploring it with specific reference to the chief locus of public life for patrician men in Venice, government service, from which all women were excluded absolutely.

A compelling reason for studying unmarried men is that there were so many of them: nearly half of male nobles who reached adulthood in the fifteenth century appear to have remained bachelors. To be precise, of 952 men from sixteen clans whose entry into adulthood can be documented, 412 (43.3%) apparently never married.[25] That is a striking percentage in a culture that assigned great dignity and importance to fatherhood, and it raises the first question: What accounts for such widespread deviation from a norm tied so eloquently and with so many practical advantages to the well-being of family and regime? The first part of an answer must be that some men did not marry because they did not live long enough to do so.[26] But among those who lived, some undoubtedly chose not to marry. There was only one Ermolao Barbaro, but in the fifteenth century growing numbers of lesser lights were similarly drawn to undistracted study and contemplation.[27] Another likely motive for elective bachelorhood was a disinclination to marry for sexual reasons. In addition to evidence of homosexual activity disclosed by the research of Patricia Labalme and Guido Ruggiero and Ruggiero's suggestions of a gay subculture, we should allow also for the choice of heterosexual alternatives to the duty-laden role of patrician husband and father.[28] There can be little doubt that some male nobles simply did not want to be patriarchs.

Nevertheless, in view of the celebration, in law, politics, cultural tradition, and new intellectual fashion, of husband- and fatherhood as the culmination of male identity for nobles, the large incidence of bachelorhood must have been the result chiefly of force of circumstance rather than choice. There is reason to see as the principal circumstance the sharpening of patrician self-consciousness around 1400, given force in the legislation noted above. In addition to widening the gap between nobles and the populace, the heavy emphasis that the new laws put on genealogy increased sensitivity to status and advantage within the ruling class. A major consequence was the attachment of heightened importance to intraclass marriage alliances, and thus to marriage settlements, featuring large and growing dowries. At a time when many noble families were confronting shortages of disposable wealth, the rise in dowries propelled by intensified matrimonial ambition took an increasingly heavy bite out of family patrimonies. A Senate act in 1420 aimed at limiting dowries specifically mentioned the hardships that large marriage settlements for daughters were causing other potential heirs, namely, the sons of the fathers amassing them.[29]

Some of the severest hardships hit the marriage prospects of sons from the patrician rank and file. James C. Davis reported that by the mid-sixteenth century, patricians followed the practice of restricted marriage, limiting the number of marriages in a sibling group in order not to disperse the collective patrimony among too many brothers with conjugal families.[30] The same calculus was likely at work in the fifteenth century, applied both to sons and to marriageable daughters. As fathers poured their families' substance into dowries in order to marry their daughters into wealthy and influential families, they thereby reduced the marriage prospects of their sons, because the funneling of the sons' prospective inheritance into their sisters' dowries made them commensurately less appealing as recipients of large dowries themselves. The effect built upon itself. As the language in the dowry-limiting law of 1420 noted, dowry inflation eroded the chances of marriage for some girls even as their sisters' marriage prospects were being enhanced.[31] Diminishing the pool of potential brides, this tendency also made the girls who remained in the pool harder to attain for male nobles of modest circumstances. Outside of the richest and most prestigious families, whose sons were likely to receive the most extravagant marriage settlements, a potential groom's eligibility seems to have rested in part on his brothers' bachelorhood—on, that is, their avoidance, willing or unwilling, of the patrimony-reducing burdens of heading families themselves.

The economics of dowry restitution also worked toward the same end. Because all the members of a fraternal group that had not been legally dissolved were liable for the restitution of the dowry of the wife of any one of them, brothers unencumbered with their own wives assured the fathers of potential sisters-in-law that the husband's family possessed resources adequate to guarantee eventual restitution of the dowry. With so much family treasure going into dowries, fathers of brides not surprisingly sought every assurance that their daughters would recover them at the end of their marriage. For their part, men sought to allay this concern by explicitly pledging their goods toward the restitution of the dowries of their brothers' wives.[32] To the economic motive should be added a potent political one. At a time when many, if not most, noble families depended materially upon the remunerative government posts filled in Great Council elections, parents seeking in their daughter's husband a political ally were likely to regard as especially attractive a potential groom with unmarried brothers. Without wifely affines of their own, those bachelor brothers-in-law might be counted on to lend their supportive votes in the council to the alliances into which their marrying brother had entered.[33]

UNFORTUNATELY, Venetians have not left much information describing their marriage strategies regarding men. Parents occasionally provided "dowries" for their sons, by which they meant property to guarantee restitution of the dowries brought by their wives. But we do not have much beyond such testamentary wishes to go on in reconstructing parental expectations for their sons' marriages.[34] It is possible, however, to make a rough reconstruction of the matrimonial activity of brothers. The following information is based on examination of ninety-one fifteenth-century sibling groups from six clans; I concentrate especially on the seventy-three groups that included at least two brothers.[35]

A couple of features are worth noting which bear upon the circumstances of bachelorhood in the nobility.[36] One is the unsurprising information that size influenced marriageability. The twenty-three fraternal groups in which all the brothers married were small, averaging 2.6 members.[37] By contrast, the forty-five groups in which some brothers married and others remained single averaged a whole brother larger, 3.7 compared with 2.6. This suggests a practice of ensuring the continuation of the line by getting one or two brothers married, then permitting, or requiring, additional brothers to marry as circumstances allowed.[38] The other and, I believe, more interesting feature is that in sixteen (more than one-third) of the forty-five groups consisting of both bachelors and husbands, the eldest brother was not among the ones who married. Although this surprising circumstance needs to be explored in greater prosopographical detail, it suggests that some families observed a discipline in which the firstborn son undertook, or was directed by a living *paterfamilias*, to work toward favorable marital circumstances for his siblings. At the very least, such a practice suggests nuance and complexity in the implementation of the patriarchal ideal among patrician sibling groups—never mind what it says about primogeniture. What is clear is that in nearly 69 percent of the families with several sons, one or more remained unmarried. This is strong evidence that the fraternal collaboration that, according to James Davis, fostered the patrimony-preserving strategy of marriage limitation among patrician sibling groups in the sixteenth century was already serving the same objective in the fifteenth. The cultural-psychological implications of this division of functions are considerable. In the century in which the patriciate fully formulated and enforced its identity as a genealogically precise hereditary ruling class, in more than two-thirds of fraternal groups some brothers were fated to be nonpropagating instruments of domestic patriarchy.

If, however, brothers met opposite destinies in the domestic environment, the divisions were not so clear-cut in political life. Unmarried men took an active part in the governmental activity that was the hallmark of their status as nobles and, according to the articulators of patrician culture, the symmetrical public counterpart to domestic patriarchy.[39] An examination of the political careers of fifty-eight men, members of fraternal groups from three clans, reveals that the 69 percent who married held an average of 4.8 offices. We might expect that of the sons-in-law of families that invested large dowries in their daughters' marriages and which expected a return in the form of support in the councils of government, where the material benefits of patrician status were distributed. What is more intriguing in the patriarchal environment is that the bachelor brothers of these married men averaged 2.7 offices.[40] To look at it from another angle, of the 239 offices accounted for by all the brothers in the sample, one-fifth (48) were held by men who never married. The sample cannot be taken as either representative or unrepresentative, but at least the office-holding record shows that as many as one-fifth of the political posts that were the distinguishing monopoly of this patriarchal governing class were entrusted to men who did not themselves perpetuate their lines or hand a patrimony on to their own sons.[41] Bachelors constituted an important element in patrician government.

Office-holding bachelors, like all nobles, were conscious of their privilege as members of the ruling class, and they surely welcomed the stipends they received from their positions. However, in a parallel of their role in the strategy of the fraternal group, office holding by bachelors also savored of instrumentalization on behalf of the larger community of which they were a second-echelon element. Indeed, their function as government officials may have been an extension of their role within the family: the function, namely, of holding government jobs and casting electoral votes in line with a family interest supervised by their fathers and married brothers. The context of the office holding of bachelors, as of all male nobles, in the fifteenth century is the growing eagerness of families to get their sons into government jobs. The eagerness is evident in an increase of more than 50 percent in the number of young men who registered their noble credentials between the first and second halves of the Quattrocento.[42] Bachelors in the council chambers and in remunerative office may have been especially valuable to their marrying brothers, whose wives' natal relatives likely regarded unmarried male in-laws as potential political allies unburdened with affinal obligations of their own.

Encouraging this instrumental characterization of the governmental role of bachelors is its confinement to the lesser offices in the governmental apparatus. Subordinate contributors to patriarchal domestic strategies, unmarried men were also locked into the lower echelons of the patriciate's official activity. At the most influential levels, the patriarchal paradigm uniting domestic with governmental authority held overwhelming sway. Among seventy-four men from fourteen clans who served between 1438 and 1455 in the Ducal Council, the Senate and its annex (Zonta), or the Council of Ten, only one was a lifetime bachelor.[43] This stark contrast between a husbandly monopoly of the important posts and the sturdy presence of bachelors in the lesser offices may owe something to the possible coincidence of bachelorhood and early death speculated upon earlier; as Robert Finlay has demonstrated, a man had to be mature and seasoned to gain election to the highest offices.[44] It may also owe something to the coincidence of powerful government position and family wealth: Finlay and other scholars have argued that political power in Quattrocento Venice was the preserve of a small oligarchy of wealthy families, of the kind that would have had the prestige and means to marry more sons than their rank-and-file counterparts.[45] Yet, even discounting these factors, the nearly complete confinement of bachelors to posts of modest prestige and power points to bachelorhood as a double liability, signifying a lesser, nonauthoritative male status in both the domestic and the official environments of ruling-class patriarchy.

NEVERTHELESS, from the perspective of "the range in sex roles and in sexual symbolism" across gender lines, the evidence of bachelors' involvement in patrician government encourages a more nuanced reading.

Certainly, with its suggestion of the instrumental inscription of bachelors in family strategy supervised by their married brothers, the seeming exclusion of unmarried men from high office suggests different layers of patriarchal privilege. Here, given the exiguousness of the sample at hand, I can only raise issues to be explored more thoroughly elsewhere. But it is worth recalling that although as many as two-fifths of adult patrician males were bachelors, they accounted for only one-fifth of the offices in the government: not an insignificant proportion, but smaller than their overall presence within male society. The inescapable uncertainty about the life span of the unmarried men cautions against making too much of these proportions. But the discrepancy seems to lend plausibility to the idea that, just as some men consciously rejected domestic patriarchy, some also had a lesser commitment to its official counterpart, their class's political vocation, than did their married brothers. Many more men than just Ermolao Barbaro likely elected not to share in either the public or the private dimension of noble patriarchy. These initial findings suggest that in both the domestic and the governmental arena of patriarchal authority, the experience of bachelors covered a variety of choices and restrictions, from intense commitment to the interests of family and regime to cool, or sometimes assertive, aloofness from them. The unmarried male population ranged from men with active political careers to office-fleeing contemplatives like Ermolao Barbaro. As Ruggiero has suggested, it also included both homosexuals cultivating a subculture of their own and sexual exploiters of the women of the populace.[46] And it probably ran the psychological gamut from economically disqualified patriarchs manqué to men who willingly declined the responsibilities of husband- and fatherhood. More than for the husbands who realized, and were defined by, the patriarchal ideal in domestic and public spheres, for bachelors the denial or rejection of patriarchy could loosen the tethers of conformity to the requirements of mainstream patrician manhood in the same degree that it closed off the highest rewards that the culture reserved for men.

So from the perspective of normative patriarchy, newly articulated in the Quattrocento as the fulcrum by which the patrician regime intensified its identity as an exclusive elite, permanent bachelors may be seen as resembling in certain respects their marrying sisters more than their marrying brothers.[47] Like noble wives, noble bachelors participated in, benefited from, were essential to, but occupied a lesser status in their class's official and domestic culture. Deprived of patriarchal authority— and, indeed, subordinated instruments of its objectives—bachelors and married women alike had less inducement than married men to identify themselves psychologically with the discipline of its requirements. Both categories could therefore construct nuances of identity along a range of possibilities not restricted by the responsibilities of dominance—albeit within parameters enjoined by a patriarchal regime and enforced by individual family heads.[48] For women, the junctions of choice lay between loyalty to natal and to marital family, and in at least some cases between marriage and religious profession.[49] Although the early findings presented here barely scratch the surface of the experience of bachelors, they encourage the hypothesis that it, too, ran a gamut, from active contribution to the purposes of family and regime to token or outright nonparticipation in the domestic and official life of the patriciate.

This is not to say that the agency of either patrician wives or bachelors threatened to subvert or even to deviate significantly from the blended purposes of family and regime. On the contrary, members of both categories could find reasons to associate themselves with their class's values and aims. Mothers especially recognized the great advantages for their children's prospects which derived from adherence to the collective interest and its discipline; bachelors characteristically directed their beneficence toward their families.[50] Nonetheless, both groups deviated from the patriarchal mainstream in sometimes convergent ways; anecdotal evidence, for instance, shows unmarried men sharing the bilateral social orientation of their married sisters as well as supporting the patrilineal aims of their married brothers.[51] Taking it all together, we may ponder the idea that bachelors shared with married patrician women a perpetually liminal status in, and at the same time an instrumental indispensability to, the social, political, and cultural order of the patrician regime.[52]

Yet in the end the similarity must not be overstated. Legal dispositions and customary values had over the centuries dug a yawning gender gulf between women and men whether married or unmarried, a gulf that deepened from around 1400 as public and private life came to be increasingly regulated by official prescriptions, obligations, and definitions, the principal purpose of which was the entrenchment of the noble regime and the families that, benefiting from inclusion in it, accepted the obligation to sustain it. As male participants in this culture, bachelors were obliged to accept some measure of the discipline imposed on all the men in noble lineages, but, in contrast with even the most economically and socially influential women, they also shared in its privileges, material and moral, which legislators and humanist commentators alike reserved to men alone. Serving in government, thereby contributing to the purposes that benefited themselves, their kinsmen, and their regime, these unmarried brothers can be seen as subaltern participants in patriarchy precisely by reason of the uncertain boundary between the public and private dimensions of the culture of this hereditary ruling class. By their activity in government, their instrumental inscription into a familial marital strategy, and their mentoring and economic contributions to the vocations of nieces and nephews, they shared in the patrician masculine identity associated with the integrated values and objectives of the patriarchal lineage in the patriarchal regime.[53]

Manuscript Sources and Abbreviations

APV: Archivio Storico della Curia Patriarcale di Venezia, Sezione Antica

ASV: Archivio di Stato, Venice

AC: ASV, Avogaria di Comun

Barbaro, Nozze: Marco Barbaro, "Libro di nozze patrizie," BMV Ital. VII, 156 (8492)

BMC: Biblioteca del Museo Correr, Venice

BMV Ital. VII: Biblioteca Marciana, Venice, MSS italiani, classe VI¹*

BO: ASV, Avogaria di Comun, Balla d'Oro†

CI: ASV, Cancelleria Inferiore, Notai†

Contratti di nozze: ASV, Avogaria di Comun, Contratti di nozze†

De Giudicato: ASV, Giudici del Proprio, De Giudicato (Diiudicatum)†

Esaminador: ASV, Giudici dell' Esaminador

di: identifying patronymic referring to a living father

Dieci, Comuni: ASV, Consiglio dei Dieci, Deliberazioni Comuni†

Dieci, Misti: ASV, Consiglio dei Dieci, Deliberazioni Miste†

MC: ASV, Maggior Consiglio, Deliberazioni§

NT: ASV, Archivio Notarile, Testamenti†

PE: ASV, Avogaria di Comun, Prove d'età†

Procurator: ASV, Giudici del Procurator

---

*Followed by codex number. ‡Followed by busta number and notary's name.
†Followed by register number. §Followed by register number and name.

Proprio: ASV, Giudici del Proprio

prot.: protocollo

PSMC: ASV, Procuratori di San Marco, Commissarie

qd: abbreviation of *quondam,* identifying patronymic referring to a deceased father

Raspe: ASV, Avogaria di Comun, Raspe[†]

Senato, Misti: ASV, Senato, Deliberazioni Miste[†]

Senato, Terra: ASV, Senato, Deliberazioni Terra[†]

Vadimoni: ASV, Giudici del Proprio, Vadimoni[†]

Voci: ASV, Segretario alle Voci, Universi, serie antica[†]

[†]Followed by register number.

✥ ✥ ✥ ✥ ✥ ✥ ✥ ✥ ✥ ✥ ✥ ✥ ✥ ✥ ✥ ✥ ✥ ✥ ✥ ✥

Notes

Introduction

1. More detailed discussion of the literature in the field can be found in Chaps. 1 and 4.

2. Richard Trexler's pioneering study of monacation in Florence, "Celibacy in the Renaissance," with its pointed discussion of families' disposal of unwanted daughters, was first published in French in 1972. I did not use it while preparing "Patrician Women" and "Dowries and Kinsmen" in the early 1970s.

3. The elements and history of this view of Venetian politics, now usually referred to as the "myth of Venice," are examined, with bibliography, in Grubb, "When Myths Lose Power"; Finlay, *Politics*, 27–37; Muir, *Civic Ritual*, 13–55; Queller, *Venetian Patriciate*, 3–28.

4. Chojnacki, "Posizione della donna."

5. Martines, "Way of Looking at Women"; Goldthwaite, "Florentine Palace." Though published in 1972, Goldthwaite's article was unavailable to me while I was writing "Patrician Women" and "Dowries and Kinsmen."

6. Stone, *Family, Sex, and Marriage*; Davis, *Society and Culture*. Stone's book had an especially powerful impact on scholars of English literature; see the introduction to Ferguson et al., *Rewriting the Renaissance*. Of the two of Davis's essays which became landmarks of women's history, "City Women and Religious Change" had been previously published, in 1973, while "Women on Top" was written for the collection.

7. Hughes, "From Brideprice to Dowry" (1978); King, "Thwarted Ambitions" (1976) and "Religious Retreat of Isotta Nogarola" (1978); and Kelly-Gadol, "Did Women Have a Renaissance?" (1977).

8. Kirshner, *Pursuing Honor*; Kirshner and Molho, "Dowry Fund." David Herlihy and Christiane Klapisch-Zuber, separately in articles and together in *Les Toscans*, addressed social and moral implications for women of Tuscan demographic patterns during the 1970s; however, it was not until the following decade that they dedicated research specifically to the position of women.

9. Betto, "Linee di politica matrimoniale"; Kuehn, "Women, Marriage, and

Patria Potestas" and " 'Cum Consensu Mundualdi' "; Hughes, "Sumptuary Law." Cohn, "Women in the Streets," first appeared as "Donne in piazza e donne in tribunale" in 1981. Klapisch-Zuber's two most powerful treatments of oppression of women in Florence, "Griselda Complex" and "Cruel Mother," were originally published in French in 1982 and 1983, respectively. An early evocation by Klapisch-Zuber of the disadvantages facing daughters, in English translation "Childhood in Tuscany," had appeared in French in 1973; she did not then, however, develop the theme as fully as she would in the 1980s.

10. Margaret King's analysis of Venetian humanist writings on marriage, "Caldiera and the Barbaros," had already appeared in 1976; Benjamin Kohl's translation of book 2 of Francesco Barbaro's treatise on marriage, "On Wifely Duties," in 1978.

11. For example, Hughes, "Sumptuary Law," emphasized legislation; Klapisch-Zuber, "Cruel Mother" and "Griselda Complex," were based mainly on *ricordanze*, or family diaries, kept by male household heads.

12. Cohn, "Donne in piazza e donne in tribunale"; Kuehn, " 'Cum Consensu Mundualdi' "; and Ruggiero, *Boundaries of Eros,* are examples.

13. The most important early writings assessing family and lineage structures in Florence were Goldthwaite, *Private Wealth* and "Florentine Palace," and Kent, *Household and Lineage.* Another important early study was Starn, "Francesco Guicciardini and His Brothers." On Venice, the subject had been broached in the even older Lane, "Family Partnerships" and *Andrea Barbarigo,* and, more recently, Betto, "Linee di politica matrimoniale." Also important in formulating a configuration of family and lineage dynamics was Hughes, "Urban Growth."

14. Gregory, "Daughters, Dowries, and the Family"; Rosenthal, "Position of Women"; Strocchia, "Remembering the Family."

15. The literature is vast, but especially prominent examples may be cited. On women's economic position, see Klapisch-Zuber, "Griselda Complex," and Chabot, "Widowhood and Poverty." On their liabilities in law, see Kirshner, "Materials for a Gilded Cage" and "Maritus Lucretur Dotem," and Kuehn, " 'Cum Consensu Mundualdi.' " On instrumentalization by families, see Chabot, "Sposa in nero," and Molho, "Deception and Marriage Strategy." On women's identification with and confinement to private space, see Romano, "Gender and Urban Geography"; Davis, "Geography of Gender"; and Hughes, "Representing the Family."

16. Some examples: Cohn, *Cult of Remembrance,* 197–201; Queller and Madden, "Father of the Bride"; Calvi, "Diritti e legami."

17. These events are treated more fully in Chojnacki, "La formazione della nobiltà" and "Social Identity."

18. See below, Chap. 2; also, Chojnacki, "Identity and Ideology."

19. Chojnacki, "Identity and Ideology." For additional discussion, see Chojnacki, "Marriage Legislation" and "Social Identity."

20. Cohn, "Social History of Women," 12–15.

21. On the state and the elites' gender concerns, see Chap. 1.

22. On the *cittadini,* see Grubb, "In Search of the *Cittadini*"; Casini, "La cittadinanza originaria"; and Zannini, *Burocrazia e burocrati.* On the law of 1420, see Chap. 2.

23. De Giudicato 1 and 2. The dowry-recovery procedure is discussed in Chap. 4.

24. The odd sum of 1,066⅔ ducats was exactly two-thirds of the maximum total of 1,600 ducats allowed under the dowry-limiting law of 1420. The remaining was the *corredo,* an outright gift to the husband and therefore not recoverable by a widow. See Chap. 3.

25. On marriage among the *cittadini* in the sixteenth century, see Bellavitis, "Famiglia 'cittadina.' "

26. My understanding of the reciprocal dynamic between structure and practice (or action), especially practice informed by individuals' and groups' "discursive knowledge" of structure, is influenced by the notion of the "duality of structure" as outlined by Anthony Giddens. People know about the structures of the social systems in which they live; they can express their knowledge in language and can act vis-à-vis the structures in ways that end up reproducing or altering them. This dynamic, the "essential recursiveness of social life," is rooted in "an intrinsic relation between agency and power." Where Giddens' ideas are especially applicable to gender relations in Venice is in his further argument that power relations are always "two-way . . . however subordinate an actor might be in a social relationship, the very fact of involvement in that relationship gives him *or her* a certain amount of power over the other" (emphasis added). Giddens, *Central Problems in Social Theory,* 4–6. These ideas, sketched in the introduction, are elaborated in Giddens' chap. 2, "Agency, Structure"; see especially 71–73, on informed agency and on the capacity of people in subordinate status to understand structures with more "penetration" than those in positions of dominance.

27. On the study of the state, see Chap. 1.

28. For a theoretical discussion, see Scott, "Gender." Examples of studies: on France, Hanley, "Engendering the State" and "Social Sites of Political Practice"; on England, Harris, "Aristocratic Women and the State" and "Women and Politics"; on Germany, Howell, "Citizenship and Gender," and Roper, *Holy Household;* on Spain, Perry, *Gender and Disorder.* On Italy, see Chap. 1.

29. See the contributions to *Origins of the State.* Important recent studies of Italian governments' concerns with gender are Calvi, *Contratto morale* and "Diritti e legami," and Rocke, *Forbidden Friendships.* Both authors focus on Florence and Tuscany.

30. See Chap. 2.

31. This sequence is discussed, with bibliography, in Chap. 1. On the dowry squeeze on working-class families in Bologna, see Carboni, *Le doti della "povertà";* my thanks to Dr. Carboni for allowing me to consult this work before publication.

32. On government efforts to exclude noble bastards, see Crescenzi, *"Esse de maiori consilio,"* and Chojnacki, "Identity and Ideology." On enforced bachelorhood, see Chap. 12.

33. Molho, *Marriage Alliance,* and Kirshner, *Pursuing Honor.*

34. Alliance: Molho, "Deception and Marriage Strategy" and *Marriage Alliance;* Fabbri, *Alleanza matrimoniale;* Betto, "Linee di politica matrimoniale."

35. Queller and Madden, "Father of the Bride"; Gregory, "Daughters, Dowries, and the Family"; Chaps. 7 and 8.

36. See Chap. 3.

37. On dowry as disinheritance, see, fundamentally, Hughes, "From Bride-price to Dowry." A contrary view is in Goody, *Development of the Family*, 255–61. For contrasting positions on Florentine practice, compare Kuehn, "Some Ambiguities," with Chabot, "Widowhood and Poverty" and "Sposa in nero." In the last study Chabot addresses the dowry system's potential for enriching women at the expense of men, countering the aims of patrilineal inheritance (423–24), but she argues that in the long trajectory of a marriage that female wealth ended up in the hands of the men of either the woman's natal or marital lineage. See also Chap. 1 for discussion of Florentine restrictions on women's rights to their dowries.

38. On widowhood, the strongest negative assessments of the situation in Florence are Chabot, "Widowhood and Poverty" and "Sposa in nero." For more positive assessments, see Calvi, *Contratto morale* and "Diritti e legami"; Rosenthal, "Position of Women"; and Crabb, "How Typical Was Alessandra Strozzi?" Klapisch-Zuber, "Cruel Mother," presents an ambiguous picture of the situation of widows in Florence.

39. See Chap. 1.

40. Klapisch-Zuber, "Cruel Mother," 117–19, 130–31. But note the complicating matter of the *tornata*, the Florentine widow's right to return to her natal family. For examples and analysis of the *tornata* in practice, see Chabot, "Sposa in nero"; Klapisch-Zuber, "Kin, Friends, and Neighbors"; and Rosenthal, "Position of Women." On Florentine women's distinctive and wide-ranging family orientation, see Strocchia, "Remembering the Family."

41. In 1309 the Great Council enacted a measure that disqualified both a woman's marital and her natal kinsmen from acting as judges or officials in civil cases regarding her or her property. The cited reason for the law was the prejudice to a husband's rights which would derive from his wife's natal kin sitting in judgment in property disputes between the spouses. See the discussion, and the text, in Guzzetti, "Le donne a Venezia," 30–31 and n. 48. See also Chap. 10.

42. On Venice, see Queller and Madden, "Father of the Bride," 695–99. In Florence, in addition to the famous example of Alessandra Strozzi, see examples in Fabbri, *Alleanza matrimoniale*, 66, and Rosenthal, "Position of Women," 374.

43. See also Chojnacki, "Cateruzza and the Patriarchs."

44. For a discussion of the relative virtues of quantitative and narrative treatments of sexual crime, see Cohn, "Sex and Violence on the Periphery," esp. 98–107.

45. Contrast the bitterness expressed by Florentine children of remarrying mothers, exemplified by the case of Giovanni Morelli, with the enduring involvement of Venetian widows in their children's upbringing. On Morelli, see Trexler, *Public Life*, 165–67; Klapisch-Zuber, "Cruel Mother," 127–30. On Venetian mothers, see Chap. 10. It is evident also that some Florentine widows remained with their children just as some Venetian ones remarried and abandoned theirs.

46. See Chap. 9; compare Florence in Herlihy and Klapisch-Zuber, *Tuscans and Their Families*, 87, 203–11.

47. Examples in Chojnacki, "Cateruzza and the Patriarchs."

48. See Chojnacki, "Social Identity."

49. Romano, "Gender and Urban Geography"; Davis, "Geography of Gender." Guzzetti's critique of the view of female containment is in her "Le donne a Venezia," 76–78.

50. Chojnacki, "Cateruzza and the Patriarchs."

51. On Alessandra Strozzi's role in Strozzi marriage arrangements, see Fabbri, *Alleanza matrimoniale,* and Gregory, "Daughters, Dowries, and the Family." Gregory has now made a large number of Alessandra Strozzi's letters available in a bilingual edition: Strozzi, *Selected Letters.*

52. On mothers giving their daughters vocational choice and arranging their marriages, see Chap. 8.

53. On men's marriage ages, see Chap. 9.

54. On the medieval church's attitudes toward women, see Dalarun, "Clerical Gaze." But note also evidence of church courts offering recourse to married women in Brucker, *Giovanni and Lusanna;* Ferraro, "Power to Decide"; and Chojnacki, "Cateruzza and the Patriarchs."

55. On what follows, see Chap. 1.

56. On marriage policy in Venice as a battleground between wealthy and poorer nobles, see Chap. 2.

57. On contention between natal and marital kin, see Klapisch-Zuber, "Cruel Mother" and "Griselda Complex"; Chabot, "Sposa in nero."

58. On identity as constructed within the web of a person's relationships, see Kuehn, "Understanding Gender Inequality." On bilaterality in Venice, see Chap. 6.

59. The influence that wives derived from their dowry wealth is the subject of several of the chapters. On the dowry (in contrast with other forms of marital assigns) as affording women economic independence, see Goody, *Development of the Family,* 259–61.

60. On husbands entrusting their widows with responsibility for their children's inheritances and upbringing, see Calvi, "Diritti e legami." On women contributing to their daughters' dowries, see Queller and Madden, "Father of the Bride." See also Chap. 8.

61. See Chojnacki, "Identity and Ideology" and "Cateruzza and the Patriarchs."

62. On the procedures, see Chojnacki, "Social Identity" and "Identity and Ideology," and Chaps. 6 and 7. On age grading, see Finlay, "Venetian Gerontocracy."

63. On electoral politics and corruption, see Cozzi, "Authority and the Law," and Finlay, *Politics.* On nobles' need and maneuverings for political office, see Queller, *Venetian Patriciate.* On sexual misbehavior, see Ruggiero, *Boundaries of Eros.*

64. See Cracco, "Patriziato e oligarchia"; Finlay, *Politics;* Cozzi, "Authority and the Law"; and Gilbert, "Venice in the Crisis."

65. See the references above, n. 49. A dissenting view, discounting the importance of alliances between affines, can be found in Everett and Queller, "Family, Faction, and Politics," and Queller and Madden, "Father of the Bride."

66. See Chaps. 9 and 11, for the collective involvement of young men in approved and disapproved activities.

67. Ruggiero, *Boundaries of Eros;* Crescenzi, *"Esse de maiori consilio."* See also Chojnacki, "Identity and Ideology," and, briefly, Chap. 2.

68. On homosexual activity, see Ruggiero, *Boundaries of Eros,* 109–45, and Labalme, "Sodomy and Venetian Justice."

69. Michael Rocke has shown that in Florence homosexual activity was largely confined to a period of young adulthood, most often followed by marriage and fatherhood; Rocke, *Forbidden Friendships,* 92–100 and passim. Whether his findings are valid also for Venice needs investigation.

70. Kuehn, "Understanding Gender Inequality," 60–61.

Chapter 1 Gender and the Early Renaissance State

This chapter originally appeared, in slightly altered form, as "Daughters and Oligarchs: Gender and the Early Renaissance State," in *Gender and Society in Renaissance Italy,* ed. Judith C. Brown and Robert C. Davis (London: Longman, 1998), 63–86.

1. Burckhardt, *Civilization of the Renaissance,* pt. 1, "The State as a Work of Art," 19–97. This chapter owes much to discussions in the seminar "Men, Women, and the State in Renaissance Europe" at the Folger Shakespeare Library in spring 1996. I gratefully acknowledge my debt to its members: Eileen Allman, Geoffrey Clark, Ross Ettle, Mack Holt, Kristin Huffman, Jeri McIntosh, Debra Ashton Meyers, and Peggy Samuels. I also wish to thank Barbara J. Harris for valuable insights and suggestions.

2. Kelly-Gadol, "Did Women Have a Renaissance?"; see the review by Judith C. Brown in *American Historical Review* 92 (1987): 938–40. For earlier studies of women, see Martines, "Way of Looking at Women," and Chap. 5, below.

3. *Women, Family, and Ritual.* Klapisch-Zuber's essays have also been gathered in *La famiglia e le donne* and *La maison e le nom.*

4. See especially "Cruel Mother" and "Griselda Complex." But see also Rosenthal, "Position of Women."

5. For similar findings see Hughes, "Representing the Family"; Kirshner, *Pursuing Honor;* and Molho, "Deception and Marriage Strategy." For a perspective that includes both instrumentalization of daughters and concern for their well-being, see Gregory, "Daughters, Dowries, and the Family," and Queller and Madden, "Father of the Bride."

6. "The 'Private,' the 'Public,' the State," S53, S56; the interpolation is from S52.

7. Ibid., S54.

8. The sociopolitical arena where oligarchies conducted alliances and rivalries that entangled the purposes and structures of both state and family is the Renaissance equivalent of the eighteenth-century "authentic public sphere" that Jürgen Habermas has identified as the site of the bourgeois critique of the aristocratic-monarchical political order; *Structural Transformation of the Public Sphere.* For outstanding studies of Italian elites, acting in concert and contestation, maneuvering to assert mastery over the public arena, see Muir, "Images of Power," and Trexler, *Public Life.* On the pervasive importance of oligarchy in its different forms, see the enduringly valuable synthesis in Jones, "Communes and Despots."

9. On changes in the concept and the practical definition of nobility from the fourteenth to the sixteenth century, see Donati, *L'idea di nobiltà,* chaps. 1–3. For a

concise survey of recent writing on Italian elites, see Lanaro Sartori, *Un'oligarchia*, 11–34.

10. For overviews, see Chittolini, "Introduzione" to idem, *La crisi degli ordinamenti comunali*, esp. 26–40, and Fasano Guarini, "Center and Periphery." For Florence, see Becker, *Florence in Transition*; for Venice, Grubb, *Firstborn of Venice*; for Ferrara, Dean, *Land and Power*.

11. Donati, *L'idea di nobiltà*, 4–15.

12. Donati notes the residual prestige of old feudal families even in Quattrocento Florence; ibid., 22 n. 24. On the quest for a nonfeudal claim to honor as a persistent imperative for republican Florence, see Trexler, *Public Life*. For a brief synthesis of recent interpretations of oligarchy, with special emphasis on "bourgeois" and "feudal" elements, see Angiolini, "I ceti dominanti," 9–16.

13. Dean, *Land and Power*, 77–91. But cf. also the comments on the uncertain success of the courts' integrative function in Dean, "The Courts," S141–44.

14. For various treatments of this theme, see, for Venice, Cozzi and Knapton, *La Repubblica di Venezia*, 117–31; for Milan, Chittolini, "L'onore dell' officiale"; for Florence, Brucker, *Civic World*, 217–22.

15. On the Milanese noble registry, see Grubb, "Memory and Identity," 382. On the feudal policy of the Visconti, see Chittolini, "Infeudazione e politico feudale." On that of the Sforza, see Bueno de Mesquita, "Ludovico Sforza and His Vassals."

16. On the post-Ciompi environment, see Brucker, *Civic World*, 60–101; Cohn, *Laboring Classes*, 65–115. For the Florentine ruling group, see Brucker, *Civic World*, 254–79, esp. 269–70 on its continuity with the thirteenth century. For the distinction between "ruling group" and "ruling class," see Kent, "Florentine *Reggimento*," 577–84. For that between "participation" and "power," see Najemy, "Guild Republicanism," 70–71; a full discussion of the post-Ciompi adjustments is in Najemy, *Corporatism and Consensus*, 268–300. On the chronology of the narrowing of the ruling group, see Witt, "Florentine Politics." A dissenting view on the oligarchical trend is in Molho, "Politics and the Ruling Class."

17. Romano, *Patricians and Popolani*, 152–58.

18. For the hypothesis of a ruling clique, see Cracco, "Patriziato e oligarchia." On legislation that had a leveling effect among patricians, see Chojnacki, "Social Identity."

19. On the effects of the war of Chioggia, see Mueller, "Effetti della Guerra di Chioggia," and Luzzatto, *Debito pubblico*, 165–76. On ennoblement of commoners and programs to assist nobles, see Chojnacki, "La formazione della nobiltà," 699–708.

20. The law on recording citizenship awards is in Ell, "Citizenship and Immigration," 230. On the laws of 1414 and 1430, see Chojnacki, "Social Identity," 343–48.

21. Molho, "State and Public Finance," S114–16.

22. On the Florentine legislation, see Herlihy, "Age, Property, and Career," 263–65; on the "daybooks" in which eligible officeholders were recorded, see idem, "Rulers of Florence," 357–59. On the competition among Florentines for public office, see also Zorzi, "I Fiorentini e gli uffici pubblici," 732–38. On eager-

ness for office in Venice, see Queller, *Venetian Patriciate*, 29–112. For a comparison of documentation practices in Florence and Venice which deemphasizes the use of public records in Florence, see Grubb, "Memory and Identity," 383–84.

23. On the Florentine ideology, see Najemy, "Guild Republicanism," 69; on Venice, see Chap. 8.

24. Herlihy and Klapisch-Zuber, *Tuscans and Their Families*, 9–10 (on Venice), 299–301 (on Florence).

25. Zorzi, "Judicial System in Florence"; Cohn, "Criminality and the State." See also Martines, *Lawyers and Statecraft*, 135–36. But cf. Stern, *Criminal Law System*, xvii–xviii, 13–14.

26. Zorzi, "I Fiorentini e gli uffici pubblici," 729–32.

27. Zorzi, "Judicial System in Florence," 55; Mazzi, "Il mondo della prostituzione," 343–44.

28. Trexler, "Florentine Prostitution," 31–34. Mazzi acknowledges the hetero-sexualizing motive but argues that Florence's rulers recognized that frequenting prostitutes was an alternative rather than an inducement to marriage; "Il mondo della prostituzione," 344–46.

29. On concern with the dangers unmarried men posed to married women, see Davidson, "Theology, Nature, and the Law," 90–96. On the circumstances under-lying disorderly behavior by young men, see Herlihy, "Some Psychological and Social Roots."

30. Mazzi, "Il mondo della prostituzione," 343, 351–56.

31. Rocke, *Forbidden Friendships*, 45, 28.

32. Ibid., 51; on antisodomy agitation preceding institution of the office, see ibid., 26–44.

33. Ibid., 53. Between 1432 and 1502 the Ufficiali convicted 2,400 men out of 15,000–16,000 implicated for sodomy; ibid., 47. However, Rocke documents con-siderable variation in penalties, prosecution, and rates of conviction throughout the fifteenth century; ibid., 54–65. Davidson observes a decline throughout Italy in governmental concern with sodomy in the fifteenth and sixteenth centuries; "Theology, Nature, and the Law," 94–96.

34. Rocke, *Forbidden Friendships*, 244, table B.5.

35. Ibid., 51–52.

36. Ibid., 106–10. See also Rocke, "Gender and Sexual Culture," 167–69.

37. Rocke, *Forbidden Friendships*, 246, table B.9.

38. Ruggiero, *Boundaries of Eros*, 9–10, 147–48, and passim.

39. Crouzet-Pavan, *"Sopra le acque salse,"* 2:802. See also Pavan, "Police des moeurs" and "Recherches sur la nuit." For other interpretations of Venetian crim-inal justice in the Trecento, see Ruggiero, *Violence in Early Renaissance Venice*, and Chojnacki, "Crime, Punishment, and the State."

40. *"Sopra le acque salse,"* 2:836–37.

41. Ibid., 838–39; Pavan, "Police des moeurs," 266–70. The statistics on pros-ecutions are from Ruggiero, *Boundaries of Eros*, 128, 134; for sodomy policy in general, see 126–35. The most systematic treatment of the state's policy on sod-omy is in Labalme, "Sodomy and Venetian Justice."

42. Labalme, "Sodomy and Venetian Justice," 242.

43. The quotations are from acts of the Council of Ten, in, respectively, ibid., 220 n. 10, and Crouzet-Pavan, *"Sopra le acque salse,"* 2:845, with discussion of the fear of divine reprisal.

44. On sodomy with male and female prostitutes, see Labalme, "Sodomy and Venetian Justice," 247–51. For cases of sodomy by married people, see Ruggiero, *Boundaries of Eros,* 118–20.

45. Ruggiero, *Boundaries of Eros,* 121–25.

46. Ibid., 149–52, 160–62.

47. The translation is in Labalme, "Sodomy and Venetian Justice," 222. She argues, however, (232–35) that nobles were more likely to get clemency. Ruggiero emphasizes the prosecution of nobles; *Boundaries of Eros,* 127–32.

48. *"Sopra le acque salse,"* 2:846.

49. The fullest discussion is in Pavan, "Police des moeurs," 242–66.

50. Lorenzi, *Leggi e memorie sulla prostituzione,* 34–37.

51. *"Sopra le acque salse,"* 2:834.

52. Romano, "Gender and the Urban Geography," 348. On locating workers in particular neighborhoods, see Cohn, *Laboring Classes,* 65–90; on the resulting restrictions on women, see idem, "Women in the Streets," 35–38.

53. Crouzet-Pavan suggests that male nobles satisfied their extramarital sexual urges with domestic slaves rather than prostitutes; *"Sopra le acque salse,"* 2:859; for examples, see Ruggiero, *Boundaries of Eros,* 40–41. Romano notes that one motive for the localization of prostitutes was to keep them away from respectable women; "Gender and Urban Geography," 345. On the Florentine brothel area, see Trexler, "Florentine Prostitution," 41–46.

54. MC 21, Leona, f. 176r; AC, Reg. 2, Capitolare, cap. 289, f. 106v. For prosecutions of male partners of sexually active nuns, see Ruggiero, *Boundaries of Eros,* 77–84.

55. The 1382 act is in MC 20, Novella (copy), ff. 410v–411r. For the penalties of 1486, see Scarabello, "Devianza sessuale," 78 n. 9; Scarabello also reports a 1455 act that the penalties of 1486 were designed to strengthen.

56. Sanudo, *Diarii,* vol. 1, col. 836.

57. On placing girls with physical and mental impairments into convents, see Molho, *"Tamquam vere mortua,"* 22–26.

58. On convents as depositories for girls without adequate marriage dowries, see (among many studies), ibid., 26–32 and passim, and Trexler, "Celibacy in the Renaissance," 17–20, 26–27.

59. On the threat to family honor from unsupervised female sexuality, see Kirshner, *Pursuing Honor,* 8–15; Molho, "Deception and Marriage Strategy," 204–12 and passim; Klapisch-Zuber, "Cruel Mother," 119–20.

60. The quotations from Tarabotti and the patriarch are in Cox, "Single Self," 536, 540. The legislative language of 1420 is reproduced in Bistort, *Magistrato alle Pompe,* 107. The Bolognese quotation is in Zarri, "Monasteri femminili e città," 365.

61. On the chartering of the Conservatori dell'Onestà dei Monasteri, see Brucker, "Monasteries, Friaries, and Nunneries," 55, and Zorzi, "Judicial System in Florence," 43. On the absorption of the Conservatori's duties by the Ufficiali di

Notte, see Rocke, *Forbidden Friendships,* 46. The quotation from Saint Antoninus is in Bizzocchi, *Chiesa e potere,* 31–32.

62. For the percentage in 1427, see Brown, "Monache a Firenze," 119; for the percentages in 1336 and 1552, Trexler, "Celibacy in the Renaissance," 16. The numerical populations are in Brucker, "Monasteries, Friaries, and Nunneries," 46.

63. Some individual convent populations grew spectacularly: the Benedictine Murate, for example, grew from 11 nuns in 1426 to 124 in 1458, to more than 200 in 1525; the Dominican S. Pietro Martire from 22 in 1427 to 60 in 1493; and the Franciscan S. Onofrio from 18 in 1439 to 79 in 1515; Brucker, "Monasteries, Friaries, and Nunneries," 47–48. The numbers and average sizes of convents are in Trexler, "Celibacy in the Renaissance," 10, 12 (tables 1 and 2).

64. Wholesale monacation caused awkward results for the government: in 1553 the magistracy that supervised nuns went unfilled because of the impossibility of finding a patrician who could meet the requirement of having no daughters, sisters, nieces, or cousins in convents. See Sperling, "Convents and the Body Politic," 12, 16. The number of convents in the 1490s is in Sanudo, *De origine,* 45; for the dates, see xx–xxi. For accounts of sexual activities in convents in the early 1400s, see Ruggiero, *Boundaries of Eros,* 76–84.

65. On the charisma of holy women, see Herlihy, "Did Women Have a Renaissance?".

66. For construction subsidies, see Brucker, "Monasteries, Friaries, and Nunneries," 54; for the abbess's claim, see Trexler, "Celibacy in the Renaissance," 6.

67. Sanudo, *Diarii,* vol. 6, col. 353. The rings are mentioned in Zarri, "Monasteri femminili e città," 375. The doge's protection of Corpus Domini is in Bornstein, "Giovanni Dominici and Venice," 156–57 n. 42.

68. This theme is explored throughout Zarri, *Le sante vive.* See especially "Pietà e profezia"; the quotation from Ercole of Ferrara is on 60. For a comprehensive discussion of the importance of convents for both republican and princely regimes, see Zarri, "Monasteri femminili e città," 360–77.

69. Zarri, "Monasteri femminili e città," 373.

70. Zarri, "Pietà e profezia," 54–55.

71. Ibid., 52 and passim; Zarri, "Monasteri femminili e città," 372–86. This question is treated most thoroughly in the title essay of Zarri, *Le sante vive,* 87–163.

72. Bizzocchi, *Chiesa e potere,* 33.

73. See Strocchia, "Learning the Virtues." See also the example of Gasparino Morosini's provision for his granddaughter in Chap. 8.

74. PSMC de ultra, B. 221, fasc. 1, Francesco Morosini, estate account book, entry for 1 February 1497/98. (The will was written on 10 November 1497.)

75. Ermolao Pisani (1469): NT 1238, Tomei, pt. 1, no. 15. Zanetta Contarini (1476): De Giudicatu, Reg. 2, f. 135r. Vito Canal: NT 558, Gambaro, nos. 171, 185.

76. Bornstein, "Giovanni Dominici and Venice," 146–48, 156–57.

77. Gill, "Open Monasteries," 24–25.

78. The "capture" of Corpus Domini is in McLaughlin, "Creating and Recreating Communities," 272–74. On the role of the princely courts in the spread of the

Clarisse, see Zarri, "Monasteri femminili e città," 363; on the Parmesan and Venetian episodes, see 371–72.

79. On the cultural and practical implications of the convention of nuns "dying" to the world, see Molho, *"Tamquam vere mortua,"* 32–44.

80. The fullest study of the Dowry Fund is in Molho, *Marriage Alliance;* for its creation, see 27–33. For a concise account of its functioning, see Kirshner and Molho, "Dowry Fund."

81. The text is reproduced in Kirshner, *Pursuing Honor,* 60.

82. Senato, Misti 53, f. 70r. See Chap. 2. A fuller analysis is in Chojnacki, "Marriage Legislation."

83. Venetian sentences are discussed in Ruggiero, *Boundaries of Eros,* 17–44, 89–108; the quotation on fathers is on 22. The bishop of Pistoia's statement is in Kirshner, *Pursuing Honor,* 10. Marco Parenti is quoted in Fabbri, *Alleanza matrimoniale,* 73. For general discussions of the intimate connection between dowries, honor, and female chastity, see Kirshner, *Pursuing Honor,* 4–11 and passim; Klapisch-Zuber, "Cruel Mother," 119–20; Molho, *Marriage Alliance,* 139–43, and "Deception and Marriage Strategy," 207–10.

84. The figures for the three periods in Florence are in Fabbri, *Alleanza matrimoniale,* 73; the rise in average dowries is in Molho, *Marriage Alliance,* 310, with a table tracking dowries recorded in *ricordanze* from an average of 1,009 florins in 1425–49 to one of 1,852 florins in 1500–1524. The Venetian figures are discussed in Chap. 4, the relationship of corredo to strictly defined dowry in Chap. 3.

85. The Tommaso and Tornabuoni-Medici dowries are in Kirshner, *Pursuing Honor,* 19–20; the figures on patrician investments are in Molho, *Marriage Alliance,* 91.

86. On false ages in Florence, see Molho, "Deception and Marriage Strategy"; on Venetian explicitness, see Chojnacki, "Social Identity," 354–55.

87. For the meanings of *alogare,* see Molho, *Marriage Alliance,* 132. The quote from Alessandra Strozzi is in Fabbri, *Alleanza matrimoniale,* 79. On parents' desire to provide honorably and generously for their daughters, see Fabbri, *Alleanza matrimoniale,* 80; Gregory, "Daughters, Dowries, and the Family," 233–37; Queller and Madden, "Father of the Bride," 705–9; and Chap. 7.

88. Giovanni Morosini's will is in NT 571, G. Gibellino, no. 106. On women's proprietorship of their dowries and its social consequences, see Chap. 7.

89. Nicolò Mudazzo's and Isabetta Mudazzo Trevisan's wills are in NT 1255, Zane, prot., ff. 184v–186v (24 July 1411) and ff. 109r–110r (26 July 1411). Isabetta's residuary legatees, after her bequests to her female relatives, were her father and, succeeding him, her brothers. In his will, Nicolò made a point of declaring that the expenses, "for food and for everything else," which he had incurred on her behalf during her widowhood, he had paid out *liberamente* so that she was "free and absolved" of any repayment.

90. Chabot, "Sposa in nero," 450–53; Kirshner, "Materials for a Gilded Cage"; Klapisch-Zuber, "Cruel Mother." On Alessandra Strozzi's contribution to her daughter's dowry, see Molho, *Marriage Alliance,* 128–29; for a positive evaluation of her social influence, see Martines, "Way of Looking at Women." See also

Rosenthal, "Position of Women," 373–74. On maternal contributions in Venice, see Queller and Madden, "Father of the Bride," 696–99, and Chap. 8.

91. For an alternative view, discounting social ambition and emphasizing the contribution of mothers, see Queller and Madden, "Father of the Bride," 694–704. On the multiform social implications of marriage alliances, see Fabbri, *Alleanza matrimoniale*, 96–110.

92. APV, Causarum matrimoniorum, B. 2, fasc. 1, doc. 5 (27 July 1457).

93. Fabbri, *Alleanza matrimoniale*, 66, 73.

94. Jacopo married in 1434, his brother Girolamo in 1432. A third brother, Marco, received his dowry of 3,000 ducats in 1419, the year before the dowry-limitation act; Barbaro, Nozze, f. 96v.

95. The Venetian figure is an extrapolation from records of dowry restitution to patrician widows or their heirs; see Chojnacki, "Social Identity," 355. Of the nubile girls in households rated in the catasto of 1480 as possessing fiscal wealth of at least 1,500 florins, 497 had Dowry Fund investments, 583 did not; Molho, *Marriage Alliance*, table 3.1, 87.

96. Antonio Strozzi's comment is in Fabbri, *Alleanza matrimoniale*, 75.

97. Chabot, "Sposa in nero," 424. On the theory and practice of the exclusion of dowered women from inheritance, see Kuehn, "Some Ambiguities."

98. Chabot, "Sposa in nero," 449–53; Klapisch-Zuber, "Griselda Complex," 224–31 and passim. The case of Lena Davizzi is in Fabbri, *Alleanza matrimoniale*, 80.

99. Molho, *Marriage Alliance*, 303–4 n. 22.

100. NT 364, Darvasio, no. 44; CI 175, Rizzo, prot., f. 35v.

101. Senato, Misti 53, f. 70r (1420); Senato, Terra 15, ff. 93v–94v (1505). The latter measure is discussed in Chap. 2.

102. Quoted in Hughes, "Sumptuary Law," 95.

103. However, the 1415 redaction protected the wife's family's interest by requiring consummation for the husband's claim to the dowry to be valid; Kirshner, "Maritus Lucretur Dotem," 116–17, 133–34. On husbands' and widowers' rights to nondotal assets, see Kirshner, "Materials for a Gilded Cage," 191–95 and passim. The restrictions on the wife's testamentary dispositions are explicitly stated in the statute; *Statuta populi*, vol. 1, lib. 2, rub. 129, p. 223. My thanks to Thomas Kuehn for making this text available to me.

104. *Statuta populi*, vol. 1, lib. 2, rub. 130, p. 224. Klapisch-Zuber, "Cruel Mother"; Chabot, "Sposa in nero," 451–52 and passim.

105. See Chap. 2.

106. Senato, Terra 28, f. 151r.

107. Bistort, *Magistrato alle Pompe*, 123, 154. For the Florentine laws, see Molho, *Marriage Alliance*, 301 n. 15.

108. "Sumptuary Law," 99.

109. See Esposito, "Strategie matrimoniali," 579–81; Klapisch-Zuber, "Les corbeilles de la mariée," 215–16 and passim; and Chap. 3.

110. Kovesi Killerby, "Practical Problems."

111. Calvi, "Diritti e legami," 487–89. The text of the 1393 law chartering the Magistrato dei Pupilli is in Morandini, "Statuti e ordinamenti," 529–35.

112. The jurists revising the Florentine statutes were apparently responding to a widespread desire to enable widows to remarry; Kirshner, "Maritus Lucretur Dotem," 134.

113. On the Milanese statutes, see Caso, "Per la storia," 524.

114. MC 22, Ursa, f. 176rv (28 December 1449).

115. Senato, Misti 53, f. 70v (22 August 1420); 55, f. 101v (22 March 1425); Senato, Terra 1, f. 115v (21 January 1443/44).

116. On bachelors in Venice, see Chap. 12.

117. Crouzet-Pavan, "*Sopra le acque salse,*" 2:875–76; Chartier, "Figures of Modernity," 15.

118. Ariès, introduction to Chartier, *History of Private Life,* 9–10.

119. Senato, Terra 28, f. 151r; the Florentine statement is translated in Molho, *Marriage Alliance,* 302.

Chapter 2 Marriage Regulation in Venice, 1420–1535

This chapter originally appeared, in slightly altered form, as "Nobility, Women, and the State: Marriage Regulation in Venice, 1420–1535," in *Marriage in Italy, 1300–1650,* ed. Trevor Dean and K. J. P. Lowe (Cambridge: Cambridge University Press, 1998), 128–51.

1. APV, Causarum matrimoniorum, B. 2, fasc. 1, doc. 5 (27 July 1457). Portions of this chapter were presented to the Annual Meeting of the American Historical Association, Washington, D.C., in 1992; the Middle-Atlantic Renaissance and Reformation Seminar, Charlottesville, Va., in 1993; and the European History Seminar, Syracuse University, in 1995. The author expresses his appreciation for valuable suggestions and criticisms received on all three occasions, with special thanks to Barbara J. Harris for invaluable advice.

2. For marriage rituals in Florence, see Klapisch-Zuber, "Zacharias, or the Ousted Father," 183–87.

3. APV, Causarum matrimoniorum, B. 2, fasc. 1, doc. 2 (5 May 1457).

4. Ibid., doc. 4.

5. Based on calculations in Luzzatto, *Storia economica,* 129–32, and Lane and Mueller, *Money and Banking,* 1:290–91.

6. According to Gabriel and Malipiero, Zaccaria left to his sons holdings in the state's funded debt (Camera degli Imprestiti), which yielded an annual return of 300 ducats, real estate bringing in 3,800 ducats in annual rents, "and a goodly sum of money to invest in commerce"; APV, Causarum matrimoniorum, B. 2, fasc. 1, doc. 5. State bonds (*prestiti*) paid interest at either 3 or 4 percent, so the Gabriels' holdings totaled somewhere between 7,500 and 10,000 ducats. With an estimated 5 percent yield from real estate, Zaccaria's holdings had a value in the neighborhood of 76,000 ducats. On prestiti, see Lane, "Funded Debt," 87–98.

7. APV, Causarum matrimoniorum, B. 2, fasc. 1, doc. 2.

8. On marriage ages for men and women in Venice, see Chap. 9. On marriage ages in Florence, see Herlihy and Klapisch-Zuber, *Tuscans and Their Families,* 203–7. On youth in brides in Florence, see Molho, "Deception and Marriage Strategy," 194, 204–10, and passim. On male honor and female chastity, see Kirshner, *Pursuing Honor,* 6–10.

9. Orsa was identified in the trial record as "Lady Orsa, daughter of the late Lord Antonio Dolfin, of the Venetian nobility" [dominam Ursiam filiam quondam domini Antonii Dolfino ex nobilibus Venetiarum]; APV, Causarum matrimoniorum, B. 2, fasc. 1, doc. 3.

10. Giustinian, *Venetiarum historia,* xviii–xv, 258, 276.

11. Ibid., 272.

12. "Distinzioni segrete che corrono tra le casate nobili di Venezia," BMV Ital. VII, 1531 (7638), ff. 2v–3r. See Romanin, *Storia documentata,* 4:305–6; Finlay, *Politics,* 92–96. On the number of patrician houses, see Chojnacki, "Social Identity," 345–46.

13. Lane, *Venice, a Maritime Republic,* 196–97, 201; see also Chap. 11.

14. MC 22, Ursa, ff. 47v–48r (26 May 1422).

15. Thirty councilors voted against the measure, and twenty-one abstained.

16. Of 478 votes cast on the first ballot, 244 were in favor of the act, 185 were opposed, and 49 abstained. On the first ballot, the combination of opposed and abstaining ballots had surpassed favorable ones by 243 to 225; on the second ballot, the nays and abstentions prevailed by 244 to 242. On the third ballot 244 yeas overcame 234 nays and abstentions. MC 19, Novella, f. 171v (28 December 1376).

17. Senato, Misti 53, f. 70rv (22 August 1420). The preamble is printed in Bistort, *Magistrato alle Pompe,* 107. Bistort (106–7) considers laws of 1334 and 1360 to have been aimed at restraining dowries, but they actually concern trousseaux and wedding gifts. For additional discussion of this law, see Chojnacki, "Marriage Legislation."

18. On the dowry, see Bellomo, *Ricerche,* 131–85; Ercole, "Istituto dotale," pt. 1:197–232; Hughes, "From Brideprice to Dowry," 278–85; Kirshner, "Wives' Claims," 256–65; Klapisch-Zuber, "Cruel Mother," 121–24; Kuehn, "Some Ambiguities," 238–41; and Chap. 6.

19. See Chap. 3. On the corredo see also Caso, "Per la storia," 523–7; Kirshner, "Materials for a Gilded Cage," 192–95; and Klapisch-Zuber, "Les corbeilles de la mariée," 216–20.

20. Bistort, *Magistrato alle Pompe,* 107.

21. Senato, Misti 53, f. 94v (30 December 1420).

22. On liberty as fundamental to the historical framing of Venice's public culture, see Crouzet-Pavan, *"Sopra le acque salse,"* 2:980–81; Tenenti, "Sense of Space and Time," 35–37.

23. Girolamo married in 1432, Jacopo in 1434; Barbaro, Nozze, f. 96v.

24. The date of the marriage is in ibid.

25. On these programs see Queller, *Venetian Patriciate,* 41–42; Chap. 11, below. On new procedures for proving noble status, see Chojnacki, "Social Identity," 343–48.

26. A law of 1392 raising the stipends of offices usually occupied by "our poorer nobles" was proposed because current stipends were so low that incumbents "were unable to live or support their families on the basis of them"; MC 21, Leona, f. 61v.

27. Barbaro, *De re uxoria,* 42–44, 50–53. For the English translation of pt. 2, see Barbaro, "On Wifely Duties."

28. MC 22, Ursa, f. 47v.

29. See Chojnacki, "Social Identity," 344, 347.

30. Bistort, *Magistrato alle Pompe*, 107.

31. Senato, Misti 53, f. 70r.

32. Maddaluzza Paruta Dolfin's dowry is in De Giudicato 2, f. 55v.

33. The two proposals received close votes in the first reading: the 2,000-ducat limit received 44 votes, the no-limit alternative, 39; the 15 abstentions prevented either side from winning a majority. On the third reading, the 2,000-ducat limit prevailed by 54 to 38 votes, with the abstentions falling to 12.

34. Antonio Dolfin's brother, Nicolò, received a dowry of 1,200 with a corredo of undetermined size from his wife, the daughter of a man described by Jacopo Gabriel and Pasquale Malipiero as "a popolano soap-maker"; APV, Causarum matrimoniorum, B. 2, fasc. 1, doc. 5. The dowry is in Vadimoni 4, f. 10v. Given the prevailing 2-to-1 ratio of dowry to corredo, as mandated in the law of 1420, it is likely that the total marriage portion was 1,800 ducats.

35. This interpretation corrects the argument in Chojnacki, "Marriage Legislation," 172–77.

36. Senato, Misti 53, f. 70rv.

37. Ibid. The statutes codified in the thirteenth century had already given married women freedom to make use of all their property, except dowry and bequests received during marriage, "as she pleases [*sicut sibi placuerit*]"; *Volumen statutorum*, lib. 1, cap. 39, p. 19v.

38. MC 22, Ursa, f. 176rv (28 December 1449).

39. Senato, Misti 53, f. 70v.

40. On marriage ages of women, see Molho, "Deception and Marriage Strategy," 194, 204–10, and passim; and Chap. 9.

41. Klapisch-Zuber, "Cruel Mother," 120–27.

42. An example of a widow bringing her children into her second marriage: In 1430, Franceschina de Castro acknowledged that her stepfather, Nicolò Vitturi, "kept me in your home from infancy until my marriage, clothed me, shod me, and treated me perfectly"; PSMC Miste, B. 307, Nicolò Vitturi, fasc. 2, parchment, 1 June 1430.

43. On male honor and unsupervised female sexuality, see Kirshner, *Pursuing Honor*, 6–10; Klapisch-Zuber, "Cruel Mother," 123; Molho, "Deception and Marriage Strategy," 206–10; Ruggiero, *Boundaries of Eros*, 16–44. On male honor and adequate provision for daughters' dowries, see Queller and Madden, "Father of the Bride," 704–5.

44. Senato, Misti 55, f. 101v.

45. Senato, Terra 1, f. 115v (21 January 1443/44).

46. Ibid.

47. MC 21, Leona, f. 169r (5 July 1407).

48. On the political implications of the myth, see Muir, *Civic Ritual*, 13–61; Finlay, *Politics*, 27–37. On the myth as republican ideology, see Silvano, *Republica de' Viniziani*.

49. E.g., Tenenti, "Sense of Space and Time," 22–33; Gaeta, "L'idea di Venezia," 632–41; but cf. Crouzet-Pavan, "*Sopra le acque salse*," 2:970–83.

50. On the nobility's central place in the myth already in the fourteenth century, see Crouzet-Pavan, "*Sopra le acque salse*," 2:971–72; on the myth's relation to patrician ideology, see Muir, *Civic Ritual*, 57.

51. Dieci, Misti 27, f. 171v.

52. Ibid., 31, ff. 109v–110r (31 August 1506). The Avogadori were to be notified within eight days of the birth. On the Libri d'Oro as the final stage in the evolution of the patriciate's exclusiveness, see Romanin, *Storia documentata*, 2:250; Kretschmayr, *Geschichte von Venedig*, 2:75–77; and Maranini, *La Costituzione di Venezia*, 2:62–65.

53. Dieci, Misti 31, f. 109v.

54. The official record was to include the given names of the newborn son and his mother, as well as the mother's surname and origin; ibid.

55. The law instructed nobles living abroad to register their sons with the Venetian government's local representatives within the eight-day period, and parish priests in Venice to transmit to the government the parental information on noble children they baptized. All these notices were then to be entered in the Avogadori's register; ibid.

56. See Chap. 12.

57. Ruggiero, *Boundaries of Eros*, 35–37, 90–91, 97–98; idem, *Binding Passions*, 3–7.

58. Sanudo, *Diarii*, vol. 41, col. 166 (11 April 1526).

59. Dieci, Misti 31, f. 110r.

60. Dieci, Comuni 2, f. 15v (26 April 1526).

61. This language appears in a law passed the previous day, which reaffirmed the requirements of the Libro d'Oro legislation of 1506; ibid., f. 14v (25 April 1526). It immediately precedes the marriage-registration act of 26 April in the register of deliberations and is a part of a single concerted legislative campaign by the Dieci, which continued into the next day as well, when another act further refined the Libro d'Oro procedures, reiterating the importance of the "acquaintance and knowledge of the mother"; ibid., f. 17rv (27 April 1526). The language of 25 April thus served as preamble to all three acts. Sanudo, *Diarii*, vol. 41, cols. 201–3.

62. Sanudo, *Diarii*, vol. 41, cols. 201–3. In his account of the promulgation of the Ten's laws in the Great Council, on 29 April, Sanudo noted that during their secret sessions the Ten determined that thirty illegitimate "suspects" who had been accorded noble status must have their credentials reexamined; col. 238.

63. Dieci, Comuni 2, f. 15v.

64. Ibid., f. 17r (*sic;* f. 16 is lacking).

65. On its significance, see Cozzi, "Domenico Morosini," 408–13 and passim, and Ventura, "Scrittori politici," 546–48.

66. Ventura, "Scrittori politici," 547; Cozzi, "Domenico Morosini," 421–27; Silvano, *Republica de' Viniziani*, 32.

67. "The state, according to Contarini, exists to ensure that through its institutions its citizens can lead happy lives in the exercise of virtue"; Gleason, *Gasparo Contarini*, 114–28; quotation on 114. See also Silvano, *Republica de' Viniziani*, 90–109; Ventura, "Scrittori politici," 551–53.

68. Dieci, Comuni 2, f. 14v.

69. Ventura, "Scrittori politici," 561.

70. The references to denigration and blemishes echo contemporary references to sodomy; see Labalme, "Sodomy and Venetian Justice," 232–34; Ruggiero, *Boundaries of Eros,* 127–34.

71. De Giudicatu, Regs. 1 and 2. For a discussion of these figures, see Chojnacki, "Social Identity," 354–56.

72. *Diarii,* vol. 1, col. 885.

73. Senato, Terra 15, ff. 93v–94v (4 November 1505).

74. Romano, *Housecraft and Statecraft,* 139–43.

75. Senato, Terra 15, ff. 93v–94v.

76. MC 22, Ursa, f. 176rv.

77. The penalty for dowries over 3,000 ducats fell on the husband: he would forfeit the excess over 3,000 and also be made to pay a fine equal to it; Senato, Terra 15, f. 93v.

78. On dowry as inheritance, see Kuehn, "Some Ambiguities," 238–41; Klapisch-Zuber, "Cruel Mother," 121–22.

79. Senato, Terra 15, f. 93v.

80. On the tensions created by a wealthy oligarchy whose members controlled the most powerful magistracies, see Cozzi, "Authority and the Law," 296–301; Gilbert, "Venice in the Crisis," 286, 290; Finlay, *Politics,* 59–81; and Gleason, *Gasparo Contarini,* 125–28. Sanudo's discussion of the passage of the 1505 law reports spirited debate in the Senate by some of the most prominent political figures of the time; *Diarii,* vol. 6, col. 253.

81. Cozzi, "Authority and the Law," 314.

82. Finlay, *Politics,* 74.

83. Senato, Terra 15, f. 93v.

84. Contratti di nozze 140/1, f. 5r (contract of Alvise Contarini and Maria Moro, 30 March 1506). Another sixteen (22%) of the seventy-two contracts registered between November 1505 and November 1507 involved dowries between 2,000 and 2,870 ducats. Thus 86 percent ranged from 2,000 to 3,000 ducats. None exceeded 3,000. Ibid., ff. 1r–66v.

85. *Diarii,* vol. 18, col. 330 (two 8,000-ducat dowries, 1514); ibid., vol. 57, cols. 478, 526 (both dowries of 10,000 ducats, 1533).

86. Senato, Terra 28, ff. 151r–152r (29 April 1535).

87. Ibid.

88. Tenenti, "Sense of Space and Time," 20–24; Tucci, "Psychology of the Venetian Merchant," 352–59; Gilbert, "Venice in the Crisis," 274–75.

89. Gilbert, "Venice in the Crisis," 274–75; Cozzi, "La donna, l'amore e Tiziano," 53–54.

90. For example, in the marriage contract between Piero Badoer and Cateruzza di Francesco Giustinian, registered on 9 February 1505/6, of the total portion of 3,000 ducats, "i do terzi de dita dote se die meter in carta, e uno terzo vadi per don de corieri, segundo consueto de la terra" [two-thirds of the said dowry should be notarized (as the wife's property), and one-third should be given (to the husband) as his corredo in keeping with the custom of our state]; Contratti di nozze 140/1, f. 4v. On the corredo, see Chap. 3.

91. Senato, Terra 28, ff. 153r–156r (12 May 1535), at f. 154v.

92. On Gritti's efforts to make public ceremonies more sober and dignified, see Muir, "Images of Power," 34–36.

93. Tafuri, *Venezia e il Rinascimento*, 162–63.

94. Contarini's coauthor, another ducal councilor named Alvise Mocenigo, was also an important governmental figure in these years, sitting regularly in the Council of Ten and the Signoria; Finlay, *Politics*, 253–54.

95. Gleason, *Gasparo Contarini*, 110, 129.

96. For different views see Tafuri, *Venezia e il Rinascimento*, 163; Gleason, *Gasparo Contarini*, 125–27; Silvano, *Republica de' Viniziani*, 26–28. Contarini's partner in the legislation, Alvise Mocenigo, was depicted by Sanudo as being a critic of Gritti's autocratic tendencies; Finlay, *Politics*, 231.

97. Contarini, *La Republica e I Magistrati*, ixr. On Contarini's view of the doge's function, see Silvano, *Republica de' Viniziani*, 95.

98. The translation is in Gleason, *Gasparo Contarini*, 122.

99. Contareno, *The Commonwealth and Gouernment*, 18. Cf. Contarini, *La Republica e I Magistrati*, xv.

100. The figure of 144 is derived from the list of extant patrician houses in 1527 in Sanudo, *Diarii*, vol. 44, cols. 569–72.

101. On persistent tensions between the wealthy elite and the noble majority, see Cozzi, "Authority and the Law," 298–301 and passim; Finlay, *Politics*, 71–81.

102. See Ventura, "Scrittori politici," 549–52, with reference to Contarini's description of these divisions. Sanudo's quotation of Gritti's statement is translated in Finlay, *Politics*, 80–81.

Chapter 3   From Trousseau to Groomgift

This chapter originally appeared, in slightly altered form, as "From Trousseau to Groomgift in Late Medieval Venice," in *Medieval and Renaissance Venice*, ed. Ellen E. Kittell and Thomas F. Madden (Urbana: University of Illinois Press, 1999), 141–65.

1. For references to the literature, see the citations in Queller and Madden, "Father of the Bride," 688 nn. 8 and 9. See, in addition, Fabbri, *Alleanza matrimoniale;* Gregory, "Daughters, Dowries, and the Family"; Kirshner, *Pursuing Honor;* and Molho, *Marriage Alliance.*

2. Queller and Madden, "Father of the Bride," 695, 703.

3. Ibid., 706.

4. Ibid., 686–87. This is the place to acknowledge that the authors make generous reference to earlier articles by me, as in their discussion of the 1,000-ducat dowry average. I am grateful to their initiative for providing an opportunity for elaboration and correction of some of the findings in my earlier studies.

5. CI 114, Marino, S. Tomà, prot. 1366–91, unfoliated.

6. Throughout this chapter sums in the various Venetian moneys of account will be converted into ducats, using equivalences in Lane and Mueller, *Money and Banking*, 131, 291.

7. CI 114, Marino, acts of 13 March 1380, 27 February 1382/83, 20 August 1382, and 20 March 1377, respectively.

8. Ibid., acts of 4 January 1384/85, 12 November 1376, 15 January 1374/75, and 22 September 1371, respectively.

9. Queller and Madden, "Father of the Bride," 704.

10. Ibid., 690–92.

11. They use a median figure of 100 ducats in their computation despite an average of 320 ducats among the nonpaternal contributions they studied. See ibid., 690 n. 16.

12. Ibid., 693 n. 22.

13. Ibid., 689, fig. 2.

14. Widows were the survivers 116 times (81.7%); widowers 26 times (18.3%). In addition to these 142, Marino's entries record 24 cases in which both spouses were dead and 2 with the survivor uncertain. (The 2 uncertain survivors corrects the number 6 in the version of this chapter published in Kittell and Madden, *Medieval and Renaissance Venice.*) See the discussion of dowry restitution in Chap. 4.

15. Probably the most famous case of a widowed mother arranging her daughter's marriage is that of Alessandra Macinghi Strozzi in Florence; see Strozzi, *Selected Letters,* 29–33; also, Phillips, *Memoir of Marco Parenti,* 150–65; Fabbri, *Alleanza matrimoniale,* 78–79 and passim. Also on widows in Florence, see Chabot, "Sposa in nero"; Crabb, "How Typical Was Alessandra Strozzi?"; Klapisch-Zuber, "Cruel Mother"; and Rosenthal, "Position of Women."

16. NT 108, Boninsegna, no. 296.

17. NT 575, Gibellino, no. 704.

18. The 2,000 ducats from Beruzza's bequest and the contribution she encouraged from Girolamo would have represented a minimum cash component of Caterina's portion, because her father's provision for her marriage may have—indeed, is likely to have—included cash in addition to real estate. I have not consulted Marco Soranzo's will.

19. Queller and Madden, "Father of the Bride," 694. Some testating widowers expressly mentioned their late wives' bequests to their daughters' marriage portions. In 1374 Marino Lion specified his own allocation for the dowry of his daughter Caterina, then added 500 lire a grossi (equal to 192 ducats) "of the goods left to me by her mother"; Procurator, Sentenze a Legge, Reg. 1, ff. 65v–66r. In 1427 Michele Navagero made marriage bequests of 1,600 and 1,000 ducats, respectively, to his daughters Paseta and Castellana, which both included "their legacies from their mother." NT 1157, Dalle Croci, prot. II, f. 14r. Queller and Madden do not indicate whether they calculated such explicit acknowledgments as paternal or nonpaternal contributions.

20. Queller and Madden, "Father of the Bride," 706–7.

21. Senato, Misti 53, f. 70rv. This act is analyzed in Chojnacki, "Marriage Legislation," and Chap. 2.

22. On the varied beneficence of men and women, see Queller and Madden, "Father of the Bride," 696, and Chap. 9.

23. Chojnacki, "Marriage Legislation," 164–66.

24. Queller and Madden, "Father of the Bride," 685–86.

25. Procurator, Sentenze a Legge, Reg. 2, ff. 56v–57r (12 February 1381/82). The corredo allocation is not mentioned by Queller and Madden.

26. Ibid. On the basis of Marco Querini's immovable wealth of 2,000 ducats, as estimated in the official cadastral survey of 1379, Queller and Madden suggest that in allocating 1,000 ducats to Franceschina's dowry Marco was "alienating half the value of [the] family's real property" ("Father of the Bride," 688). His total wealth must have been considerably greater than 2,000 ducats, however, if he contemplated total marriage portions of 1,500 ducats to each of at least two daughters—to say nothing of the seven sons Queller and Madden have identified ("Father of the Bride," 685 n. 2).

27. Queller and Madden, "Father of the Bride," 705.

28. Queller and Madden do not quote the language of Regina's paternal bequest. If, like many other fathers, he allocated it simply "for her marriage" (*pro suo maritare*), then he doubtless envisaged its division into dowry and corredo, as did the many other fathers such as Marco Querini who made the proportions explicit. The importance of the distinction is conveyed by a scribal error in the records of the Giudici del Procurator, in 1381. Recording the judges' authorization that a testator's daughter draw the amount her father had specifically left for her dowry, the scribe wrote *pro suo maritare*—then crossed out *maritare* and wrote instead *repromissa*, that is, dowry. Procurator, Sentenze a Legge, Reg. 1, ff. 65v–66r.

29. On the evolution, see Chojnacki, "Social Identity."

30. Fundamental studies of the the the dowry are Bellomo, *Ricerche*, 131–85, and Ercole, "Istituto dotale," 1:197–232. For early dowry practice in Venice, see Zordan, "I vari aspetti."

31. In Florence, also, a widow was entitled to her entire dowry; see Kirshner, "Materials for a Gilded Cage," 184–85. In Milan, the widowed mother of a male heir regained her entire dowry except her wedding regalia; see Caso, "Per la storia," 525.

32. On the corredo in general, see Ercole, "Istituto dotale," 1:201–3; Zordan, "I vari aspetti," 133; Besta, *La famiglia*, 145. More specifically pertinent studies are Caso, "Per la storia," and Klapisch-Zuber, "Les corbeilles de la mariée."

33. CI 87, Gaffaro, parchment no. 23.

34. On the case vecchie, see Romanin, *Storia documentata*, 4:305–6; on their identification as the *longhi*, see Finlay, *Politics*, 92–96.

35. On the admission in 1303 of the Lion and six other houses after the fall of Acre, see BMV Ital. VII, 719 (7425), f. 75v. On the Lion's prominence in the 1350s, see Lazzarini, *Marino Faliero*, 205 and passim.

36. *Volumen statutorum*, lib. 3, cap. 28, 29, p. 49v bis; see also Chap. 5, below. On the general principle of ensuring the wife's dowry, see Kirshner, "Wives' Claims."

37. For example, in 1415 Girardo Dandolo, acknowledging receipt of his wife's dowry of 120 lire di grossi (1,200 ducats) "in solid cash [*de bonis denariis*]," secured it with bonds from Marco Dandolo, who pledged his property as surety for 800 ducats of the sum; Orsato Giustinian, who pledged his for the remaining 400; and Orsato's father, Marco Giustinian, who assumed responsibility as counterpledge (*contraplezius*) of both sureties. CI 229, Della Valle, prot., ff. 34r–35r.

38. In 1356 *nobilis vir* Marino Avonal "gave, assigned, and transacted [*dedit, et assignavit, atque transactavit*]" to his wife real estate appraised by the Giudici del

Esaminador as worth 1,000 lire a grossi (385 ducats), "for her entire dowry [*pro tota sua repromissa*]" of the same amount. She was fully invested with the property sixteen months later. CI 115, Marino, S. Tomà, prot. IV, no foliation, 5 January 1357/58.

39. On the corredo as advertising the prestige of the bride's family, see Esposito, "Strategie matrimoniali," 580–81; Klapisch-Zuber, "Les corbeilles de la mariée"; for a different emphasis, see Klapisch-Zuber, "Griselda Complex."

40. CI 117, Marcella, prot. C, f. 7r.

41. NT 1189 (notary unnoted), no. 83.

42. NT 1154, Bruto, no. 32.

43. NT 1023, Cavazza, no. 23.

44. Bistort, *Magistrato alle Pompe*, 332. On 106 Bistort erroneously states that this was a limit on dowries.

45. Romanin, *Storia documentata*, 3:280–82.

46. Ibid., 280.

47. The law of 1360 went on to prescribe limits for expenditure on apparel and jewelry by married and unmarried women and even men; ibid., 281–82. The law of 9 June 1334 was soon followed by another one, on 20 June, which described in great detail the types of clothing regarded as excessive; Bistort, *Magistrato alle Pompe*, 333–52. Also on laws restraining nuptial extravagance, see Newett, "Sumptuary Laws," 261–64. For a general interpretation of sumptuary expenditure as gender-specific social gesture, see Hughes, "Sumptuary Law"; see also Kovesi Killerby, "Practical Problems."

48. On the dominance of the case vecchie in the Senate, see Chojnacki, "La formazione della nobiltà," 667–69.

49. He added to his own dowry bequest another 500 lire a grossi (192 ducats) that his late wife had bequeathed to him. Procurator, Sentenze a Legge, Reg. 1, ff. 65v–66r.

50. PSMC Miste, B. 2, Giovanni Morosini, copy of the will in the unpaginated register of the estate's administration.

51. NT 1255, Zane, prot., ff. 184v–186v.

52. On the economic effects of the war of Chioggia, see Luzzatto, *Debito pubblico*, 161–76, and Mueller, "Effetti della Guerra."

53. CI 54, Crescimbeni, prot. "1403," f. 15r.

54. Ibid.

55. CI 36, Campion, prot. II, f. 125v.

56. BMC, Codici Cicogna, no. 3427/11, parchment dated 8 January 1343/44. For fourteen as the age of majority for unmarried women, see the Great Council act of 2 May 1299, reproduced in Bistort, *Magistrato alle Pompe*, 324.

57. The type of lira was not specified. If it was in lire a grossi, then the 1,000 lire would be equal to 385 ducats. If it was in lire di piccoli, then it would be equal to 313 ducats. For interpretations of references to unspecified lire, see Lane and Mueller, *Money and Banking*, 131–33.

58. CI 241, Zane, prot. "1388–1428," f. 51v.

59. The law is reprinted in Newett, "Sumptuary Laws," 252–53 n. 14. A *pelanda* was a "garment with long and wide sleeves"; Sella, *Glossario*, 424. On the

costliness of *pelande*, see Caso, "Per la storia," 530–31. I have been unable to determine the meaning of "denisado." The word may be a variant of *nasiciis*, which according to Bistort was one of the most costly fabrics, so much so that its use was permitted only to brides; see the lengthy discussion in Bistort, *Magistrato alle Pompe*, 334–38 n. 1; also Vitali, *La moda*, 261–62.

60. The barrier-raising legislation and its effects are discussed, with reference to the Serrata, in Chojnacki, "Social Identity," 341–48. For evidence of alliance-seeking marriage strategies in the Mocenigo clan, see Betto, "Linee di politica matrimoniale," 54–55 and passim.

61. Queller, *Venetian Patriciate*, 29–50. Also on office holding as a major noble concern in the Quattrocento, see Cozzi, "Authority and the Law," 297–301; Finlay, *Politics*, 72–81. The preamble to a Great Council measure of 1490 stated flatly that "the majority of our nobles support their families by office holding." MC 12, Stella, f. 109v.

62. The doge and his son, Nicolò Venier, gave notarized acknowledgment that they had received the last installment of this immense dowry on 22 December 1393; Doge Antonio pledged his property toward its restitution. CI 17, Belancini, prot. IV, no foliation. Like other dowry receipts, this one is silent on the *corredo*.

63. CI 193, Soris, prot. 1410, f. 2r (17 April 1410). The Cinquecento genealogist Marco Barbaro identified Bragadin's daughter, named Isabetta, as a *bastarda*; Barbaro, Nozze, f. 151v.

64. Queller and Madden, "Father of the Bride," 709.

65. CI, Miscellanea, Testamenti Diversi, B. 27, no. 2697.

66. For examples of fathers favoring daughters' marriage portions at the expense of sons, see Chap. 7.

Chapter 4   Getting Back the Dowry

This chapter originally appeared, in slightly altered form and in Italian, as "Riprendersi la dote: Venezia ca. 1360–1530," in *Tempi e spazi di vita femminile nella prima età moderna*, ed. Silvana Seidel Menchi, Anne Jacobson Schutte, and Thomas Kuehn (Bologna: Il Mulino, 1999).

1. For a recent assessment, see Judith C. Brown, introduction to Brown and Davis, *Gender and Society*, 1–15.

2. Klapisch-Zuber, "Cruel Mother" and "Griselda Complex"; Chabot, "Sposa in nero" and "Widowhood and Poverty"; Molho, *Marriage Alliance* and "Deception and Marriage Strategy"; Kirshner, *Pursuing Honor*. On statutes restricting women's rights, see Kirshner, "Materials for a Gilded Cage" and "Maritus Lucretur Dotem."

3. Calvi, "Diritti e legami" and "Reconstructing the Family"; Kuehn, "Some Ambiguities" and "Understanding Gender Inequality." See also Molho et al., "Genealogia e parentado"; Baxendale, "Exile in Practice," 740–45; Rosenthal, "Position of Women"; Crabb, "How Typical Was Alessandra Strozzi?"; Gregory, "Daughters, Dowries, and the Family."

4. Chabot, "Sposa in nero."

5. See, in addition to the references above, Hughes, "From Brideprice to Dowry." For a recent summary, see Chap. 1.

6. CI 114, Marino, S. Tomà, prot. 1366–91.

7. De Giudicato 1 and 2.

8. The dates of dowry payments to husbands are given in only 142 of the 168 cases. The dates refer to the original conveyances of dowries repaid between 1366 and 1390 to widows or their designees. Amounts given in other moneys have been converted into ducats, using conversion tables in Lane and Mueller, *Money and Banking*, 131, 291.

9. Only 122 of the 139 Quattrocento diiudicatus cases give precise dowry totals. De Giudicato 1 and 2.

10. Contratti di nozze 140/1, ff. 1r–66v. This figure represents the two-thirds portion of the total marriage settlement which was designated as dowry strictly speaking, exclusive of the *corredo* (see below).

11. On the evolution of the corredo into a premium for the husband, see Chap. 3, above.

12. For a brief review, see Chap. 1.

13. The dowry-recovery procedures are in *Volumen statutorum*, lib. 1, caps. 54–62, pp. 24v–29v. For a review of the relevant statutes and their application, see Bellavitis, "Famiglia 'cittadina.' "

14. The documentation was to be presented to the court by the widow's *fideiussor*, or guarantor, whom she had convinced of the validity of her claim. The statutory correction of Doge Andrea Dandolo in 1343 required that the *fideiussor's* brief (*breviarium*) could no longer merely be notarized but must be subscribed by the Giudici del Proprio. *Volumen statutorum*, lib. 6, cap. 7, p. 89v.

15. Ibid., lib. 1, cap. 60, p. 27v.

16. Ibid., lib. 6, cap. 17, p. 93v.

17. On Florence, see Chabot, "Sposa in nero," 438–40.

18. NT 1255, Zane, prot., ff. 184v–86v. For other examples, see NT 670, Marino, no. 116; NT 1157, Croci, prot. 2, f. 14r; NT 1233, Sorio, no. 257; NT 558, Gambaro, no. 86; NT 1149, Benedetto, no. 16; CI, Miscellanea Testamenti, B. 27, nos. 2578 and 2697.

19. On the remarriage of widows in Florence, see Klapisch-Zuber, "Cruel Mother," 120, 125–27. In the seventeenth and eighteenth centuries, Florentine widows were chosen as guardians of their children in 75.4 percent of cases; see Calvi, "Diritti e legami," 490–91.

20. "Nihil tamen noceat hoc in repromissa viduantis." *Volumen statutorum*, lib. 4, cap. 34, p. 76v.

21. Proprio, Testimoni, Reg. 4, f. 14r (Grimani); Vadimoni 8, f. 30rv (Priuli). The reference to Leonardo Priuli's will is to the probated copy, dated 24 December 1478, but it was actually written in March 1477. See the following note.

22. "Item Marie dilectissime uxori mee integre dimitto dotem suam quam habui, ducatorum triamillia, quamquam uxorem meam oro ut dictam dotem quandocumque non est ei numorum necessitas ad filiorum nostrorum utilitatem in mea comissaria per quinquennium si ei placuerit remanere permittat. Insuper ei dimitto vestimenta et res suas quas habuit a patre suo, et item quas feci quae omnia eidem libere remanere volo et pro suis haberi. Exceptis omnibus meis iocalibus et zoiis quae in meo residuo remanere et computari volo. Item eidem

dimitto viduando vitum et vestitum prout meis comissariis videbitur condic-
tionibus suis convenire; plusque [?] ei dimittere si plus aut necessitas sua exigeret,
aut facultati meae conveniret. Cui quidam dillectissime uxori meae commendo
charissimum filium nostrum Zacariam omnesque alios filios et filias nostras
nascituras ut patri amisso et matris et patris loco illorum curari suscipiret."
    I have deciphered the text from Vadimoni 8, f. 3orv and a more elegantly
legible copy, in Priuli's own hand, bearing the date *"kalendis martii"* 1477, in NT
1239, Tomei, no. 413.
    23. Maria's 1475 marriage to Leonardo Priuli is in Barbaro, Nozze, f. 368v; her
1479 marriage to the widower Piero Loredan is in ibid., f. 246r.
    24. BO 164/3, f. 140v. She was identified in the registration record as Maria
Loredan, widow of Leonardo Priuli. I have found no record of any children from
her second marriage. On the participation of mothers in the Barbarella, or Balla
d'Oro, see Chap. 6.
    25. In a group of 859 marriages of patrician women in the Quattrocento, only
74, 8.6 percent, were remarriages of widows. Barbaro, Nozze. The 859 cases are
marriages of women from, or into, sixteen selected noble clans; see Chap. 10.
    26. Vadimoni 1, 4, 5, 8, 9; Proprio, Testimoni, Reg. 4; Proprio, Parentelle, Reg.
1; CI 126, Buosi, parchments. These 138 claims are part of the total sample of 163
fifteenth-century vadimoniums studied; the other 25 are not clear about the beginning date of the marriage.
    27. *Volumen statutorum*, lib. 1, cap. 54, p. 25v. As one example, Alberto Badoer,
filing his mother's vadimonium in 1477, documented her dowry with a dowry
receipt of 1442; the scribe then noted: "Datum infra XXXta annos cum ipse dominus Albertus Badoer quondam domini Danielis uti scriptus in curia pro domina
Helena eius matre juravit in anima sua nescivisse legem." Vadimoni 8, f. 13r.
    28. *Volumen statutorum*, lib. 1, cap. 54, p. 24v.
    29. Widows themselves lodged their claims in 106 (87.6 percent) of the 121
vadimoniums involving living women. The other 15 were filed by the widows'
proctors, usually family members. The following table shows the survival of
spouses at vadimonium filings:

	Cases	%
Wife survives, husband dead	121	74.2
Husband survives, wife dead	6	3.7
Wife dead, husband uncertain	14	8.6
Both deceased	22	13.5
Total	163	100

    30. MC 22, Ursa, f. 17orv. Only 158 of the 163 fifteenth-century vadimonium
claims studied indicate clearly the type of documentation presented.
    31. E.g., De Giudicato 1, f. 12r; 2, ff. 13r, 13v, 18r, etc. Among 105 diiudicatus
awards for which the documentation was indicated, 10.1 percent used marriage
contracts. (This diiudicatus figure should not be confused with the 22 percent of
vadimonium claims based on contracts, as discussed here.)
    32. Eighty-five (28.1 percent) of 302 vadimoniums and diiudicatus from the

fifteenth century involved the dowries of deceased women and were therefore handled by the women's executors or beneficiaries. Note that this group does not include the fourteenth-century diiudicatus that are part of the total in table 2.

33. Information from the 42 of the 163 Quattrocento vadimoniums that were filed for deceased women; see the table in note 29, above.

34. *Volumen statutorum*, lib. 4, cap. 28, p. 74v. For examples of married women filing their mother's vadimonium, see Vadimoni 4, ff. 20r, 15r. In the latter instance, Agnesina, wife of Nicolò Loredan, filed for her one-sixth share of the dowry of her mother seven months after her brother, Arsenio Vitturi, had filed for his one-sixth share; ibid., f. 11r.

35. Unmarried daughters were to succeed equally with unemancipated brothers to movables but not immovables, as long as their share was adequate to provide them with a suitable dowry. *Volumen statutorum*, lib. 4, cap. 25, p. 71v.

36. On women's testamentary bequests, see Chap. 5.

37. Zanetta had named Nicolò as an executor in her will of 1443, fifteen years before the vadimonium but nineteen years after she married; Vadimoni 4, f. 11v. In another example, Antonio Tron, as one of the *commissari* named in the will of his sister, the late Orsa Tron Foscarini, filed the vadimonium in 1460 for the dowry that had been conveyed to Orsa's late husband thirty-two years earlier, in 1428; Proprio, Testimoni, Reg. 4, f. 34v.

38. For examples of both husbands and wives choosing their spouses as executors, see Chap. 7, below. For Florentine husbands choosing their wives as executors, see Calvi, "Diritti e legami."

39. *Volumen statutorum*, lib. 1, cap. 34, p. 17v; lib. 4, cap. 24, p. 71v; MC 21, Leona, f. 233v.

40. *Volumen statutorum*, lib. 3, caps. 28 and 29, pp. 49v^2 and 49v^3. (The pagination repeats p. 49 twice.)

41. De Giudicato 1 and 2. The total number of diiudicatus judgments examined in these fifteenth-century registers is 139. This total includes the 122 mentioned earlier, as well as another 17 in which the original amount of the dowry (though not the sum authorized in the judgment) is unclear or absent.

42. The first three deductions are in *Volumen statutorum*, lib. 1, cap. 55, p. 25v. On the contributions of mothers to their daughters' dowries, see Queller and Madden, "Father of the Bride," and Chap. 8.

43. On the provision of widows' garb in Florence, see Chabot, "Sposa in nero," 433–36.

44. Kirshner, "Wives' Claims."

45. Twenty-nine of the 139 diiudicatus judgments included such assignments of secondary liability.

46. This information is derived from an analysis of 83 marriage contracts or notarized dowry receipts from 1427 to 1541.

47. Proprio, Testimoni, Reg. 4, f. 18rv.

48. "Son debitor a Prospera Arimondo mia consorte." Vadimoni 4, f. 45r.

49. *Volumen statutorum*, lib. 4, cap. 34, p. 17v; MC 21, Leona, f. 233v.

50. One example of the formula: in 1407 Paolo Orio gave a notarized security to Elisabetta, "uxori sue dilecte, de tota illa repromissa que tempore sue desponsa-

tionis pro ea sibi dari promissa fuit, que repromissa fuit hucusque in toto libre duecentequinquaginta due denariorum venetorum grossorum [equal to 2,520 ducats]." Vadimoni 1, f. 2v.

51. On the Florentine practice, see Molho, *Marriage Alliance,* 319–24.

52. Contratti di nozze 142/3, f. 188rv. If the fund in which the 2,000 ducats were invested should be liquidated, Marcantonio would be able to choose a substitute government fund or invest them in a bank; in any case they were to remain Morosina's *fondo dotal.*

53. Esaminador, Vendizioni, Reg. 7, 15r–16r. The 6,000 ducats were designated not as dowry but as *dimissoria,* or inheritance, which, though under the husband's administration, was considered the wife's property outside the strict limits of the dowry. The part of the marriage portion designated as *dimissoria* was not subject to the dowry limit of 1,600 ducats set in 1420, and another act on the same day reaffirmed a wife's right to the income from her *dimissoria.* Senato, Misti 53, f. 70rv.

54. "Si veramente che xe la dita dona Issabeta per nexun tempo vora chel dito ser tomado so mario faza scriver ala camera de imprestedi ducati mille de quella moneda, el dito ser tomado sia tenuto a farli scriver." Proprio, Testimoni, Reg. 4, f. 22r (1453). Of the 1,000 ducats in cash that Laura Montorio's mother contributed to her dowry, "500 ducats are to be invested in a [government] fund as the wife's dowry security." Contratti di nozze 142/3, f. 173v (1530). Of the 1,600-ducat dowry that Girolamo Soranzo was to receive from his bride, Marina Tron, "400 are to be earmarked for the dowry's restitution." Contratti di nozze 140/1, f. 9r (1506).

55. Contratti di nozze 142/3, f. 234rv. Regina Barbaro's dowry in 1412 included 500 ducats' worth of prestiti shares for which Regina's bridegroom was to "have a dowry receipt notarized indicating their current price." Vadimoni 4, f. 25v. Subsequently, the groom documented receipt of the 400 prestiti ducats, which equaled 232 gold ducats, "at the rate of 58 percent."

56. The government periodically reaffirmed the principle. The Great Council had passed a law to that effect in 1291, and a copy of it was inserted into the capitulary of the Giudici del Proprio, who had jurisdiction in dowry restitution. Vadimoni, B. 2, pp. 34–35. The stricture was reiterated in a dowry-limiting act of 1505; Senato, Terra 15, f. 93v.

57. On Florence, see Molho, *Marriage Alliance,* 324. On the practice in Venice, see Crouzet-Pavan, *"Sopra le acque salse,"* 1:447–58.

58. *Volumen statutorum,* lib. 1, cap. 61, p. 27v.

59. Ibid., lib. 3, cap. 28, p. 49v[2].

60. CI 70, Darvasio, prot. "1398," no foliation, 9 August 1398. The court action was initiated by Marina's father, Piero Zancani.

61. Contratti di nozze 142/3, f. 199v. The total dowry was 3,000 ducats.

62. "A modo cum plenissima virtute et potestate intromittendi, habendi, tenendi, dandi, donandi, vendendi, committendi, et proprio possidendi, vel quicquid aliud inde tibi placuerit faciendi." The two apartments were contiguous (*insimul coniuncta*). CI 15, Nicolò Benedetto, parchment, 14 November 1365.

63. CI 70, Darvasio, unfoliated fascicle beginning 17 June 1412; the act confirming his wife's ownership is dated 30 October 1413. On the meaning of *domus a statio* as noble residence, see Crouzet-Pavan, *"Sopra le acque salse,"* 1:471–526.

64. For Jacopo Morosini, CI 70, Darvasio, prot. "1409," f. 31r (1410). Lucia was confirmed in possession of it after being invested *ad proprium* by the judges. For Luca Falier, Vadimoni 4, 11r (1457). Luca also assigned to Maria an inn (*hostellum*) and an adjacent house in Mirano. In both cases the term for rental property is *domus a sergentibus,* used in Venice to describe modest habitations, usually rented out by the owner. See Crouzet-Pavan, *"Sopra le acque salse,"* 1:471–72 n. 13.

65. Contratti di nozze 142/3, ff. 124v–125r (1529).

66. Vadimoni 4, f. 54v.

67. CI 96, Griffon, prot. II, f. 25r.

68. An example of four brothers pledging is in Proprio, Testimoni, Reg. 4, f. 26r. Examples of three are in ibid., f. 32v; and Vadimoni 4, ff. 19rv, 25rv, 54v, 64v.

69. Only the movable portion of the father's estate was to be used for this purpose. *Volumen statutorum,* lib. 4, cap. 24, p. 71v; see also lib. 1, cap. 56, p. 26v.

70. E.g., the wills of Ermolao Pisani in 1469/70 and Prodocimo Arimondo in 1473/74: NT 1238, Tomei, series 2, no. 15; NT 1239, Tomei, no. 606.

71. Vadimoni 4, ff. 25v–26v. For another example of fathers providing housing and living expenses to their sons and daughters-in-law, see Esaminador, Vendizioni, Reg. 7, ff. 15r–16r.

72. Kuehn, *Emancipation,* 143–44.

73. He made two such declarations, at payments of the two installments of the dowry. CI 17, Belancini, prot. IV, no foliation, acts of 6 February 1392/93 and 22 December 1393.

74. "Ha da sij de beni de so mare e de so madona ducati mille e zinquezento zoe mvᶜ." Vadimoni 4, ff. 25v–26v.

75. The sum was 42 lire di grossi, "o circha," equal to 420 ducats. The judgment was against Francesco Loredan; the maternal grandmother identified herself as Agnesina Loredan, widow of Bernabò Loredan. Ibid., ff. 29v–30v.

76. Other examples are in ibid., ff. 58v–59v.

77. Ibid., Reg. 5, f. 10v (Piero Bragadin and Maria Contarini).

78. Ibid., ff. 4v–5r.

79. Ibid., Reg. 8, ff. 38v–40r (1479); Contratti di nozze 142/3, f. 95v (1528).

80. Additional examples of women securing the dowries of their sons and grandsons on their property: Vadimoni 4 ff. 48v, 64v; 5, f. 10r; 8, ff. 42r–43v; Proprio, Testimoni, Reg. 4, ff. 17r, 23v–24r, 26r; Contratti di nozze 140/1, f. 3v; 142/3, ff. 46rv, 161v–162r, 173v–174r, 205v–206r.

81. On women's contributions to their daughters' dowries, see Queller and Madden, "Father of the Bride," 695–99, and Chap. 6.

82. For Isabetta Corner, CI 162, Colonna, prot. 1457, ff. 4v–5r. For Laura Bragadin, Contratti di nozze 142/3, ff. 265v–265 rbis.

83. For Agostino Coppo, Vadimoni 4, f. 25v. For Giovanni Dolfin, Vadimoni 8, ff. 42r–43v.

Chapter 5   Patrician Women in Early Renaissance Venice

This chapter originally appeared, in slightly altered form, as "Patrician Women in Early Renaissance Venice," *Studies in the Renaissance* 21 (1974): 176–203.

1. Cecchetti, "La donna nel medioevo," 344.

2. Power, "Position of Women," 433; Herlihy, "Land, Family, and Women," 89. See also Herlihy's more comprehensive statement *Women in Medieval Society.*

3. M. Petiot, as quoted in Ariès, *Centuries of Childhood,* 356.

4. Goldthwaite, "Florentine Palace," 1011. Discussing household relations during this period, David Herlihy notes the contemporary view that the upbringing of children was "too much dominated by women," with unfortunate results for the children's characters. In any case, Herlihy goes on, a wife, usually years younger than her husband, "enjoyed a more intimate, and usually a longer contact with her children"; moreover, wives normally survived into a grandmotherly widowhood, during which they "lived with their married sons, aided in the management of their homes and the raising of their children." Herlihy does not, however, state that this was a recent development. "Some Psychological and Social Roots," 148–49.

5. On women in Germanic and Roman law, see Herlihy, "Land, Family, and Women," 89–91; Pertile, *Storia del diritto,* 3:232–44. On property aspects, see Ercole, "Istituto dotale," and Brandileone, "Studi preliminari."

6. The rules governing succession to intestate individuals are in *Volumen statutorem,* lib. 4, caps. 24–27, pp. 70v–74v.

7. On the fraterna, see Fumagalli, *Il diritto di fraterna;* also Besta, *La famiglia,* 207–9; Pertile, *Storia del diritto,* 3:282; and, on Venice, Ferro, *Dizionario del diritto,* 5:276–78.

8. "Filie . . . sint contente dote sua." *Volumen statutorum,* lib. 4, cap. 25, p. 73v. See also Ercole, "Istituto dotale," pt. 1:212–22.

9. See the discussion, with full bibliographical references, in Lane, "Enlargement of the Great Council," esp. 252 ff. On the extent of the restrictiveness of the measures, see Chojnacki, "In Search of the Venetian Patriciate," 52–58. In the present chapter, *family* refers to the conjugal (or nuclear) domestic group made up of parents and children, married or unmarried; *lineage* is a consanguineal kin group whose members' knowledge of their relationships stems from their knowledge of their descent from a common ancestor; *clan* is a consanguineal kin group whose members exhibit a sense of community but whose common ancestor is too far back in the past to be traced accurately. (The older Venetian patrician houses are clans in this sense.) See Fox, *Kinship and Marriage,* 36–40, 49–50; Murdock, *Social Structure,* 46–75.

10. The evolving requirements for demonstration of patrician status are in AC, Reg. 14, ff. 3r–12v, and BMV Ital. VII, 196 (8578), ff. 1r–5r. The legislation is summarized in Merores, "Grosse Rat," 76–81; Lane, "Enlargement of the Great Council," 254–58; Chojnacki, "In Search of the Venetian Patriciate," 52–53.

11. NT 571, Giorgio Gibellino, "carte varie," dated 28 April 1401. Another example: in 1416 Nicolò di Giovanni Morosini instructed that his unmarried sister be given the means of marrying "cum honore et prout congruit conditionem domus mee honorificentius." NT 1234, Francesco Sorio, no. 509.

12. The sample is taken from a group of 305 wills written by members of the Morosini clan or by wives of Morosini men. I simply selected the first fifty married males and the first fifty married females alphabetically. The total number of bequests is 235 for the men, 215 for the women. The wills are in various funds

of the ASV, especially NT, CI, and the *commissarie* (accounts of estate administration) in PSMC.

In several cases an individual testator (or testatress) wrote more than one of the wills in the sample. Thus the fifty women's wills were written by thirty-seven women, and the fifty men's wills by forty-four men; so bequests in later wills cancel out those in the earlier ones. For present purposes, however, the way legacies were finally paid is less important than testators' intentions at the time of the will. The evidence of wills written at different points in the testators' life cycles and in those of their beneficiaries makes the sample more representative by accounting for changes in those intentions.

13. This can be seen more easily in tabular form:

	Men's Bequests		Women's Bequests	
	No.	%	No.	%
To natal kin	65	27.7	107	49.7
To marital kin	156	66.4	96	44.7
To affinal kin	14	5.9	12	5.6
Totals	235	100	215	100

It should be noted that bequests to kinsmen dominated in women's wills. Occasionally, a woman would make a small bequest to a friend—for example, Orsa Morosini's 1425 legacy of 20 ducats to "amice mee" Chiara Contarini (CI 24, Rolandino Bernardo, 16, f. 75v, no. 209). But except for such rare exceptions (as well as more frequent nonkinship bequests listed in the category of pious charity), bequests by women generally remained within the web of kinship.

14. The specificity of men's bequests to children, as compared with the generality in women's wills, suggests that fathers had more precise intentions regarding the economic destinies of individual children.

15. This inference is reinforced by the fact that men's bequests to mothers and sisters outnumbered those to fathers and brothers by 16 to 4. For the fraterna in action in Venice, see Lane, "Family Partnerships."

16. Two of the women and four of the men with living spouses mentioned previous marriages. It should be noted that women married younger than men did and tended to survive their husbands more frequently than the reverse; this was a general trend, not just reflected in these wills, so widowed women would tend to be younger than widowed men. On marriage ages, see Chap. 8; on widows' survival, see Chap. 4.

17. On the developmental cycles of families, see Fortes, introduction to Goody, *Developmental Cycle*, 2–4, and Laslett, introduction to Laslett and Wall, *Household and Family*, 32–34.

18. Women were legally entitled to full restitution of their dowry upon the death of their husbands; however, many men still specifically authorized repayment of the dowry in the wills, presumably to spare their future widows the inconveniences involved in the dowry-restitution procedure. In addition, large numbers of men made bequests to their wives over and above the dowry, as an

inducement to them not to remarry, so that the children of the marriage would be cared for by their mother, and without a stepfather from another lineage. In such bequests the condition that the widow not remarry is often explicit. On widows' rights to dowry restitution, see Ercole, "Istituto dotale," pt. 2:222 ff.

19. The statutes did require mothers to contribute to their sons, however. *Volumen statutorum*, lib. 5, cap. 28, p. 74v. See also Pertile, *Storia del diritto*, 4:91–95.

20. Fortes, "Structure of Unilineal Descent Groups," 32.

21. Ibid., 33.

22. The male testators in the sample made thirty-nine bequests to secondary natal male kin but only four bequests to primary natal kinsmen. Women distributed their bequests more evenly: twenty-two to secondary but twenty-six to primary natal male kin. Pertile (*Storia del diritto*, 4:76–79) discusses the principles behind favoring male kin in succession beyond the elementary family. In fact, the sons of a deceased brother in a fraternal group were entitled, collectively, to one share of their paternal grandfather's patrimony—their father's share. They thus carried into the next generation their father's participation in the joint patrimony with his brothers.

23. These patterns can be more clearly seen in tabular form:

	Men's Bequests	Women's Bequests
To primary natal males	4	26
To primary natal females	16	34
To secondary natal males	39	22
To secondary natal females	6	25

The relatively large number of bequests by men to their primary natal female relatives is an indication of the interest men had—and legally were obliged to have—in their sisters' dowries and of their desire to provide for their widowed mothers' well-being.

24. Ercole, "Istituto dotale," pt. 1:212–13, 231–35; Ferro, *Dizionario*, 4:383.

25. Ercole, "Istituto dotale," pt. 1:238–46; Ferro, *Dizionario*, 4:385; *Volumen statutorum*, lib. 2, cap. 8, p. 17v; lib. 4, cap. 25, pp. 71v–72v. On dowry responsibility, see also Chap. 6, below.

26. "Tam masculis, quam foeminis virginibus, maritatis, & viduis, omnium mobilium & immobilium aequaliter successio deferatur." *Volumen statutorum*, lib. 4, cap. 28, p. 74v.

27. On wives' property in general, see Pertile, *Storia del diritto*, 3:320–32; Ercole, "Istituto dotale," pt. 2:179–90. Pertile makes the general observation that men were favored over women as heirs to their mothers; *Storia del diritto*, 4:92–95. This does not seem to have been the case in Venice.

28. *Volumen statutorum*, "Liber promissionis maleficii," caps. 2–3, p. 129v; lib. 6, cap. 79, p. 125v.

29. ASV, Signori di Notte al Criminal, Processi, Reg. 7, ff. 2r–3r; Reg. 8, f. 39v.

30. Cecchetti notes cases where female beauty appeared to influence judicial

decisions: a fine was reduced for a father who had a *"bella* e nubile" daughter (Cecchetti's emphasis); a man who cut ("amputavit") the hair of a woman against her will was fined 100 lire. "La donna nel medioevo," 38–39.

31. *Volumen statutorum*, consultum no. 39, 169v. On women and the law in general, see Pertile, *Storia del diritto*, 3:232–44.

32. On the male precedence over real property, see Ercole, "Istituto dotale," pt. 1:289–94; Pertile, *Storia del diritto*, 3:239; Niccolai, "Consorzi nobiliari," 318.

33. See the discussion of the tradition of male *tutela*, and its apparent weakening as early as the late Roman period, in Herlihy, "Land, Family, and Women," 89–91. Pertile (*Storia del diritto*, 3:232 ff.) discusses the Germanic *mundium*, or protective power over women, and its endurance in the Middle Ages. He notes, however (239–40 n. 37), that there is no mention of it in the statutes of the Veneto region.

34. "Mulier . . . quae non steterit cum eius viro, et ipsa de predicto eius viro, conquesta fuerit." *Volumen statutorum*, consultum no. 8, 144v.

35. In 1340 Beriola, wife of Marco Erizzo, had a receipt drawn up acknowledging her husband's payment to her of 12½ soldi di grossi, "which you were required to give me for my food and clothing expenses during the current half year, as indicated in a court document signed by the Giudici del Procurator." The court document referred to was dated 10 December 1317. CI 114, Marino, S. Tomà, prot. 1335–1350, no pagination, dated 1 January 1339/40.

36. PSMC De Citra, B. 179, Micheletto Morosini, parchment 9 June 1343. On the competence of the Giudici del Procurator, see Da Mosto, *Archivio di Stato*, 1:93.

37. PSMC De Citra, B. 179, Micheletto Morosini, parchment 9 June 1343.

38. Ibid., parchment 15 May 1348. The will also alludes to another child, now deceased. Caterina's will in the postplague year 1352 makes no reference to any children, living or dead. NT 1023, Passamonte, no. 17.

39. The fullest discussion of women's property and its status during marriage is in Ercole, "Istituto dotale," pt. 2:167–90. See also Brandileone, "Studi preliminari," 274–89 and passim; Pertile, *Storia del diritto*, 3:320–61; Besta, *La famiglia*, 143–69. On Venice, see Mueller, "Procurators of San Marco," 175–84; also Chap. 2.

40. *Volumen statutorum*, lib. 1, cap. 39, p. 19v. See also Pertile, *Storia del diritto*, 3:327, 352. Ercole suggests that in Venice this right did not extend to the "parafernal goods"—that is, the *corredum*, or trousseau—that accompanied the dowry; "Istituto dotale," pt. 1:204–5. According to him, the husband had control over such possessions; however, the statutes he cites (205 n. 1) do not appear to sustain this conclusion.

41. CI 242, Giacomo Ziera, 5, prot., f. 1v. Giovanni had no sons, though he was generous in his will to his brothers' sons. The main study of the Venetian funded debt is the "Introduzione" to Luzzatto, *I prestiti*, reprinted as Luzzatto, *Debito pubblico*.

42. For interest payments on Monte shares, see Lane, "Funded Debt," 87.

43. Other examples: in 1348 Andreasio di Michele Morosini bequeathed 50 lire to each of his five married daughters. PSMC Miste, B. 182a, Andreasio Mo-

rosini, prot. (no pagination). In the same year, Andrea Morosini *miles* bequeathed to his married sister the income from 2,000 lire in Monte shares during her lifetime. PSMC De Citra, B. 180, Andrea Morosini, prot. I, ff. 5r–11r.

44. Of the 305 wills in the sample, 196 were written by wives or widows. Of these, 74 identified living daughters in their wills, of whom 40 were married.

45. *Volumen statutorum*, lib. 1, cap. 39, p. 19v. See also Ercole, "Istituto dotale," pt. 1:197–98; Besta, *La famiglia*, 143–51.

46. Pertile put it in a nutshell: "The wife kept proprietorship over the dowry, so much so that in certain places she also gained all or some of the income from it, depending on arrangements made between the spouses. However, income from the dowry normally belonged to the husband, according to the Roman law principle that the dowry was 'for bearing the burdens of matrimony' " [della dote la moglie conservava la proprietà, tanto che in qualche luogo ne faceva suoi anche i frutti, in tutto o in parte, secondo che gli sposi avean convenuto; ma comunemente l'usufrutto della dote spettava al marito giusta le leggi romane *ad sustinendum onera matrimonii*]. *Storia del diritto*, 3:324.

47. In 1349 Goffredo di Francesco Morosini bequeathed to his wife a lifetime annuity of 50 ducats as interest for his use of her dowry. NT 576, Giovanni de Comasini, no. 95. Ercole observes that "as a wife and mother the wife had the right, during the marriage, to share in the income from the dowry" [come moglie e madre essa (i.e., the wife) aveva diritto di partecipare di fatto, durante il matrimonio, del godimento della sostanza dotale]. "*Istituto dotale*," pt. 2:181.

48. For the general obligation, see *Volumen statutorum*, lib. 1, cap. 34, p. 17v: "omnia bona viri sunt obligata mulieri." On the deposit, see ibid., lib. 3, cap. 29, p. 49v² (erroneously paginated 50v), and lib. 6, cap. 31, pp. 101v–102v. If the obligated property was real estate and the husband wanted to sell it, he was to offer it to his wife first; if she declined it, he could make the sale to a third party, but the payment would have to be deposited with the Procuratori. On a related matter, see Mueller, "Procurators of San Marco," 175–76. Pertile discusses the husband's obligation under the term *antefactum; Storia del diritto*, 3:327–34). Brandileone suggests that the antefactum amounted to a fraction, usually one-half, of the dowry amount; "Studi preliminari," 273–74; this was not true of Venice.

49. The cosigner was usually a relative. For example, Elena Morosini cosigned with her son, Andrea; CI 21, Boninsegna, prot. 2, f. 51v. Leonardo Morosini cosigned with his brother Paolo; ASV, Raccolta Stefani, Archivio genealogico, Cassa 33, "Morosini."

50. The statutes were clear on the obligation of the widow's father-in-law when the husband was unemancipated. *Volumen statutorum*, lib. 1, cap. 56, p. 26v; see also Ercole, "Istituto dotale," pt. 2:236–37. In practice the fathers of emancipated sons also were assessed the balance. For example, when Marina, widow of Pangrazio da Molin, filed for restitution of her dowry in 1368, the estate of her father-in-law, Benedetto da Molin, was required to satisfy the deficiency in Pangrazio's estate, even though the latter was a *filius divisus*. CI 114, Marino, S.Tomà, prot. 1366–91, 10 May 1368.

51. CI 114, Marino, S.Tomà, prot. 1366–91, 19 March 1371. It is not clear whether the widow was the son's mother or stepmother.

52. *Volumen statutorum*, lib. 1, cap. 34, p. 17v. This was reaffirmed in 1471; ibid., Consultum no. 47, 175v–176v. See also Ercole, "Istituto dotale," pt. 2:222–23, 255–57.

53. "Dabitur potestas mulieri in iudicatu suo de proprietatibus & bonis viri tollendis." *Volumen statutorum*, lib. 1, cap. 56, p. 26v. Moreover, the judges awarding the property were to award to the widow that property of the husband which was "contiguous or most useful" to her. Ibid., cap. 61, pp. 27v–28v.

54. Parents usually instructed in their wills that their daughters marry in their early teens, at twelve to fourteen years in the mid-fourteenth century, at fourteen to fifteen years in the mid-fifteenth. This corresponds to Tuscan practice; see Herlihy, "Some Psychological and Social Roots," 146. Regarding husbands predeceasing their wives, this general demographic tendency is documented in the dowry-restitution records: if the husband died first, his widow received her dowry; if the wife died first, her heirs received it. Of 110 patrician marriages indicated in this source as terminated between 1366 and 1380, 77 ended with the death of the husband, only 33 with the death of the wife. CI 114, Marino, S. Tomà, prot. 1366–91. See now the fuller documentation of this pattern in Chap. 4.

55. Tomasina Zane's investment is in CI 20, Giovanni Bon, fascicle 4, dated 21 March 1380. Beria Morosini's will is in NT 574, Giorgio Gibellino, no. 595.

56. This largesse, already noted in wills, extended to business contracts, too. For example, Pietro Zane got an investment loan of 240 lire from his mother, Beriola, in 1337; CI 114, Bartolomeo prete, prot. 1, dated 25 August 1337. Nicolò Dolfin received a similar loan, in the amount of 1,000 lire a grossi, from his mother, Cecilia; CI 14, Betino, prot. 4, dated 25 April 1353.

57. Cf. Herlihy, *Women in Medieval Society*, 5–6. On Florence, see Martines, *Social World*, 37–38. Dante was already censorious about a rise in dowries in his time; referring to the time of his great-great-grandfather Cacciaguida, he wrote:

Non faceva, nascendo ancor paura
La figlia al padre, chè il tempo e la dote
Non fuggian quinci e quindi la misura.
Paradiso XV, 103–5

See also Ercole, "Istituto dotale," pt. 1:280–81.

58. The midcentury dowry average was extracted from fifty patrician marriages contracted between 1346 and 1366; the later average was extracted from twenty-five patrician marriages contracted between 1370 and 1386. CI 114, Marino, S. Tomà, prot. 1366–91, which includes records of dowry payments presented as evidence by widows reclaiming their dowries. These data have now been expanded and include the fifteenth century; see Chap. 4.

59. On this and other dowry legislation, see Chap. 2. For similar measures elsewhere in Italy, see Pertile, *Storia del diritto*, 3:322. Pertile notes that the intent of such measures was to prevent sons being deprived of their shares of the patrimony by dowry increases for their sisters.

60. Ercole, "Istituto dotale," pt. 1:282–84. Recall that the dowry's purpose was to enable the husband to bear the *onera matrimonii*.

61. See Chap. 2. On disproportionate endogamy among the twenty-four

oldest clans, the *case vecchie*, see now Chojnacki, "Marriage Legislation," 173–75. For a Florentine instance of dowry-engineered social mobility, see Brucker, "The Medici," 10–11.

62. On the impact on Venetian trade of events in transalpine Europe, see Cessi, "Le relazioni commerciali"; on the devastation of private wealth by forced loans during periods of crisis, see Luzzatto, *Storia economica*, 141–45. The resulting shares in the state debt (Monte) could be negotiated as dowry payments.

63. The exact figures, based on bequests explicitly for dowry purposes, are in the following table:

	1331–70	1371–1410	1411–50
From fathers	6	24	11
From mothers	1	11	16

For a fuller discussion, see Chap. 6.

64. In tabular form:

	Men's Wills		Women's Wills	
	No.	%	No.	%
To 1330	8	57.1	6	42.9
1331–70	22	44	28	56
1371–1410	40	33.1	81	66.9
1411–50	34	28.3	86	71.7

65. According to Beloch, the plague struck Venice eleven times between 1347 and 1400; *Bevölkerungsgeschichte Italiens*, 3–4.

66. These multiple women's wills, whatever their other implications, do not account for mothers outstripping fathers in fifteenth-century dowry bequests (above, n. 63). Among the testators who bequeathed dowries to their daughters, only two men and one woman wrote two wills.

67. Of the 305 Morosini wills examined, 87, more than one-quarter of the total, were written by thirty-six individuals who drew up more than one will. Of these thirty-six, twenty-eight (77.8 percent) were women.

68. For example, Ratolica Giustinian invested in an overseas commercial venture with her son-in-law in 1138. Morozzo della Rocca and Lombardo, *Documenti del commercio*, 1:74. On Genoese women's business dealings in the early thirteenth century, see Bonds, "Genoese Noblewomen."

69. For example, Alice Contarini was active in the small loan business in 1320; CI 73, Egidio, S. Sofia, prot. I, acts dated 15 April and 20 November 1320. Caterina Michiel made at least one loan of 300 lire; CI 79, Favacio, prot., dated 14 February 1359/60.

70. In 1420 Ingoldise Morosini entered into a soap-making partnership with Giovanni di Spagna ("contraximus in simul societates seu compagnias in arte saponaria"); CI 24, Rolandino Bernardi, prot. 2, f. 56rv.

71. Palma Signolo made such an investment in 1311; CI 10, Michele Bondemiro, prot., f. 3v. Leonarda Morosini received in 1348 a return on her investment

in an earlier voyage to Alexandria; CI 114, Marino, S. Tomà, prot. 1335–50, dated 5 August 1348. On the state-run galleys, see Lane, "Venetian Shipping during the Commercial Revolution" and "Family Partnerships."

72. See above, n. 55.

73. NT 670, Alessandro Marino, no. 126.

74. Examples: In 1439, Caterina, wife of Moisè Contarini, bequeathed 3,000 ducats' worth of Monte shares to her father, to be distributed to her brothers; NT 1115, Benedetto dalle Croci, no. 68. In 1388/89, Cristina, wife of Giovanni Morosini, willed 1,000 ducats to her husband; NT 921, Saiabianca, no. 494. In 1426, Maria, wife of Nicolò Morosini, bequeathed 2,000 ducats for her daughter's dowry; NT 746, Naresi, no. 83.

75. Friedl, "Position of Women," 108. Her findings accord with the Venetian case: a formal structure, male-dominated, still leaves room for female influence, largely because of economic power. My thanks to Stanley Brandes for this reference.

76. One of numerous examples: Piero di Giovanni Morosini in 1383 named his wife, Franceschina, as one of his executors and bequeathed her some Monte shares and the income from his real estate on the condition that she not remarry. NT 571, Giorgio Gibellino, no. 169.

77. NT 108, Giovanni Boninsegna, no. 296 (22 October 1388).

78. "Pro salute anime sue et mee." In another place she asked him to free the slave "ob amorem dei et salutem anime sue." Ibid. On the sexual activity between masters and their female slaves and the resentment of their wives, see Origo, "Domestic Enemy," 343–44.

79. NT 1233, Pietro Zane, ff. 141v–142v (5 August 1417).

80. On this theme in a Florentine context, see Goldthwaite, "Florentine Palace," 1011.

81. A fraterna would thus embrace several families of the same line—brothers' families and those of their sons. See Lane, "Family Partnerships," 37; Pertile, Storia del diritto, 3:282. On the Florentine case, Goldthwaite, Private Wealth, should be read in conjunction with Starn, "Francesco Guicciardini and His Brothers," and Kent, Household and Lineage.

82. This is one of the elements of the "myth of Venice," on which there is a large literature. See, for example, Fasoli, "Nascita di un mito," and Gaeta, "Alcune considerazioni sul mito."

83. See, for example, Fortes, "Structure of Unilineal Descent Groups," 26: "The more centralized the political system the greater the tendency seems to be for the corporate strength of descent groups to be reduced or for such corporate groups to be non-existent." For this principle in Italy, see Goldthwaite, Private Wealth, 253, and Tamassia, La famiglia italiana, 111.

84. NT 721, Andrea Marevidi, no. 226.

85. Marriage contracts for the fourteenth and fifteenth centuries are scarce. One between the Sanudo and Morosini families in 1343/44 illustrates the complex interweaving of two families' economic interests in the connection. Museo Correr, Venice, Codici Cicogna, no. 3427/11. On this contract, see Chap. 3.

86. "Family Partnerships," 38–39.

87. Per grande amor e raxion chio o portado sempre a quella caxa. NT 1062, Lorenzo della Torre, no. 300. Gasparino's first wife, the sister of these beneficiaries, was already dead in 1371, when Gasparino returned her dowry to her family. CI 114, Marino, S. Tomà, prot. 1366–91, dated 17 December 1371. By the time of the 1374 will Gasparino had remarried.

88. See the example of Andrea Barbarigo and his affines from the Cappello family, in Lane, *Andrea Barbarigo,* 27–30. Especially interesting is Andrea's relationship with his mother-in-law (29).

89. Barbaro, Nozze, ff. 322v–326r, 39v–40r, 103r–104v.

Chapter 6 Dowries and Kinsmen

This chapter originally appeared, in slightly altered form, as "Dowries and Kinsmen in Early Renaissance Venice," *Journal of Interdisciplinary History* 5 (1975): 571–600.

1. There is disagreement among historians of law about the degree to which Roman dowry practice, as opposed to Germanic institutions such as the Lombard *faderfio,* survived in the early Middle Ages. By the twelfth century, however, the Roman institution seems to have regained ground lost in earlier centuries; and the comeback involved more of a blending with Germanic law than a wholesale rejection of it. See Brandileone, "Studi preliminari," 231 ff. For dowry worries in early Renaissance Italy, see Martines, *Social World,* 19, 37–38, and Lane, *Andrea Barbarigo,* 39.

2. The dowry figures are taken from CI 114, Marino, S. Tomà, prot. 1366–91. This source records the repayment of dowries to widows or their heirs upon the death of husband or wife. The entries usually mention the date on which the dowry had been paid to the husband, normally at or around the time of the wedding. The fifty cases studied represent marriages contracted between 1346 and 1366.

In this and in all other monetary references, the various Venetian moneys have been converted into ducats, using the conversion tables in Lane and Mueller, *Money and Banking,* 131, 291. Correspondences are also noted in the records of estates administered by the Procuratori di S. Marco: in 1347 the gold ducat was worth 2.63 lire a grossi, the Venetian money of account; PSMC Miste, B. 70a, Nicolò Morosini, account book, f. 2r.

3. The standard had already risen in the late fourteenth century and would continue to rise. See Chaps. 4 and 5.

4. For the legislation, see Chap. 2.

5. See Heers, *L'Occident,* 294–99; Luzzatto, "Costo della vita," 285–87. For a graphic tracing of the changing relations between gold and silver Venetian moneys, see Cipolla, *Studi,* 44–47.

6. The data are fragmentary, regionally selective, and sometimes contradictory. See Miskimin, *Economy of Early Renaissance Europe,* 89–92; Lopez, "Trade of Medieval Europe," 343–47; Luzzatto, *Economic History,* 138–46.

7. See Genicot, "Crisis," 688–94. On Venetian economic fortunes in the fifteenth century in general, see Luzzatto, *Economic History,* 150–55; in greater detail, idem, *Storia economica,* 146–79. The 1342 figure is in idem, "Costo della

vita," 290. The equivalence of the *staio* is in Lane, *Venetian Ships and Shipbuilders*, 246. In 1390 the estate of Simone Morosini sold nine *staia* of wheat to the grain office for 1 lira, 10 soldi di grossi; (1 lira di grossi equaled 10 ducats); PSMC Miste, B. 128, Simone Morosini, Register, fol. 5r. The 1432 figure comes from Lane, *Andrea Barbarigo*, 67–68.

8. On wheat prices as general index, see Heers, *L'Occident*, 295; Luzzatto, "Costo della vita," 286. See the regional variations in grain prices in Genicot, "Crisis," 683. On dowries, see Ercole, "Istituto dotale," pt. 1:280–84.

9. The main study of prestiti and their economic impact is Luzzatto, *I prestiti*; see esp. clx–clxxv. More briefly, see idem, *Storia economica*, 140–45. See also Lane, "Funded Debt," 87–98; Cessi, "La finanza veneziana."

10. A measure authorizing a revision of the fisc's estimate of private wealth, passed after the war of Chioggia, indicated that the total could be as much as 1.5 million lire less than the total of 6 million lire reached in the previous estimate of 1379, at the beginning of the war (Luzzatto, *Storia economica*, 145). But see the cautionary comments of Cessi, "La finanza veneziana," 192–98.

11. Luzzatto, *Storia economica*, 147–48; Lane, "Funded Debt," 87–89.

12. "Propter importabilem sumptum dotium." Especially noteworthy in the act are the suggestions that this practice was of relatively recent origin ("orta sit") and the clear indication that high dowries damaged a man's other heirs—presumably the male ones. See Chap. 2.

13. Ercole, "Istituto dotale," pt. 1:197–98. See also Besta, *La famiglia*, 143–51.

14. Ercole, "Istituto dotale," pt. 1:212–13, 218–31. The main study of the fraterna is Fumagalli, *Il diritto di fraterna*. See also Besta, *La famiglia*, 207–9; Pertile, *Storia del diritto*, 3:282, 322. On the fraterna in Venetian practice, see Ferro, *Dizionario del diritto*, 5:276–78.

15. "La dote è un diritto della figlia, cui il padre non può mai sottrarsi." Ercole, "Istituto dotale," pt. 1:334.

16. PSMC Miste, B. 127, Leone Morosini, parchment no. 2. On convents as brothels, see Gilbert, "Venice in the Crisis," 275; also Chap. 1.

17. *Volumen statutorum*, lib. 2, cap. 8, p. 17v. See also Ercole, "Istituto dotale," pt. 1:238–46, and Ferro, *Dizionario del diritto*, 4:385–86.

18. On the responsibility of mothers, see Pertile, *Storia del diritto*, 4:93–94; Ercole, "Istituto dotale," pt. 1:237. The reference to mothers' kin is in Ferro, *Dizionario del diritto*, 4:386: "L'avo ed ascendenti materni sussidiariamente sono tenuti a costituire la dote alla nipote in mancanza degli ascendenti paterni, e della madre." I have not encountered this principle in any other source.

19. In a fiscal census (*estimo*) conducted in 1379, the Morosini estimates ranged from 500 to 38,000 lire a grossi (equal to 192–14,615 ducats). The basis of the estimate was real property. The Morosini in the *estimo* dwelt in twenty-four different parishes, in five of Venice's six *sestieri*, or administrative zones. Luzzatto, *I prestiti*, doc. 165, 141–86. I have isolated more than twenty different lineages within the clan. For the terms *clan* and *lineage* I follow Fox, *Kinship and Marriage*, 49–50. For a fuller discussion, See Murdock, *Social Structure*, 46–78. The 140 women's wills are, of course, distinct from 62 wills of Morosini daughters, twelve of whom married Morosini males.

20. See *Volumen statutorum,* lib. 4, caps. 25–26, p. 735. For the principle that dowries were women's only claim on their fathers' estates, see Tamassia, *La famiglia italiana,* 292–95.

21. Thirty-six of the forty-two men mentioned children, totaling 129. Thirty-four of the thirty-seven women mentioned children, a total of 91. Included in these figures are unborn children of pregnant wives—whether mentioned in the wives' or in the husbands' wills.

22. Thus, of the eighteen mothers whose husbands were still living when the women wrote their wills, four were pregnant with their first child, four mentioned one child, three mentioned two children, one mentioned four, one mentioned seven, and the remaining five made general reference to their children without specifying their names or numbers. Taking another perspective, five of the thirty-seven female testators mentioned grandchildren, against six of the forty-two men; and ten of the women mentioned living parents, against eight of the men.

23. NT 466, Benedetto Gibellino, no. 5; NT 1230, Federico Stefani, no. 207; NT 721, Andrea Marevidi, no. 145; NT 746, Marciliano de' Naresi, no. 83.

24. Based on 102 bequests in specific amounts; the remaining 23 dowry bequests did not specify amounts.

25. For examples of economic and political returns on dowry investments, see, respectively, Lane, *Andrea Barbarigo,* 28–29, and idem, "Family Partnerships," 38–39.

26. In Roman law during the republic, a wife might be absorbed into her husband's family or not; by the empire, the tendency was for her not to be so—to remain, rather, either under her natal *paterfamilias* or, if none existed, to be *sui iuris.* In either of the latter two cases, she was not considered agnatically related to her husband's family. See Crook, *Law and Life,* 103–4, and Nicolas, *Introduction,* 80–83. In Lombard law, wives passed over to their husbands' families by reason of the husbands' purchase of the *mundium*—roughly, protective domination—from the wives' fathers; by the time of the restoration of Roman law, however, this practice no longer prevailed in the Veneto, if, indeed, it ever had. See Pertile, *Storia del diritto,* 3:234–40. In practice, women retained ties both to their natal and to their marital families and lineages.

27. Succession to an intestate father excluded married daughters, whose share of the patrimony had already been advanced in the form of dowries. Married daughters were, however, admitted to equal shares in the succession to their intestate mothers' property, since this did not have the patrimonial character. See *Volumen statutorum,* lib. 4, cap. 25, p. 73v, cap. 28, p. 74v. The same relationship holds true regarding emancipated and unemancipated sons; Cessi, *Statuti veneziani,* 297, gloss 173. On general bequest patterns, see n. 40.

28. Besta, *La famiglia,* 149–50; Tamassia, *La famiglia italiana,* 289. In 1060 Venetian women were already regarded as the proprietors of their dowries; Leicht, "Documenti dotali," 294. The statute governing inheritance from intestate mothers is in *Volumen statutorum,* lib. 4, cap. 28, p. 74v.

29. There was a momentary decline in the period 1351–70, from which twenty-two wills survive, as compared with twenty-eight for 1331–50, sixty-five for 1371–90, and fifty-six for 1391–1410. However, this relative decline can be

attributed to the mortality itself; moreover, the great leap in the period 1371–90 strengthens the argument advanced below.

30. This is consistently apparent in the wills. For example, Marco di Gentile Morosini in 1359 instructed that his daughter Beriola come into her inheritance at age eleven; NT 1023, Ariano Passamonte, no. 3. Moisè di Piero Morosini specifically instructed that his daughters marry at age twelve; NT 572, Giorgio Gibellino, no. 23. One exception was Silvestro di Marco Morosini, who in 1432 instructed that his daughters were not to marry until age sixteen; he increased their dowry legacies by 250 ducats for every year they waited after that. This may suggest a changing attitude in the fifteenth century. NT 486, Francesco Gibellino, no. 45. See also Tamassia, *La famiglia italiana*, 197–98.

31. To cite just two examples: Beruzza, wife and then widow of Marco Soranzo, who was still unmarried in 1374, wrote wills in 1380, 1385, 1388, and 1401. NT 108, Giovanni Boninsegna, no. 84; NT 921, Nicolò Saiabianca, no. 519; NT 108, Giovanni Boninsegna, no. 296; NT 575, Giorgio Gibellino, no. 704. Beruzza's nubility in 1374 is indicated in the will written that year by her brother, Gasparino di Bellello Morosini; NT 1062, Lorenzo della Torre, no. 300. Another example is Cristina, wife and then widow of Vettor di Lodovico Morosini, who wrote wills in 1382, 1399, 1423, and 1432. CI 36, Giovanni Campion, 3, 1, no. 71; NT 571, Giorgio Gibellino, no. 118; NT 560, Francesco Gritti, no. 346; NT 215, Giovanni Campisano, no. 34.

32. That is, the thirty-one possibilities either had no children or named their parents as executors (an indication of relative youth) or both.

33. This was Agnesina, widow of Marco di Gentile Morosini; CI 143, Stefano Pianigo, no. 41, dated 7 January 1359/60. Her husband's will, cited above, n. 30, is dated 21 August 1359.

34. In the pre-1331 period, six of the wills were written by women, one by a pregnant testatrix.

35. Wives outlived their husbands in the great majority of cases. Of 142 cases of surviving spouses recorded between 1366 and 1390, wives were the survivers in 116 (81.7%), husbands in 26 cases (18.3%); CI 114, Marino, S. Tomà, prot. 1366–91. These figures amplify those given in the original version of this essay. For a fuller discussion, see Chap. 4.

36. Increased state-bond (prestiti) holdings may have increased dowry amounts. From 1343 to 1381 the state's indebtedness, and thus the amount invested in it by citizens, jumped over 1,100 percent; and although it oscillated thereafter, by 1438 it was nearly 16 times greater than in 1343; Lane, "Funded Debt," esp. 88. As noted above, shares in the Monte could be negotiated for dowry purposes.

37. To protect wives' dowries, the statutes required a deposit by the husband in the amount of his bride's dowry. They also assigned priority among all claims on a man's estate—including those of his children and his creditors—to dowry restitution and made the husband's ascendants and descendants financially liable if the husband's estate was not sufficient to repay the entire dowry of his widow (*Volumen statutorum*, lib. 1, caps. 34, 56, 61, 62, pp. 17v, 26v–29v). An example of enforcement of the statutes is that of Marina, widow of Pangrazio di Benedetto da Molin. Although her late husband had been emancipated ("filius divisus") from

his father, the latter was nevertheless forced to make up the difference when Pangrazio's own estate was inadequate to Marina's dowry claim. CI 114, Marino, S. Tomà, prot. 1366–91, n.p., 10 May 1368. A wife was unable to invest her dowry without her husband's consent; but in compensation he was obliged to pay her interest when he invested it. *Volumen statutorum,* lib. 1, cap. 39, p. 19v, lib. 3, cap. 28, p. 48v; NT 579, Giovanni de Comasini, no. 95: will of Goffredo di Francesco Morosini, 21 February 1348/49.

38. In strict anthropological terms, of course, a husband was just as much a member of two conjugal families as his wife. Legally, however, a man could belong to a marital conjugal family and still be under his father's *patria potestas,* with all its economic effects. In any case, descent in Venice was patrilineal; to the extent that Venetian husbands remained unemancipated from their fathers, as seems to have been the rule, it seems fair to speak of extended families in the male line, even when common residence did not prevail. See Murdock, *Social Structure,* 2–10.

39. See above, n. 27.

40. Based on examination of the bequests in the first fifty (by alphabet) wills of married women in the sample. Of 215 total bequests to first- and second-degree relatives, 107 (49.7%) went to natal kin, 96 (44.7%) to marital kin, and 12 (5.6%) to affines. These bequests are analyzed more fully in Chap. 5.

41. Friedl, "Position of Women," 108.

42. Tamassia, *La famiglia italiana,* 111–14. See also the valuable discussion in Herlihy, "Family Solidarity."

43. NT 1189, Piero Cavazza, no. 83; NT 571, Giorgio Gibellino, "Carte Varie," dated 28 April 1401. Gasparino's bequest complemented real estate that Franceschina had been left by her late father.

44. NT 571, Giorgio Gibellino, "Carte Varie," 28 April 1401. In his will of 1348, Andreasio di Michele Morosini bequeathed all of his real estate to his four sons with the provision that if they all died without issue, the property was to be sold, at a discount of 25 percent off the assessed value, to "aliquibus vel alicui de propinquioribus, de stipite, prolis mee" [any of my sons' nearest agnate kin]. PSMC Miste, B. 182a, Andreasio Morosini, account book, n.p. For similar sentiments, see the wills of Nicolò Morosini dottor in 1379 and of Albertino di Marino Morosini in 1450: CI 97, Francesco Gritti, no. 1; NT 986, Francesco Rogeri, no. 110.

45. PSMC Miste, B. 182a, Andreasio Morosini, account book, n.p.

46. In this respect the Venetian lineage, as well as the clan to which it belonged, contrasts with the consorteries of Lombardy and Tuscany. See Niccolai, "Consorzi nobiliari," 119–24 and passim. On the restrictions that corporate kin groups, such as the consortery, place on relations with affines, see Wolf, "Kinship, Friendship, and Patron-Client Relations," 5.

47. Of the other three, two are unclear about the testators' relationship to the legatee, and one bequest went to the daughter of the testator's brother-in-law; it is not clear whether a sister's husband or a wife's brother is meant.

48. CI 168, Marco de' Rafanelli, no. 93.

49. Legally, the fraterna lasted for two generations of the male line; Lane, "Family Partnerships," 37; Pertile, *Storia del diritto,* 3:282. The principle of grandfatherly bequests was prescribed in the statutes: *Volumen statutorum* (lib. 4, cap.

25, p. 72v) stated that the unmarried and orphaned granddaughters, through the male line, of intestate men possessed a right to shares of their grandfathers' estates for dowry purposes, in effect, the shares that their deceased fathers would have inherited had they been alive. The principle was important enough to have been included in the additions and amendments to the statutes carried out under Doge Andrea Dandolo in 1343 (lib. 6, cap. 53, p. 110v).

50. The statute makers devised a long and complex set of principles to guarantee that the son of an intestate father made a sufficient amount available to his unmarried sister for her dowry. *Volumen statutorum*, lib. 4, cap. 25, p. 71v; Ercole, "Istituto dotale," pt. 1:241–46; Pertile, *Storia del diritto*, 3:322.

51. NT 1062, Lorenzo della Torre, no. 300.

52. Cum honore et prout congruit conditionem domus mee honorificientius maritetur. NT 1234, Francesco Sorio, no. 509.

53. On the chronology of patrilineal traditions, however, see the debate between Leyser, "German Aristocracy" and "Debate: Maternal Kin," and Bullough, "Early Medieval Social Groupings."

54. He bequeathed 100 ducats to his "madona" for her daughter's dowry; NT 1233, Francesco Sorio, no. 257. For "madona" as mother-in-law, see Boerio, *Dizionario*, 381.

55. "E in caxo che si al maridar de mie fie le non avesse tanto che le podese ben maridar segondo la so condition, voio che lo i se posse azonzar la parte che i tocasse de questo mio residuo in la so impromesse per maridarle meio." NT 1255, Pietro Zane, prot., fol. 194r.

56. However, one of them, Giovanni di Marino Morosini, was very generous in 1397 to his brothers' sons. CI 242, Giacomo Ziera, 5. prot., c. iv.

57. Novella's will is in CI 24, Rolandino Bernardi, 16. c. 67, no. 184; her husband Giovanni's is in PSMC Miste, B. 2, Giovanni Morosini, account book, n.p. A counterexample can be found in the 1413 will of Maria, widow of Matteo Morosini, who bequeathed 500 ducats toward the dowry of her son's daughter without reference to either her own daughter or that daughter's children, even though her daughter was to act as Maria's executor. However, the daughter was living with her husband in Negroponte (Euboea), and distance may have weakened contacts; the daughter was to be an executor only if she returned to Venice. CI 24, Bernardi, 16. c. 41, no. 99.

58. Based on examination of primary-kin executors in ninety-seven wives' and widows' wills—those in the sample whose first names begin with the letters A–E. The results are shown in the table below:

Executor	67 Wives' Wills		30 Widows' Wills		All Women	
	No.	%	No.	%	No.	%
Parents and siblings	91	52.2	32	42.7	123	49.5
Husbands	53	30.5	—	—	53	21.3
Children	30	17.3	43	57.3	73	29.2
Total	174	100	75	100	249	100

It is noteworthy that one out of every five wives (fourteen of sixty-seven) declined to name her husband among her executors.

59. For example, Tomasina, widow of Albano Zane, made business loans to her father, Andrea di Dardi Morosini, at least twice in the 1380s. CI 20, Giovanni Bon, fasc. 4, n. p., 21 March 1380; fasc. 5, n. p., 27 April 1382.

60. The quotation is from Fortes, "Structure of Unilineal Descent Groups," 34. Fortes contrasts these principles governing the family, the nucleus of the "complementary line of filiation" which ties husband and wife together, with those that govern the descent group's interests—law and public institutions.

61. Making provision for her unborn child in her 1385 will, Cristina, wife of Antonio Querini, bequeathed it 300 ducats if a boy, but only 200 if a girl. CI 22, Miscellanea Testamenti, Notai Diversi, no. 747.

62. This is the same group as that used above, n. 58. Excluded from consideration are unborn children and generalized bequests to groups unspecified as to number, for example, legacies "to all my children."

63. Evidence is the tendency in wives' choices of executors, indicated above, n. 58, and the patterns of their bequests, analyzed above, n. 40.

64. See Herlihy, "Family Solidarity"; Goldthwaite, *Private Wealth*, esp. 255–58; and Starn, "Francesco Guicciardini and His Brothers."

65. For reasons of space, I have not discussed the growing practice, engaged in by both men and women, of bequeathing money to the dowries of poor girls, both patrician and plebeian. The Morosini wills include thirty-four such generalized bequests, or almost one for every ten wills. The impulse behind these and the bequests to kinswomen which we have been considering were doubtless encouraged by the dowry inflation of the time. However, there is a difference between eleemosynary beneficence *ad pias causas* and specific contributions to kinswomen among the other bequests to family and friends. The former fall into the category of generalized charity which was growing in importance at this time. See Pullan, *Rich and Poor*, 183 and passim.

Chapter 7 Wives and Husbands

It originally appeared, in slightly altered form, as "The Power of Love: Wives and Husbands in Late Medieval Venice," in *Women and Power in the Middle Ages,* ed. Mary Erler and Maryanne Kowaleski (Athens: University of Georgia Press, 1988), 126–48.

In honor of the fifty-year marriage of Signe and Steve Chojnacki.

1. NT 558, Gambaro, nos. 123, 124. Research for this essay was supported principally by the American Council of Learned Societies and the College of Arts and Letters, Michigan State University. I express my gratitude to both bodies.

2. Vittoria's later marriages are noted in Barbaro, Nozze, f. 432r. Valerio's concern that his bequest to Vittoria might be contested is apparent in his wording: "volo, quod non obstantibus, neque impedientibus aliquibus condicionibus neque oppositionibus, que quo iure, modo, et forma opponi et fieri possent contra hanc presentem meam ordinationem et voluntatem, dicta Vittoria semper et in omni statu et termino, *et tam viduando quam non viduando,* et in quocumque alio statu

et termino esse posset et declarari, semper habeat et habere debeat totum illud quod sibi dimitto" (emphasis added).

3. Vittoria's mother, Zacca Vitturi, in her will of 1417 mentions both Vittoria and a son, Nicolò; NT 1157, Croci, prot. I, f. 25v. This Nicolò registered his son, then eighteen, in the Balla d'Oro lottery for admission to the patrician Great Council in 1442; they were both probably still living when Vittoria testated in 1445. BO 163, f. 396r. On registration for the Great Council and the Balla d'Oro, see Chaps. 10 and 11.

4. In an earlier will of 1427, Vittoria had followed the same pattern, making Valerio her sole executor and universal heir (except for a 5-ducat bequest to a daughter of her late brother, Piero Vitturi) but requesting burial "in the tomb of my father and kinsmen [*propinquorum meorum*]." She also committed 10 ducats toward the placement of a marble tablet on the tomb. NT 852, Rizoto, no. 349.

5. The tension between loyalty to natal families and to marital families, especially for women, is an important theme in the writings of Diane Owen Hughes and Christiane Klapisch-Zuber. See Hughes, "From Brideprice to Dowry" and "Representing the Family," esp. 10–11, and Klapisch-Zuber, "Cruel Mother."

6. Guido Ruggiero has advanced useful speculations on husband-wife affection in Venice in the context of the tension between marital and extramarital sexual urgings. See *Boundaries of Eros*, esp. 64.

7. Hughes, for example, sees growing lineage consciousness leading to the shift from brideprice to dowry; "From Brideprice to Dowry," 287–88. Klapisch-Zuber and David Herlihy argue that family interest led fathers to hasten very young daughters onto the marriage market in order to procure sons-in-law at a time when eligible men were in short supply; *Tuscans and Their Families*, 223. Elsewhere, however, Klapisch-Zuber raises questions about the supply-and-demand approach; "Griselda Complex," 215–17. She also cites cases of Florentine men so eager for matrimonial alliances that they forced their widowed sisters to remarry even when doing so meant abandoning young children of the first marriage; "Cruel Mother." For discussions of psychological and cultural factors, see Goldthwaite, "Florentine Palace," 1009–10, and Kirshner, *Pursuing Honor*.

8. On marriage in Venice, in addition to the observations in Ruggiero, *Boundaries of Eros*, see Betto, "Linee di politica matrimoniale," and Chap. 6. Political implications are discussed in Finlay, *Politics*, esp. 82–89; economic calculations in Davis, *Venetian Family*. Frederic Lane treated marriage from different angles in many writings, including *Andrea Barbarigo* and several essays in *Venice and History*.

9. On brides' ages, see Chap. 9, below. For an example of a prospective groom contracting his marriage: Contratti di nozze 111/1 no. 5 (Arimondo-Michiel, 1488). Marriage contracts in Venice have yet to be studied systematically.

10. This sample, a tiny fragment of the huge testamentary holdings in the Venetian State Archives, is the current state of an ongoing survey of the wills of sixteen patrician clans which I am making as part of the research for a general study of patrician marriage. The 361 examined for the present discussion, exclud-

ing wills written by single and widowed members of the clans, were drawn up by 104 husbands and 257 wives.

11. The thesis, generally based on prescriptive literature, that affection among family members was an innovation of the early modern period, at least in Europe, is controversial. For statements of it, see Stone, *Family, Sex, and Marriage,* and Flandrin, *Families in Former Times.* For criticisms of it, see Ozment, *When Fathers Ruled,* and Herlihy, *Medieval Households,* 112–30. The evidence studied for the present discussion suggests strongly that, in Venice, husbands and wives experienced, or at least were moved to express, mutual affection well before the religious developments that Stone in particular and also Flandrin regard as contributing to the emergence of "companionate" family life.

12. Valerio noted that 1,200 ducats of Vittoria's dowry was secured by "my real estate in [the parish of] S. Giacomo dall'Orio, *which I received from her as part of the dowry"* [possessionibus et proprietatibus meis de sancto Jacobo de Luprio *quas habui ab ea in dotem*]; emphasis added. Although 1,200 ducats indicated a substantial amount of property, it is unlikely that this dowry included any of the Vitturis' own residences. The total dowry of 2,400 ducats greatly exceeded the limit of 1,600 imposed by the Senate on marriage settlements in 1420; the act is partially reproduced in Bistort, *Magistrato alle Pompe,* 107 ff. Bistort also discusses other legislation that attempted to hold back the dowry tide; see Chap. 2.

13. Hughes, "From Brideprice to Dowry," 288–90; Herlihy and Klapisch-Zuber, *Tuscans and Their Families,* 224–25.

14. See Chojnacki, "Social Identity."

15. Barbaro, *De re uxoria,* 41. On Barbaro, see King, "Caldiera and the Barbaros," 31–35. In 1422 the Great Council passed a measure denying patrician status to sons of patricians and low-status women; MC 22, Ursa, ff. 47v–48r. On the prestige value of marriage and wives in male-dominated societies, see Ortner and Whitehead, "Introduction," 21.

16. On the status of prospective husbands as a factor in the calculus of marriage, see Chap. 3.

17. Ha abudo asa piui de quello havera tutti suo fradelli; CI 175, Rizzo, prot., f. 35v (will of Francesco Loredan, 22 January 1458/59). Morosina, widow of Marco Querini, noted that her daughters' dowries had been constituted partly at the expense of their brothers' inheritance: "Le son sta marida e ben e ha abudo de quell de suo fradelli"; NT 1149, Benedetto, unnumbered will, 6 March 1461.

18. Senato, Terra 28, f. 151r.

19. See Chap. 4. Observation of Florentine practice prompts Klapisch-Zuber to be skeptical of the dowry's significance as a share of the paternal estate; "Griselda Complex," 216.

20. The father who wanted his daughters to be content was Vito da Canal in 1448: "Pro eo, quod eis dedi in dotem ipse habent causam remanendi bene contente et non se condolendi de aliquo"; NT 558, Gambaro, no. 171. As early as 1393, Antonio Morosini instructed his executors to reserve a certain portion of his bequest to his daughter "as a legacy, not as her dowry" [pro so legato e non per docta]; NT 640, Bordo, unnumbered. Heiresses appear to have had immediate

access to legacies not encumbered by dowry regulations; this subject, however, needs more study.

21. Examples of mothers who encouraged further dowry inflation by allocating more for their daughters' dowries than for their sons' legacies: Maria Balbi in 1438, and Chiara Moro in 1490. NT 558, Gambaro, no. 54; NT 41, Bonamico, no. 54. In her will of 1464, Petronella Morosini commanded not only her own wealth but that of her mother in the interest of her daughter Paolina's marriage by appointing the Procuratori di San Marco to administer Paolina's one-third share of Petronella's estate as well as 1,000 ducats that Petronella's mother had bequeathed to her granddaughter, which would now enrich Paolina's marriage portion. Petronella expressed concern that her husband, Zilio Morosini, would be dilatory in arranging Paolina's marriage, which Petronella wanted concluded by the girl's fifteenth birthday. Noteworthy is Petronella's confidence that her contribution to Paolina's marriage portion was great enough to compel Zilio to bow to the Procurators' arrangements for his daughter's marriage. NT 1239, Tomei, no. 600 (2 September 1464).

22. E.g., Lucia Priuli in 1489 and Elisabetta Vitturi in 1483. NT 727, Moisis, no. 92; NT 66, Busenello, no. 232.

23. Most women with children made them the principal beneficiaries, but women also made alternative provisions in the event that the children died before reaching adulthood. While some favored husbands as secondary legatees, others gave all to their natal kinsmen. Agnesina Arimondo in 1411 provided that if her two children failed to reach their majority (her son at age twenty, her daughter at marriage), her mother and her sister, a nun, were to receive lifetime annuities from Agnesina's estate, which at their deaths would go to her four brothers—and not a ducat for her husband; NT 364, Darvasio, no. 291. More characteristic were the arrangements of Maria Soranzo, who provided for the possibility that her children would not reach adulthood by giving one-quarter of her *residuum* each to her mother, her husband, her three brothers together, and charity; NT 558 Gambaro, no. 54.

24. An example of a husband's efforts: in 1365 Leonardo Morosini bequeathed his wife 200 lire a grossi provided she kept half of her dowry in the family ("lasando la mitade de la so enpromessa in la chasa a utilitade de so fioli"); NT 1023, Caresini, no. 13. In the fifteenth century the inducements were proportionately higher; see below, n. 52.

25. For some preliminary observations, see Chojnacki, "Posizione della donna." On fashion and its significance, see Herald, *Renaissance Dress in Italy;* Hollander, *Seeing through Clothes;* and Lurie, *Language of Clothes.* On the social forces behind sumptuary legislation, see the valuable study of Hughes, "Sumptuary Laws."

26. Bistort, *Magistrato alle Pompe,* 123, 154.

27. On the displays of trousseaux, see Vecellio, *Habiti,* 126v. A rare look into newlyweds' expenses is offered by the account book of Moisè Venier, who in 1438 recorded expenditures of more than 147 ducats on the apparel of his wife, Cateruzza Vitturi, in the first three months of their marriage; PSMC Miste, B. 3a,

Moisè Venier, red leather account book, ff. 1r–3r. An act of the Senate in 1420 had set a limit of 500 ducats on husbands' expenditures on their wives' apparel during the first five years of marriage; Senato, Misti 55, f. 103v. In Florence, husbands' gifts of clothing to their wives were seen as only temporary concessions; see Klapisch-Zuber, "Griselda Complex." For an instance of a Venetian father urging restraint upon his daughters in their expenditures (thus testifying to their freedom in the matter), see the 1447 will of Francesco Morosini, in which, after endowing the daughters with dowries of as much as 1,800 ducats and making them his residuary heirs, he "prayed and commanded them, in true paternal obedience, not to spend their wealth on vain and empty things but rather *in honorem dei et proximi.*" PSMC Miste, B. 158a, Francesco Morosini, parchment, 5 April 1448. On male ambivalence regarding women's dress, see Hughes, "Sumptuary Laws," 95–99.

28. In contrast to this hypothesis, Georg Simmel, in his famous treatise on the subject, saw fashionable dress as a sign of conformity, associated with subordinate status, which induces persons to seek security in the group. In arguing his point, however, Simmel noted that women in Renaissance Italy, unlike their German contemporaries, enjoyed "full play for the exercise of individuality"; therefore, according to his thesis, there should have been no "particularly extravagant Italian female fashions," in contrast to the situation in Germany; *Georg Simmel,* 308–9. Simmel's characterization of Italian Renaissance costume runs counter to all authoritative testimony; see, for a sampling, Hughes, "Sumptuary Laws," 88–92. For comments on the forging of female identity within social and cultural boundaries, especially the family, see Davis, "Boundaries and the Sense of Self."

29. On gender identity as contingent, something continuously being shaped by historical circumstances, see Scott, "Gender."

30. Examples of other men who either made their wives their only executors or instructed that, in any dispute among executors, the wife's side should prevail: Marino Arimondo, 1477, Donato Arimondo, 1499, Marco Pisani, 1504: CI Miscellanea Testamenti, Notai Diversi, B. 27, no. 2578; NT 66, Busenello, nos. 126, 264.

31. Hughes ("From Brideprice to Dowry," 284) and Klapisch-Zuber ("Cruel Mother," 124–25) note men's characteristic concern for the sons of their sisters. For the role of maternal uncles in Venice, see Chap. 10.

32. Testating fathers normally left detailed instructions on the investment of their assets until their daughters were of age to be married, preferably—in the words of Andrea Arimondo in 1427, echoing others—"to a Venetian patrician" [in uno zentilomo de Veniesia]; CI, Miscellanea Testamenti, Notai Diversi, B. 27, no. 2697. Similarly, Michele Navagero, in the same year, asserted that his daughter Suordamor "se debia maridar in zentilhomo"; NT 1157, Croci, prot. II, f. 14r.

33. Andrea Arimondo, who wanted his daughter to marry a "zentilomo" (see n. 32 above), authorized his executors to decide whether his estate had enough to marry off any additional daughters or put them into convents: "Non habiando la summa de dener sel fusse piu de una sia lor [i.e., the executors'] liberta de munegar e maridar qual a lor parera." Lorenzo Loredan in 1440 made similar arrangements: "Item, volio che mia fia Biancha e Loredana siano maridade o munegade

segondo aparera . . . a deschrizion de mie chomessarii"; NT 558, Gambaro, no. 86. Giovanni Morosini, however, in 1437 noted "bitterly [*con amaritudine*]" that his estate was so impoverished that he could not afford even a convent dowry, let alone a marriage dowry, for his daughter Marietta; NT 1232, Stefani, no. 314.

34. Examples of fathers' solicitude: Lorenzo Loredan left it up to his daughters to decide whether they wanted to "serve God or marry." Leonardo Priuli provided dowry money for any daughters who "might want to marry" [nubere vellent]. Respectively, NT 1186, Groppi, no. 71; prot., no. 38. Michele Navagero, who wanted his daughter to marry a patrician (above, n. 32), also gave her the option to enter a convent ("munegar"). A rare fourteenth-century father giving his daughter the same choice was Marino Morosini, who in his 1380 will made Agnesina heir to half his *residuum* for her marriage or her religious vocation, "as she chooses" [como la dita Agnesina mia fia alezera]; PSMC Miste, B. 167, Marino Morosini, parchment, 6 January 1379/80.

35. I am preparing a detailed discussion of trends in marriage ages and their larger significance. Broadly speaking, the preferred age for brides rose from the preteens or early teens in the fourteenth century to the middle to late teens in the fifteenth. See, briefly, Chap. 6. For intriguing information on changing measures of female maturity discernible in prosecutions of sexual offenses against young women, see Ruggiero, *Boundaries of Eros*, 102.

36. This is a general impression given by women's wills and has not yet been systematically investigated. Examples of mothers who gave daughters the option: Cristina Morosini (1423), NT 560, Gritti, no. 346; Sterina Lando (1458), NT 727, Moisis, no. 142. On the other hand, some mothers made their preferences clear and forceful: Orsa da Canal declared in 1440 that, if they were not married by age seventeen, "those daughters are to get nothing from my residuary estate" [nichil habere debeant ipse filie femine de dicto meo residuo]; NT 558, Gambaro, no. 84.

37. Francesca Zeno, wife of Piero Morosini, contemplated with apparent tranquillity the lay single state chosen by her daughter Chiara; Chiara would enter into her inheritance as Francesca's residuary legatee either when she married or, if she did not, at age twenty. BMC, MSS P.D./C, no. 916/10 (1427). Isabetta, widow of Barbon Morosini, wanted her bequest to her granddaughter to stand even if the young woman "wants to remain in the secular world, neither marrying nor joining a convent" [vuol star in nel mondo sença maridarse, o munegarse]; NT 1156, Croci, no. 517 (1450). The dangers to daughters' virtue and family honor are explicitly raised in the Senate act of 1420 attempting to limit dowries. For male fears of the dangers presented by unmarried lay women, see Klapisch-Zuber, "Cruel Mother," 122–23, and Kirshner, *Pursuing Honor*, 9–10 and passim.

38. The discrepancy between this figure and the larger group of husbands' wills discussed above is a result of my having noted the language of husbands' references to their wives only in the recent stages of my research in the wills. The indications from such tiny documentation will need to be verified in examination of a much larger sampling of husbands' wills. Even in this small sample, however, the consistent difference between the wills of fourteenth- and fifteenth-century husbands strongly suggests a tendency in patrician society at large.

39. Respectively, "my dearest wife," "my dear beloved consort," "my most

beloved consort." Quotations from wills of Jacopo Morosini, 1448, Donato Arimondo, 1499, and Alvise Lando, 1481. NT 558, Gambaro, no. 168; NT 66, Busenello, no. 126; NT 1186, Groppi, no. 72.

40. I found not one use of the term *consorte* in the thirty-eight wills written before 1427, when it was used by Andrea Arimondo; CI, Miscellanea Testamenti, Notai Diversi, B. 27, no. 2697. For an example from Tuscany of the more traditional, lineage-focused use of the term, see Klapisch-Zuber, "Kin, Friends, and Neighbors," 76.

41. NT 41, Bonamico, no. 150 (will of Nicolò Pisani, 1493); NT 1157, Croci, prot. II, f. 29r (will of Daniele Vitturi, 1440).

42. In his 1499 will, for example, Donato Arimondo referred to his wife, Bianca, variously as "mia chara chonsorte," "mia chara e dileta chonsorte," "mia dileta chonsorte," and just plain "Madona Biancha"; NT 66, Busenello, no. 126.

43. "Et al osequio mio non voio el ne vegni ne mia moier ne fiuoli ne fie per no i dar pena sora pena": will of Francesco Loredan, 1459, NT 179, Rizzo, prot., f. 35v.

44. Bene volio che la chognoscha lamor lio senper portato: will of Donato Arimondo, 1499, NT 66, Busenello, no. 126.

45. Ala qual sono tropo ubligato, si per lo bon portamento chomo per assa danari, oltre la dote, ho abuto de i suo; NT 558, Gambaro, no. 168.

46. In a 1431 will, for example, Sebastiano Vitturi endowed a mansionary to pray for his soul and that of his wife, Suordamor; NT 1157, Croci, prot. I, f. 88v.

47. Donato also wanted to include two natal kinsmen, sons of his late brother, in the tomb, but only his and Bianca's names were to be inscribed on it; NT 66, Busenello, no. 126. Bianca's will of 1490 is NT 41, Bonamico, no. 30.

48. The procedure for recovering dowries is spelled out in the Venetian statutes: *Volumen statutorum*, lib. 1, cap. 62, pp. 28v–29v. Legislation on marriage and dowries in the fourteenth to sixteenth centuries periodically altered it; see Chap. 2, above. Elaborate documentation of dowry claims is evident in, for example, Vadimoni 4, ff. 29v–30v (claim of heirs of the late Franceschina Barbaro, May 14, 1460). On dowry rules and practice, see Chap. 4.

49. Francesco Barbaro declared that the upbringing of children was a wife's most serious duty (*De re uxoria*, 92), but fathers' concern for the maternal care of children was surely interwoven with fear that a mother's remarriage would transfer her loyalty and her wealth to a new family—a transfer, Klapisch-Zuber notes, that was urged by widows' brothers in Florence; "Cruel Mother." For examples of Venetian fathers who conditioned their bequests to wives on the latter's remaining, unmarried, with the children, see the wills of Michele Navagero, 1427, and Sebastiano Vitturi, 1431; NT 1157, Croci, prot. II, f. 14r, prot. I, f. 88v.

50. "Volio la sia tratada come la persona mia." Marino left her 400 ducats over and above her dowry, the use of his "caxa granda," in which her widowed sister could also live, at Marino's expense, or—if they preferred another nearby house—remodeling expenses; CI, Miscellanea Testamenti, Notai Diversi 27, no. 2578.

51. Marino's will was written in 1477; he had married in 1432. Donato's will dates from 1499; his wedding was in 1462. For the wedding dates, Barbaro, Nozze, ff. 8v, 9v.

52. Michele Navagero (1427), testating with young children, bequeathed his

wife, over and above her dowry, 400 ducats if she remained unmarried but 200 if she remarried; NT 1157, Croci, prot. II, f. 14r. Sebastiano Vitturi (1431) at first left his wife 400 ducats "tam viduando quam non" but, later in the will after providing for his adopted son, apparently thought better of it and made the bequest conditional upon her remaining single and caring for the young man; ibid., prot. I, ff. 88v–90r. Lorenzo Loredan (1441) conditioned a supradowry bequest of 200 ducats to his wife upon her caring for their children, but if there were no children, then she had it free and clear and would be free to marry; NT 558, Gambaro, no. 86.

53. "Per haver abudo bonissima chompagnia da lui sino al presente e molto meio spiero per lavegnir"; NT 1186, Groppi, no. 82. Maddaluzza had two married sisters, alternative beneficiaries, but they got only 100 ducats each.

54. Lucrezia was apparently a rich widow, since Sebastiano moved in with her at their marriage in 1497. NT 66, Busenello, no. 246; Barbaro, Nozze, f. 369v.

55. "I son ubiga piu cha criatura di sto mondo per lestremi afani la porta chon mi per chason de la mia infirmita e dano dela soa persona che a tuti puo eser manifesto non chomo muier ma chomo sciava"; NT 1157, Croci, prot. II, f. 29.

56. CI 175, Rizzo, prot., f. 35v.

57. For a discussion of the effects of kinship, marriage, and "prestige structures" on gender definitions, see Ortner and Whitehead, "Introduction," 21–24.

58. For instances of women linking their natal and marital families, see Chap. 10.

59. A preliminary statement on these matters can be found in Chojnacki, "Posizione della donna."

Chapter 8   Motherhood, Gender, and Patrician Duty

This chapter originally appeared, in slightly altered form, as " 'The Most Serious Duty': Motherhood, Gender, and Patrician Culture in Renaissance Venice," in *Refiguring Woman: Perspectives on Gender and the Italian Renaissance,* ed. Marilyn Migiel and Juliana Schiesari (Ithaca, N.Y.: Cornell University Press, 1991), 133–54.

1. Barbaro, *De re uxoria,* 92. The translation is based on that of Benjamin G. Kohl: Barbaro, "On Wifely Duties," 220. Barbaro's discussion makes clear that he uses *educatio* in the sense that includes general upbringing as well as pedagogy. On Barbaro, see King, "Caldiera and the Barbaros," 31–35. Research for this essay was supported by the American Council of Learned Societies, the Gladys Krieble Delmas Foundation, and the College of Arts and Letters and Department of History, Michigan State University.

2. On Venice's uninterrupted subscription to family principles of Roman law, see Zordan, "I vari aspetti."

3. *De re uxoria,* 63; Kohl's translation, 193.

4. The fullest discussion of patrician political practice is in Finlay, *Politics.* On the establishment of the hereditary principle in the patriciate, see Lane, "Enlargement of the Great Council." See also Chap. 11.

5. See the germinal essay of Joan Kelly-Gadol, "Did Women Have a Renaissance?" (1977). The broad strokes of Kelly's essay are given historical nuance in Stuard, "Dominion of Gender." For other considerations of change in the position

of women during the Middle Ages and Renaissance, see the introduction to Bennett, *Women in the Medieval English Countryside;* Wiesner, *Working Women in Renaissance Germany;* and Howell, "Citizenship and Gender."

6. My views of gender in historical analysis have been especially influenced by Ortner and Whitehead, "Introduction"; Rosaldo, "Woman, Culture, and Society" and "Use and Abuse of Anthropology"; Elshtain, *Public Man, Private Woman;* Flax, "Postmodernism and Gender Relations"; and Scott, "Gender."

7. The complex interaction between gender, social placement, and individual identity is variously explored in Greenblatt, "Fiction and Friction"; and Davis, "Boundaries and the Sense of Self."

8. This essay is part of a larger project exploring patrician politics, society, and culture, with special attention to gender, especially as it related to the liminal groups of women and young men. See Chaps. 7 and 11.

9. On marriage in the patriciate, see Finlay, *Politics,* esp. 81–96; Betto, "Linee di politica matrimoniale"; and Chaps. 2–4.

10. On governmental definitions of the status requirements of patrician wives, see Chojnacki, "Marriage Legislation." Barbaro ranked the pedigree of the mother at least as high as that of the father in producing worthy offspring; *De re uxoria,* 41.

11. See Chap. 2.

12. On electioneering, see Finlay, *Politics;* on dependence on political office, Queller, *Venetian Patriciate.*

13. On assembling dowries, see Chap. 6, above. For non-Venetian perspectives, see Hughes, "From Brideprice to Dowry"; Kirshner and Molho, "Dowry Fund"; and Klapisch-Zuber, "Griselda Complex."

14. In the fifteenth century marriage portions usually consisted of two-thirds strict dowry to be returned to the wife and one-third *corredo* (*corredum*), at that time an outright gift to the husband. The complex and evolving relationship of dowry to *corredo* (the latter in its twin dimensions as trousseau and as gift to the husband) is addressed in Chap. 3.

15. On the mechanisms guaranteeing women's rights to their dowries at marriage's end, see Chap. 4. See also Kirshner, "Wives' Claims," and Kuehn, "Some Ambiguities."

16. On the authority of fathers, see Kuehn, *Emancipation.*

17. NT 575, Gibellino, no. 675, 9 May 1401.

18. On the continuing relationships between fathers and sons after the latter's emancipation, see Kuehn, *Emancipation.*

19. Gasparino's unusual generosity toward Maria runs exactly counter to the remarrying "cruel mother" syndrome analyzed in the Florentine context by Christiane Klapisch-Zuber in her influential essay of that name. Whereas the cruelty of the mother in Klapisch-Zuber's typology consisted in her willing or coerced abandonment of her children upon remarriage, Gasparino, though solicitous of his grandchildren by Maria, nevertheless benignly supported the prospect of her remarriage. It seems unlikely that a remarrying Venetian mother was more likely than her Florentine counterpart to continue caring for the children of her first marriage. Gasparino himself was accustomed to cherish ties to in-laws even

after remarriage. In an earlier will of 1374, written during his second marriage, he had bequeathed 50 ducats to each of the brothers of his deceased first wife "per grande amor e raxion chio o portado sempre a quella caxa" [because of the great love and interest I have always had for that house]. NT 1062, Della Torre, no. 300, 14 April 1374.

20. Vojo la se dia a quelo zentilomo venizian che sia dexevele ala so condizion e che sia de conttentto e azetto a mi fiuoli Nicolò Benedetto e Antuonio. E semelmentre sia azeto a miy cosini Barbon e Bernardo morexini e mio coxin german Zanin Morexini, hover a la plu parte de questi. NT 571 "carte varie" 18 April 1401. (The 4 May will added codicils to the basic text of the 18 April will.)

21. The example of a father mediating equitably the legacies to his sons by their different predeceased mothers represents another alternative to the child-abandoning widow discussed as a model of Florentine wifehood by Klapisch-Zuber in "Cruel Mother." The remarrying widow was only one of several maternal typologies; in addition to women who, like Gasparino's three wives, preceded their husbands to the grave, many mothers remained head of household after their husband's death, giving a distinctive cast to their discharge of that role. See the discussion later in this chapter.

22. Kent, *Household and Lineage*, 29–36, 58–60.

23. On the Balla d'Oro (or Barbarella) exercise establishing patrician adulthood, see Chaps. 10 and 11, below. In 1405 the Great Council passed a law requiring candidates for office to be identifed not only by given name and surname but by patronymic as well; MC 21, Leona, f. 127r.

24. Klapisch-Zuber, "Cruel Mother" and "Kin, Friends, and Neighbors"; Hughes, "From Brideprice to Dowry" and "Representing the Family"; Strocchia, "Remembering the Family." See also Weissman, *Ritual Brotherhood,* 33.

25. Female testators often advertised their double affiliation: "Ego Victoria filia qd. domini Andree Victuri *ad presens* uxor nobilis viri domini Valerii Geno" [I, Vittoria, daughter of the late Lord Andrea Vitturi, *at present* wife of the noble Lord Valerio Zeno]; NT 857, Rizoto, no. 349, 31 July 1427 (emphasis added). "Mi Franceschina fia fo del nobel homo messer Domenego Loredan *al prexente* spoxa del nobel homo miser Nicholo Chapelo" [I, Franceschina, daughter of the late noble messer Domenico Loredan, *at present* spouse of the noble messer Nicolò Capello]; NT 1238, Tomei, pt. 2, no. 239, 2 December 1404 (emphasis added). The allusion to the temporariness of marital ties suggests a more durable natal than marital identification for these women. Other wives, however, emphasized the marital family connection: Briseida Pisani, wife of Nicolò Bragadin, while retaining close ties to her mother and brother (naming them as testamentary executors and leaving them bequests), nevertheless identified herself as "ego Briseida consors viri nobilis domini Nicolai Bragadeno" [I Briseida, consort of the noble Lord Nicolò Bragadin]; NT 1238, Tomei, pt. 2, no. 17, 10 July 1438.

26. Fortes, "Structure of Unilineal Descent Groups," 34. On functional bilaterality in formally unilineal descent groups, see Goody, *Development of the Family,* 6, 236; also, Chap. 10.

27. See Chap. 11.

28. Official testimony about the dependence of a majority of patricians on

office holding is in MC 34, Stella, f. 109v. The fullest treatment of governmental careerism in the patriciate is in Queller, *Venetian Patriciate*.

29. On the tension between youthful expansiveness and adult conformity, see Trexler, *Public Life*, chap. 5, and Chap. 11 in this volume.

30. Among testating parents in the sample of wills, thirty-four identified specific ages for their daughters' marriages. Their preferences ranged from age eleven or twelve to twenty, with a median age of fourteen to sixteen. See, briefly, n. 53 below.

31. In 1497 Francesco Morosini made a bequest to his daughter who lived in a convent, "che io amo come lanima mia propria" [whom I love as my very soul]. He urged the convent authorities, to whom he left a large bequest, to treat her well, "because I have allowed no harm to befall her from the time she entered that convent, in order to be a good father to her who is my most sweet daughter and my very heart." PSMC De Ultra, B. 221, fasc. I, Francesco Morosini, Register, 10 November 1497.

32. Not yet systematically documented, this tendency emerges anecdotally. Isabetta Trevisan, married in 1417 to Filippo Foscari, named as executors of her 1419 will her father and a paternal uncle as well as her husband. Pregnant, she bequeathed to the unborn child 600 ducats, which, if the child did not reach adulthood, were to go to her father and uncle, who in any case were named her residuary heirs; her husband was to get only 100 ducats. NT 367, Angeletus, unnumbered, 4 January 1418/19; Barbaro, Nozze, f. 189v. Maria Barbarigo, who married in 1450, also named as executors of the will she drew up during her pregnancy in 1451 her father, a paternal uncle, and her husband. She bequeathed 200 ducats to her husband but the same amount each to her father and her mother and 100 ducats to one of her brothers; her remaining 100 ducats she left to the child she was carrying, but if it died before age fourteen, the money was to go to her brothers. NT 558, Gambaro, no. 220, 17 December 1451; Barbaro, Nozze, f. 368v.

33. On male honor and female vocations, see Kirshner, *Pursuing Honor.*

34. Senato, Misti 53, f. 70r. This act, aimed at restraining dowry inflation, is discussed at length in Chap. 2. On motives for consigning daughters to convents, see Trexler, "Celibacy in the Renaissance." Questions about the effectiveness of the religious life in guaranteeing male honor by preserving female chastity are raised by the evidence of sexual activity in convents presented in Ruggiero, *Boundaries of Eros,* chap. 4, "Sex Crimes against God."

35. Nonetheless, Gasparino was more explicit than most about his lineage ties to the men he charged with arranging Franceschina's marriage. Men usually assigned the responsibility for their daughters' marriages to their executors, who normally included a large proportion of agnates, though by no means agnates alone. For example, Lorenzo Loredan: "Volio che mia fie . . . siano maridade o munegade segondo aparera a dischrezio de mio chomessarii" [I want my daughters to be married or placed in a convent, at the discretion of my executors], who were his three brothers, his wife, her father, and his sons when they reached age fourteen; NT 558, Gambaro, no. 86, 10 May 1441. Similarly, Andrea Arimondo provided that when his daughter turned fifteen, "lasso libertas ala maor parte de mii

commessarii . . . al suo maridar a uno zentilomo de Veniesia" [I give liberty to the majority of my executors (to make the appropriate arrangements) at her marriage to a Venetian noble]; CI, Miscellanea Testamenti, Notai Diversi, B. 27, no. 2697, 13 August 1427. His executors were his mother, his four brothers, his wife, her parents, and her brother. On the involvement of wives and their natal kin in the determination of their children's future, see the discussion later in this chapter.

36. This sample is not scientific but the product of study over several years of all the wills I could read. Most but not all were drawn up by members, by birth or marriage, of sixteen patrician clans whose social and political experiences I am reconstructing in detail. I know of no statistical breakdown of surviving Venetian wills; but extensive work with the card index of wills in the ASV, as well as with the testament files of dozens of notaries, gives the overpowering impression that women left wills far more often than men.

37. The Venetian statutes governing inheritance in cases of intestacy reflected patrilineal principles, favoring, first, children, then ascendants in the male line. Fathers who conformed to those principles could thus entrust their estates to the enforcements of the statutes. *Volumen statutorum*, lib. 4, caps. 24–27, pp. 70v–74v. Mothers, whose intestacy was governed largely but not completely by the same rules, had reason in their more complex social placement to make their intentions testamentarily explicit; ibid., cap. 28, p. 74v.

38. For differences in men's and women's patterns of testation, see Chap. 6.

39. See n. 35; also Chap. 7.

40. Chap. 10.

41. NT 575, Giorgio Gibellino, no. 704, 15 November 1401. Beruzza was the married sister whom Gasparino Morosini wanted to prepare his granddaughter Franceschina for marriage. The preference for men as heirs to immovable property and women as heirs to movables was clearly stated in the statutes governing intestacy; *Volumen statutorum*, lib. 4, cap. 15, p. 71v. On similar rules in Florence, see Kuehn, "Some Ambiguities," 28 n. 4.

42. Chap. 10; Finlay, *Politics*, 87–89. Diane Owen Hughes argues that the dowry regime diminished bilateral ties; she also notes, however, that men retained an interest in the woman to whose dowry they had contributed as well as in the affines it produced; "From Brideprice to Dowry," 284, 290.

43. On family and kin boundaries as the frame of adult identity, see Davis, "Boundaries and the Sense of Self."

44. For example, in 1430 Cristina Falier, widow of Nicolò Barbarigo, invested 1,300 ducats with her son, Andrea, who acknowledged that it was "pro meis utilitatibus" [for my use]; CI 122, Marevidi, prot., f. 15v. In a marriage contract of 1451, Marina, widow of Tomaso Donà, "se hobliga la mittade de tuti i suo beni" [pledges one-half of all her property] as security for repayment of the dowry that her son, Nicolò, was to receive from his wife-to-be, Isabetta Querini; the total dowry to be repaid was 1,200 ducats; Vadimoni 4, ff. 58v–59v.

45. The exact percentage of adult male patricians who married, 56.7 percent, was gained by comparing marriage lists in Barbaro, Nozze, with registrations for the Balla d'Oro among sixteen sample clans for the period 1410–90. This involved 952 registrants, of whom 540 (56.7%) married. BO 162, 163, 164. The practice

among patricians of limiting male marriage for purposes of preserving the property of a group of brothers is discussed for the sixteenth through eighteenth centuries in Davis, *Venetian Family,* 93–106. Davis cites sources asserting that the practice began in the mid-sixteenth century; the evidence just noted, however, suggests that it was already in effect in the fifteenth.

46. CI 56, Griffon, prot. I, f. 76v. In return for this maternal generosity, Barbarella transferred to her mother all her rights of succession to her father's estate. This case shows how, by discharging a paternal responsibility, a mother could lay claim to a child's share of the paternal estate.

47. NT 1439, Tomei, no. 600: "ma tuto quel parera a diti commisarii sia fato in chaxo el padre dilatase el suo maridar" [but my executors should take whatever action they deem appropriate in the event that her father delays arranging her marriage].

48. Paolina's marriage to Luca Falier in 1466, when she could not have been more than fifteen (calculated from Petronella's will of 1464), is in Barbaro, Nozze, f. 327r.

49. NT 68, Bonicardi, no. 210, 16 May 1479.

50. Francesca Loredan Capello bequeathed 400 ducats to each of her daughters; but "ista condicio sit et intellagatur in filiabus meis que maritaverintur. Ille vero que monacaverintur *aut starent honesta in domo* habeant ducatos trecentos" [this provision should be understood as applying to my daughters who marry. Those indeed who became nuns *or live chastely at home* are to have 300 ducats]. NT 1238, Tomei, pt. 2, no. 292 bis, 6 October 1473; emphasis added. See also the wills of Isabetta Gritti da Lezze (ibid., no. 220, 4 May 1465); Fantina Contarini Morosini (NT 486, Gibellino, no. 204, 11 July 1435); and Isabetta Morosini, who bequeathed 100 ducats to her granddaughter "o per so maridar, o se lie volese andar munega in monastier de oservancia voio lie i abia e posa far quelo lie vora, *e cusi se la vuol star in nel mondo sença maridarse, o, munegarse*" [either for her marriage or, if she chooses, to become a nun in an observant convent, I want her to have them to use as she wishes; *and likewise if she elects to live a secular life without marrying or becoming a nun*]. NT 1156, Croci, no. 517, 23 October 1450; emphasis added.

51. Although I have found no fathers explicitly endowing spinsterhood for their daughters, Prodocimo Arimondo instructed that his daughter Pellegrina, "que ducit vitam spiritualem" [who is leading a spiritual life], was to live not in a convent but with her brothers, "et habeat vitum de bonis meis et vestitum et bene tractetur" [and she is to have food and clothing from my estate, and be well treated]; NT 1239, Tomei, no. 606, 27 February 1473/74. More in line with the growing tendency to allow daughters vocational choice, Lorenzo Loredan left it "in libertade dele do mie fie zoe Chataruzza e Ixabela se quelle volesse servir a dio" [up to my two daughters, namely, Cateruzza and Isabella, if they wish to serve God], in which case each was to receive 400 ducats; but "se veramente quelle volesse esser maridada, abiano de beni dela mia comesaria ducati 600 per suo dote" [if indeed they wish to marry, each is to receive 600 ducats from my estate for their dowries]; NT 1186, Groppi, no. 71, 29 April 1476. More munificently, Alvise Zane left his daughter Michela his entire residuary estate for her marriage portion, unless his wife bore a son, in which case Michela would get only (!)

3,500 ducats; but if Michela "vellet monacare solum habere debeat ducatos 1500" [wishes to become a nun, she is to have only 1,500 ducats]; NT 68, Bonicardi. no. 316, 7 April 1485.

52. Davis, "Boundaries and the Sense of Self," 61. That essay lays out the components of the complex issue, central to social and cultural history and especially to the benefits of a gender-sensitive approach to it, of the tension between individual identity and the group membership that both restricts and gives it shape. The conceptual and methodological problems involved in attending to both sociocultural context and the vagaries of individual circumstance and experience require much discussion, but they are helpfully clarified by Davis's essay.

53. Of 361 wills of married patricians, most mentioned the age of majority (conventionally age fourteen) as the preferred marriage age. But among thirty-three parents who between 1350 and 1500 specified marriage ages for their daughters, those testating between 1350 and 1400 ranged in their specifications from eleven to seventeen years, with a median preferred age of thirteen; the preference of those testating between 1401 and 1450 ranged from age thirteen to twenty, with a median of fifteen; and between 1451 and 1500 from fourteen to eighteen, with a median of sixteen.

54. The evidence is mixed on mothers' preferences; some seem to have favored early marriage for their daughters, possibly to free them from their fathers' control; but others favored delaying marriage, to give the daughters greater maturity in choosing and adapting to marriage.

55. Ruggiero, *Boundaries of Eros,* 137–40. For a different perspective, see Labalme, "Sodomy and Venetian Justice," 232–35.

56. See Chap. 10, and now Chojnacki, "Identity and Ideology."

57. Senato, Terra, f. 151r.

58. Rosaldo, "Woman, Culture, and Society," 21.

Chapter 9   Adolescence and Gender

This chapter originally appeared, in slightly altered form, as "Measuring Adulthood: Adolescence and Gender in Renaissance Venice," *Journal of Family History* 17 (1992): 371–95.

1. NT 1238, Tomei, pt. 2, no. 9. Agnesina noted that the will was written "by my own hand [*de mia propria man*]." Research for this chapter was supported by the American Council of Learned Societies, the Gladys Krieble Delmas Foundation, and the All-University Research Fund of Michigan State University. An early draft was revised during the tenure of an Andrew W. Mellon Fellowship at the National Humanities Center. I wish to express my gratitude to all these institutions. I also wish to signal my debt to Barbara A. Hanawalt for valuable advice.

2. NT 1149, Benedetto, no. 170.

3. Rossiaud, "Prostitution, jeunesse et société," and Otis, "Prostitution in Late Medieval Perpignan," illustrate differences in male and female coming-of-age experiences in late medieval southern France: respectively, young men engaging in gang rape, young women in a phase of prostitution.

4. For explorations of identity in context, see Davis, "Boundaries and the Sense of Self," "Fame and Secrecy," and "Ghosts, Kin, and Progeny," and the ex-

change between Finlay, "Refashioning of Martin Guerre," and Davis, "On the Lame." See also Greenblatt, *Renaissance Self-Fashioning*, chap. 1.

5. On various aspects of youth, see Davis, "Reasons of Misrule"; Trexler, "Ritual in Florence"; Duby, "Au XIIᵉ siècle"; and Chap. 11.

6. The definition of the age of majority is in *Volumen statutorum*, lib. 2, cap. 1, p. 32v. The Great Council act of 1299 is in Bistort, *Magistrato alle Pompe*, 324.

7. Van Gennep, *Rites of Passage*, 66. See also Glucksman, "Rites de passage."

8. Paolino, *Trattato de regimine*, 68; Barbaro, *De re uxoria*, 37. On Barbaro's ideas about marriage in the Venetian context, see King, "Caldiera and the Barbaros."

9. The 614 wills, drawn from the NT, CI, and PSMC funds of the ASV, are only a small sampling of the immense testamentary holdings for the late medieval–early Renaissance period. They represent no scientific selection, though most were drawn up by members of sixteen patrician houses that I have studied in detail. The study of wills continues, but the 614 provide the basis for initial charting of patrician tendencies.

10. Giovanni Morosini: NT 364, Darvasio, no. 363; Marino Pisani: NT 727, Moisis, no. 1; Piero Morosini: NT 1154, Bruto, no. 52; Petronella Falier Morosini: NT 1239, Tomei, no. 60; Orsa Soranzo da Canal: NT 558, Gambaro, no. 84.

11. Herlihy and Klapisch-Zuber, *Tuscans and Their Families*, 223; Klapisch-Zuber, "Cruel Mother"; Hughes, "From Brideprice to Dowry" and "Representing the Family"; Kirshner and Molho, "Dowry Fund"; Kirshner, *Pursuing Honor*; Molho, "Deception and Marriage Strategy."

12. NT 575, Gibellino, no. 675.

13. Systematic information about births is lacking before the sixteenth century. However, by comparing references to children and pregnancy in the date-specific wills of married women with the dates of their marriages, as registered in the most reliable list of pre-1500 patrician marriages, we can get anecdotal evidence that young brides indeed conceived soon after marrying. Istriana Balbi Bon, married in 1456, described herself in her will of 1458 as "approaching childbirth [*propinque partum*]"; Barbaro, Nozze, f. 40v; NT 727, Moisis, no. 21. Sterina Foscari Lando, also married in 1456, already had a daughter when she testated in 1458; Barbaro, Nozze, f. 231v; NT 727, Moisis, no. 142. Andriana Balbi da Mula, married in 1495, attested her pregnancy already in February of the following year; Barbaro, Nozze, f. 40v; NT 41, Bonamico, no. 1. Suordamor Balbi Zane, married in 1469, already had a son named Bernardo by April 1470; Barbaro, Nozze, f. 40v; NT 1239, Tomei, no. 690.

14. Silvestro: NT 486, Gibellino, no. 45; Vida: NT 1238, Tomei, pt. 1, no. 83. Vida wrote her will in 1435; she had been married only in 1428; Barbaro, Nozze, f. 244v.

15. Of the thirty-four age-specifying parental preferences, one was from the first half of fourteenth century; it specified age thirteen to fifteen. Eleven were from 1351–1400, with a median age of thirteen; fourteen were from 1401–50, with a median of fifteen; and eight were from 1451–1500, with a median preferred age of sixteen. Additional evidence of the receding age of female maturity in popular conception may be found in the changing parameters of the term *puella* in cases of rape of underage girls; see Ruggiero, *Boundaries of Eros*, 102. In a will of

1374, Gasparino Morosini, whose solicitude toward his granddaughter in his 1401 will was noted above, wanted his daughter to marry at age twelve; when he testated anew in 1389, the preferred age had risen to thirteen. NT 1062, Della Torre, no. 300; NT 571, Gibellino, no. 182.

16. On the social implications of marriage, see above, Chap. 2. On mothers' influence on fathers, see Chap. 7.

17. An act of the Senate in 1420 limiting dowries in order to permit more girls to marry expressly noted the threat; the act is discussed in Chap. 2. See also Kirshner, *Pursuing Honor*, 5–15; Molho, "Deception and Marriage Strategy," 206–10; and Klapisch-Zuber, "Cruel Mother," 119. Evidence of notorious sexual activity in convents, however, raises the question how securely male honor was protected by a daughter's monacation; see Ruggiero, *Boundaries of Eros*, 76–84. The attribution to late medieval men of a model derived from ethnographic study of modern Mediterranean cultures is problematic, especially so when the model is applied to elites such as the Italian urban patriciates. Julian Pitt-Rivers notes that even in contemporary Spain aristocratic women do not suffer a loss of honor by violating sexual mores that, for peasant women, are ironclad; Pitt-Rivers, "Honour and Social Status," 71.

18. In a will of 1342, Leone Morosini provided for the marriage portion of his daughter and for the child his pregnant wife was carrying; if the latter was born a boy, he was to get the bulk of Leone's estate; if a girl, she was to be put into a convent, in order not to diminish the older daughter's dowry by claiming one of her own; PSMC Miste, B. 127, Leone Morosini, parchment no. 2. A century later, Lorenzo Loredan echoed the practice of many testating fathers by authorizing his executors to decide whether his daughters should be "maridade o munegade [married or placed in a convent]." NT 558, Gambaro, no. 86. On the convent as an expedient for settling unmarriageable daughters, see the references in Chap. 1.

19. Hughes, "From Brideprice to Dowry"; Kirshner and Molho, "Dowry Fund"; Klapisch-Zuber, "Cruel Mother"; Riemer, "Women, Dowries, and Capital Investment"; Trexler, "Celibacy in the Renaissance."

20. PSMC Miste, B. 167, Marino Morosini, parchment, 6 January 1379/80.

21. After providing for the marriage portion of his elder daughter, Franceschina, Nicolò Morosini in 1380 noted that he "delegated my dear second daughter, Chiara, to the service of Jesus Christ"; NT 679, Antonio Bellancini, prot., f. 9r.

22. Herlihy, *Medieval Households*, 143.

23. "Libertade" is in the will of Lorenzo Loredan, in 1472; NT 1186, Groppi, no. 71. Francesco Navagero: NT 1233, Soris, no. 224. In 1485 Alvise Zane allocated at least 3,500 ducats for the marriage portion of his daughter, Michela, but if instead she preferred the religious life [velet monacare], she was to get only 1,500 ducats; NT 68, Bonicardi, no. 316.

24. NT 486, Gibellino, no. 204.

25. Franceschina Capello: NT 1238, Tomei, pt. 2, no. 292 bis. Isabetta da Lezze: ibid., no. 220. Isabetta Morosini: NT 1156, Croci, no. 517.

26. See, among many discussions, Cozzi, "Authority and the Law"; Finlay, *Politics*; Queller, *Venetian Patriciate*; and Chap. 11.

27. Barbaro thought that men who waited until age thirty-seven to marry would have fewer but more robust children; *De re uxoria*, 39. Fra Paolino, the fourteenth-century moralist, urged men to wait at least until age twenty-one "in order not to impede their further growth [*azò k'el no embrige en lo so creser*]"; Paolino Minorita, *Trattato de regimine*, 69. On the other hand, note the Florentine Giovanni Morelli's warnings about the dangers of late marriage for men, in Trexler, *Public Life*, 166.

28. Men's marriage ages were calculated by comparing the marriage dates in Barbaro, Nozze, with the records of grooms' earlier registrations for the Barbarella (also known as the Balla d'Oro), the lottery offering winners early admission to the Great Council. When registering, young patricians had to provide evidence or testimony that they had reached age eighteen and were of legitimate patrician birth. Those age declarations were quite specific, with most registrants indicating their age as eighteen, others specifying a year or two beyond that, and an occasional registrant indicating his imminent eighteenth birthday. Of course, fraud and inaccuracy occurred, but no more than in other age registration exercises. The source for this information is BO 162, 163, 164. On the Barbarella, see Chaps. 10 and 11.

29. An act of the Great Council in 1490 stated that "the majority [of patricians] live and support their families" by office holding; MC 24, Stella, f. 109v. See also Queller, *Venetian Patriciate*, chap. 2. On the division between prominent and dependent patricians, see Finlay, *Politics*, 59–81, and Cracco, "Patriziato e oligarchia."

30. Finlay, "Venetian Gerontocracy"; Chap. 11.

31. Chap. 11; Herlihy, "Some Psychological and Social Roots"; Ruggiero, *Boundaries of Eros*, 160–62.

32. On the role of the young in affirming and enhancing cultural values by their untainted embodiment of those values, see Trexler, "Ritual in Florence," and Chap. 11.

33. See Chaps. 10 and 11.

34. Bowmen earned a stipend of 60 ducats per year and enjoyed the opportunity to gain trading profits of an additional 40–140 ducats; Queller, *Venetian Patriciate*, 34–39.

35. In 1431 the Senate explicitly declared that bowmen had to prove that they were twenty exactly as did winners of the Barbarella lottery (who, even if they won the competition shortly after registering at age eighteen, still had to wait until their twentieth birthday to enter the Great Council); Senato, Misti 58, f. 77v. In the records of age proofs, it appears that those appointed bowmen on galleys (*galie*) did indeed prove that they were twenty, but bowmen assigned to round ships (*naves*) needed to prove only eighteen, PE 178/2, ff. 141 ff. This difference has not been noted in the literature and merits examination.

36. The classic but outdated study of the *calza* companies is Venturi, "Compagnie della Calza." On the companies' role in public festivities, see Muraro, "Le feste a Venezia." On the importance of collective ritual in Venetian public life, see Muir, *Civic Ritual*.

37. BMC, Codici Cicogna, 3278, fasc. 24, cc. 25r–29r.

38. Ages were calculated using the Barbarella registrations of the young men who signed the Modesti statutes on 20 February 1486/87. For example, Girolamo da Pesaro did not register for the Barbarella until 30 November of that year, when he was identified as eighteen years old; BO 164, f. 294r. (In cases where more than one person with the same given and family names registered for the Barbarella in the same general period, and where the Modesti reference lacks the distinguishing patronymic, I assumed that the one closest to age eighteen was the Modesti member, since the statutes identify the signatories as "adolescentes."

39. On the special character of the liminal or threshold period of the passage to adulthood, see Chap. 11.

40. Of 1,065 young men from sixteen clans studied who registered for the Barbarella between 1408 and 1497, 678, or 64 percent, had living fathers at the time; data from BO 162, 163, 164. Probably a result of the tendency of early Quattrocento patricians to marry in their late twenties, this contrasts with the Florentine situation, where, as Herlihy and Klapisch-Zuber have shown, men of the patriciate tended to marry in their thirties and were consequently more likely than their Venetian counterparts to leave their sons fatherless in their late teens. Herlihy and Klapisch-Zuber, *Tuscans and Their Families*, 244–50; Herlihy, "Some Psychological and Social Roots," 147–48.

41. The large numbers of applicants for the limited bowman posts created constant pressure on the government to expand the program; in 1500, for example, 120 to 130 men were selected from 250 applicants; Queller, *Venetian Patriciate*, 36.

42. Senato, Misti 53, f. 70r. See also Chap. 2.

43. Dieci, Misti 27, ff. 171v–172r.

44. Figures culled from BO 162, 163, 164, and Barbaro, Nozze.

45. Davis, *Venetian Family*, 93–106.

46. For examples of parents who commented upon their sons' difficulties owing to the effort to assemble large dowries for their daughters, see Chap. 7, n. 17. The Senate act of 1420 limiting dowries also took note of the effect of large dowries on sons' prospects; Chojnacki, "Marriage Legislation," 165.

47. The statutory principle was that "omnia bona viri sunt obligate mulieri" [the husband's entire estate is obligated to the wife]; *Volumen statutorum*, lib. 1, cap. 4, p. 17v. On the liability of the husband's agnate kin for restitution of the wife's dowry, see above, Chap. 4. For the principle in the Italian context generally, see Kirshner, "Wives' Claims." For examples of fathers providing explicitly for their sons' "dowries," see NT 670, Marino, no. 167 (Piero Morosini); NT 1238, Tomei, pt. 1, no. 15 (Ermolao Pisani); and NT 1239, Tomei, no. 606 (Prodocimo Arimondo).

48. Ruggiero, *Boundaries of Eros*, 161. For a different perspective on homosexuality in Venice, see Labalme, "Sodomy and Venetian Justice."

49. King, *Venetian Humanism*, 195–205.

50. The formulation of Natalie Davis, according to which individual identity becomes clarified not so much in the absence of but rather in defining friction with the pressures to conform to social and cultural structures, seems to me especially fruitful for viewing male experience in the Venetian patriciate, with its highly

organized patriarchal, patrilineal, and patrimonial structures; Davis, "Boundaries and the Sense of Self."

51. On the disciplining of youth in patrician government and society, see Chap. 11; see also the contrasting interpretation, emphasizing public indulgence of youthful misbehavior, of Ruggiero, *Violence in Early Renaissance Venice,* chap. 10. Parental dismay over misbehaving sons is occasionally displayed in wills. See, for example, those of Daniele and Chiara Loredan, who cut their son Giovanni out of their wills because of his misbehavior, and of Nicolò Mudazzo, who required his son Piero to mend his ways and marry in order to share in Nicolò's estate. NT 1157, Croci, prot. 2, ff. 35r (Daniele), 150r (Chiara); NT 1255, Zane, prot., ff. 184v–186v (Nicolò).

52. For anthropological evidence of the prestige attached to marriage for men in patriarchal societies, see Ortner and Whitehead, "Introduction," 21–24. In Venice, the favored role of the father in rituals inducting young men into adult patrician society underscores the public importance of legal generativity in this carefully patrilineal group; Chojnacki, "Social Identity," 344–45.

53. On the dowry as inheritance and its implications for gender roles and family property, see, variously, Hughes, "From Brideprice to Dowry," 278–82; Klapisch-Zuber, "Cruel Mother," 121–22; and Kuehn, "Some Ambiguities." These titles represent only a small sample of a large literature on an issue central to gender, family, and property in the late medieval Italian cities.

54. Although married only two years earlier and with her father still living, Arimonda Arimondo Marino, pregnant and testating in 1479, named her husband, Marco Marino, as her sole executor; she also expressed her wish to be buried alongside him in the tomb of his choice and bequeathed her dowry and other goods to "mio caro e dolze marito [my dear, sweet husband]." NT 68, Bonicardi, no. 8; the date of their marriage is in Barbaro, Nozze, f. 9r. Similarly committed to her husband, naming him as her only executor and secondary beneficiary after her children, was Lucia Priuli Girardo, who had been married less than a year at the drawing up of her will. NT 66, Busenello, no. 232; Barbaro, Nozze, f. 369v. But other young wives remained tied to their natal families well into marriage. Chiara da Lezze Zane, married two years and pregnant, apparently with her first child, named her mother and brothers as her executors along with her husband, referring to them as "peramabiles [most beloved]," but giving her husband no affectionate term, and making the brothers her residuary heirs after a 300-ducat bequest to the child she was carrying—with no bequest to her husband. NT 1233, Soris, no. 159 (1412); Barbaro, Nozze, f. 453v. Franceschina Loredan Capello, married three years, in her will of 1464 named as her executors her husband, her sister and the latter's husband, and her mother to whom alone she gave determining authority in the administration of the estate. NT 1238, Tomei, pt. 2, no. 292; Barbaro, Nozze, f. 245r.

55. Francesco Barbaro identified the upbringing of children as the central duty of motherhood, devoting several paragraphs to the importance of a mother breastfeeding her own children in order to launch their childhood properly; *De re uxoria,* 95–98. Barbaro's urgings suggest that many mothers were indeed consigning, or

were obliged to consign, the care and nourishment of their infant children to nurses, as was the custom in Florence; Klapisch-Zuber, "Blood Parents and Milk Parents." There is no study of infant care or of wet-nursing in Venice, although references were made in wills to children's nurses.

56. Above, n. 10. The daughter, Paolina, was married in 1466 to Luca Falier; Barbaro, Nozze, f. 327r. Petronella's marriage to Zilio Morosini had taken place in 1450; ibid., f. 325v. Zilio had registered for the Barbarella in 1443, at the declared age of eighteen; BO 163, f. 306v.

57. "Filie mee maritari aut monacari debeant quando videbitur ipsi Christine earum matri"; NT 68, Bonicardi, no. 134. Filippo and Cristina had been married in 1461; Barbaro, Nozze, f. 368v. For the marriages of Michela Zane and of her parents, Alvise and Cecilia Zane (1474), see ibid., ff. 455r and 454v. Alvise Zane's will, of 1485, is in NT 68, Bonicardi, no. 316.

58. The ages of mothers are calculated from the dates of their weddings, as recorded in Barbaro, Nozze, and assume a wedding age of fifteen. Simone Arimondo's Barbarella registration is in BO 163, f. 13r; his parents' wedding in 1423 is in Barbaro, Nozze, f. 8v. Antonio Zane's registration is in BO 164, f. 353v; his parents' wedding in 1460 is in Barbaro, Nozze, f. 454v. Jacopo Balbi's registration is in BO 163, f. 96r; his parents' wedding in 1438 is in Barbaro, Nozze, f. 40v. On the activity of mothers in the Barbarella, see Chap. 10.

59. Bianca swore in 1461 that Lorenzo was entitled to take his place in the Great Council because he had turned twenty-five; PE 169/1, f. 104r. Yet Bianca and Lorenzo's father, also named Lorenzo, had married only in 1440, a date consistent with young Lorenzo's Barbarella registration, assertedly at age eighteen, only one year earlier than the Great Council entry in 1460. Barbaro, Nozze, f. 325v; BO 163, f. 311v. It appears that the Avogadori di Comun, responsible both for Barbarella registrations and for validations of Great Council eligibility, slipped or winked at this one. Antonio Zulian, in contrast with Lorenzo Morosini, won the Barbarella lottery and thus entered the Great Council at twenty rather than twenty-five. His mother was about thirty-nine at the time. PE 169/1, f. 23r; Barbaro, Nozze, f. 450v.

60. An example of the activity of mothers in promoting the family's private interest is their serving as pledges for the restitution of the dowries of their daughters-in-law, as examined in Chap. 4. To cite one instance: in a marriage contract of 1451, Marina, widow of Tomaso Donà, pledged half of her goods, movable and immovable, toward the restitution of the dowry of her son Nicolò's wife-to-be, Isabetta Querini; Vadimoni 4, ff. 58v–59v.

Chapter 10   Kinship Ties and Young Patricians

This chapter originally appeared, in slightly altered form, as "Kinship Ties and Young Patricians in Fifteenth-Century Venice," *Renaissance Quarterly* 38 (1985): 240–70.

1. By now the literature is very large. Among recent works especially pertinent and helpful for the present study are Brucker, *Renaissance Florence*, esp. chap. 3; Herlihy and Klapisch-Zuber, *Les Toscans et leurs familles*; Klapisch-Zuber, "La

Mère cruelle"; Kent, *Household and Lineage;* Kent, *Rise of the Medici* and "Floren-tine *Reggimento";* Trexler, *Public Life;* Hughes, "Urban Growth" and "From Bride-price to Dowry." There are many more.

2. Although patrician social structure still lacks a thorough examination, im-portant contributions have been made to the study of the patrician family: see, notably, Finlay, *Politics,* which integrates family and kinship into patrician politics; see esp. 81–96. Among other works on the patrician family are Davis, *Venetian Family;* King, "Caldiera and the Barbaros"; Betto, "Linee di politica matrimo-niale"; Loenertz, *Les Ghisi;* and Lane, *Andrea Barbarigo* and "Family Partnerships." More characteristically focused on divisions by political interest and wealth are Gilbert, "Venice in the Crisis"; Cozzi, "Authority and the Law"; and Cracco, "Patriziato e oligarchia." For a comparison of recent writing on Venice and Flor-ence, see Brucker, "Tales of Two Cities."

3. This crude formulation does not address many nuances in the anthropolog-ical literature on the subject, which cannot be gone into here. See, for helpful discussions, Murdock, *Social Structure,* 15–16, 91–92; Evans-Pritchard, "Descent and Kinship"; Fortes, "Structure of Unilineal Descent Groups," 30 and passim. The whole issue is given wide-ranging consideration, discussing Europe in com-parative context, in Goody, *Development of the Family,* esp. 10–33 and appendixes.

4. On this pivotal event, called the Serrata, or closing, of the Great Council, see Lane, "Enlargement of the Great Council"; Merores, "Der grosse Rat," 75–81 and passim; Chojnacki, "In Search of the Venetian Patriciate"; and Ruggiero, "Modernization and the Mythic State."

5. A strain of legislation beginning in 1407 toughened the rules for establish-ing patrician credentials. See now Chojnacki, "Social Identity."

6. An example of the former: Nicolò Morosini Dottor, testating in 1379, offered a 10 percent discount to Morosini cousins or their male heirs who might want to buy his residence. CI 97, Francesco Gritti, 12, no. 1. An example—one of many—of the latter: another Nicolò Morosini asked in his will of 1446/47 to be buried in the "archa de cha Mauroceno" [tomb of the Morosini] at S. Trinità; NT 1157, Benedetto dalle Croci, prot. II, f. 152rv.

7. The concern with inherited status found expression in sharpened distinc-tions within the patriciate as well, as political lines were drawn between the class's most venerable houses, the *case vecchie* or *longhi,* and relatively more recent arrivals, the *case nuove* or *curti.* See Finlay, *Politics,* 92–96; Chojnacki, "In Search of the Venetian Patriciate," 49–50; Romanin, *Storia documentata,* 4:305–6.

8. For the dowry as currency in such connections, see Hughes, "From Bride-price to Dowry," 284, 287–88. More generally, exogamy and its bilateral effects are a central concern in Goody, *Development of the Family;* for the central Middle Ages, see Duby, *Knight, the Lady, and the Priest,* 94, 104–5, 244–45.

9. The instituting law was passed by the Great Council on 25 November 1319, and a 1356 act of the Council of Ten, noting that the eighteen-year age minimum was being violated, decreed a fine of 200 lire for offenders. AC, Reg. 2, Capitolare, ff. 67v–68r, 69v. Occasional mention is made of the Balla d'Oro in the Avogaria di Comun's fourteenth-century Raspe registers of criminal proceedings, but no rec-

ords of Balla d'Oro registrations from that century appear to have survived. I believe that systematic Balla d'Oro record keeping began only in the fifteenth century: a Great Council act of 1414, which elaborated Barbarella procedures, specifically mandated the keeping of registration information "in uno quaterno," suggesting that documentation had hitherto been haphazard; MC 21, Leona, ff. 241v–242r. On the Barbarella and age grading, see Law, "Age Qualification," 128–31, and Chap. 7.

10. In a sample of 138 nobles from sixteen clans who entered the Great Council between 1444 and 1454, nearly half, 65 (47.1%), made it by winning the Barbarella lottery. Of the rest, 37 (26.8%) got in after election as civil court advocates and the remaining 36 (26.1%) took their hereditary places at age twenty-five. PE 178, ff. 1r–103v. The latter two categories included many unsuccessful Balla d'Oro competitors, so the proportion of registrants among young patricians was more than the one-half who won. Among these same clans (listed below, n. 12) there were 417 registrants during 1408–50 but 648 during 1451–97—an increase of more than 50 percent in the latter half century. BO 162, 163, 164.

11. On office seeking in the Quattrocento, see Cozzi, "Authority and the Law," 298 ff.; on the maneuvering that accompanied it, see Finlay, *Politics*, 59–81 and passim. However, nobles' desire for remunerative offices should be considered alongside evidence that burdensome posts were shunned. See Queller, "Civic Irresponsibility"; also below, n. 14.

12. The sixteen clans are Arimondo, Balbi, Canal, Lando, Loredan, Morosini, Mudazzo (or Muazzo), Mula, Navagero, Pisani, Polani, Priuli, Ruzzini, Vitturi, Zane, Zulian. They were chosen to represent large, middling, and small clans from the three divisions of the nobility by antiquity, the *case vecchie* or *longhi*, the *case nuove* or *curti*, and a subdivision of these latter, the *case ducali*, which monopolized the dogeship in the fifteenth and sixteenth centuries. See the references above, n. 7. The terms *clan* and *lineage* are used here in the following sense: the clan is a unilineally connected cluster of lineages whose common ancestry may be shadowy or even mythical and whose relationships to one another are consequently vague; the relationships within the lineage, by contrast, are genealogically precise. See Middleton and Tait, "Lineage and the Lineage System," 155–56; Fortes, "Structure of Unilineal Descent Groups," 25; Goody expresses reservations about the use of *clan* and especially *lineage* in the European context; *Development of the Family*, 227–32. In the sense indicated above, however, they fit the Venetian patriciate.

13. The long-term economic problems of the patriciate appear to have begun in earnest with the shocks dealt individual finances by the demands of the war of Chioggia against the Genoese (1378–81). See Mueller, "Effetti della Guerra"; Luzzatto, *Storia economica*, 141–45; Cessi, "Finanza veneziana"; Lane, *Venice, a Maritime Republic*, 189–96. On the decline of commerce, see Lane, *Venice, a Maritime Republic*, 285–93.

14. See above, n. 11. The Great Council acted already in 1386 to spread the benefits of office holding around the entire class [ut omnes participent de honoribus et beneficiis terre]. Another act, of 1392, stated that certain minor offices

322 ➤ Notes to Pages 209–210

were designated for "our impoverished nobles [*nostris pauperibus nobilibus*]."
MC 21, Leona, ff. 14r, 61v. An indication of the eager pursuit of government-sponsored economic opportunities is Senate measures of 1417 and 1431 aimed at regulating intense competition among young patricians for bowman posts on government vessels. Senato, Misti 50, f. 33r; 58, f. 81v. These posts gave young nobles the chance to trade at ports of call. Lane, *Andrea Barbarigo*, 17–18; Finlay, *Politics*, 69.

15. On the fraterna, see Pertile, *Storia del diritto*, 4:128–33. On the institution in Venice, see Lane, "Family Partnerships," 37 and passim; also Davis, *Venetian Family*, 7–8 and passim.

16. The Balla d'Oro law of 1414, mentioned above, and other measures of the period toughened procedures for proving patrician status. For example, a law of 1430 regulated council admission of men who bypassed the Balla d'Oro; MC 22, Ursa, f. 88r.

17. A Great Council act of 1422 disqualified sons of women of low condition; MC 22, Ursa, ff. 47v–48r. On dowries, see Hughes, "From Brideprice to Dowry," 287–90; also Chap. 6.

18. Another sign of the tightening of pedigree requirements: in 1408 the fine for a false claim of patrician descent was raised from 300 to 500 lire. MC 21, Leona, f. 181v.

19. "Quod pater dicti juvenis, si tunc vixerit, et erit in civitate Veneciarum, teneatur presentare dictum talem eius filium." MC 21, Leona, f. 241v. On fathers' legal authority—the *patria potestas*—see Kuehn, *Emancipation*, 25–26 and passim. On patriarchal authority in practice in Florence, see Kent, *Household and Lineage*, 33 ff.

20. Fathers absent, candidates were to be presented "per unum aut duos ex propinquioribus." MC 21, Leona, f. 241v. For example, in 1413 Nicolò di Bartolomeo da Canal was presented by his uncle, Giovanni di Fantin da Canal, because his father was then serving as Venetian consul in Tunis; BO 162, f. 49r. In 1451 Marco di Paolo Loredan was presented by an uncle because his father was serving as *podestà* and captain at Belluno; BO 163, f. 289v. (Paolo Loredan's office, not specified in the BO entry, is in Voci 4, f. 56).

21. Davis, *Venetian Family*, traces this tendency across many generations of the Donà dalle Rose clan.

22. It contrasts with the Florentine case, where young men were likely to be fatherless by their late teens. Herlihy and Klapisch-Zuber, *Les Toscans et leurs familles*, 394 ff., esp. 411. See also on the present subject: Herlihy, "Vieillir à Florence" and "Mapping Households."

23. Sponsors outnumber registrants because nonparent sponsors often come in pairs; see the quotation above, n. 20.

24. It is risky to assume traceable blood relationships among men of the same surname, especially in the large clans, such as the Loredan, the Priuli, and above all the Morosini. However, most of the sponsors who shared candidates' surnames (the category called "Paternal Kin" in table 12) probably belonged to the candidate's specific lineage within the clan; see examples below. On *clan* and *lineage*, see above, n. 12.

323 Notes to Pages 212–214

25. BO 164, f. 274v. Nicolò himself had been enrolled in 1453; BO 163, f. 341v; Girolamo apparently never registered. Another example: Antonio qd Donato Arimondo, himself a Balla d'Oro registrant in 1412, enrolled his eighteen-year-old brother Paolo in 1417. A third brother, Marino, sponsored still another, Nicolò, in 1435. BO 162, f. 7v; I could find no record of Marino's ever having himself been registered.

26. For example, Nicolò qd Giovanni da Mula was twenty-nine when he sponsored his brother Alvise in 1464 (preceding note). Nicolò's birthdate, as documented by "his father's ledger [*libro patris sui*]" at his registration, was 9 May 1435 (making him exactly eighteen years, seven months when he registered on 3 December 1453); BO 163, f. 341v.

27. *Volumen statutorum,* lib. 3, cap. 4, p. 411. See also Davis, *Venetian Family,* 85–95; Lane, "Family Partnerships."

28. The two sponsoring da Mula uncles, Angelo and Benedetto qd Antonio, also attested to the authenticity of the handwriting in the "librum qd patris," which had recorded Giovanni's birthdate as 18 March 1413, making him eighteen and a half at his registration. BO 162, f. 108v. Uncle Angelo da Mula had previously registered another deceased brother's son, Francesco qd Giovanni, in 1424. Ibid. Other examples: Piero qd Daniele da Canal registered "eius nepotem" Bernardo qd Giovanni da Canal in 1458; BO 163, f. 201v. Nicolò qd Bernardo Navagero, presenting his late brother Andrea's son Bernardo in September 1474, knew enough about family matters to testify that Bernardo would turn eighteen the following 13 October; BO 164, f. 275r.

29. See references above, n. 20.

30. For example, in 1417 Antonio qd Lorenzo Loredan and Lorenzo qd Bartolomeo Loredan sponsored the registration of Lodovico qd Tomaso Loredan, identified only as "their kinsman [*eorum attinentem*]." BO 162, f. 85v. In many cases even that vague connection is absent.

31. BO 164, f. 55rv. Piero had also served as a guarantor at the 1481 registration of Nicoletto's older brother Giovanni; ibid.

32. The common ancestor was Marino di Vitale Lando, four of whose sons registered for the Balla d'Oro. One of these was Giovanni, father of Piero, the sponsor at the 1493 registration; Giovanni himself registered in 1441; BO 163, f. 294r. Another of Marino's sons was Girolamo, grandfather of that Girolamo di Piero enrolled in 1493; at this elder Girolamo's registration, in 1436, his father, the common ancestor Marino, was already dead. BO 162, f. 88r. The registration of 1493 is in BO 164, f. 214v.

33. See Finlay, *Politics,* 90–96 and passim.

34. Ibid., 84–87. On large clans' advantages, see Chojnacki, "In Search of the Venetian Patriciate," 67–70. The political personality that such rules recognize in the patrician *casa* warrants using the term *clan* to characterize it.

35. An analysis of the office-holding experience of a sample of young patricians in the second half of the Quattrocento reveals that 88 percent of those who held public office got their first posts before age thirty-five. (Data from Voci 6.)

36. Genealogical information culled chiefly from BO 162, 163, 164, and 165, and from Barbaro, Nozze. A simplified genealogy of the Landos discussed

here, leaving out siblings not mentioned ("R" and the year indicate Barbarella registration):

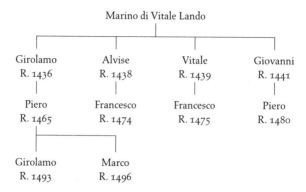

The registration of Vitale qd Marino (1439) is in BO 163, f. 294r; those of Piero di Girolamo (1465), Francesco di Alvise (1474), Francesco di Vitale (1475), Piero qd Giovanni (1480), and Marco qd Piero (1496; see below, n. 62) are in BO 164, f. 214rv.

37. Voci 6, ff. 102r, 34v, 30v. I assume that Piero was eighteen or nineteen at his BO registration in 1480.

38. Among other posts, he was *podestà* at Verona (1470) and *avogadore di comun* (1472); Voci 6, ff. 16v, 7r. The genealogist Cappellari reports that he was *provveditore* with the Venetian forces at a siege of Trieste in 1462 and ambassador to the duke of Milan in 1474. Cappellari also credits him with philosophical writings. G. A. Cappellari-Vivaro, "Il Campidoglio Veneto," BMV Ital. VII, 16 (8305), f. 203.

39. Voci 6, f. 7r. Alvise had been elected an *avogadore* the previous year, as well. On the importance of the Avogadori di Comun, see Cozzi, "Authority and the Law," 303–5 and passim.

40. See Betto, "Linee di politica matrimoniale," 53–54 and passim; and Chaps. 5 and 7. Mothers' significance as Barbarella presenters grew throughout the century: before 1451 they supplied one of every 10.7 sponsors; after 1450 they were one of every 5.5. The reasons for the increase include families' growing concern to get younger brothers—less likely to have living fathers—into the Great Council as soon as possible and also the growing stature of women in patrician society.

41. A constantly repeated theme in husbands' wills is economic inducement to wives to devote chaste widowhood to raising their children. The examples are countless: for example, testament of Lorenzo qd Bartolomeo Loredan, 10 May 1441 (actually written 1440); NT 558, Antonio Gambaro, no. 86. See also Chap. 8, above. On the complexity of the widow's orientation to lineage and family in Florence, especially as concerned dowry and children, see Klapisch-Zuber, "La Mère cruelle." On the same subject, Trexler, *Public Life,* 165 ff.

42. See above, n. 17.

43. For example, Elena, widow of Benedetto Morosini, registered her son Piero in 1463 with another son, Antonio, as a guarantor. Another example: at the

325 ⬧ Notes to Pages 216–219

registration of Piero qd Luca Pisani in 1467, Piero's mother was the sponsor; his older brother Nicolò stood surety. BO 164, ff. 217r, 282v.

44. BO 164, f. 204v.

45. For example, the registrations of Francesco qd Cristoforo da Canal (1442) and Andrea qd Nicolò Loredan (1468). BO 163, f. 200v; BO 164, f. 203v. In both cases, mothers sponsored, and fathers' brothers guaranteed.

46. Klapisch-Zuber, "La Mère cruelle," and Hughes, "From Brideprice to Dowry," 287–88, discuss married women's lineage orientation. See also Goody, *Development of the Family*, 225, and Chaps. 5 and 7.

47. BO 164, ff. 126v, 127r. Delfina's paternity, and thus her sibling tie to Andrea Dolfin, are in Barbaro, Nozze, f. 104v. Another example: Foscarina, widow of Agostino qd Piero Priuli, in 1479 registered her son Leonardo with the guarantees of two of her brothers, Francesco and Bernardo qd Piero Foscarini. BO 164, f. 139v; Barbaro, Nozze, f. 368v. Specific relationships can be established using the patronymics in both the BO registers and Barbaro, Nozze.

48. For the marriage date, Barbaro, Nozze, f. 388v (1422). In any case, the marriage dated at least from 1424, eighteen years before the couple's first son, Ruggero, was enrolled (by his father) in the Barbarella in 1442. BO 163, f. 370r. Piero Ruzzini's registration (1459) is in BO 163, f. 371r; that of his brother Giorgio (1448), f. 370r.

49. BO 164, f. 127r; the young candidate's name was Cristoforo qd Giovanni qd Cristoforo. In another interesting combination, the sponsoring uncle here, Francesco da Canal, was joined by a cosponsor, Francesco qd Marco Priuli—brother of the young registrant's mother. Barbaro, Nozze, f. 104v.

50. Marco's son was named Antonio; his registration took place on 22 November, that of his cousin Giorgio on 2 December. BO 163, f. 370r. Similarly, instead of recruiting her brothers to guarantee her son's registration in 1479 (above, n. 47), Foscarina Priuli could have asked her late husband's brother, Maffeo, who would register his own son, Cristoforo, two years later. BO 164, f. 140r.

51. See Klapisch-Zuber, "La Mère cruelle," 1101–2; also Chap. 5.

52. Above, Chap. 5.

53. Barbarella Vitturi's son was Piero; her brother, Tomaso Duodo: BO 162, f. 141v; Barbaro, Nozze, f. 432v. Maddaluzza Arimondo's son was Simone; her brother, Nicolò Capello: BO 163, f. 13v; Barbaro, Nozze, f. 8v. Agnesina Loredan's son was Andrea; her brother, Domenico Vitturi: BO 164, f. 203v; Barbaro, Nozze, f. 264v.

54. That is, the categories labeled "Other Maternal Kin" and "Other."

55. Hughes, "From Brideprice to Dowry," 284, notes the stake that brothers of richly dowered brides had in the fortunes of their sisters' families. See also Chap. 5.

56. Francesco di Alvise Lando sponsored by Antonio Valier, 1474; Paolo qd Giovanni Lando sponsored by Francesco Foscari, 1493; and Marco qd Piero Lando sponsored by Giorgio Corner, 1496. BO 164, f. 214rv. All three matrimonial connections are in Barbaro, Nozze, f. 231v.

57. Francesco di Alvise's brothers had been (Marino, in 1472) and would be (Girolamo, in 1480) sponsored by their father. BO 164, f. 214rv. Paolo qd Giovanni

was sponsored by both Francesco Foscari and his own brother, Piero Lando. Marco qd Piero was a younger brother of the Girolamo di Piero Lando whose registration in 1493 had been sponsored by their cousin once removed, the future doge, Piero qd Giovanni Lando; above, nn. 32, 36.

58. Another example of the same thing: Piero qd Benedetto da Mula himself was alive when his wife's brother, Piero Querini, sponsored the registrations of da Mula's two sons, Angelo in 1484 and Girolamo in 1486. BO 164, f. 274v; Barbaro, Nozze, f. 270v.

59. BO 163, f. 294r (Alvise), BO 164, f. 214r (Piero). Also in the latter year, Alvise di Francesco Lando, from a different Lando lineage, was enrolled by his sister's husband, Jacopo qd Andrea Foscarini; BO 164, f. 214r. Both marriage connections are in Barbaro, Nozze, f. 231r.

60. BO 164, f. 214r; Barbaro, Nozze, f. 23r. Note that Jacopo Bembo belongs to the "Other" category of Table 13, while as a mother's brother Antonio Valier belongs to "Other Maternal Kin." Other examples of sponsoring brothers-in-law: Andrea qd Paolo Zane was presented by his sister's husband, Vitale Lando, in 1457. BO 163, f. 46r; Barbaro, Nozze, f. 231v. Bertuccio qd Cristoforo da Canal was registered in 1441 by his sister's husband, Marco Magno. BO 163, f. 200r; Barbaro, Nozze, f. 104r.

61. Canal-Gritti: BO 63, f. 200r (1436); Barbaro, Nozze, f. 103r. (Note that Filippo da Canal was still alive when his Gritti brother-in-law registered Filippo's son.) Loredan-Bragadin: BO 164, f. 206r; Barbaro, Nozze, f. 245r (1458).

62. BO 164, f. 214v, Barbaro, Nozze, f. 231v (Lando-Corner, 1471), f. 231r (Lando-Soranzo, 1454). See the genealogical chart above, n. 36.

63. Barbaro, Nozze, f. 323v; BO 163, f. 306r. A simplified genealogy may help clarify what follows:

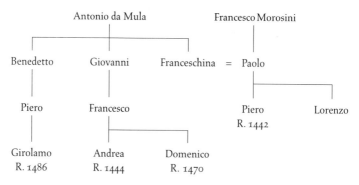

64. BO 163, f. 341v. Andrea's father, Francesco qd Giovanni da Mula, was living at the time and presumably had at least a hand in the selection of Paolo Morosini as his son's sponsor.

65. BO 164, f. 274r. The long interval between the registrations of Andrea and Domenico di Francesco (1444–70) is explained by their being half brothers, sons of two mothers, as documented in their BO entries.

66. A further sign of the strength of these matrimonial ties is that Girolamo's

other sponsor in 1486 was Piero qd Girolamo Querini, brother of the young candidate's mother. Barbaro, Nozze, f. 270v. As noted above, n. 57, this Piero Querini had also sponsored the registration of Girolamo da Mula's elder brother, Angelo, in 1484. It is interesting that the two sponsors of Girolamo da Mula in 1486, Lorenzo Morosini and Piero Querini, had a close relationship of their own besides their mutual marriage ties to the da Mulas: in his will of 1486, Lorenzo identified Piero as someone "whom I always considered a brother [*quem semper habui loco fratris*]." PSMC de Ultra, B. 221, Lorenzo Morosini.

67. One more example: at the 1471 registration of Piero di Nicolò Arimondo, one of the guarantors was Bernardo qd Nicolò da Pesaro. The connection between registrant and guarantor was that Bernardo da Pesaro was the son of a daughter of Nicolò di Fantin Arimondo, a brother of young Piero's grandfather. Candidate and guarantor were thus cousins twice removed through the female line. BO 164, f. 2r; Barbaro, Nozze, f. 8r.

68. For example, when Piero di Benedetto da Mula was elected an advocate in the Corte del Forestier in 1446, his guarantor for good conduct in office was Piero di Paolo Morosini, whose BO registration four years earlier had been guaranteed, as noted above, by Piero da Mula's father, Benedetto. Voci 4, f. 16r.

69. Examination of the marriages of the sixteen sample clans, as recorded in Barbaro, Nozze, shows a drop in the percentage of the men's marriages with nonpatrician women. From 1400 to 1450, 41 of 421 (9.7%) married brides from the populace; from 1451 to 1500, the number was 40 of 460 (8.5%). However, this is a complex business, requiring careful analysis; the percentage of patrician women marrying *popolani*, by contrast, rose between the two periods, from 0.7 percent (3 of 404 marriages) to 2 percent (9 of 455). Even in the latter period, the incidence of patrician women's hypogamy is tiny. Nevertheless, the increase could reflect growing difficulties of contracting good intraclass marriages for girls at a time of increased status consciousness and rising dowries. See Betto, "Linee di politica matrimoniale," 53–59, and Chaps. 3 and 4.

70. Barbaro, Nozze, ff. 8v–9r, 40v–41v. The diffusion of spouses is even more significant in view of both clans' having contracted multiple marriages with certain other very large clans. The Arimondos married four spouses from each of the Contarini, Pesaro, and Loredan clans; the Balbi four each from the Contarini and Morosini.

71. Paolo Arimondo: BO 162, f. 7v; Barbaro, Nozze, f. 8r (Arimondo-Lion). Francesco Morosini: BO 163, f. 307v, Barbaro, Nozze, f. 314v (Morosini-Corner).

72. BO 164, f. 282v. The other guarantor, seconding Cristoforo Duodo, was Domenico Duodo, husband of Giovanni Pisani's sister and thus the candidate's uncle once removed. Barbaro, Nozze, f. 361r. The two Duodo guarantors were cousins, sons of two brothers. The Duodo-Pisani connection, perhaps strengthened by collaborations such as this BO registration, endured: in 1470, a nephew of the guarantor Domenico Duodo—his brother's son, Francesco qd Piero Duodo— married a daughter of Luca Pisani, son of Giovanni, the sponsor in this 1467 BO registration. Barbaro, Nozze, f. 362r.

73. BO 164, f. 127r; Barbaro, Nozze, ff. 104v (Canal-Priuli), 367v (Priuli-Bondumier).

74. BO 164, f. 214r; Barbaro, Nozze, ff. 231v (Corner-Lando), 405r (Soranzo-Corner). The other sponsor of Marco Lando's registration was another Soranzo, Andrea qd Marco, connected to the candidate in another way, one not dependent on the Corner alliance: he was the son of a sister of Marco Lando's grandfather. Barbaro, Nozze, f. 231r.

75. Between 1506 and 1526 the Council of Ten enacted measures mandating careful recording of all patrician births and marriages; see Chap. 2, above. By mid-century Marco Barbaro was compiling his monumental collection of historico-genealogical material, especially the "Libro di Nozze" and his "Arbori dei Patritii Veneti," with copies at the BMV and the ASV. On Barbaro and the various versions of his work, see Cicogna, *Delle inscrizioni veneziane*, 6:21–26.

76. Goody, *Development of the Family*, 16, 226, and passim. Hughes ("From Brideprice to Dowry," 290) sees the dowry regime strengthening the lineage and weakening bilaterality, although she also notes men's interest in the fortunes of their dowered sisters' marital families (284).

77. In 1260 an act of the Great Council had listed as interested parties ineligible to take part in deliberations touching individuals their "Propinqui, vz Germani, Consanguinei, Nepotes, Filii Fratris, vel Sororum, Soceri et Generi, et Avunculi, Fratres Patris, vel Matris vel Cognati." AC, Reg. 2, Capitolare, f. 66v.

78. The strength of ties through marriage caused the Great Council in 1409 to add "cognati, germani, consanguinei et alii attinentes qui non sunt de eadem domo" to the lineage kin who could not sit on the Council of Ten at the same time. MC 21, Leona, f. 189v.

79. A proposal of 1403 to replenish the patriciate by giving noble status to a member of the citizen class each time a noble clan died out failed to get beyond the Ducal Council. Both proponents and opponents of this measure regarded the patriciate as consisting of certain identified clans. ASV, Collegio, Notatorio, Reg. 3, f. 111v.

80. Until then, only the mother's given name had been recorded. The new practice went into effect in 1431; see BO 162. The requirement that the Avogadori di Comun ascertain the names of mothers of young men seeking to enter the Great Council had been passed in 1422; MC 22, Ursa, ff. 47v–48r.

81. On the government's responses to patrician economic need, see, in addition to the references regarding office holding above, Pullan, "Occupations and Investments."

Chapter 11   Political Adulthood

This chapter originally appeared, in slightly altered form, as "Political Adulthood in Fifteenth-Century Venice," *American Historical Review* 91 (1986): 791–810.

1. Piero was born on 11 January 1420/21; BO 163, f. 214v. For his elections as *avogadore* (1476) and as *procuratore*, see Voci 6, ff. 71, 87v. He was elected to the Forty in June 1450 but did not prove his eligibility by age until the following 1 February. Voci 4, f. 126v; PE 178, f. 74v. Among his other offices were *signore di notte* (a police post), *provveditore al sale* (supervisor of the salt trade), *governador*

delle entrade, and official of the Rason Vecchie (both finance offices). Voci 4, f. 3v; Voci 6, ff. 46v, 73r, 140v.

Parts of this essay were presented in a paper read at the 1984 annual meeting of the American Historical Association in Chicago. I wish to thank the American Council of Learned Societies, the Gladys Krieble Delmas Foundation, and the Department of History and the College of Arts and Letters, Michigan State University, for supporting the research on which it is based; and Gene Brucker, David Herlihy, Margaret L. King, Christiane Klapisch-Zuber, Edward Muir, Gordon T. Stewart, Emily Z. Tabuteau, and Richard C. Trexler for their helpful comments on earlier versions of it.

2. For a full description of the disturbance in the trial record, see Raspe 3649/9, pt. 1, f. 7rv. The ages of the guilty nobles were traced in BO 162 and 163.

3. For discussions of Venice's governmental reputation, see Muir, *Civic Ritual,* chap. 1, and Finlay, *Politics,* 27–37. For classic statements, see Bouwsma, "Venice and the Political Education," 445–46, and Gaeta, "Alcune considerazioni sul mito." For contemporary Florentine views of Venice, see the many references in Brucker, *Civic World;* Gilbert, "Venetian Constitution"; and Pecchioli, "Il mito di Venezia."

4. For the issues in Venetian Renaissance politics, see Finlay, *Politics;* Cozzi, "Authority and the Law"; Gilbert, "Venice in the Crisis"; and Muir, *Civic Ritual.* On the preference for mature government officials, see Finlay, "Venetian Gerontocracy." On the role of the young elsewhere in Europe, see Davis, "Reasons of Misrule"; Rossiaud, "Prostitution, jeunesse et société"; Duby, "Au XIIᵉ siècle"; Trexler, *Public Life* and "Ritual in Florence"; and Klapisch-Zuber, " 'Mattinata' in Medieval Italy."

5. The indictment asserts that the regime, and, specifically, the Avogaria di Comun, suffered "great ignominy" and the whole Great Council "no small scandal" as a consequence of the young miscreants' "presumption, disobedience, assault, and violent fury [*impetu ac violento furore*]." Raspe 3651/11, ff. 80v–81r (16 March 1460). For similar language in the 1446 episode, see Raspe 3649/9, pt. 2, f. 14r.

6. MC 22, Ursa, ff. 148v (1443), 173v (1449); MC 23, Regina, f. 138rv (1474).

7. "Multitudo puerorum nobilium," MC 22, Ursa, f. 148v; "nobiles juvenes," MC 23, Regina, f. 138rv. *Nobiles juvenes* is also used in the Raspe trial records as a blanket term for the boisterous council fugitives.

8. Twenty-four of the young men were younger than twenty-five years; twenty-six were between the ages of twenty-five and twenty-eight; seven ranged from twenty-nine to thirty-two; three more were thirty-three or thirty-four; and the remaining one was thirty-eight years old. The ages are in BO 163 and 164.

9. At the ducal election of 1462, the number of voters dropped from 1,063 to 930 (12.5%) when the councilors younger than thirty left the hall; at that of 1485, from 679 to 601 (11.5%). MC 23, Regina, f. 44v; MC 24, Stella, ff. 60r–61v.

10. On Paolo Zane, see PE 178, f. 8r; on Luca Pisani, see Voci 4, f. 123v. Piero Balbi's tenure as captain at Brescia had been preceded by his election the previous year to the financial office of the Misseteria; PE 169, ff. 90r, 106v. All three held other offices in later years.

11. The houses, or clans, in the sample were chosen to represent numerically small, medium, and large representatives of the categories into which contemporaries grouped patrician houses according to their antiquity: the *case vecchie*, or old houses, the *case nuove*, or new houses, and an influential subgroup of the latter, the *case ducali*, or ducal houses, which monopolized the dogeship in the fifteenth and sixteenth centuries. For the comments of contemporaries on these distinctions, see Finlay, *Politics*, 92–96; Chojnacki, "In Search of the Venetian Patriciate," 49–50. For lists of the case vecchie and case ducali, see Romanin, *Storia documentata*, 4:305–6. The houses in the sample are Morosini, Polani, Zane (vecchie); Lando, Loredan, Priuli (ducali); Arimondo, Balbi, da Canal, Mudazzo, da Mula, Navagero, Pisani, Ruzzini, Vitturi, Zulian (nuove).

12. Data from Voci 4, Voci 6, PE 169, and PE 178.

13. The civil court advocacies were more important as stepping stones into the Great Council than as legal-service offices; Sanudo, *De origine*, 144–45.

14. Cozzi, "Domenico Morosini," 422–23.

15. The view, stated here, that the patrician regime continued to evolve during the fourteenth and fifteenth centuries runs counter to a persistent tradition that holds it as essentially fixed in composition and ideology by the early fourteenth. For a recent example of the traditional view, see Ruggiero, "Modernization and the Mythic State." For views of continuing development, see Cracco, *Società e stato;* Chojnacki, "In Search of the Venetian Patriciate"; and Law, "Age Qualification."

16. On governmental regulation of marriage and dowries, see Bistort, *Magistrato alle Pompe*, 90–113. On patrician marriage, see Betto, "Linee di politica matrimoniale," and Chap. 6. On the *scuole*, see Pullan, *Rich and Poor*, pt. 1. On the *compagnie* (which merit a modern study), see Venturi, "Compagnie della Calza."

17. These figures are drawn from Voci 4 and 6. They do not include ambassadorships, temporary military posts, or ad hoc commissions, nor do they take account of multiple tenants of individual offices such as the Forty, whose membership was expanded in 1400 to 80, in 1442 to 120, and in 1492 to 160, as the court ramified into specialized jurisdictions. See Kretschmayr, *Geschichte von Venedig,* 2:103.

18. On the patrician population, see Sanudo, *De origine*, 146; on the number of officeholders, see Finlay, *Politics*, 59. The officeholder number (831, to be exact) refers to the number of men in office, not to the number of offices.

19. On penalties for avoiding office, see Queller, "Civic Irresponsibility." The need to attract officials was constantly cited in preambles to acts raising stipends; see, for example, MC 20, Novella (copy), f. 5v (18 April 1350); MC 21, Leona, ff. 61v–63v (10 August 1392); MC 22, Ursa, f. 12v (3 September 1415); MC 24, Stella, f. 59rv (11 September 1485).

20. In an indication that office holding by young men was viewed as serving more to provide political conditioning for them than to contribute importantly to the functioning of the state, the Great Council in 1487 lowered the age requirement of the neighborhood-patrolling *capi sestieri* from thirty to twenty-five, "in view of the insignificance [*pocha importantia*] of the office." MC 24, Stella, f. 91v.

21. For examples of such complaints, see MC 22, Ursa, f. 152r (1445); Dieci, Misti 15, ff. 46v–47r (1455). The plot of 1433 is described in the "Cronaca copiata da Gasparo Zancaruol," BMV Ital. VII, 2570 (12462), ff. 142v–143r. The ages of the conspirators were drawn from BO 162 and 163.

22. On the economic impact of the war of Chioggia, see Luzzatto, *Storia economica,* 144–45; Mueller, "Effetti della Guerra"; and Cessi, "Finanza veneziana." On economic strains throughout the Trecento, see Luzzatto, *Storia economica,* 135–39; Cessi, "Introduzione storica"; and Cracco, *Società e stato,* chap. 4.

23. Any noble able to persuade two-thirds of the Forty that he was "fiscally destitute [*impotentem ad solvendum . . . imprestita et impositiones*]" could keep his seat in the Great Council and, crucially, his eligibility for office. MC 20, Novella (copy), ff. 434v–435v (3 October 1383).

24. Senato, Misti 52, ff. 33r (1417), 84v (1418); Senato, Misti 58, f. 81v (1431). On the bowmen, see Finlay, *Politics,* 69, and Law, "Age Qualification," 131–34.

25. See Cozzi, "Authority and the Law," 298–300; Finlay, *Politics,* 59–81.

26. The principle is stated clearly in legislative preambles. In one example, the Great Council asserted its intention "that all share in the honors and benefits of our polity [*de honoribus et beneficiis terre*]"; MC 21, Leona, f. 14r (1385). In another, it noted that "the ducal regime [*ducale dominium*] is accustomed magnanimously to come to the aid of its needy noble citizens, especially those impoverished through no fault of their own [*illis qui non suo defectu ad inopiam devenerunt*]"; ibid., f. 22v (1388).

27. Ibid., f. 61v (1392). This act identified "certain lesser offices to which our poorer nobles are regularly [*continue*] elected," the stipends of which, however, "are inadequate for a livelihood [*nullo modo possunt ex illis vivere*]."

28. In 1442, the Great Council created eleven new rectorships in Venice's Italian mainland territories because, as the act's preamble noted, "it enhances the honor of our regime to provide that our nobles may live under our care [*sub umbra nostra*]." MC 22, Ursa, f. 141r. In 1488, the election of a second treasurer for Ravenna was authorized because, "since the number of patricians [*zentilhomeni nostri*] has increased and increases daily, it is appropriate and necessary to ensure that the largest number possible [*quel piui numero se pono*] may serve in the offices and rectorships of the regime." MC 24, Stella, f. 92v.

29. There are indications, not yet systematically studied, that mainland expansion, the internal politics of Doge Francesco Foscari (1423–58), and the dependence on government jobs of a large segment of the patriciate were all connected. However, early-fifteenth-century Venetian political history still awaits its modern student.

30. The fundamental studies of the Serrata are Merores, "Der grosse Rat," and Lane, "Enlargement of the Great Council." See also Cracco, *Società e stato,* 331–50; Chojnacki, "In Search of the Venetian Patriciate"; and Ruggiero, "Modernization and the Mythic State."

31. For legislation addressing the social status of mothers of claimants to noble status, see MC 19, Novella, f. 171v (1376), and MC 22, Ursa, ff. 47v–48r (1422). The latter act required, among other provisions, that the Avogadori di Comun

"diligently determine who was or is the mother" of anyone wishing to prove his eligibility for Great Council membership. Natal family names of mothers of Balla d'Oro registrants, however, were not recorded until 1431; BO 162.

32. For legislation-tightening procedures, see MC 21, Leona, ff. 169r (1407), 181v (1408), and 241v–242r (1414), MC 22, Ursa, ff. 43v, 45r (1421), and 88r (1430).

33. The first proof of credentials which I have found in the Avogadori's Raspe records, which begin in 1324, does not come until 1342; Raspe 3642/2, f. 29r. Such proofs remained rare for several decades thereafter, picking up frequency only in the 1370s, when the Avogadori's research became more elaborate. For an example of thorough investigation of a claimant's credentials, see Raspe 3644/4, f. 27rv (1381). The number of rejections on the basis of illegitimacy grew in consequence of the law of 1376 disqualifying bastards from Great Council membership; MC 19, Novella, f. 171v. By the second decade of the fifteenth century, cases of claimants failing to prove their credentials appear with regularity in the Avogadori's records. See Raspe 3647/7, ff. 9v–10r (1417), 65v (1419), 105v–106r (1421).

34. For the laws requiring patricians to register births and marriages, see Dieci, Misti 31, ff. 101rv, 109v–110r (1506), Dieci, Comuni 2, ff. 14v–17v (1526); Contratti di nozze 140/1, unfoliated initial sheets reproducing a Senate act of 4 November 1505. On this legislation, see Maranini, *Costituzione di Venezia*, 2:55–67.

35. The Ducal Council's rejection in 1403 of a proposal to replace each patrician family that died out with one of the "more worthy" citizen families is symptomatic of the tendency toward exclusivism. ASV, Collegio, Notatorio, Reg. 3, f. 111v.

36. The growing caste consciousness is apparent in the language of legislation. Uncredentialed interlopers were seen as threatening to "blemish [*maculare*] the reputation, status, and honor" of the regime or to "denigrate and stain the reputation" of the Great Council. MC 21, Leona, f. 241v (1414); MC 22, Ursa, f. 82r (1430).

37. Finlay, *Politics*, 59–81.

38. On cooperation between affines, see Chap. 10.

39. Van Gennep, *Rites de passage*. For a history and analysis of van Gennep's ideas, see Glucksman, "Rites de passage," and Fortes, "Ritual and Office."

40. "The neophyte in liminality must be a *tabula rasa*, a blank slate, on which is inscribed the knowledge and wisdom of the group." Thus "[liminality] can be seen as potentially a period of scrutinization of the central values and axioms of the culture in which it occurs." Turner, *Ritual Process*, 103, 167. See also Fortes, "Ritual and Office," 83–84.

41. She notes, however, that when transplanted from village to city, the French abbeys of misrule lost some of their solidarity. Davis, "Reasons of Misrule," 113. See also Rossiaud, "Prostitution, jeunesse et société," 298–300.

42. Trexler, "Ritual in Florence," 245, and more generally in *Public Life*. For a discussion of Italian youth groups regulating marriage by means of ritual in a manner similar to that discussed by Davis for France (above, previous note), see Klapisch-Zuber, " 'Mattinata' in Medieval Italy," esp. 282.

43. The term *adolescentes* is less frequently encountered in the Venetian documents than *juvenes* or *giovani*. One use of *adolescentes* which suggests its contemporary meaning is its application to the charter members of the Modesti, one of the *compagnie della calza*, who drew up their statutes in 1487. The ages of eight of the sixteen signatories are traceable in BO 164: of these, seven were seventeen and one sixteen years old when the statutes were drawn up. The statutes are in BMC, Codici Cicogna 3278, fasc. 24, ff. 25–29.

44. On the Balla d'Oro, see Maranini, *Costituzione di Venezia*, 2:42–43. Maranini errs, however, in asserting that before 1441, registrants, as opposed to Great Council entrants, had to be at least twenty years old. See also the excellent discussion in Law, "Age Qualification," 128–33.

45. AC, Reg. 2, Capitolare, ff. 67v–68r. Frederic Lane suggested that heredity may have been established in fact by 1298; "Enlargement of the Great Council," 255 and corresponding n. 83, pp. 272–73. Merores mistakenly put the act instituting the Balla d'Oro in 1321 rather than 1319; "Der grosse Rat," 79.

46. AC, Reg. 2, Capitolare, f. 69v. This act, passed by the Forty on 9 December 1356, does not appear in the Great Council records.

47. "Cum beneficium nostri consilii maioris sit solenissimum [sic], et pro conservatione status et honoris dominationis nostre . . . de ipso non veniant persone qui habeant maculare famam, statum, et honorem tanti domini; Equidem cum novis casibus nuperime occursis et sequitis, nova sint remedia adhibenda." MC 21, Leona, ff. 241v–242r (18 March 1414).

48. The registrants were members of the sixteen sample houses; see above, n. 11. The 1,065 registrations are found in BO 162, 163, and 164. Registration records begin (in BO 162) in 1408, apparently as a result of some retroactive recording after the passage of the 1414 act. BO 164 carries registrations to 1497.

49. The steady rise is apparent in a breakdown of registrations from 1410 to 1490 into four twenty-year periods: from 1411 to 1430, 158 men registered; from 1431 to 1450, 254 registered; from 1451 to 1470, 252; and from 1471 to 1490, 292.

50. The law of 1414 restricted the Balla d'Oro competition to sons of Great Council members. Men able to document their legitimate birth to fathers who, though noble, had never formally joined the council could themselves take council membership at age twenty-five but were ineligible for the Balla d'Oro.

51. Sanudo, *De origine*, 145–46. Sanudo's description shows that the spare instructions in the instituting act of 1319 had become elaborated by the later 1400s. For the act of 1319, see AC, Reg. 2, Capitolare, ff. 67v–68r.

52. The doge's participation was not prescribed in the act of 1319 or mentioned in that of 1414; however, the latter addresses registration rather than the sortition ceremony itself. The ratio of winners to losers, 1 to 4, was spelled out in a law of 1441. MC 22, Ursa, f. 138r (26 November 1441).

53. On the different routes, see Sanudo, *De origine*, 145–46. Roughly half of the 246 men from the sixteen sample houses who joined the Great Council between September 1444 and August 1464 (118, or 48%) entered as winners of the Barbarella, one-quarter (65, or 26.4%) by gaining election as civil court advocates, and only the remaining one-quarter (63, or 25.6%) on reaching age twenty-five; PE 169, 178.

54. On the ritual importance of the doge, see Muir, *Civic Ritual*, 256–62. On charismatic qualities of political leaders, see Geertz, "Centers, Kings, and Charisma," 124 and passim.

55. Commenting on the significance of fixed dates, Barbara Myerhoff notes that rites of transition are especially helpful in solving social problems and perpetuating the social order by socializing and integrating members "when seasonal rituals are contained within or coordinated with rites of passage. . . . Then the individual initiate is presented with a paradigm for his or her future; collective tensions are overcome, and the calendar, by which the society understands its long and short history, is articulated with transitions being marked for the individual." Myerhoff, "Rites of Passage," 112–13. I owe this reference to Lisa M. Fine of Michigan State University.

56. On the seventeenth-century celebrations, see Bistort, *Magistrato alle Pompe*, 275–76.

57. For an application to rituals of transition of the theory of cognitive dissonance, the value of the prize is enhanced by the suffering undergone to attain it; see Myerhoff, "Rites of Passage," 121. This idea is pertinent to the Venetian instance, where four-fifths of every year's Barbarella candidates were denied the prize, leading to such cases as that of Domenico Priuli, who registered just in time for the lottery of December 1452 but did not gain the golden ball until 1457; or that of Paolo Loredan, who registered in 1453 but also did not win until 1457. BO 163, ff. 216r, 290r; PE 169, ff. 14v, 27r.

58. Sanudo, *De origine*, 146.

59. The fifteenth century witnessed increasing differentiation between sons of Great Council members and men whose fathers, though eligible for membership, had never formally proved their eligibility. This distinction, little noted in the literature, created an official stratification within the patriciate, strengthened the fusion between patrician status and active participation in government, and encouraged continuity from father to son in the sociopolitical strategies of families. For the special status of sons of council members, see MC 23, Regina, f. 27v (28 January 1458/59); Dieci, Misti 31, f. 101rv (19 August 1506).

60. MC 21, Leona, ff. 241v–242r.

61. In the 755 registrations sponsored by either the candidate's father or mother, 1,342 guarantors participated. See Chap. 10, above.

62. Of the 1,342 guarantors studied, 873 (65%) came from nonparental lineages. For a general discussion of kin involvement in Barbarella registrations, see ibid. The guarantors from other lineages were likely tied to the families of registrants by bonds of patronage, possibly reinforced by spiritual kinship, whose strength is hinted at by an act of the Council of Ten in 1505 forbidding nobles to stand as godfathers (*copatres*) at the baptisms and confirmations of other nobles' children. Dieci, Misti 30, f. 191r.

63. The family stake is apparent in measures enjoining fathers to control their sons' behavior: an act of 1443 made fathers liable for fines levied on youngsters cavorting in the council chamber; MC 22, Ursa, f. 148v.

64. Raspe 3649/9, ff. 12rv, 135r; Raspe 3651/11, f. 81r.

65. Dieci, Misti 11, ff. 64r–71v; "Cronaca Zancaruol" (above, n. 21), ff. 142v–143r.

66. This information emerges from examination of the careers of 149 men from the sixteen sample houses who registered for the Balla d'Oro from 1467 to 1475. One hundred went on to hold government office; of these, sixty-nine got their first posts while still in their twenties; BO 164, Voci 6.

67. Baldassare di Marco Lando, age twenty at his Barbarella registration in 1451 (where it was stated that he was born in 1431), was elected to the financial office of the Misseteria in 1456. Domenico di Antonio Zane, registered for the Balla d'Oro, assertedly at age eighteen, in 1450, was elected a silver official in 1457; BO 163, ff. 194v, 45v; PE 169, ff. 3v, 23. Antonio di Fantin Arimondo, registered at eighteen in November 1480, was elected *podestà* at Noale in February 1486/87. BO 164, f. 2v; Voci 6, f. 30r.

68. Electees usually proved their ages by reference to their Balla d'Oro registrations, on file after 1414 in the records of the Avogaria di Comun, but sometimes by testimony of relatives and friends, as in the Barbarella registrations. It is not clear, for example, why Andrea Navagero, elected a meat-market supervisor (*ufficiale alle beccarie*) in 1456, called on Nicolò Bondumier and Benedetto Gritti to testify that he was twenty-five instead of simply producing the record of his Balla d'Oro registration in early 1448. The likelihood is that by involving them in the proof of his office-holding credentials, Andrea was strengthening his relationship with them, which went back at least as far as 1448 in the case of Gritti, who had registered Andrea for the Barbarella. BO 163, f. 274v; PE 169, f. 6r. I have been unable to establish ties of kinship between the Gritti and Navagero families.

69. PE 177, the first register in the series recording proofs of age, opens with the texts of a Great Council act of 1430 and a Senate act of 1431 requiring more careful official scrutiny of age and genealogical credentials for council membership and office holding. The acts, reproduced in the inside cover of the register, are MC 22, Ursa, f. 88r (5 March 1430) and Senato, Misti 58, f. 77v (1 September 1431). Another act revealing the heightened concern with credentials is one requiring the use of patronymics to identify precisely the candidates in elections to office. MC 21, Leona, f. 127rv (19 February 1403/4).

70. Finlay, "Venetian Gerontocracy." The registers in the series beginning with PE 169 record proofs of age of Balla d'Oro winners and civil court advocates (who both had to be twenty), of Great Council entrants at age twenty-five, and of electees to offices with age requirements of twenty-five and thirty. The series beginning with PE 177 contains, in addition, age proofs for *patroni* of the merchant galley fleets (who had to be thirty) and for galley crossbowmen (who had to be twenty).

71. In 1410, young Paolo Valier was so eager to take a seat on the Forty that he induced a woman to impersonate his mother and testify falsely—in his mother's bedchamber—that he had reached the required age of thirty; Raspe 3646/6, f. 89. Seats on the Forty were so ardently pursued by young men that many claimed to have reached the requisite age of thirty when only in their thirtieth year, calculating from conception rather than birth—which, said the Council of Ten in 1506,

"absurdissimum est." The Ten therefore specified that age requirements for all offices were met only after the appropriate birthday had been reached ("etatem completam et non inceptam"). Dieci, Misti 31, ff. 122v–123r.

72. There are repeated references in the fifteenth century to nobles' dependence on office. In 1490, the Great Council frankly acknowledged that it was the means by which "the majority live and support their families." MC 24, Stella, f. 109v.

73. Factional and familial jockeying is the chief theme of Finlay, *Politics*.

74. Turner, *Ritual Process*, 94.

75. Ibid., 95.

76. Eisenstadt, "Archetypal Patterns of Youth," 32–33. Myerhoff also notes that "the liminal person comes to stand for all that is universal, innate, whole, and unified"; "Rites of Passage," 117. Turner contrasts adult society and liminal youths as representing two different models of human relationships. The first is the "structured, differentiated, and often hierarchical system of political-legal-economic positions with many types of evaluation, separating men in terms of 'more' or 'less.'" The second type, "which emerges recognizably in the liminal period, is . . . society as an unstructured or rudimentarily structured and relatively undifferentiated *comitatus*, community, or even communion of equal individuals." *Ritual Process*, 96.

77. Much traditional writing, focusing on the "myth" of Venetian governmental wisdom, has treated the patriciate as an undifferentiated bloc. More recently, the work of Cozzi, Cracco, Finlay, and Gilbert, among others, has traced divisions, rendering a more complex, nuanced picture of the patriciate acting as a cohesive group in some matters and dividing into factions, interest groups, and economic levels in others. For a useful formulation of the double character of social groups—outwardly unified, inwardly varied—see the discussion of "group and grid" in Douglas, *Natural Symbols*, 56–61.

78. MC 23, Regina, ff. 7v–8r (13 July 1455); MC 24, Stella, f. 109v (21 September 1490).

79. Finlay, *Politics*, 59–81; Cracco, "Patriziato e oligarchia." For other recent discussions of differences within the class, see Chojnacki, "In Search of the Venetian Patriciate"; Cozzi, "Authority and the Law"; Cracco, *Società e stato*; Gilbert, "Venice in the Crisis"; and Hocquet, *Voiliers et commerce*.

80. Discussing Florence in the same period, Anthony Molho has observed that the emphasis of recent historians on prosopography has obscured elements of class conflict; "Cosimo de' Medici," 9. His words have cautionary value also for Venice, but assessment of the social and factional components of Venetian political history requires careful reconstruction of the membership of these groups in order to scrape away the effects of the long tradition of generalization about the undifferentiated patrician regime.

81. On the case vecchie and case nuove (also referred to as the longhi and the curti), see above, n. 11. But note the corrective comments of Merores, "Der grosse Rat," 64–70.

82. In the important area of matrimonial choice, the case vecchie (among

the sixteen-clan sample studied) chose 44.4 percent of their children's spouses from outside their own numbers. Barbaro, Nozze. See now Chojnacki, "Marriage Legislation."

83. The Great Council fugitives of 1442 included members of the Barozzi, Bembo, and Contarini clans, all case vecchie, but also Nicolò Paruta, member of a family ennobled in 1381. In the episode of 1446 young men bearing such ancient names as Pisani, Zane, and Loredan were implicated, but so were Francesco Lippomano and Girolamo Vendramin, also sons of families ennobled in 1381. Raspe 3649/9, pt. 1, f. 7v; pt. 2, f. 14r. The electoral conspirators of 1433 included members of the oldest houses such as Giovanni Soranzo and Zaccaria Contarini but also Marco Cicogna, of the inductees of 1381; "Cronaca Zancaruol," f. 142v. For the thirty men ennobled with their families after the war of Chioggia in 1381, see *Raphayni de Caresinis chronica*, ed. Ester Pastorello, *Rerum italicarum scriptores*, 2d ed., vol. 12, pt. 2, fasc. 1–2 (Bologna, 1923), 57. See also Chojnacki, "In Search of the Venetian Patriciate," 57. The signatories of the statutes of the *calza* company of the Modesti, drawn up on 20 February 1486/87 (the year after a tense struggle between vecchi and nuovi over the dogeship), included vecchie (Badoer, Bembo, Bragadin, Zorzi) and nuove (Trevisan, Venier, Loredan, Malipiero) families. BMC, Codici Cicogna, 3278, fasc. 24, f. 29. On the events of 1486, see Romanin, *Storia documentata*, 4:305–6. On the *compagnie della calza*, see Venturi, "Compagnie della Calza."

84. Writers on liminality have noted the tension between the "creativity and innovation" characteristic of neophytes in the liminal state and adult society's view of this freedom as "dangerous and anarchical, and [having] to be hedged around with prescriptions, prohibitions and conditions." For the statement on creativity, see Myerhoff, "Rites of Passage," 117; for that on danger and anarchy, see Turner, *Ritual Process*, 109.

85. Finlay also observes that restricting high position to men of mature years encouraged shared values at the center of power by grouping there men who shared the experience of directing Venetian government and defining its goals. "Venetian Gerontocracy," 174.

Chapter 12   Patrician Bachelors

This chapter originally appeared, in slightly altered form, as "Subaltern Patriarchs: Patrician Bachelors in Renaissance Venice," in *Medieval Masculinities: Regarding Men in the Middle Ages*, ed. Clare A. Lees (Minneapolis: University of Minnesota Press, 1994), 73–90.

1. Davis, "Women's History in Transition," 90. An earlier version of this essay was read at the annual meeting of the American Historical Association in December 1989. It was written in the peerless scholarly environment of the National Humanities Center, with the support of fellowships from the Andrew Mellon Foundation and the National Endowment for the Humanities, to both of which I express my deep gratitude. I also gratefully acknowledge my indebtedness to Laura M. Noren for research assistance and to Judith M. Bennett, Monica E. Chojnacka, and Barbara J. Harris for valuable suggestions on earlier drafts.

2. The specific issue addressed here, namely, differentiation among males within patriarchal structures, has importance for gender in all historical contexts. However, the factors I discuss are inseparable from the peculiar social and political character of Venice's patrician regime as it developed in the fourteenth and fifteenth centuries. On the importance of attending to the distinctiveness of different contexts, see Geertz, "Local Knowledge."

3. For varied approaches to gender, see Ortner, "Is Female to Male as Nature Is to Culture?"; Scott, "Gender"; and Connell, *Gender and Power.*

4. On the interplay of structure and practice, or action, in a process labeled "structuration," see Giddens, *Central Problems in Social Theory,* esp. 1–48. For an application to gender issues, see Connell, *Gender and Power,* 61–64.

5. For further discussion of this dynamic, see Chap. 8.

6. For an excellent illustration of changes in conceptions of what constituted marriage in Florence as a result of statutory adjustments regarding property claims between husbands and wives, see Kirshner, "Maritus Lucretur Dotem."

7. For a consideration of how human agents' consciousness of the structures in which they act works to change those structures, see Giddens, *Central Problems in Social Theory,* 198–225. For the way specific structures helped shape individual identity in sixteenth-century France, see Davis, "Boundaries and the Sense of Self."

8. Useful summary comments can be found in Bennett, *Women in the Medieval English Countryside,* 3–9. See also the essays in Bridenthal, Koonz, and Stuard, *Becoming Visible.*

9. Kelly-Gadol, "Did Women Have a Renaissance?" The continuing influence of her essay is evident in the introductions and various essays in Ferguson, Quilligan, and Vickers, *Rewriting the Renaissance,* and in Migiel and Schiesari, *Refiguring Woman.* For examples of its heuristic application to specific contexts, see Brown, "Woman's Place Was in the Home," and Terpstra, "Women in the Brotherhood."

10. See Chojnacki, "Marriage Legislation," and Chaps. 2 and 11.

11. A law of 1414 required fathers, if alive and in Venice, personally to register their sons for government service; MC 21, Leona, ff. 241v–242r. A law of 1443 authorized fines and the loss of office-holding privileges for fathers whose sons misbehaved during meetings of the Great Council; MC 22, Ursa, f. 148v. A law imposing a limit on marriage settlements identified fathers as the agents of a ruinous rise in marriage settlements; Senato, Misti 53, f. 70rv.

12. MC 21, Leona, f. 127rv.

13. A fine authorized in 1463 for excessive expenditure on dress by women was to be imposed on the "husbands, fathers, or others with authority over the offending women" [maritis, sive patribus, vel illis sub quorum potestate contrafacientes mulieres essent]; Senato, Terra 5, f. 46r.

14. On legal distinctions favoring men in earlier centuries, see Zordan, "I vari aspetti."

15. For orientation to the establishment and chronology of the regime, see Lane, "Enlargement of the Great Council"; Law, "Age Qualification"; and Choj-

nacki, "In Search of the Venetian Patriciate" and above, Chap. 11. For a dissenting view, see Ruggiero, "Modernization and the Mythic State."

16. Lane, "Enlargement of the Great Council," 258.

17. See Law, "Age Qualification."

18. Chojnacki, "Social Identity."

19. Chojnacki, "Marriage Legislation," 167–71.

20. Muir, *Civic Ritual*, 119–22.

21. Barbaro, *De re uxoria.* See King, "Caldiera and the Barbaros," and *Venetian Humanism*, 92–98.

22. Barbaro, *De re uxoria*, 63.

23. Barbaro, *De coelibatu.* See King, *Venetian Humanism*, 197–202; Branca, "Un trattato inedito."

24. On Barbaro's rejection of his Venetian identity, see King, *Venetian Humanism*, 198–205. Branca states that Ermolao fully accepted the dignity of the married state for men other than himself; "Un trattato inedito," 86.

25. This information is derived from two sources. The first is the records of the Balla d'Oro, or Barbarella, the exercise by which patrician youths established their credentials for adult membership in the ruling class, providing proof of legitimate patrician birth and attainment of age eighteen. A total of 952 young men from sixteen clans who presented their credentials from 1410 to 1490 constituted the basic population for this analysis; their acts of presentation are in BO 162, 163, 164. Their marital activity was then tracked in the most complete available list of patrician marriages, Barbaro, Nozze. It is important to note, however, that the Barbaro compilation includes marriage notices for 132 men who did not register for the Barbarella. Adding these men would enlarge the population to 1,084, making it more complete, but it would also add disproportionally to the percentage of husbands, as there is no comparable source identifying men who failed to register for the Barbarella but remained single. For that reason, I have limited the analysis to Barbarella registrants. The sixteen clans examined are as follows: Arimondo, Balbi, da Canal, Lando, Loredan, Morosini, Mudazzo, da Mula, Navagero, Pisani, Polani, Priuli, Ruzzini, Vitturi, Zane, Zulian. My test of the accuracy of Barbaro's compilation of marriages will be presented elsewhere. On this manuscript, see Cicogna, *Delle inscrizioni veneziane*, 6:24; on the Barbarella, see Chaps. 10 and 11.

26. To note this is to recognize that the entire inquiry rests on a basic uncertainty, deriving from the impossibility of determining the percentage of men who reached documented "political" adulthood but died before attaining the normal marriage age of around thirty; on men's age at marriage, see Chap. 9. Although it is unwarranted to assume in all cases that men who died in their twenties would have married had they survived into their thirties, the bachelorhood of many of them may indeed have been the result not of the choices or forces examined here but simply of premature, that is, prenuptial, death. Some support for this conclusion comes from the fact that many more "bachelor" brothers than "husband" brothers fail to appear in the office-holding records; the complexities of interpreting this information are discussed below. However, because the great majority of

bachelors did, like husbands, hold office at one time or another, it is necessary to account for their persistent adult presence and their bachelorhood. In the absence of any sure means of determining who among the bachelors were prevented from marrying by death, I treat bachelors as an undifferentiated category.

27. The valuable "Profiles" of Venetian humanists in King, *Venetian Humanism*, 315–449, show that most either married or embraced clerical careers. The choice of the latter vocation may reflect a desire, like that of Ermolao, to avoid familial entanglements. In addition, as King notes (277), the prominent humanists came from the wealthiest and most influential tier of the patriciate; on the greater frequency of marriage among that tier, see below. For one prominent patrician humanist's ambivalence about the tension between the desire for study and the duty of public service, see the references to Leonardo Giustinian in Labalme, *Bernardo Giustiniani*, 9–10.

28. Labalme, "Sodomy and Venetian Justice"; Ruggiero, "Sodom and Venice," in *Boundaries of Eros*, 109–45. Michael Rocke, studying homosexuality in Florence, has noted an age-specific, temporary homosexual experience turning into a heterosexual alternative as men grew to full maturity; Rocke, "Il controllo della omosessualità," 708–9.

29. "Divitum substantia attenuator in maximum damnum et preiuditium suorum heredum" [the economic substance of dowry-providing fathers is reduced, entailing severe damage and prejudice for their heirs]; Senato, Misti 53, f. 70rv. The preamble of the act is reprinted in Bistort, *Magistrato alle Pompe*, 107. This legislation is discussed at length in Chojnacki, "Marriage Legislation," 164–66 and passim, and Chap. 2. In her will of 1391, Pellegrina Venier Basadona acknowledged with loyal gratitude that "my father took so little account of his need to provide for his many children that he gave me a marriage settlement worth more than half his worldly goods" [mio pare non aver respeto a la so condizion de tanti fioli et fie ch el me de tanta de dote et coriedi plu de la mitade de zo che lo avena al mondo]. She therefore made him her residuary heir, entreating her husband not to be aggrieved. NT 364, Darvasio, no. 44. For other evidence of daughters' dowries favored over sons' inheritance, see Chap. 7.

30. Davis, *Venetian Family*, 93–106.

31. The preamble to the law of 1420 noted that fathers of richly endowed wives were consequently "forced to imprison their [other] daughters in convents, amid the latter's well-warranted tears and wailing" [coguntur in monasteriis carcerare, cum dignis lacrimis et plantibus ipsarum]. Bistort, *Magistrato alle Pompe*, 107.

32. An example of brothers committing themselves and their property toward the restitution of the dowry of their brother's wife: "The noble lords Nicolò and Piero da Mosto, with their heirs, declare that they have received their sister-in-law, Isabetta, and her entire dowry, pledging all their property, movable and immovable, present and future" [Manifestum fecerunt viri nobiles domini Nicolaus et Petrus de Musto . . . cum suis heredibus quod receperunt eam dictam dominam Isabetham cognatam suam et totem suam repromissam predictam super omnibus et singulis bonis suis mobilibus et immobilibus presentibus et futuris]; Vadimoni 4, f. 25r. On the other hand, some brothers who married sought to keep

their wives' dowries separate from the substance shared with their brothers in the *fraterna,* or collectively held patrimony. In a *divisio,* or agreement dissolving the shared fraternal inheritance, by which in 1416 Piero Soranzo was economically separated from his brothers Donato and Jacopo, the three brothers explicitly excepted marriage portions from the goods that they were dividing: "dowries, trousseaux, and other marital assigns are and should remain the property of him or those of us who now possess them" [que dos sive repromissa, correda, et provissiones sint et esse debeant illius et illorum nostrum qui habuit, habet, aut habuerunt vel habent]; CI 71, Dotto, prot., ff. 21v–22r.

33. The marriage ties of brothers could also be knotted together in more complex coalitions. That is more likely to have happened in made marriages than in the calculations of fathers of daughters with large dowries. For cases of brothers-in-law from different families combining, see Chap. 6. On widespread patrician dependence upon political office, see Queller, *Venetian Patriciate,* 29–50.

34. In a will of 1469 (?) Ermolao Pisani made his two sons his residuary heirs, "with the understanding that before the distribution of my estate, my son Giovanni is to have one thousand gold ducats, since his brother had more than that for his dowry" [hoc declarato quod Ihoannes (*sic*) filius meus primo et ante omnia et super partem habeat ducatos mille auri eo quod plus habuit in doctem . . . frater suus]; NT 1238, Tomei, pt. 1, no. 15. In a rare instance of a father requiring his son to marry, Nicolò Mudazzo, testating in 1420, conditioned his son Piero's share in his estate and inclusion among his executors upon the young man's marrying; NT 1255, Zane, prot., f. 184v.

35. The fraternal groups were reconstituted using the Barbarella registration records in BO 162, 163, 164. Their matrimonial experience was taken from Barbaro, Nozze. The fraternal groups ranged in size from 2 to 9; the average was 3.26 brothers, the median, 3, and the most frequently encountered (modal) size was 2 brothers (twenty-three of the seventy-three groups). The information available on these men is not precise enough or extensive enough to warrant a lot of reporting, and it proved impossible to get an adequate grip on the variables of numbers of brothers, presence of sisters, and family wealth and influence to be able to come to any sensible conclusions about any one of these with reference to the others. Thus, of the five cases in which no brother married, four (80%) had sisters who married, which might be expected as an influential circumstance of wholesale male bachelorhood. But any conclusions along those lines are undercut by the fact that of the twenty-three cases in which all brothers married, seventeen (73.9%) had sisters who married, close to the same percentage as in the nonmarrying groups. Among the forty-five fraternal groups that included both bachelors and husbands within the group, the proportion with marrying sisters was 71.1 percent (n = 32). These percentages seem too close to warrant any conclusions, especially in the absence of consistent information about family wealth and prestige. Finally, the lack of complete information on brothers who did not marry, and of any consistent information at all on sisters who did not marry, keeps us in ignorance of the total composition of the sibling groups.

36. The information may be schematically displayed as follows:

Marital Activities in 73 Fraternal Groups

	No.	%
All brothers marry	23	31.5
Eldest marries; at least one other a bachelor	29	39.7
Eldest a bachelor; at least one other marries	16	21.9
None marries	5	6.9
Total	73	100

37. The information in tabular form:

Average Sizes by Category among 73 Fraternal Groups

All brothers marry	2.6
Eldest marries; at least one other a bachelor	4
Eldest a bachelor; at least one other marries	3.3
None marries	2.2

38. We should note, however, that six of these forty-five divided groups consisted of two brothers, only one of whom married.

39. This information comes from reconstruction of the governmental careers of fifty-eight men who came of age in the 1460s and 1470s, members of seventeen multiple-brother groups from the Arimondo, Balbi, and da Canal clans. The nucleus of the sample is the men from those clans who registered for the Barbarella from 1465 to 1475; to this core were added their brothers, older and younger. The governmental activity of these men was reconstructed from Voci 6 and PE 169, 170, 171. Marriages were compiled from Barbaro, Nozze, and BO 164, 165.

40. The forty men who married (69%) were collectively elected to office 191 times, averaging about 4.8 offices per husband. The eighteen bachelor brothers (31%) accounted for forty-eight offices, an average of 2.7 per man.

41. Offices held by unwed men who subsequently married are counted in the husbands' total. I do not mean to suggest that the marital state as such was either a qualification for or a disqualification from office but precisely the reverse: that participation in the government was a consequence of patrician male birth rather than of marital vocation.

42. In the sixteen sample houses, 417 young men registered between 1408 and 1450; between 1451 and 1497 the number rose to 648, a 55 percent increase; BO 162, 163, 164.

43. Voci 4. This register was used for the examination because, unlike Reg. 6, which was examined above, it includes the high offices. To the seventy-four whose marital status could be identified should be added three whose identities or marital status remain uncertain. Only fourteen of the sixteen sample clans appear, because the Mudazzo and the Navagero clans had no men elected to the offices considered. Many of the men encountered held two or all three of the offices considered, sometimes for many terms.

44. Finlay, "Venetian Gerontocracy." However, many of the politically active bachelors held posts reserved for men in their thirties, that is, well into the normal age of marriage for men.

45. Evidence seems to bear out this surmise. Of thirteen holders of high office from six clans examined in detail, ten belonged to fraternal groups in which all brothers married, only three having any bachelor brothers. The clans are the Arimondo, Balbi, da Canal, Lando, da Mula, and Vitturi. It was impossible to reconstruct the sibling groups of an additional three men from these clans. Note that the five Balbi men belonged to only two groups. On the presence of an oligarchy at the patriciate's center, see Cozzi, "Authority and the Law"; Cracco, "Patriziato e oligarchia"; and Finlay, *Politics,* 59–81 and passim.

46. Ruggiero, *Boundaries of Eros.*

47. For discussions of the informal power of married noble women in Venice, see Romano, *Patricians and Popolani,* 131–39; and Chaps. 7 and 8.

48. On the capacity of members of nondominant groups to construct identities by consciously adapting to the constraints imposed on them, see the comments regarding women in Davis, "Boundaries and the Sense of Self," 61–63.

49. See Chap. 8.

50. On mothers, see Chaps. 8 and 9. On the family orientation of bachelors, one example may stand for many: in his will of 1502 the unmarried Francesco Morosini, who, having registered for the Barbarella in 1471, was then probably approaching age fifty, divided his estate between his married sister, to whom he willed 50 ducats, and his brother, whom he designated as his residuary heir; NT 66, Busenello, no. 160. His Barbarella registration is in BO 164, f. 218r.

51. Scattered evidence shows unmarried men supporting the political careers of their sisters' sons and contributing to the dowries of their sisters' daughters. On the other hand, see the words of a bachelor who took responsibility for fraternal nieces: Antonio da Canal, testating in 1519, named as his executors and universal heirs the three daughters of his late brother, Girolamo, "whom I have always regarded as my own daughters" [le qual o sempre tenute et reputate mie fie proprie]; NT 66, Busenello, no. 43. For the effects of the bilateral social orientation of patrician wives, see Chap. 10.

52. The role of liminal age and gender groups in the articulation of the political and social culture of Florence's patrician regime is a central theme in Trexler, *Public Life.* On liminality in Venice, see Chap. 11.

53. They can be seen as achieving a kind of publicly defined, encouraged, and rewarded generativity, in Erik Erikson's sense of "concern for establishing and guiding the next generation"; Erikson, *Identity,* 138. See also Levinson et al., *Seasons of a Man's Life,* 196 ff.

Bibliography

Angiolini, Franco. "I ceti dominanti in Italia tra Medioevo ed Età Moderna: Continuità e mutamenti." *Società e storia* 10 (1980): 909–18.

Ariès, Philippe. *Centuries of Childhood: A Social History of Family Life.* Translated by Robert Baldick. New York, paperback edition, n.d.

———. Introduction to Chartier, *History of Private Life,* 3:1–11.

Arnaldi, Girolamo, and Manlio Pastore Stocchi. *Storia della cultura veneta.* Vol. 3, *Dal primo Quattrocento al Concilio di Trento.* Vicenza, 1981.

Barbaro, Ermolao. *De coelibatu, De officio legati.* Edited by Vittore Branca. Florence, 1969.

Barbaro, Francesco. *De re uxoria liber in partes duas.* Edited by Attilio Gnesotto. Padua, 1915.

———. "On Wifely Duties." Translation by Benjamin G. Kohl of part 2 of *De re uxoria.* In *The Earthly Republic: Italian Humanists on Government and Society,* ed. Benjamin G. Kohl and Ronald G. Witt, with Elizabeth B. Welles, 189–228. Philadelphia, 1978.

Baxendale, Susannah Foster. "Exile in Practice: The Alberti Family in and out of Florence." *Renaissance Quarterly* 44 (1991): 720–56.

Becker, Marvin B. *Florence in Transition.* Vol. 2, *Studies in the Rise of the Territorial State.* Baltimore, 1968.

Bellavitis, Anna. "La famiglia 'cittadina' veneziana nel XVI secolo: Dote e successione. Le leggi e le fonti." *Studi veneziani,* n.s., 30 (1995): 55–68.

Bellomo, Manlio. *Ricerche sui rapporti tra coniugi: Contributo alla storia della famiglia medievale.* Milan, 1961.

Beloch, Karl Julius. *Bevölkerungsgeschichte Italiens.* Vol. 3. Berlin, 1961.

Bennett, Judith M. *Women in the Medieval English Countryside.* New York, 1987.

Besta, Enrico. *La famiglia nella storia del diritto italiano.* Milan, 1962.

Betto, Bianca. "Linee di politica matrimoniale nella nobiltà veneziana fino al XV secolo. Alcune note genealogiche e l'esempio della famiglia Mocenigo." *Archivio storico italiano* 39 (1981): 3–64.

Bistort, Giulio. *Il Magistrato alle Pompe nella Repubblica di Venezia.* 1912. Reprint, Bologna, 1969.

345

Bizzocchi, Roberto. *Chiesa e potere nella Toscana del Quattrocento.* Bologna, 1987.

Boerio, Giuseppe. *Dizionario del dialetto veneziano.* Venice, 1856.

Bohannan, Paul, and John Middleton, eds. *Kinship and Social Organization.* Garden City, N.Y., 1968.

Bonds, William N. "Genoese Noblewomen and Gold Thread Manufacturing." *Medievalia et Humanistica* 17 (1966): 79–81.

Bornstein, Daniel. "Giovanni Dominici, the Bianchi, and Venice: Symbolic Action and Interpretive Grids." *Journal of Medieval and Renaissance Studies* 23 (1993): 143–71.

Bouwsma, William J. "Venice and the Political Education of Europe." In Hale, *Renaissance Venice,* 445–56.

Branca, Vittore. "Un trattato inedito di Ermolao Barbaro: Il De coelibatu libri." *Bibliothèque d'Humanisme et Renaissance* 14 (1952): 83–98.

Brandileone, Francesco. "Studi preliminari sullo svolgimento storico dei rapporti patrimoniali fra coniugi in Italia." In Francesco Brandileone, *Scritti di storia del diritto privato,* 1:229–319. Bologna, 1931.

Bridenthal, Renate, Claudia Koonz, and Susan M. Stuard, eds. *Becoming Visible: Women in European History.* 2d ed. Boston, 1987.

Brown, Judith C. "Monache a Firenze all'inizio dell'età moderna. Un'analisi demografica." *Quaderni storici* 85 (1994): 117–52.

———. "A Woman's Place Was in the Home: Women's Work in Renaissance Tuscany." In Ferguson, Quilligan, and Vickers, *Rewriting the Renaissance,* 206–24.

Brown, Judith C., and Robert C. Davis, eds. *Gender and Society in Renaissance Italy.* London, 1998.

Brucker, Gene. *The Civic World of Early Renaissance Florence.* Princeton, 1977.

———. *Giovanni and Lusanna: Love and Marriage in Renaissance Florence.* Berkeley, 1986.

———. "The Medici in the Fourteenth Century." *Speculum* 32 (1957): 1–26.

———. "Monasteries, Friaries, and Nunneries in Quattrocento Florence." In *Christianity and the Renaissance: Image and Religious Imagination in the Quattrocento,* ed. Timothy Verdon and John Henderson, 42–62. Syracuse, N.Y., 1990.

———. *Renaissance Florence.* 2d ed. Berkeley, 1983.

———. "Tales of Two Cities: Florence and Venice in the Renaissance." *American Historical Review* 88 (1983): 599–616.

Bueno de Mesquita, D. M. "Ludovico Sforza and His Vassals." In *Italian Renaissance Studies,* ed. E. F. Jacob, 184–216. London, 1960.

Bullough, D. A. "Early Medieval Social Groupings: The Terminology of Kinship." *Past and Present* 45 (1969): 3–18.

Burckhardt, Jacob. *The Civilization of the Renaissance in Italy.* Translated by S. G. C. Middlemore. 1878. Reprint, London, 1990. (Original German ed., 1860.)

Calvi, Giulia. *Il contratto morale: Madri e figli nella Toscana moderna.* Bari, 1994.

———. "Diritti e legami: Madri, figli, stato in Toscana (XVI–XVIII secolo)." *Quaderni storici* 86 (1994): 487–510.

———. "Reconstructing the Family: Widowhood and Remarriage in Tuscany in the Early Modern Period." In Dean and Lowe, *Marriage in Italy,* 275–96.

Carboni, Mauro. *Le doti della "povertà": Risparmio, donne e doti fra assistenza e previdenza. Il Monte del Matrimonio di Bologna (1583–1796).* Bologna, forthcoming.

Casini, Matteo. "La cittadinanza originaria a Venezia tra i secoli XV e XVI: Una linea interpretativa." In *Studi veneti offerti a Gaetano Cozzi,* 133–50. Venice, 1992.

Caso, Anna. "Per la storia della società milanese: I corredi nuziali nell'ultima età viscontea e nel periodo della Repubblica Ambrosiana (1433–1450), dagli atti del notaio Protaso Sansoni." *Nuova rivista storica* 65 (1981): 521–51.

Cecchetti, Bartolomeo. "La donna nel medioevo a Venezia." *Archivio veneto* 31 (1886): 33–169, 307–49.

Cessi, Roberto. "La finanza veneziana al tempo della guerra di Chioggia." In Cessi, *Politica ed economia,* 179–248.

———. "Introduzione storica." In *La regolazione delle entrate e delle spese (sec. XIII–XIV),* ed. Roberto Cessi, documenti finanziari della Repubblica di Venezia, 1st ser., vol. 2, pt. 1. Padua, 1925.

———. *Politica ed economia di Venezia nel Trecento.* Rome, 1952.

———. "Le relazioni commerciali tra Venezia e le Fiandre nel secolo XIV." In Cessi, *Politica ed economia,* 71–172.

———. *Gli statuti veneziani di Jacopo Tiepolo del 1242 e le loro glosse.* Venice, 1938.

Chabot, Isabelle. " 'La sposa in nero': La ritualizzazione del lutto delle vedove fiorentine (secoli XIV–XV)." *Quaderni storici* 86 (1994): 421–62.

———. "Widowhood and Poverty in Late Medieval Florence." *Continuity and Change* 3 (1988): 291–311.

Chartier, Roger. "Figures of Modernity: Introduction." In Chartier, *History of Private Life,* 3:15–19.

———, ed. *A History of Private Life.* Vol. 3, *Passions of the Renaissance.* 1986. Eng. trans., Cambridge, Mass., 1989.

Chittolini, Giorgio, ed. *La crisi degli ordinamenti comunali e le origini dello stato del Rinascimento.* Bologna, 1979.

———. "Infeudazione e politico feudale nel ducato visconteo-sforzesco." In Giorgio Chittolini, *La formazione dello stato regionale e le istituzioni del contado: Secoli XIV–XV,* 36–100. Turin, 1979.

———. "L'onore dell'officiale." In *Florence and Milan: Comparisons and Relations,* ed. Sergio Bertelli et al., 1:101–33. Florence, 1989.

———. "The 'Private,' the 'Public,' the State." In *Origins of the State in Italy,* S34–61.

Chojnacki, Stanley. "Cateruzza and the Patriarchs: Wifehood and Selfhood in Renaissance Venice." In *Culture and Self in Renaissance Europe,* ed. William J. Connell. Berkeley, forthcoming.

———. "Crime, Punishment, and the Trecento Venetian State." In Martines, *Violence and Civil Disorder,* 184–228.

———. "La formazione della nobiltà dopo la Serrata." In *Storia di Venezia,* vol. 3, *La formazione dello stato patrizio,* ed. Girolamo Arnaldi et al., 641–725. Rome, 1997.

———. "Identity and Ideology in Renaissance Venice: The Third Serrata." In *Venice Reconsidered,* ed. John Martin and Dennis Romano. Baltimore, forthcoming.

——. "In Search of the Venetian Patriciate: Families and Factions in the Fourteenth Century." In Hale, *Renaissance Venice*, 47–90. London, 1973.

——. "Marriage Legislation and Patrician Society in Fifteenth-Century Venice." In *Law, Custom, and the Social Fabric in Medieval Europe: Essays in Honor of Bryce Lyon*, ed. Bernard S. Bachrach and David Nicholas, 163–84. Kalamazoo, Mich., 1990.

——. "La posizione della donna a Venezia nel Cinquecento." In *Tiziano e Venezia*, 65–70.

——. "Social Identity in Renaissance Venice: The Second Serrata." *Renaissance Studies* 8 (1994): 341–58.

Cicogna, Emmanuele Antonio. *Delle inscrizioni veneziane.* 6 vols. Venice, 1824–53.

Cipolla, Carlo M. *Studi di storia della moneta.* Vol. 1, *I movimenti dei cambi in Italia dal secolo XIII al XV.* Pavia, 1948.

Cohn, Samuel K., Jr. "Criminality and the State in Renaissance Florence, 1344–1466." *Journal of Social History* 14 (1981): 211–33.

——. *The Cult of Remembrance and the Black Death: Six Renaissance Cities in Central Italy.* Baltimore, 1992.

——. "Donne in piazza e donne in tribunale a Firenze nel Rinascimento." In *Studi storici* 22 (1981): 515–33.

——. *The Laboring Classes of Renaissance Florence.* New York, 1980.

——. "Sex and Violence on the Periphery: The Territorial State in Early Renaissance Florence." In Cohn, *Women in the Streets*, 98–136.

——. "The Social History of Women in the Renaissance." In Cohn, *Women in the Streets*, 1–15.

——. "Women in the Streets, Women in the Courts in Early Renaissance Florence." In Cohn, *Women in the Streets*, 16–38.

——. *Women in the Streets: Essays on Sex and Power in Renaissance Italy.* Baltimore, 1996.

Connell, R. W. *Gender and Power.* Stanford, 1987.

Contareno, Cardinall Gasper. *The Commonwealth and Gouernment of Venice.* Translated by Lewes Lewkenor. London, 1599.

Contarini, Gasparo. *La Republica e i magistrati di Vinegia.* Venice, 1544.

Cox, Virginia. "The Single Self: Feminist Thought and the Marriage Market in Early Modern Venice." *Renaissance Quarterly* 48 (1995): 513–81.

Cozzi, Gaetano. "Authority and the Law in Renaissance Venice." In Hale, *Renaissance Venice*, 293–345.

——. "Domenico Morosini e Il 'De bene instituta re publica.'" *Studi veneziani* 12 (1970): 405–58.

——. "La donna, l'amore e Tiziano." In *Tiziano e Venezia*, 47–63.

Cozzi, Gaetano, and Michael Knapton. *La Repubblica di Venezia nell'età moderna: Dalla guerra di Chioggia al 1517.* Vol. 12, pt. 1 of *Storia d'Italia diretta da Giuseppe Galazzo.* Turin, 1986.

Crabb, Ann Morton. "How Typical Was Alessandra Macinghi Strozzi of Fifteenth-Century Florentine Widows?" In *Upon My Husband's Death: Widows in the Literatures and Histories of Medieval Europe*, ed. Louise Mirrer, 47–68. Ann Arbor, Mich., 1992.

Cracco, Giorgio. "Patriziato e oligarchia a Venezia nel Tre-Quattrocento." In *Florence and Venice: Comparisons and Relations,* ed. Sergio Bertelli et al., vol. 1, *Quattrocento,* 71–98. Florence, 1979.

———. *Società e stato nel medioevo veneziano, secoli XII–XIV.* Florence, 1967.

Crescenzi, Victor. *"Esse de maiori consilio": Legittimità civile e legittimazione politica nella Repubblica di Venezia (secc. XIII–XVI).* Rome, 1996.

Crook, J. A. *Law and Life of Rome.* London, 1967.

Crouzet-Pavan, Elisabeth. *"Sopra le acque salse": Espaces, pouvoir et société à Venise à la fin du Moyen Age.* 2 vols. Rome, 1992.

Dalarun, Jacques. "The Clerical Gaze." In *A History of Women in the West,* vol. 2, *Silences of the Middle Ages,* ed. Christiane Klapisch-Zuber, 15–42. Translated by Arthur Goldhammer. Cambridge, Mass., 1992.

Da Mosto, Andrea. *L'Archivio di Stato in Venezia.* Bibliothèque des *Annales institutorum,* vol. 5. Rome, 1937.

Davidson, Nicholas. "Theology, Nature, and the Law: Sexual Sin and Sexual Crime in Italy from the Fourteenth to the Seventeenth Century." In Dean and Lowe, *Crime, Society, and the Law,* 74–98.

Davis, James C. *A Venetian Family and Its Fortune, 1500–1900.* Philadelphia, 1975.

Davis, Natalie Zemon. "Boundaries and the Sense of Self in Sixteenth-Century France." In Heller et al., *Reconstructing Individualism,* 53–63.

———. "Fame and Secrecy: Leon Modena's *Life* as an Early Modern Autobiography." In *The Autobiography of a Seventeenth-Century Venetian Rabbi: Leon Modena's Life of Judah,* ed. and trans. Mark R. Cohen, 50–70. Princeton, 1988.

———. "Ghosts, Kin, and Progeny: Some Features of Family Life in Early Modern France." In *The Family,* ed. Alice S. Rossi et al., 87–114. New York, 1978.

———. "On the Lame." *American Historical Review* 93 (1988): 572–603.

———. "The Reasons of Misrule." In Davis, *Society and Culture,* 97–123.

———. *Society and Culture in Early Modern France.* Stanford, 1975.

———. " 'Women's History' in Transition: The European Case." *Feminist Studies* 3 (1976): 83–103.

Davis, Robert C. "The Geography of Gender in the Renaissance." In Brown and Davis, *Gender and Society,* 19–38.

Dean, Trevor. "The Courts." In *Origins of the State in Italy,* S136–51.

———. *Land and Power in Late Medieval Ferrara: The Rule of the Este, 1350–1450.* Cambridge, 1988.

Dean, Trevor, and K. J. P. Lowe, eds., *Crime, Society, and the Law in Renaissance Italy.* Cambridge, 1994.

———, eds. *Marriage in Italy, 1300–1650.* Cambridge, 1998.

Donati, Claudio. *L'idea di nobiltà in Italia: Secoli XIV–XVIII.* Bari, 1988.

Douglas, Mary. *Natural Symbols: Explorations in Cosmology.* 2d ed. New York, 1982.

Duby, Georges. "Au XIIᵉ siècle: Les Jeunes dans la société aristocratique." *Annales: économies, sociétés, civilisations* 19 (1964): 835–46.

———. *The Knight, the Lady, and the Priest.* Translated by Barbara Bray. New York, 1983.

Eisenstadt, S. N. "Archetypal Patterns of Youth." In *The Challenge of Youth,* ed. Erik H. Erikson, 29–50. Garden City, N.Y., 1965.

Ell, Stephen R. "Citizenship and Immigration in Venice, 1305 to 1500." Ph.D. diss., University of Chicago, 1976.

Elshtain, Jean Bethke. *Public Man, Private Woman*. Princeton, 1981.

Ercole, Francesco. "L'istituto dotale nella pratica e nella legislazione statutaria dell'Italia superiore." *Rivista italiana per le scienze giuridiche* 45 (1908): 191–302; 46 (1910): 167–257.

Erikson, Eric H. *Identity: Youth and Crisis*. New York, 1968.

Esposito, Anna. "Strategie matrimoniali e livelli di richezza." In *Alle origini della nuova Roma: Martino V (1417–1431), Atti del Convegno*, ed. Maria Chiabò et al., 571–87. Rome, 1992.

Evans-Pritchard, E. E. "Descent and Kinship." In Bohannan and Middleton, *Kinship and Social Organization*, 151–54.

Everett, James E., and Donald E. Queller. "Family, Faction, and Politics in Early Renaissance Venice: Elections in the Great Council, 1383–87." *Studies in Medieval and Renaissance History*, n.s., 14 (1993): 1–31.

Fabbri, Lorenzo. *Alleanza matrimoniale e patriziato nella Firenze del '400: Studio sulla famiglia Strozzi*. Florence, 1991.

Fasano Guarini, Elena. "Center and Periphery." In *Origins of the State in Italy*, S74–96.

Fasoli, Gina. "Nascita di un mito." In *Studi storici in onore di Gioacchino Volpe*, 1:455–79. Florence, 1958.

Ferguson, Margaret W., Maureen Quilligan, and Nancy Vickers, eds. *Rewriting the Renaissance: The Discourses of Sexual Difference in Early Modern Europe*. Chicago, 1986.

Ferraro, Joanne M. "The Power to Decide: Battered Wives in Early Modern Venice." *Renaissance Quarterly* 48 (1995): 492–512.

Ferro, Marco. *Dizionario del diritto comune e veneto*. 10 vols. in 5. Venice, 1778–81.

Finlay, Robert. *Politics in Renaissance Venice*. New Brunswick, N.J., 1981.

———. "The Refashioning of Martin Guerre." *American Historical Review* 93 (1988): 553–71.

———. "The Venetian Republic as a Gerontocracy: Age and Politics in the Renaissance." *Journal of Medieval and Renaissance Studies* 8 (1978): 157–78.

Flandrin, Jean-Louis. *Families in Former Times*. Translated by Richard Southern. New York, 1979.

Flax, Jane. "Postmodernism and Gender Relations in Feminist Theory." *Signs* 12 (1987): 621–43.

Fortes, Meyer. Introduction to *The Developmental Cycle in Domestic Groups*, ed. Jack Goody, 1–14. Cambridge, 1958.

———. "Ritual and Office in Tribal Society." In Glucksman, *Essays on the Ritual of Social Relations*, 53–88.

———. "The Structure of Unilineal Descent Groups." *American Anthropologist* 55 (1953): 17–41.

Fox, Robin. *Kinship and Marriage*. Harmondsworth, England, 1967.

Friedl, Ernestine. "The Position of Women: Appearance and Reality." *Anthropological Quarterly* 40 (1967): 97–108.

Fumagalli, Camillo. *Il diritto di fraterna nella giurisprudenza da Accursio alla codificazione.* Turin, 1912.

Gaeta, Franco. "Alcune considerazioni sul mito di Venezia." *Bibliothèque d'Humanisme et Renaissance* 23 (1961): 58–75.

———. "L'idea di Venezia." In Arnaldi and Pastore Stocchi, *Storia della cultura veneta,* vol. 3, pt. 3, 565–641.

Geertz, Clifford. "Centers, Kings, and Charisma: Reflections on the Symbolics of Power." In Geertz, *Local Knowledge,* 121–46.

———. "Local Knowledge: Fact and Law in Comparative Perspective." In Geertz, *Local Knowledge,* 167–231.

———. *Local Knowledge: Further Essays in Interpretive Anthropology.* New York, 1983.

Genicot, Léopold. "Crisis: From the Middle Ages to Modern Times." In *The Cambridge Economic History of Europe,* vol. 1, *The Agrarian Life of the Middle Ages,* 2nd edition, ed. M. M. Postan, 660–741. Cambridge, 1966.

Giddens, Anthony. *Central Problems in Social Theory: Action, Structure and Contradiction in Social Analysis.* Berkeley-Los Angeles, 1979.

Gilbert, Felix. "The Venetian Constitution in Florentine Political Thought." In *Florentine Studies: Politics and Society in Renaissance Florence,* ed. Nicolai Rubinstein, 463–500. London, 1968.

———. "Venice in the Crisis of the League of Cambrai." In Hale, *Renaissance Venice,* 274–92.

Gill, Katherine. "Open Monasteries for Women in Late Medieval and Early Modern Italy: Two Roman Examples." In *The Crannied Wall: Women, Religion, and the Arts in Early Modern Europe,* ed. Craig A. Monson, 15–47. Ann Arbor, Mich., 1992.

Giustinian, Pietro. *Venetiarum historia vulgo Petro Iustiniano Iustiniani filio adiudicata,* ed. Roberto Cessi and Fanny Bennato. Venice, 1964.

Gleason, Elisabeth G. *Gasparo Contarini: Venice, Rome, and Reform.* Berkeley-Los Angeles, 1993.

Glucksman, Max. *Essays on the Ritual of Social Relations.* Manchester, England, 1962.

———. "Les Rites de Passage." In Glucksman, *Essays on the Ritual of Social Relations,* 1–52.

Goldthwaite, Richard A. "The Florentine Palace as Domestic Architecture." *American Historical Review* 72 (1972): 977–1012.

———. *Private Wealth in Renaissance Florence: A Study of Four Families.* Princeton, 1968.

Goodman, Dena. "Public Sphere and Private Life: Toward a Synthesis of Current Historiographical Approaches to the Old Regime." *History and Theory* 31 (1992): 1–20.

———. *The Republic of Letters: A Cultural History of the French Enlightenment.* Ithaca, N.Y., 1994.

Goody, Jack. *The Development of the Family and Marriage in Europe.* Cambridge, 1983.

Greenblatt, Stephen. "Fiction and Friction." In *Reconstructing Individualism*, 30–52.

———. *Renaissance Self Fashioning: From More to Shakespeare.* Chicago, 1983.

Gregory, Heather. "Daughters, Dowries, and the Family in Fifteenth Century Florence." *Rinascimento,* 2d ser., 27 (1987): 215–37.

———, ed. and trans. *Selected Letters of Alessandra Strozzi.* Berkeley, 1997.

Grubb, James S. *Firstborn of Venice: Vicenza in the Early Renaissance State.* Baltimore, 1988.

———. "In Search of the *Cittadini.*" In Martin and Romano, *Venice Reconsidered.*

———. "Memory and Identity: Why Venetians Didn't Keep *Ricordanze.*" *Renaissance Studies* 8 (1994): 375–87.

———. "When Myths Lose Power: Four Decades of Venetian Historiography." *Journal of Modern History* 58 (1986): 43–94.

Guzzetti, Linda. "Le donne a Venezia nel XIV secolo: Uno studio sulla loro presenza nella società e nella famiglia." *Studi veneziani,* n.s., 35 (1998): 15–88.

Habermas, Jürgen. *The Structural Transformation of the Public Sphere: An Inquiry into a Category of Bourgeois Society.* Translated by Thomas Burger. Cambridge, Mass., 1989.

Hale, J. R., ed. *Renaissance Venice.* London, 1973.

Hanley, Sarah. "Engendering the State: Family Formation and State Building in Early Modern France." *French Historical Studies* 16 (1989): 4–27.

———. "Social Sites of Political Practice in France: Lawsuits, Civil Rights, and the Separation of Powers in Domestic and State Government, 1500–1800." *American Historical Review* 102 (1997): 27–52.

Harris, Barbara J. "Aristocratic Women and the State in Early Tudor England." In *State, Sovereigns, and Society in Early Modern English History: Essays in Honour of A. J. Slavin,* ed. Charles Carlton et al., 3–24. New York, 1998.

———. "Women and Politics in Early Tudor England." *Historical Journal* 33 (1990): 259–81.

Heers, Jacques. *L' Occident aux XIVe et XVe siècles: Aspects économiques et sociaux.* Paris, 1966.

Heller, Thomas C., et al., eds. *Reconstructing Individualism: Autonomy, Individuality, and the Self in Western Thought.* Stanford, 1986.

Herald, Jacqueline. *Renaissance Dress in Italy.* Atlantic Highlands, N.J., 1982.

Herlihy, David. "Age, Property, and Career in Medieval Society." In Herlihy, *Women, Family, and Society,* 261–78.

———. "Did Women Have a Renaissance? A Reconsideration." *Medievalia et Humanistica,* n.s., 13 (1985): 1–22.

———. "Family Solidarity in Medieval Italian History." In Herlihy et al., *Economy, Society, and Government, in Medieval Italy,* 173–84.

———. "Land, Family, and Women in Continental Europe, 701–1200." *Traditio* 18 (1962): 89–120.

———. "Mapping Households in Medieval Italy." *Catholic Historical Review* 58 (1972): 1–24.

———. *Medieval Households.* Cambridge, Mass., 1985.

——. "The Rulers of Florence, 1282–1530." In Herlihy, *Women, Family, and Society,* 353–80.

——. "Some Psychological and Social Roots of Violence in the Tuscan Cities." In Martines, *Violence and Civil Disorder,* 129–54.

——. "Vieillir à Florence au Quattrocento." *Annales: économies, sociétés, civilisations* 24 (1969): 1338–52.

——. *Women, Family, and Society in Medieval Europe: Historical Essays, 1978–1991.* Providence, R.I., 1995.

——. *Women in Medieval Society: The Smith History Lecture, 1971.* Houston, 1971.

Herlihy, David, and Christiane Klapisch-Zuber. *Les Toscans et leurs familles.* Paris, 1978.

——. *Tuscans and Their Families: A Study of the Florentine Catasto of 1427.* New Haven, 1985.

Herlihy, David, et al., eds. *Economy, Society, and Government in Medieval Italy: Essays in Memory of Robert L. Reynolds.* Kent, Ohio, 1969.

Hocquet, Jean-Claude. *Voiliers et commerce en Méditerranée.* Vol. 2 of *Le Sel et la fortune de Venise.* Villeneuve-d'Ascq, 1979.

Hollander, Anne. *Seeing through Clothes.* New York, 1978.

Howell, Martha C. "Citizenship and Gender: Women's Political Status in Northern Medieval Cities." In *Women and Power in the Middle Ages,* ed. Mary Erler and Maryanne Kowaleski, 37–60. Athens, Ga., 1988.

Hughes, Diane Owen. "Distinguishing Signs: Ear-Rings, Jews, and Franciscan Rhetoric in the Italian Renaissance City." *Past and Present* 112 (1986): 3–59.

——. "From Brideprice to Dowry in Mediterranean Europe." *Journal of Family History* 3 (1978): 262–95.

——. "Representing the Family: Portraits and Purposes in Early Modern Italy." *Journal of Interdisciplinary History* 17 (1986): 7–38.

——. "Sumptuary Law and Social Relations in Renaissance Italy." In *Disputes and Settlements: Law and Human Relations in the West,* ed. John Bossy, 69–99. Cambridge, 1983.

——. "Urban Growth and Family Structure in Medieval Genoa." *Past and Present* 66 (1975): 3–28.

Jones, Philip. "Communes and Despots: The City-State in Late-Medieval Italy." *Transactions of the Royal Historical Society,* 5th ser., 15 (1965): 71–96.

Kelly-Gadol, Joan (Joan Kelly). "Did Women Have a Renaissance?" In *Becoming Visible: Women in European History,* ed. Renate Bridenthal and Claudia Koonz, 137–64. Boston, 1977. Reprinted in *Women, History, and Theory: The Essays of Joan Kelly,* 19–50. Chicago, 1984.

Kent, Dale. "The Florentine *Reggimento* in the Fifteenth Century." *Renaissance Quarterly* 28 (1975): 575–638.

——. *The Rise of the Medici: Faction in Florence, 1426–1434.* Oxford, 1978.

Kent, F. W. *Household and Lineage in Renaissance Florence: The Family Life of the Capponi, Ginori, and Rucellai.* Princeton, 1977.

King, Margaret L. "Caldiera and the Barbaros on Marriage and the Family: Humanist Reflections of Venetian Realities." *Journal of Medieval and Renaissance Studies* 6 (1976): 19–50.

———. "The Religious Retreat of Isotta Nogarola (1418–1466)." *Signs* 3 (1978): 807–22.

———. "Thwarted Ambitions: Six Learned Women of the Renaissance." *Soundings* 59 (1976): 280–304.

———. *Venetian Humanism in an Age of Patrician Dominance.* Princeton, 1986.

Kirshner, Julius. "Maritus Lucretur Dotem Uxoris Sue Premortue in Late Medieval Florence." *Zeitschrift der Savigny-Stiftung für Rechtsgeschichte, Kanonistische Abteilung* 77 (1991): 111–55.

———. "Materials for a Gilded Cage: Non-Dotal Assets in Florence, 1300–1500." In *The Family in Italy from Antiquity to the Present,* ed. David I. Kertzer and Richard P. Saller, 184–207. New Haven, 1991.

———. *Pursuing Honor While Avoiding Sin: The Monte delle Doti of Florence.* Quaderni di *Studi Senesi* 41. Milan, 1978.

———. "Wives' Claims against Insolvent Husbands in Late Medieval Italy." In Kirshner and Wemple, *Women of the Medieval World,* 256–303.

Kirshner, Julius, and Anthony Molho. "The Dowry Fund and the Marriage Market in Early Quattrocento Florence." *Journal of Modern History* 50 (1978): 403–38.

Kirshner, Julius, and Suzanne F. Wemple, eds. *Women of the Medieval World: Essays in Honor of John H. Mundy.* Oxford, 1985.

Kittell, Ellen E., and Thomas F. Madden, eds. *Medieval and Renaissance Venice.* Urbana, Ill., 1999.

Klapisch-Zuber, Christiane. "Blood Parents and Milk Parents: Wet Nursing in Florence, 1300–1530." In Klapisch-Zuber, *Women, Family, and Ritual,* 133–64.

———. "Childhood in Tuscany at the Beginning of the Fifteenth Century." In Klapisch-Zuber, *Women, Family, and Ritual,* 94–116.

———. "Les corbeilles de la mariée." In Klapisch-Zuber, *La maison et le nom,* 215–27.

———. "The 'Cruel Mother': Maternity, Widowhood, and Dowry in Florence in the Fourteenth and Fifteenth Centuries." In Klapisch-Zuber, *Women, Family, and Ritual,* 117–31.

———. "L'enfance en Toscane au début du XV siècle." *Annales de Démographie Historique* (1973): 99–122. Eng. trans., "Childhood in Tuscany."

———. *La famiglia e le donne nel rinascimento a Firenze.* Bari, 1988.

———. "The Griselda Complex: Dowry and Marriage Gifts in the Quattrocento." In Klapisch-Zuber, *Women, Family, and Ritual,* 213–46.

———. "'Kin, Friends, and Neighbors': The Urban Territory of a Merchant Family in 1400." In Klapisch-Zuber, *Women, Family, and Ritual,* 68–93.

———. *La maison et le nom: Stratégies et rituels dans l'Italie de la Renaissance.* Paris, 1990.

———. "The 'Mattinata' in Medieval Italy." In Klapisch-Zuber, *Women, Family, and Ritual,* 261–82.

———. "La 'Mère cruelle': Maternité, veuvage et dot dans la Florence des XIVe–

XVe siècles." *Annales: économies, sociétés, civilisations* 38 (1983): 1097–1109. Eng. trans., "The Cruel Mother."

———. "Parenti, amici, vicini." *Quaderni storici* 33 (1976): 953–82.

———. "Il pubblico, il privato, l'intimità: Una introduzione." *Ricerche storiche* 16 (1986): 451–58.

———. *Women, Family, and Ritual in Renaissance Italy.* Translated by Lydia G. Cochrane. Chicago, 1985.

———. "Zacharias, or the Ousted Father: Nuptial Rites in Tuscany between Giotto and the Council of Trent." In *Women, Family, and Ritual,* 178–212.

Kolsky, Stephen. "Bending the Rules: Marriage in Renaissance Collections of Biographies of Famous Women." In Dean and Lowe, *Marriage in Italy,* 227–48.

Kovesi Killerby, Catherine. "Practical Problems in the Enforcement of Italian Sumptuary Law, 1200–1500." In Dean and Lowe, *Crime, Society, and the Law,* 99–120.

Kretschmayr, Heinrich. *Geschichte von Venedig.* 3 vols. Orig. publ. 1905–34. Aalen, 1964.

Kuehn, Thomas. " 'Cum Consensu Mundualdi': Legal Guardianship of Women in Quattrocento Florence." In Kuehn, *Law, Family, and Women,* 212–37.

———. *Emancipation in Late Medieval Florence.* New Brunswick, N.J., 1982.

———. *Law, Family, and Women: Toward a Legal Anthropology of Renaissance Italy.* Chicago, 1991.

———. "Some Ambiguities of Female Inheritance Ideology in the Renaissance." In Kuehn, *Law, Family, and Women,* 238–57.

———. "Understanding Gender Inequality in Renaissance Florence: Personhood and Gifts of Maternal Inheritance by Women." *Journal of Women's History* 8 (1996): 58–80.

———. "Women, Marriage, and *Patria Potestas* in Late Medieval Florence." In Kuehn, *Law, Family, and Women,* 197–212.

Labalme, Patricia H. *Bernardo Giustiniani: A Venetian of the Quattrocento.* Rome, 1969.

———. "Sodomy and Venetian Justice in the Renaissance." *Legal History Review* 52 (1984): 217–54.

Lanaro Sartori, Paola. *Un'oligarchia urbana nel Cinquecento veneto: Istituzioni, economia, società.* Turin, 1992.

Lane, Frederic C. *Andrea Barbarigo, Merchant of Venice, 1418–1449.* Baltimore, 1944.

———. "The Enlargement of the Great Council of Venice." In *Florilegium Historiale: Essays Presented to Wallace K. Ferguson,* ed. J. G. Rowe and W. H. Stockdale, 237–74. Toronto, 1971.

———. "Family Partnerships and Joint Ventures in the Venetian Republic." In Lane, *Venice and History,* 36–55.

———. "The Funded Debt of the Venetian Republic, 1262–1482." In Lane, *Venice and History,* 87–98.

———. "Venetian Shipping during the Commercial Revolution." In Lane, *Venice and History,* 3–24.

———. *Venetian Ships and Shipbuilders of the Renaissance.* Baltimore, 1934.

———. *Venice, a Maritime Republic.* Baltimore, 1973.

———. *Venice and History.* Baltimore, 1966.

Lane, Frederic C., and Reinhold C. Mueller. *Money and Banking in Medieval and Renaissance Venice.* Vol. 1, *Coins and Moneys of Account.* Baltimore, 1985.

Laslett, Peter. Introduction to *Household and Family in Past Time,* ed. Peter Laslett and Richard Wall, 1–89. Cambridge, 1972.

Law, John Easton. "Age Qualification and the Venetian Constitution: The Case of the Capello Family." *Papers of the British School at Rome* 39 (1971): 125–37.

Lazzarini, Vittorio. *Marino Faliero.* Florence, 1963.

Leicht, Pier Silverio. "Documenti dotali dell' alto medioevo." In Leicht, *Scritti vari di storia del diritto italiano.* Vol. 2, pt. 2. Milan, 1943–48.

Levinson, Daniel J., et al. *The Seasons of a Man's Life.* New York, 1979.

Leyser, Karl. "Debate: Maternal Kin in Early Medieval Germany: A Reply." *Past and Present* 49 (1970): 126–34.

———. "The German Aristocracy from the Ninth to the Early Twelfth Century: A Historical and Cultural Sketch." *Past and Present* 41 (1968): 25–53.

Loenertz, R. J. *Les Ghisi, dynastes vénitiens dans l'Archipel, 1207–1390.* Florence, 1975.

Lopez, Robert S. "The Trade of Medieval Europe: The South." In *The Cambridge Economic History of Europe,* vol. 2, *Trade and Industry in the Middle Ages,* ed. M. Postan and E. E. Rich, 257–354. Cambridge, 1952.

Lorenzi, Giovanni Battista, ed. *Leggi e memorie venete sulla prostituzione.* Venice, 1870–72.

Lurie, Alison. *The Language of Clothes.* New York, 1981.

Luzzatto, Gino. "Il costo della vita a Venezia nel Trecento." In Gino Luzzatto, *Studi di storia economica veneziana,* 285–97. Padua, 1954.

———. *Il debito pubblico della Repubblica di Venezia, dagli ultimi decenni del XII secolo alla fine del XV.* Milan, 1963.

———. *An Economic History of Italy.* Translated by Philip J. Jones. New York, 1961.

———. *La storia economica di Venezia dall'XI al XVI secolo.* Venice, 1961.

———, ed. *I prestiti della Repubblica di Venezia (secolo XIII–XV).* Documenti finanziari della Repubblica di Venezia, 3d ser., vol. 1, pt. 1. Padua, 1929.

Maranini, Giuseppe. *La Costituzione di Venezia.* 2 vols. 1927–31. Reprint, Florence, 1974.

Martin, John, and Dennis Romano, eds. *Venice Reconsidered.* Baltimore, forthcoming.

Martines, Lauro. *Lawyers and Statecraft in Renaissance Florence.* Princeton, 1968.

———. *The Social World of the Florentine Humanists, 1390–1460.* Princeton, 1963.

———. "A Way of Looking at Women in Renaissance Florence." *Journal of Medieval and Renaissance Studies* 4 (1974): 15–28.

———, ed. *Violence and Civil Disorder in Italian Cities, 1200–1500.* Berkeley, 1972.

Mazzi, Maria Serena. "Il mondo della prostituzione nella Firenze tardo medievale." *Ricerche storiche* 14 (1984): 337–63.

McLaughlin, Mary Martin. "Creating and Recreating Communities of Women:

The Case of Corpus Domini, Ferrara." In *Sisters and Workers in the Middle Ages,* ed. Judith M. Bennett et al., 261–88. Chicago, 1989.

Merores, Margarete. "Der grosse Rat von Venedig und die sogenannte Serrata vom Jahre 1297." *Vierteljahrschrift für Sozial- und Wirtschaftsgeschichte* 21 (1928): 33–113.

Middleton, John, and David Tait. "The Lineage and the Lineage System." In Bohannan and Middleton, *Kinship and Social Organization,* 155–59.

Migiel, Marilyn, and Juliana Schiesari, eds. *Refiguring Woman: Perspectives on Gender and the Italian Renaissance.* Ithaca, N.Y., 1991.

Miskimin, Harry A. *The Economy of Early Renaissance Europe, 1300–1460.* Englewood Cliffs, N.J., 1969.

Molho, Anthony. "Cosimo de' Medici: Pater Patriae or Padrino?" *Stanford Italian Review* (Spring 1979): 5–33.

———. "Deception and Marriage Strategy in Renaissance Florence: The Case of Women's Ages." *Renaissance Quarterly* 41 (1988): 193–217.

———. *Marriage Alliance in Late Medieval Florence.* Cambridge, Mass., 1994.

———. "Politics and the Ruling Class in Early Renaissance Florence." *Nuova Rivista Storica* 52 (1968): 401–20.

———. "The State and Public Finance: A Hypothesis Based on the History of Late Medieval Florence." In *Origins of the State in Italy, 1300–1600,* S97–135.

———. "*Tamquam vere mortua:* Le professioni religiose femminili nella Firenze del tardo medioevo." *Società e storia* 43 (1989): 1–44.

Molho, Anthony, et al. "Genealogia e parentado: Memorie del potere nella Firenze tardo medievale: Il caso di Giovanni Rucellai." *Quaderni storici* 86 (August 1994): 365–403.

Morandini, Francesca. "Statuti e ordinamenti dell'Ufficio dei pupilli nel periodo della Repubblica fiorentina (1388–1534)." *Archivio storico italiano* 113 (1955): 522–51; 114 (1956): 92–117; 115 (1957): 87–104.

Morozzo della Rocca, Raimondo, and Antonino Lombardo, eds. *Documenti del commercio veneziano nei secoli XI–XIII.* 2 vols. Turin, 1940.

Mueller, Reinhold C. "Effetti della Guerra di Chioggia (1378–1381) sulla vita economica e sociale di Venezia." *Ateneo Veneto,* n.s., 19 (1981): 27–41.

———. "The Procurators of San Marco in the Thirteenth and Fourteenth Centuries: A Study of the Office as a Financial and Trust Institution." *Studi veneziani* 13 (1971): 105–220.

Muir, Edward. *Civic Ritual in Renaissance Venice.* Princeton, 1981.

———. "Images of Power: Art and Pageantry in Renaissance Venice." *American Historical Review* 84 (1979): 16–52.

Muraro, Maria Teresa. "La festa a Venezia e le sue manifestazioni rappresentative: Le compagnie della calza e le *momarie.*" In Arnaldi and Pastore Stocchi, *Storia della cultura veneta,* vol. 3, pt. 3, 315–41.

Murdock, George Peter. *Social Structure.* New York, 1949.

Myerhoff, Barbara. "Rites of Passage: Process and Paradox." In *Celebration: Studies in Festivity and Ritual,* ed. Victor Turner, 108–35. Washington, 1982.

Najemy, John. *Corporatism and Consensus in Florentine Electoral Politics.* Chapel Hill, N.C., 1982.

———. "Guild Republicanism in Trecento Florence: The Successes and Ultimate Failure of Corporate Politics." *American Historical Review* 84 (1979): 53–71.

Newett, M. Margaret. "The Sumptuary Laws of Venice in the Fourteenth and Fifteenth Centuries." In *Historical Essays by Members of the Owens College, Manchester,* ed. T. F. Tout and James Tait, 245–78. London, 1902.

Niccolai, Franco. "I consorzi nobiliari ed il Comune nell'alta e media Italia." *Rivista di storia del diritto italiano* 13 (1940): 117–47, 292–342, 397–477.

Nicholas, Barry. *An Introduction to Roman Law.* Oxford, 1961.

The Origins of the State in Italy, 1300–1600. Supplement to the *Journal of Modern History* 67 (1995). Also published as *The Origins of the State in Italy, 1300–1600,* ed. Julius Kirshner. Chicago, 1996.

Origo, Iris. "The Domestic Enemy: The Eastern Slaves in Tuscany in the Fourteenth and Fifteenth Centuries." *Speculum* 30 (1955): 321–66.

Ortner, Sherry B. "Is Female to Male as Nature Is to Culture?" In Rosaldo and Lamphere, *Woman, Culture, and Society,* 67–87.

Ortner, Sherry B., and Harriet Whitehead. "Introduction: Accounting for Sexual Meanings." In *Sexual Meanings: The Cultural Construction of Gender and Sexuality,* ed. Sherry B. Ortner and Harriet Whitehead, 1–27. Cambridge, 1981.

Otis, Leah Lydia. "Prostitution in Late Medieval Perpignan." In Kirshner and Wemple, *Women of the Medieval World,* 137–60.

Ozment, Steven. *When Fathers Ruled: Family Life in Reformation Europe.* Cambridge, Mass., 1983.

Paolino Minorita, Fra. *Trattato de regimine rectoris.* Edited by Adolfo Mussafia. Florence, 1868.

Pavan, Elisabeth (Elisabeth Crouzet-Pavan). "Police des moeurs, société et politique à Venise à la fin du Moyen Age." *Revue historique* 264 (October–December 1980): 241–88.

———. "Recherches sur la nuit vénitienne à la fin du moyen âge." *Journal of Medieval History* 7 (1981): 339–56.

Pecchioli, Renzo. "Il 'mito' di Venezia e la crisi fiorentina intorno al 1500." *Studi storici* 3 (1964): 451–92.

Perry, Mary Elizabeth. *Gender and Disorder in Early Modern Seville.* Princeton, 1990.

Pertile, Antonio. *Storia del diritto italiano.* 2d ed. Turin, 1894.

Phillips, Mark. *The Memoir of Marco Parenti: A Life in Medici Florence.* Princeton, 1987.

Pitt-Rivers, Julian. "Honour and Social Status." In *Honor and Shame: The Values of Mediterranean Society,* ed. J. G. Peristiany, 19–77. Chicago, 1966.

Power, Eileen. "The Position of Women." In *The Legacy of the Middle Ages,* ed. G. C. Crump and E. F. Jacob, 401–33. Oxford, 1926.

Pullan, Brian. "The Occupations and Investments of the Venetian Nobility in the Middle and Late Sixteenth Century." In Hale, *Renaissance Venice,* 379–408.

———. *Rich and Poor in Renaissance Venice: The Social Institutions of a Catholic State, to 1620.* Cambridge, Mass., 1971.

Queller, Donald E. "The Civic Irresponsibility of the Venetian Nobility." In Herlihy et al., *Economy, Society, and Government in Medieval Italy,* 223–35.

——. *The Venetian Patriciate: Reality versus Myth.* Urbana, Ill., 1986.

Queller, Donald E., and Thomas F. Madden. "Father of the Bride: Fathers, Daughters, and Dowries in Late Medieval and Early Renaissance Venice." *Renaissance Quarterly* 46 (1993): 685–711.

Riemer, Eleanor S. "Women, Dowries, and Capital Investment in Thirteenth-Century Siena." In *The Marriage Bargain,* ed. Marion A. Kaplan, 59–79. New York, 1985.

Rocke, Michael. "Il controllo dell'omosessualità a Firenze nel XV secolo: Gli *Ufficiali di Notte.*" *Quaderni storici* 66 (1987): 701–23.

——. *Forbidden Friendships: Homosexuality and Male Culture in Renaissance Florence.* New York, 1996.

——. "Gender and Sexual Culture in Renaissance Italy." In Brown and Davis, *Gender and Society,* 150–70.

Romanin, Samuele. *La storia documentata di Venezia.* 3d ed. 10 vols. Venice, 1972–75.

Romano, Dennis. "Gender and the Urban Geography of Renaissance Venice." *Journal of Social History* 23 (1989): 339–53.

——. *Housecraft and Statecraft: Domestic Service in Renaissance Venice, 1400–1600.* Baltimore, 1996.

——. *Patricians and Popolani: The Social Foundations of the Venetian Renaissance State.* Baltimore, 1987.

Roper, Lyndal. *The Holy Household: Women and Morals in Reformation Augsburg.* Oxford, 1989.

Rosaldo, Michelle Zimbalist. "The Use and Abuse of Anthropology: Reflections on Feminism and Cross-Cultural Understanding." *Signs* 5 (1980): 389–417.

——. "Woman, Culture, and Society: A Theoretical Overview." In Rosaldo and Lamphere, *Woman, Culture, and Society,* 17–42.

Rosaldo, Michelle Zimbalist, and Louise Lamphere, eds. *Woman, Culture, and Society.* Stanford, 1974.

Rosenthal, Elaine G. "The Position of Women in Renaissance Florence: Neither Autonomy nor Subjection." In *Florence and Italy: Renaissance Studies in Honour of Nicolai Rubinstein,* ed. Peter Denley and Caroline Elam, 369–81. London, 1988.

Rossiaud, Jacques. "Prostitution, jeunesse et société dans les villes du Sud-Est au XVe siècle." *Annales: économies, sociétés, civilisations* 31 (1976): 289–325.

Ruggiero, Guido. *Binding Passions: Tales of Magic, Marriage, and Power at the End of the Renaissance.* New York, 1993.

——. *The Boundaries of Eros: Sex Crime and Sexuality in Renaissance Venice.* New York, 1985.

——. "Modernization and the Mythic State in Renaissance Venice: The Serrata Revisited." *Viator* 10 (1979): 245–56.

——. *Violence in Early Renaissance Venice.* New Brunswick, N.J., 1980.

Sanudo, Marino. *I diarii di Marino Sanuto.* Edited by Rinaldo Fulin et al. 58 vols. Venice, 1879–1903.

——, il giovane. *De origine, situ et magistratibus urbis Venetae ovvero la città di Venetia.* Edited by Angela Caracciolo Aricò. Milan, 1980.

Scarabello, Giovanni. "Devianza sessuale ed interventi di giustizia a Venezia nella prima metà del XVI secolo." In *Tiziano e Venezia*, 75–84.

Scott, Joan W. "Gender: A Useful Category of Historical Analysis." *American Historical Review* 91 (1986): 1053–75.

Sella, Pietro. *Glossario Latino Italiano: Stato della Chiesa–Veneto–Abruzzi*. Vatican City, 1944.

Silvano, Giovanni. *La "Republica de' Viniziani": Ricerche sul repubblicanesimo veneziano in età moderna*. Florence, 1993.

Simmel, Georg. *Georg Simmel on Individuality and Social Forms: Selected Writings*. Edited by Donald N. Levine. Chicago, 1971.

Sperling, Jutta. "Convents and the Body Politic in Late Renaissance Venice." Ph.D. diss., Stanford University, 1995.

Starn, Randolph. "Francesco Guicciardini and His Brothers." In *Renaissance Studies in Honor of Hans Baron*, ed. Anthony Molho and John A. Tedeschi, 411–44. Florence, 1971.

Statuta populi et communis Florentiae, anno salutis mccccxv. 3 vols. Freiburg, 1778–83.

Stern, Laura Ikins. *The Criminal Law System of Medieval and Renaissance Florence*. Baltimore, 1994.

Stone, Lawrence. *The Family, Sex, and Marriage in England, 1500–1800*. London, 1977.

Strocchia, Sharon T. "Learning the Virtues: Convent Schools and Female Culture in Renaissance Florence." In *Women's Education in Early Modern Europe: A History, 1500–1800*, ed. Barbara J. Whitehead, 3–46. New York, 1999.

———. "Remembering the Family: Women, Kin, and Commemorative Masses in Renaissance Florence." *Renaissance Quarterly* 42 (1989): 635–54.

Strozzi, Alessandra. *Selected Letters of Alessandra Strozzi*. Bilingual edition. Translated by Heather Gregory. Berkeley, 1997.

Stuard, Susan M. "The Dominion of Gender: Women's Fortune in the High Middle Ages." In Bridenthal, Koonz, and Stuard, *Becoming Visible*, 153–74.

Tafuri, Manfredo. *Venezia e il Rinascimento: Religione, scienza, architettura*. Turin, 1985.

Tamassia, Nino. *La famiglia italiana nei secoli decimoquinto e decimosesto*. Milan, 1910.

Tenenti, Alberto. "The Sense of Space and Time in the Venetian World of the Fifteenth and Sixteenth Centuries." In Hale, *Renaissance Venice*, 17–46.

Terpstra, Nicholas. "Women in the Brotherhood: Gender, Class, and Politics in Renaissance Bolognese Confraternities." *Renaissance and Reformation* 26 (1990): 193–212.

Tiziano e Venezia: Convegno internazionale di studi, Venezia 1976. Vicenza, 1980.

Trexler, Richard C. "Celibacy in the Renaissance: The Nuns of Florence." In Trexler, *Women of Renaissance Florence*, 6–30.

———. "Florentine Prostitution in the Fifteenth Century: Patrons and Clients." In Trexler, *Women of Renaissance Florence*, 31–65.

———. *Public Life in Renaissance Florence*. New York, 1980.

———. "Ritual in Florence: Adolescence and Salvation in the Renaissance." In *The*

Pursuit of Holiness in Late Medieval and Renaissance Religion, ed. Charles Trinkaus and Heiko A. Oberman, 200–264. Leiden, 1974.

———. *The Women of Renaissance Florence.* Vol. 2 of *Power and Dependence in Renaissance Florence.* Binghamton, N.Y., 1993.

Tucci, Ugo. "The Psychology of the Venetian Merchant in the Sixteenth Century." In Hale, *Renaissance Venice,* 346–78.

Turner, Victor. *The Ritual Process: Structure and Anti-Structure.* Ithaca, N.Y., 1969.

van Gennep, Arnold. *Rites de passage.* Paris, 1909. Eng. trans., *The Rites of Passage.* Translated by Monika B. Vizedom and Gabrielle L. Caffee. London, 1960.

Vecellio, Cesare. *De gli habiti antichi e moderni di diuerse parti del mondo.* Venice, 1590.

Ventura, Angelo. "Scrittori politici e scritture di governo." In Arnaldi and Pastore Stocchi, *Storia della cultura veneta,* vol. 3, pt. 3, 513–63.

Venturi, Lionello. "Le Compagnie della Calza (sec. XV–XVI)." *Nuovo archivio veneto,* n.s., 16 (1908): 161–221; 17 (1909): 140–233.

Vitali, Achille. *La moda a Venezia attraverso i secoli.* Venice, 1992.

Volumen statutorum, legum, ac iurium D. Venetorum. Venice, 1564.

Weissman, Ronald F. E. *Ritual Brotherhood in Renaissance Florence.* New York, 1982.

Wiesner, Merry E. *Working Women in Renaissance Germany.* New Brunswick, N.J., 1986.

Witt, Ronald G. "Florentine Politics and the Ruling Class, 1382–1407." *Journal of Medieval and Renaissance Studies* 6 (1976): 243–67.

Wolf, Eric R. "Kinship, Friendship, and Patron-Client Relations in Complex Societies." In *The Social Anthropology of Complex Societies,* ed. Michael Banton, 1–22. New York, 1966.

Zannini, Andrea. *Burocrazia e burocrati a Venezia in età moderna: I cittadini originari (sec. XVI–XVII).* Venice, 1993.

Zarri, Gabriella. "Monasteri femminili e città (secoli XV–XVIII)." In *La chiesa e il potere politico dal medioevo all'età contemporanea,* Storia d'Italia: Annali, 9, ed. Giorgio Chittolini and Giovanni Miccoli, 359–429. Turin, 1986.

———. "Pietà e profezia alle corti padane: Le pie consigliere dei principi." In Zarri, *Le sante vive,* 51–85.

———. *Le sante vive: Profezie di corte e devozione femminile tra '400 e '500.* Turin, 1990.

Zordan, Giorgio. "I vari aspetti della comunione familiare di beni nella Venezia dei secoli XI–XII." *Studi veneziani* 8 (1966): 127–94.

Zorzi, Andrea. "I Fiorentini e gli uffici pubblici nel primo Quattrocento: Concorrenza, abusi, illegalità." *Quaderni storici* 66 (1987): 725–51.

———. "The Judicial System in Florence in the Fourteenth and Fifteenth Centuries." In Dean and Lowe, *Crime, Society, and the Law,* 40–58.

Index

Adimari family (Florence), 45
adolescence, 185–205; female, 187–93,
201–3; male, 187, 198, 203–4, 235
adulthood, 185–205; changes in, 186; female: —criteria, 187; —parents and, 161,
201; —stages of, 201 (*see also* uxorial cycle); —varied, 189, 201; male: —and fathers, 210; —and patrician status, 186;
—public nature of, 187, 193–97, 229–43;
—stages of, 174, 194–97, 200–201;
—varied, 193, 198–200, 203–4
affection: between spouses, 154–68; of husbands, 161, 165; language of, 161–63; in
marriage strategies, 11–12
affines: in Barbarella, 215, 219–24; relations between, 131, 167, 220–22
age, 161, 228; in government policy, 34–36;
of majority, 185–86; and patrician status,
30–31. *See also* marriage, age at
agnates, 116
Antoninus, Archbishop (Florence), 38–39
Ariès, Philippe, 51
Arimondo clan: Andrea, 93; Antonio, 222;
Bianca, 163–64; Donato, 163–64; Fantin,
222; Maddaluzza, 93, 202, 218; Marietta,
93; Marino, 164; Simone, 93
Avogadori di Comun: as guardians of patrician status, 65, 233, 237; in marriage regulation, 62–63, 65, 68, 72, 86; and
youthful disorders, 227–28

bachelors, 244–56; compared to women,
244–45, 246, 254–55; and dowry infla-

tion, 11, 250–52; and family strategy, 22,
252–53; in fraternal groups, 251–52; and
marriage alliances, 250–51; numbers of,
198–99, 249; and patriarchy, 244–56; political activity of, 252–54; sexual behavior of, 22, 64, 249; status of, 66, 253;
varied, 255
Balbi clan, 131, 222; Alvise (Lodovico), 222;
Elena, 202; Nicoletto, 212; Piero, 229;
Piero di Alvise, 212
Balla d'Oro. *See* Barbarella
Barbarella, 206–44; age requirement, 198;
and bilaterality, 217–18, 220–24; families and, 208–9, 236–37; evolution of,
208, 235; guarantors in, 215–24, 237; kin
in, 212–26; legislation on, 208–9, 224,
235–36; and male adulthood, 174, 195,
235; and marriage, 222–24; mothers in,
19, 100, 202–3; and patrician status,
224–26, 235–36; procedures, 209, 236–
37; relationships in, 237–38; as rite of
passage, 214; sponsors in, 210–15
Barbarigo, Secondo, 78
Barbaro, Ermolao, *De coelibatu,* 248–49
Barbaro, Francesco, *De re uxoria,* 89, 156–
57, 169, 187, 247–48
Barbo, Gabriella, 110
bastards: as dishonoring Great Council, 59;
political exclusion of, 11, 22, 56, 65
Bembo clan: Andrea, 90–92; Jacopo, 220
Betto, Bianca, 4
bilaterality: in Barbarella, 218, 220–24; and
lineage, 19, 224; marriage and, 207;

Morosini clan (*cont.*)
  vella, 148–49; Paolo di Alessandro, 85;
  Paolo di Francesco, 221; Paolo di Nicolò,
  222; Petronella, 178–79, 187–88, 202;
  Piero, 187; Piero di Marino, 85; Silvestro,
  189; Zilio, 178–79, 202
  mothers: and affines, 215–18; in Barbarella,
  215–18, 225; and children, 160, 169–82;
  and children's adulthood, 202–3; and
  children's gender identity, 176–77; and
  daughters, 178–79, 190; and daughters'
  dowries, 76, 80, 110–11, 126, 136, 139–
  44; and daughters' marriages, 144, 177–
  80, 202; and daughters' vocations, 161,
  179, 191–92, 204–5; importance of, 10;
  influence of, 173–82, 190; and patrician
  status, 56, 59, 64, 171, 247; and regime,
  64; responsibilities of, 201–3; and sons,
  176–77, 181; status of, 209
Mudazzo (Muazzo) clan: Elena, 98–99;
  Elisabetta, 218; Nicolò, 45, 98–99
Muir, Edward, 236
myth of Venice, 63, 228

Navagero, Francesco, 191
nobility, 55–56, 64
nuns: and marriage market, 38; numbers
  of, 39; sexual activities of, 37–38; and
  state, 37–42. *See also* convents

office-holding, 239; age requirements, 231,
  239; bachelors and, 252–53; competition
  for, 239–40; by husbands, 252–53; levels
  of, 231; lineage and, 213; and male adulthood, 193–96; marriage and, 222; patricians' dependence on, 174, 231, 208–9; as
  patrician welfare, 225–26, 232–33; regulation of, 240–41; young men and, 195–
  96, 200, 229–30
Origins of the State in Italy, 27–28
Osanna of Mantua, 40
Otto di Guardia (Florence), 32

Paolino di Venezia, 187
Parenti, Marco, 44
patria potestas, 169, 246
patriarch of Venice, 38–39
patriarchy, 6–7, 116; and elite hegemony,
  31; in gender structure, 20; ideology of,
  4, 197, 200–201; institutions of, 181–82;

and male identity, 170, 175, 246; polymorphousness of, 17–19, 48–49; public
  and private, 16, 43, 169; and women's
  position, 5, 177
patrician status, 242; heredity in, 117, 233;
  legislation on, 16, 30, 233, 235–36, 247;
  and male identity, 246; parents and, 233
patriciate, 2, 73; changes in, ca. 1400, 156,
  230, 246; dowries of, 9, 69–70, 152; economic difficulties of, 232–33; exclusiveness of, 7, 156, 235; and gender, 8, 205;
  governmental orientation of, 195, 225–
  26, 231; groupings within, 21–22, 54–
  56, 62, 74, 198, 240–41; ideology of, 58–
  59, 63, 174–75; inner elite in, 196, 241;
  marriage alliances in, 92, 171; regulation
  of, 8; relationships in, 21, 220, 223; size
  of, 231, 233; unity of, 21, 63; welfare programs for, 58, 195–96, 232–33. *See also*
  office-holding; patrician status
patriliny: and bilaterality, 20; and dowries,
  47, 95, 130; in gender structure, 20; and
  inheritance, 116; kinship context of, 206–
  26; and male identity, 4; and marriage,
  211–12, 224; in patriciate, 117, 207
pelanda (cloak), 90–91
Pisani clan, 130; Ermolao, 41; Giovanni,
  223; Luca, 229; Marino, 187
Pollini clan: Francesco, 85; Lucia, 85
popolo: dowries of, 9; intermarriage with
  patricians, 8–9, 60; and marriage regulation, 60; patrician status and, 30; in sodomy prosecution, 36
Power, Eileen, 115
pregnancy, 140–42
prestiti, 45, 133. *See also* funded debt
Priuli clan: Cristina, 202; Filippo, 202; Francesco, 223; Girolamo, 69; Leonardo, 99–
  100; Lucrezia, 166; Marcantonio, 106;
  Maria, 99–100; Morosina, 106; Piero,
  227–28, 243; Sebastiano, 166; Zaccaria,
  100
Procuratori di San Marco, 107, 124, 178,
  227–28, 243
prostitution: in Florence, 32; in Venice, 36–
  37
puberty, 187, 196

Quarantia (Forty), Council of, 227
Queller, Donald E., 21, 77, 91–92, 195; and

Library of Congress Cataloging-in-Publication Data

Chojnacki, Stanley.
    Women and men in Renaissance Venice : twelve essays on patrician
society / Stanley Chojnacki.
        p.   cm.
    Includes bibliographical references and index.
      ISBN 0-8018-6269-8 (alk. paper) — ISBN 0-8018-6395-3 (pbk. : alk. paper)
      1. Marriage—Italy—Venice—History.   2. Man-woman relationships —
Italy—Venice—History.   3. Family—Italy—Venice—History. 4. Aristocracy
(Social class)—Italy—Venice—History.   5. Renaissance—Italy—Venice.   I.
Title: 12 essays on patrician society. II. Title.

HQ630.15.V47C48 2000
306.7'0945'31—dc21   99-038575